Beyond the Symbol Model

SUNY Series in Speech Communication
Dudley D. Cahn, Jr., editor

Beyond the Symbol Model

Reflections on the Representational Nature of Language

EDITED BY

John Stewart

State University of New York Press

Published by
State University of New York Press, Albany

© 1996 State University of New York

For information, address State University of New York Press,
State University Plaza, Albany, N.Y., 12246

Production by Diane Ganeles
Marketing by Nancy Farrell

Library of Congress Cataloging-in-Publication Data

Beyond the symbol model : reflections on the representational nature
    of language / [edited by] John Stewart.
        p.   cm. — (SUNY series in speech communication)
    Includes bibliographical references and index.
    ISBN 0-7914-3083-9. — ISBN 0-7914-3084-7 (pbk.)
    1. Language and languages—Philosophy.   2. Semiotics.
    3. Representation (Philosophy.   I. Stewart, John Robert, 1941–
    II. Series.
    P106.B466   1996
    401—dc20   95-39476
                                                            CIP

10 9 8 7 6 5 4 3 2 1

Contents

Part III. Resuscitations of Semiotic Dimensions

Part IV. Continuing the Conversation

Editor's Introduction

This book is a collection of contributions to an interdisciplinary conversation about the nature of language. Participants include two philosophers, three psychologists, a professor of comparative literature, a semiotician, a sociolinguist, and three communication theorists. All are interested in the promises and pitfalls of characterizing language as a representational system, and all have published extensively on these matters.

This collection will be of interest to scholars and students who work with language or discourse and who believe either that language can fruitfully be characterized semiotically as a representational system of signs and symbols or that postmodern critiques of representationalism raise important questions about the nature of language. This group includes communication theorists and critics, linguists, psycholinguists, sociolinguists, ethnographers, and philosophers committed to the linguistic turn. Some more or less explicit view of the nature of language underlies each of the various theoretical approaches taken by such scholars. These views of language may be thought of as more or less representational, and they guide the diverse theoretical, critical, and empirical projects these scholars undertake. As a result, there are not only philosophical but also theoretical, critical, and empirical concerns addressed in the following chapters. This book as a whole is meant to encourage students and scholars with these interests to reflect on their assumptions about the nature of language and to take seriously the criticisms by some postmodern philosophers of the dominant belief that language is fundamentally a system of signs and symbols.

This work was conceived of as a companion volume to the editor's *Language as Articulate Contact: Toward a Post-Semiotic Philosophy of Communication* (Albany: State University of New York Press, 1995), which examines semiotic conceptualizations of language from the perspective of the critiques of representation developed by Heidegger, Gadamer, Bakhtin, and Buber. Because language theory is of central interest to scholars across the human studies, and because the argument made in *Language as*

1

Articulate Contact is controversial, I asked a dozen scholars from half a dozen disciplines to comment from their own perspectives about the efficacy of representational accounts of the nature of language. Each author included here has developed from his or her philosophical, critical, or empirical work a perspective on language that may be characterized as semiotic or post-semiotic, and each argues for the coherence and utility of this perspective.

The chapter authors' contributions to this larger conversation can be profitably read with or without reference to the earlier volume. These papers stand on their own as investigations of at least two prominent ways of thinking about language that inform and influence work in all the human studies. Some of the chapters that follow complement and extend the argument made in *Language as Articulate Contact*. There and in this book's first chapter I contend that semiotic accounts of language have been uncritically accepted from the fifth century B.C. through at least the early twentieth century, that such accounts are fatally representational, that these views of language can no longer be sustained in light of postmodern critiques, and that language theorists need to continue developing a postsemiotic account of language that is anchored in the verbal/nonverbal, speaking/listening event that constitutes conversation or dialogue. Other chapters focus more narrowly on arguments for and against the symbol model in works by Wittgenstein, Merleau-Ponty, Nietzsche, or Lyotard. Still other chapters argue that it is impossible to develop any coherent "postsemiotic" account of the nature of language or that with some small revisions, the symbol model can still prove useful. The final chapter indicates how the entire book might be understood in relation to other attempts to move "beyond" dominant points of view.

This book is assertively interdisciplinary. As a result, subject matter specialists may be disappointed by the fact that there are so few chapters written by philosophers, for example, or by linguists, semioticians, or discourse analysts. Part of my rationale for the selection of chapter authors is that this conversation about the nature of language crosses disciplinary boundaries and that voices from each of the perspectives offered here need to be heard by their interlocutors in other fields. Much more fully developed and nuanced arguments supporting each chapter's case may be found in other works, but one purpose of this book is to collect a sample of these diverse perspectives so that narrowly focused viewpoints may be broadened.

The four chapters making up Part I, "Alternatives to Representational Accounts of Language and Meaning," present arguments from communication theory, philosophy, and psychology that traditional understandings of the nature of language need to be drastically revised. In chapter 1, I review and critique five theoretical commitments entailed by the claim that language is a semiotic system and then sketch a postsemiotic account of the nature of language. I argue that semiotic and postsemiotic views are incommensurable, which is to say that one cannot coherently maintain both that language is representational and that it is constitutive. My account of language as constitutive articulate contact affirms that: (a) language should be treated first and foremost as event, not system (as "languaging"); (b) this event embodies the distinctive dynamic of human being, which is understanding; (c) this ongoing process of understanding-via-languaging is the human's way of constituting world ("world-building-and-rebuilding" or simply "worlding"); (d) this understanding occurs in contact between persons, which is to say that the event is irreducibly dialogic or interpersonal; and (e) this understanding-in-contact is articulate, which means both that it accomplishes differentiation or categorization and that it occurs paradigmatically as oral-aural contact.

In chapter 2, philosopher Gary Madison develops a "postsemiological" account of language that is friendly to the one outlined in chapter 1. He emphasizes that since language is "not a 'thing' but a *way of being*," it is impossible to treat it as an object external to humans. Madison also points out that although this view requires thinkers to give up correspondence tests of truth-value, there remain available tests of *practice* that enable communicators to choose between "true" and "false" accounts and stories.

The following chapter by psychologist and communication theorist John Shotter argues against representational accounts of two fundamental phenomena, knowledge and theory. With the help of Vygotsky, Bakhtin/Volosinov, Billig, and especially the Wittgenstein of the *Philosophical Investigations,* Shotter claims that accounts of knowledge as representation may suffice for what Gilbert Ryle called "knowing-that" and "knowing-how," but not for the more fundamental knowledge from within that Shotter terms "knowledge of a third kind." Theory, Shotter argues, has been treated as a representation of knowing-that and knowing-how, an approach that renders it blind to the constitutive nature of the language game of theorizing itself. Theorists have pursued the Greek and Enlightenment goals of perfect knowledge of the inner workings of phenomena without acknowledging the extent to which their projects are, in Garfinkel's terms, context-dependent, ongoing practical accomplishments. Because they are accomplishments, one cannot ask what supposedly "underlies" them as a signified underlies a signifier. Human scientists might better attend to the everyday, conversational, mundane and professional joint-actions that constitute theorizing and attempts to generate knowledge. Social constructionism is a growing movement in the human sciences that studies these activities, and in the final section of his chapter, Shotter reviews how social constructionists describe the *basis* for evaluating knowledge claims, a *method* for studying them, and a *site* or focus for investigating this kind of knowing.

The final chapter in Part I is made up of two psychologists' arguments for a "collaborative theory of meaning" based on their empirical studies of everyday discourse. Gillian L. Roberts and Janet Beavin Bavelas study relationships between verbal and nonverbal behaviors and interpretations. They maintain that analysis of empirical observations is vital to any theory of the nature of language and meaning and that their observations reveal pervasive and important events in which interlocutors' coconstruct linguistic and communicative meaning. They offer close readings of nine examples of actual communicating that reveal implicit, explicit, and problematic semantic collaboration.

Taken together, the first four chapters illustrate common themes present in postrepresentational views of the nature of language that are emerging in communication, philosophy, and psychology. They also indicate what is at stake intellectually when they contrast subject/object analyses of language as a *system* or *code* employed by humans to represent their more fundamental and primary "thoughts" or "meanings," with postmodern analyses that treat language as the human's way-of-being, the *primary* means humans have of sense-making, interpreting or understanding. In other words, they argue from different perspectives that language can and should be treated as an ontologically, not just epistemologically consequential process, as the primary way humans work out who we are, not simply as an instrument or tool that humans use to represent mental contents or other designata. This view that communication is ontologically constitutive rather than merely representational of realities allegedly constituted otherwise or elsewhere has obvious ethical and political implications. These implications are not extensively developed in these chapters, but Michel Foucault, among many others, has written and spoken at length about them, and his works contribute to several important threads of the larger conversation.[1]

Part II, "Postmodern Rediscoveries," consists of two chapters that discuss watershed contributions in the history of postmodern critiques of representational accounts of language. The author of chapter 5, Comparative Literature professor Ernst Behler, is currently at work on a twenty–volume edition of Nietzsche's corpus. He argues that there is in Nietzsche's work "a fundamental reflection on language, in a continuous process of questioning the problems of expression and communication in a basic manner." The chapter lays out the conceptual connections between Nietzsche's account of language and his critiques of metaphysics and reason. Behler reveals in Nietzsche's work an important struggle with the Two Worlds commitment of the symbol model. He shows how, especially in Nietzsche's *On Truth and Lie in a Nonmoral Sense*, both reality and reason are interpreted *rhetorically*.

In the following chapter, communication theorist Andrew R. Smith argues that Jean-François Lyotard's work develops a critique of Peircean semiotics that can politically inform communication research. Lyotard's discourse theory is presented as fundamentally agonistic, partly by way of a dialogue between a follower of C. S. Peirce and a Lyotardian. The final section of the chapter addresses the concerns of anthropologists and communication scholars who are working out the status of communication ethnography. Smith argues that Lyotard's deconstruction of the discourse subject may contribute to the development of the emerging "ethnography of differends."

Part III is made up of three arguments for the continued efficacy of symbol model analyses of language and meaning. In chapter 7, semiotician D. S. Clarke anchors his defense of the symbol model on the usefulness and wisdom of analysis-into-atoms and working from simple-to-complex systems. He maintains that language philosophers should focus on the logically necessary, as contrasted with the contingent, features of language use, and that the most primitive of these elements may aptly be termed *natsigns* (natural signs). In the following section of the chapter, Clarke describes some of the "transactional" features of language that are "less central for semiotic as a branch of philosophy." He concludes that even these transactional features yield to semiotic analysis, primarily because of the presence within them of "sentence radicals with subject-predicate structure."

Chapter 8 consists of communication theorist Wendy Leeds-Hurwitz's explanation and application of a *social* account of symbols. She argues against chapter 1 that the symbol model can still serve language and communication analysts, so long as symbols are acknowledged to be collaboratively constructed. Leeds-Hurwitz uses the extended example of a nonverbal symbol—a necklace—to explore various layers of meaning and three dimensions of use—polysemy, bricolage, and intertextuality. She maintains that there is no need to move *beyond* symbol theory and that her social model of symbols can stay at the center of analyses of verbal and nonverbal communication.

Chapter 9 also argues that attempts to jettison the symbol model are premature. Sociolinguist John Wilson attempts to refute the claim in chapter 1 that language cannot be both a way of being constitutive of humanity and a system instrumentally employed by already constituted humans to represent cognitions and accomplish other goals. Wilson supports his argument with close readings of utterances from audio-recorded everyday discourse. He demonstrates how a word like "So" in the utterance used as an example in chapter 1 may fruitfully be described as a "marker" functioning symbolically. He also explores relations between "discourse and the life world" by describing some ways discourse markers reveal how text is adapted to its context. Wilson's central claim is that "model of language as an independent symbolic system, systemically interacting with talk in the world will suffice."

The final chapter offers a provocative comment on the entire attempt to move "beyond" the symbol model. Philosopher Marcelo Dascal reviews volumes by Skinner, Bernstein, Freud, Nietzsche, Fromm, and others who attempt to critique a dominant metaphor and propose a path that in some way transcends it. In the best tradition of scholarship as conversation, Dascal's observations provide the impetus for each chapter author—and reader—to reframe or otherwise responsively change his or her arguments.

Brief introductions to each chapter highlight similarities and differences among the authors' perspectives. Few issues are settled in this conversation among diverse voices, but many recurrent themes emerge, and it becomes obvious how one's view of the nature of language materially affects his or her ontology, ethics, and politics. My hope is that this work might contribute to ongoing dialogue among researchers in the human studies who share many interests and concerns. I am convinced that scholars working with language need to acknowledge in their practices even more often than the authors noted here, that language is indeed "collaborative," "transactional," "social," and "communicative" and that there is a pervasive and consequential connection between how humans speak and listen and who we are.

Note

1. One reviewer faults these essays for being insufficiently political. From a Critical Theory perspective, philosophical ideas necessarily have political consequences, and every author who reflects on the nature of language ought explicitly to consider these consequences. This book's approach to this issue is, for the most part, more traditional. In the past, many works of considerable philosophical importance were not explicitly political, even though much was legitimately and fruitfully said by both their authors and commentators about these works' political implications. So, for example, although *Truth and Method* is silent on most directly political issues, in the 1980s Gadamer spoke and wrote extensively about German politics in the 1920s and 1930s, Heidegger's Nazism, and contemporary political realignments in post-Cold War Europe [see, for example, *Hans-Georg Gadamer on Education, Poetry, and History: Applied Hermeneutics*, ed. Dieter Misgeld and Graeme Nicholson (Albany: State University of New York Press, 1992.)]. In a similar way, political implications of the views of language developed in this volume could usefully be addressed in future works.

Foucault's position on the semiotic/postsemiotic question is complex and will also have to be the subject of future research. His comments about language and power, however, obviously extend some of the arguments about the ontological primacy of language made in these chapters. See, e.g., Michel Foucault, *The Archeology of Knowledge and the Discourse on Language*, trans. A. M. Sheridan Smith (New York: Pantheon Books, 1972).

Part I

Alternatives to Representational Accounts of
Language and Meaning

1

The Symbol Model vs. Language as Constitutive Articulate Contact

John Stewart

Since the mid-twentieth century, postmodern philosophers of various stripes have been questioning the efficacy of representational accounts of knowledge and representational accounts of language. In one influential volume, Richard Rorty exploits the metaphor of "mirroring" to expose serious problems inherent in the widespread beliefs held by philosophers and many other human scientists that

> [t]o know is to represent accurately what is outside the mind; so to understand the possibility and nature of knowledge is to understand the way in which the mind is able to construct such representations. [and that] Philosophy's central concern is to be a general theory of representation, a theory which will divide culture up into the areas which represent reality well, those which represent it less well, and those which do not represent it at all (despite their pretense of doing so.)[1]

Rorty combines insights from Wittgenstein, Heidegger, and Dewey to argue persuasively that it is a mistake to understand knowing as "mirroring" something separate from the knower. He points out that these three philosophers expressed this insight primarily as a claim about the nature of language. The three "hammer away at the holistic point," Rorty writes, that words do not take their meanings "by virtue of their representative character" or "their transparency to the real." To profit from these thinkers' works, "we have to understand speech not only as not the externalizing of inner representations, but as not a representation at all."[2]

Both Rorty's supporters and his critics have recognized that arguments like his against "systematic" theorizing and for a conception of philosophy as "the conversation of humankind" turn on a radical rethinking of the nature of language. For example, Richard J. Bernstein locates both the impetus for and the resistance to much of postmodernism in what he calls "Cartesian Anxiety," the conviction that either there is a fixed foundation for knowledge—objectivism—or we cannot escape the intellectual and moral chaos of relativism.[3] With the help of Rorty, Gadamer, Habermas, and Arendt, Bernstein argues that this anxiety can only be dissolved by adopting "a dialogical model of rationality" anchored in a view of language as *praxis*. Cultures need "to foster and nurture those forms of communal life in which dialogue, conversation, *phronesis*, practical discourse, and judgment are concretely embodied in our everyday practices. This is the *telos* that is common to the visions of Gadamer, Habermas, Rorty, and Arendt."[4] Importantly, both poles of Bernstein's Cartesian dilemma depend on representationalist assumptions. Objectivism relies on the assumption that knowledge and language can represent "reality" accurately, and relativism terrifies because it asserts that there is no bedrock reality for knowledge and language to represent. Thus, Bernstein argues, the escape from this anxiety begins with the recognition that knowledge and language are not representational but constitutive, which is to say that human worlds are coconstructed in the everyday practices of "dialogue, conversation, *phronesis*, practical discourse." On his view, language does not "represent" aspects of these human worlds; as praxical dialogue it brings them into being.

These arguments against representationalism echo and develop Martin Heidegger's claim that "Language is the house of Being." As Heidegger put it, "In its [language's] home [the hu]man dwells. Those who think and those who create with words are the guardians of this home. Their guardianship accomplishes the manifestation of Being insofar as they bring the manifestation to language and maintain it in language through their speech."[5] Two centrally important claims are made here. The first is that language "accomplishes the manifestation of Being" rather than *representing* Being that has somehow already and elsewhere been accomplished. This is a radically different picture from the one developed in most western language scholarship. As Heidegger noted, Aristotle's *De Interpretatione* established the classical, representational view of language, which was that "the letters are signs of sounds, the sounds are signs of mental experiences, and these are signs of things." Due to Aristotle's influence, "The sign relation constitutes the struts of the structure [of language]. . . . It has remained the standard for all later considerations of language, although with numerous modifications."[6] Heidegger believed that it was important to attend to this classical view because it prevents language scholars and laypeople from recognizing that *The essential being of language is Saying as Showing.* [and] Its showing character is not based on signs of any kind."[7] In other words, Heidegger argued that the dominant, representational model of language obscures the extent to which language is constitutive.

Heidegger's second centrally important claim was that this constitutive character of language can be grasped only when language is understood as *process* or *event* rather than *system*. This means, first, that "If we take language directly in the sense of something that is present, we encounter it as the act of speaking, the activation of the organs of speech, mouth, lips, tongue. Language manifests itself in speaking. . . ."[8] But in addition, "speaking is at the same time also listening. . . . Listening accompanies and surrounds not only speaking such as takes place in conversation. The simultaneousness of speaking and listening has a larger meaning. Speaking is of itself a listening. Speaking is listening to the language which we speak."[9] Thus in several of Heidegger's works, language was described as *coconstitutive* or *communicative*. Rather than being treated as a "system" that "represents" meanings, thoughts, or things, language became the interpersonal speaking-and-listening event that accomplishes the manifestation of Being. In other words, the phenomenon that has classically been viewed as (the system of) language was refigured as *speech communicating*.

Heidegger's student, Hans-Georg Gadamer affirms and develops his mentor's insights when he criticizes the representational *"concept of language* that modern linguistics and philosophy of language take as their starting point," because it inadequately captures "the language that lives in speech."[10] Gadamer emphasizes that from his perspective language "is no longer a system of [representational] symbols or a set of rules of grammar and syntax,"[11] and that "as long as [language] is even conceived as a symbolic form, it is not yet recognized in all its true dimensions."[12] In several of his works Gadamer mounts a sustained critique of representational accounts of language and an argument for understanding how language occurs as dialogue or conversation in which "matters of fact (*Sacheverhalte*)" and other features of human worlds are coconstituted in address-and-response.[13] A number of twentieth-century philosophers have echoed aspects of Gadamer's, Heidegger's, Bernstein's, and Rorty's views, so that there is now a widespread recognition that at least several versions of postmodernism centrally involve a critique of representational accounts of the nature of knowledge and the nature of language.[14]

Heidegger's comments about "sign relations" and Gadamer's reference to the model of language as "a symbolic form" demonstrate that a central target of this general critique is the view that language is a *semiotic system*, that is, a system of signs and/or symbols. Since signs and symbols are universally understood as entities that somehow "stand for" or "depict" something else, critiques of representational accounts of the nature of language are critiques of accounts of language as a semiotic system. But oddly enough, this point has not been widely recognized. Despite the prominence and plausibility of postmodern arguments against representationalism, scholars in many disciplines continue to characterize language semiotically. For example, according to contemporary linguist Julia Kristeva,

> the idea that the fundamental core of *la langue* resides in the *sign* has belonged to various thinkers and schools of thought, from ancient Greece through the Middle Ages *and up to the present time* [italics added]. In fact, every speaker is more or less conscious of the fact that language symbolizes or *represents* real facts by *naming* them. The elements of the spoken chain—for the moment let us call them words—are associated with certain objects or facts that they *signify*.[15]

Although Kristeva acknowledges at least one other point of view "based on a philosophical critique of the very concept of the sign,"[16] she nonetheless treats semiosis as one essential feature of language.

Scholars in several disciplines concur with Kristeva about the fundamentally semiotic nature of language. For example, sociologist Norbert Elias maintained that to understand virtually anything, humans must be able to distance themselves from physical reality: "they must, as it were, mentally ascend to a level of synthesis above that of its existence here and now as a heap of matter."[17] Various types of symbolic representations allow humans to do this, and languages are the most important. The need for communicable symbols "extends to the whole fund of knowledge of a language community and ultimately of humanity, including functions, situations, processes, and symbols themselves." In fact, Elias wrote, "communication by means of symbols, which may differ from society to society, is one of the singularities of humankind. . . . One may rightly say that all this is obvious."[18] Psycholinguist Charles E. Osgood echoed the same sentiments when he defined what he took to be the six essential criteria that characterize language. The fourth is The Semantic Criterion, which holds that the production of identifiably different and nonrandomly recurrent physical linguistic forms (e.g., words) follows nonrandom rules of reference to events in other channels. "This criterion," Osgood explained, "implied that for anything to be a language it must function so as to *symbolize* (represent for the organism) the non-necessarily-*here* and the not-necessarily-*now*."[19]

Some contemporary communication scholars also persist in the belief that their object of study is a representational, semiotic system. For example, in a widely cited essay, Gary Cronkhite argues that the discipline of communication is united by its focus upon "human symbolic activity," and that "all words, with the possible exceptions of onomatopoeic [sic] words, are pure *symbols*."[20] Cronkhite acknowledges criticisms of the referential nature of "treatments of meaning as symbolic," but he claims to avoid this problem by asserting that "a *symbol system* (e.g., the English language) represents *systems* of environmental, social, and cognitive entities and relationships in far more complex ways than direct symbol-referent correspondences."[21] In a similar vein, Michael T. Motley begins his examination of the construct of communicative intent with a review of "some extremely common, if not quite universal assumptions found in even the most elementary discussions" of his subject matter.[22] The first of these virtually universal postulates is that "communication is characterized by symbolic behaviors, that is to say, that communication involves the transmission and/or reception of symbols." "Traditionally, *symbols* have been defined as signs arbitrarily related to their referents," Motley notes. And "the cognitive process of preparing a message for transmission to another requires, among other things, that we select signs from among a repertoire of possibilities. Signs thus selected and transmitted *function as symbols*. . ."[23] (pp. 2–3).

Some prominent writers have set out systematically to correct what they acknowledge are oversimplifications in semiotic characterizations of language and communication. For example, semiotician Umberto Eco attempts to articulate key features of what he calls a "general semiotics" that embraces "text, semiosis, significant practice, communication, discourse, language, effability, and so on."[24] A central part of Eco's work is meant to "disentangle" the concept of sign "from its trivial identification with the idea of coded equivalence and identity" and to restore the centrality of interpretation to what he calls the semiosic process. Eco demonstrates that the essential feature of the sign has been expressed in the antique formulation *aliquid stat pro aliquo*, something stands for something else. The symbol has been characterized similarly, he notes, although this construct typically foregrounds the vagueness and openness of *aliquo*: "with symbols and by symbols one elucidates what is always beyond one's reach."[25] Using the example of a badge worn at one's buttonhole, Eco emphasizes that something is a sign or symbol "only inasmuch as it *does not stand for itself*. It does not stand for its molecular composition, its tendency to fall down, its capability of being packaged and transported. It stands for something which is outside itself."[26]

Eco argues that the problem with the classic formula is that it obscures the importance of human interpretation in semiosis, where interpreting a sign means defining "the portion of continuum which serves as its vehicle in its relationship with the other portions of the continuum derived from its global segmentation by the content. It means to define a portion through the use of other portions, conveyed by other expressions."[27] The outcome of this interplay among signs is the elucidation of reality, which Eco calls "the world" or "the pulp itself of the matter which is manipulated by semiosis."[28] In the final chapter of *Semiotics and the Philosophy of Language*, Eco describes the "seven semiotic requirements" that actually make a sign a sign, the first six of which are aspects of the *aliquid stat pro aliquo* formulation and the seventh of which is the aspect of interpretation. Thus Eco's project to revise the oversimplified identification of semiosis with "the idea of coded equivalence and identity" (Cronkhite's referentialism) ultimately reaffirms most features of historical analyses, including the ontological claim that in the process of semiotic representation, human meaning connects with "the pulp itself of the matter which is manipulated by semiosis." In other words, this prominent and influential effort to revise the dominant, simplistically representational concept of the sign ultimately concludes that a sign is indeed, at its root, "something that stands for something else."

As these and other writers develop their views of the nature of language, substantive differences arise. Kristeva often relies on Saussure's *Cours de linguistique générale,* but she also distances herself from some of its conclusions. Elias rejects aspects of the Cartesian-Kantian analyses that inform many of the semiotic accounts of language that preceded his. Cronkhite and Motley cite with approval C. K. Ogden and I. A. Richards's classic, *The Meaning of Meaning*, but their views of communication move significantly beyond the telementational perspective outlined in that work. Eco concurs at some points with Kristeva and Elias and disagrees with them at others. It is clear, in short, that semiotic accounts of language are not all of a piece; they differ in important ways, and each of these authors would accept some claims made in complementary writings and reject others.

The Symbol Model

Despite their substantive differences, however, these and many other philosophers, linguists, semioticians, and communication theorists share some common commitments. These commitments make up what I call the symbol model, the model summarized by the claim that language is fundamentally a semiotic system, a system of signs and/or symbols.

Some scholars who embrace this perspective, including D. S. Clarke, the author of chapter 7 of this book, argue against using the term "sym-

bol" to label such a model. They take pains to distinguish generally between signs and symbols, and to differentiate among specific types of signs,
for example, "decisigns," "natsigns," and comsigns."[29] Thus, these writers
claim, it is both imprecise and misleading to group semiotic programs
together under the "*symbol* model" rubric. But as the citations from Osgood, Elias, Cronkhite, and Motley indicate, "symbol" is the term most
frequently used by scholars in a variety of disciplines to characterize the
basic nature of language. Scores of these writers continue in the 1990s to
argue that the human animal is distinctive because of its ability to "symbolize" and that language is essentially, in Kenneth Burke's words, a "conventional, arbitrary symbol system."[30] Thus I have chosen the term "symbol model" to label not only these programs but also those that foreground
"sign" rather than "symbol" vocabulary, because both sets of approaches
adhere in varying degrees to five interrelated theoretical commitments.

As I have already indicated, the first commitment of the symbol model
is an ontological one. These accounts presume that there is a fundamental
distinction between two realms or worlds, the world of the sign and the
signified, symbol and symbolized, name and named, word and thought,
aliquid and *aliquo*. Although writers have described significant—although
sometimes contradictory—differences between signs and symbols, these
two phenomena are ontologically similar because they are both primary
semiotic units, which means that they are viewed as fundamentally different from, and most often ontologically subordinate to, whatever they signify or symbolize.

Descriptions of the symbol model's two realms or worlds differ, and in
some cases theorists argue that they are virtually indistinguishable or inseparable, or even, in some cases, that there is no distinction. But once the
semiotic assumption has been made, a structural a priori has been established, and even those who argue for inseparability must struggle to make
their accounts of language coherent with what has been termed the
"Janus-faced" character of language.[31] I call this basic ontological claim the
commitment to "Two Worlds." It holds that there is a difference in kind
between the linguistic world, or the world of "signifiers," and some other
world—that of "things," "mental experiences," "ideas," "concepts," or
other "signifieds."

The four additional commitments that make up the symbol model
follow from this one. Commitment 2 is the belief that the linguistic world
consists of identifiable units or elements (phonemes, morphemes, words,
utterances, speech acts) that are its atoms or molecules. The third commitment is the claim that the relationship between these units of language
and the units that make up the other of the two worlds is some sort of
representational or symbolizing relationship.[32] Commitment 4 is the belief

that these ontologically distinct, representationally functioning units make up a system, the system called "language." The final commitment asserts that language is a tool or instrument humans use to accomplish their goals. Some version of these five commitments is entailed by the decision to characterize language semiotically. In other words, *some version of these five commitments necessarily follows as a consequence of using "sign" or "symbol" vocabulary to describe the nature of language.*

Commitment #1: Two Worlds

These five commitments are interrelated in several ways. First, as I noted, the two worlds claim is most basic. As reviews of the history of linguistics demonstrate in detail, this claim embodies the ontology first established in Platonic and Aristotelian formulations of the nature of language.[33] The basic distinction between linguistic and nonlinguistic worlds was articulated explicitly in the influential Aristotelian formula that Heidegger cited: "Spoken words are the symbols of mental experience and written words are the symbols of spoken words."[34] This became the medieval canon linking *aliquid* and *aliquo*, which was developed into John Locke's claim that words are "signs" that signify "ideas," and the connection in Wittgenstein's *Tractatus Logico-Philosophicus* between "propositions" and the "objects of thought" that they "picture."[35] In Kristeva's words cited earlier, the distinction is between "language" and "real facts." Elias distinguished between "symbols" and "physical reality" or "a heap of matter." For Osgood the two worlds consist of "physical forms" and "events in other channels" or present "symbols" and "the not-necessarily here and the not-necessarily now." Cronkhite's terms are "symbols" or "symbol systems" and "environmental, social, and cognitive entities," and, for the most part, Motley is satisfied with the distinction between "symbols" and "referents." In places, Eco speaks of two different "portions of the continuum," but at others he distinguishes between the sign and "the world (the continuum, the pulp itself of the matter which is manipulated by semiosis)." This sample of perspectives illustrates some of the diversity that characterizes expressions of the commitment to two worlds.

Eco's is not the only work in which this commitment to two worlds appears to be modified or even rejected, only to resurface. Early in the *Cours*, for example, Saussure labeled the two phenomena *concept* and *sound image* and claimed that both were psychological entities, which would mean, in the present vocabulary, that they were parts of *one* world. This claim was central to Saussure's argument that language is constituted solely of *differences* among units in the single system. But despite the conceptual centrality of this claim, Saussure contradicted it by treating concept and sound image as ontologically distinct, both when he discussed the fact that sound images were "temporal" but ideas were not,[36] and when he argued that there is a *representational* relationship between concept and sound image.[37] This set of moves is typical. Theorists who treat language semiotically sometimes acknowledge the potential problems created by their commitment to two worlds, but when they explore in detail the nature of the "symbol" or "signifier" and the "symbolized" or "signified," in virtually all cases they postulate at one point or another an ontological distinction between them.

Once the existence of two realms or worlds has been posited, and one wishes to carry on the conversation, one requirement for coherence is that the theorist explain the nature of each world—what each is made up of or resembles. Most language scholars have approached this issue by beginning with analysis rather than synthesis, which has led them to identify the *units* that purportedly constitute each world. Thus arises commitment #2, to some form of atomism. Then, once one has asserted the existence of two different worlds consisting of two different sets of units, coherence further demands that one explain how units in one world relate to units in the other. This question has been answered with the claim that one set of units somehow *represents* (signifies, symbolizes) the other—commitment #3. At this point, language has been characterized as a semiotic *system* consisting of units in one world that in some way represent units in another—commitment #4. Given the existence in the human world of this more-or-less objective system, coherence then demands that one give an account of how humans orient to this system. Commitment #5 is a response to this question: Humans use the system instrumentally to accomplish their goals.

Commitment #2: Atomism

As was noted, the commitment to atomism is embodied in the decision to approach language by dividing it into units. This move has been popular since the first primitive pictographs isolated some visible features of notable events and the letters of the first alphabets designated specific phonemes. In each case, consequential decisions were made to mark some elements of communicative experience *and to ignore others*. For example, pre-Socratic Greeks graphically represented not only distinctions between closely related consonants, such as /p/ and /b/, but also between related vowels, such as /e/ and /æ/. But although their system marked differences between voiced and unvoiced consonants and front, medial, and back vowels, it included no units to highlight the differences between, for example, a threatening greeting and a welcoming one or a serious question and an ironic one. Thus the atomism commitment has not only focused attention on parts rather than wholes, it has also highlighted some kinds of parts and ignored others with as much or more semantic and pragmatic importance. This reductive feature of the atomism commitment is one reason the symbol model distorts the phenomenon it purports to explain.

The commitment to treat language atomistically has been most apparent in theorists' dependence on examples of single words to support their claims about the semiotic character of language. The literature from pre-Socratic times to the present is replete with claims that "horse," "tree," "ox," "chair," "table," "cat," "hat," and "mat" are all paradigm examples of units of language that, when analyzed carefully, will reveal the basic character of language itself. At best, of course, these analyses can only account for some aspects of the operation of one category of language units, concrete nouns. To generalize from these to language itself, theorists have had to assume that concrete nouns were the paradigmatic units of language, and that all other units can be compared to or contrasted with them. From at least Aristotle forward, abstract nouns, adverbs, prepositions, conjunctions, and even sentences and propositions have been analyzed in terms of, or in ways parasitic on, the analysis of concrete nouns. Several critics have noted the indefensibility of this way of proceeding, and, as a result, especially in the twentieth century, some theorists have concentrated on phonemes, utterances, or speech acts. But these phenomena are also typically treated as discrete units that, in various combinations, make up language. In this way, commitment #2 persists even in some of the most recent accounts of language.

Commitment #3: Representational

The commitment to representationalism follows directly. Given two worlds or realms, each made up of units, one is led to ask how units of one relate to units of the other. Everyday experience has often appeared to offer a hint: Names represent individual persons; therefore, early theorists speculated, isn't it probable that other words function similarly? Fortunately, it almost immediately became apparent to most theorists that it would be difficult to locate the "thing named" for many categories of words, including negative terms, articles, prepositions, and conjunctions. But unfortunately, rather than reexamining the basic assumption that words function representationally, scholars typically have looked for ways to salvage their semiotic analyses. One strategy has been to argue that problematic words only represented by virtue of their connection with other, concrete terms. This strategy led to the tortuous efforts to analyze "categorematic" and "syncategorematic" terms that peaked in the late Middle Ages. A second approach has been to generate various kinds of entities for these prob- lematic terms to represent, such as John Locke's "the absence of some- thing," which, he postulated, was the representamen or thing-named for the word "nothing."[38] Gilbert Ryle labeled this strategy "the 'Fido'-Fido fallacy," because it holds that every meaningful expression must signify an extra-linguistic correlate, as "Fido" signifies Fido.[39] But Ryle failed to point out that his criticism undermined not just referential theories of word meaning but all semiotic, representational accounts of language. Partly as a result, these accounts persist.

A third strategy has been to distinguish various kinds of representa- tional relationships, including those that are logical, psychological, cul- tural, or communicative. Wittgenstein argued in the *Tractatus*, for exam- ple, that words were representations in the sense of the German term *Darstellung* ("model," "presentation," "exhibition"—a logical representa- tion) but not in the sense of *Vorstellung* ("picture"—a sensory representa- tion). But this distinction did not alter the basic structure of the symbol model. Virtually all contemporary dictionaries, encyclopedia, and glossaries define a symbol as something that stands for or represents something else. And the claim persists in each articulated version of the symbol model that the representing unit from world$_1$ in some way stands for (signifies, sym- bolizes, represents) another unit from world$_2$.

Commitment #4: System

Theorists frequently overlook the significance of the fact that semiotic characterizations of language picture it as a system rather than a process, event, or mode of human being. In the late nineteenth century, Wilhelm von Humboldt attempted to redirect language scholarship by arguing that theorists should focus on *energeia* or *activity*, not *ergon*, or *product*.[40] But he stopped considerably short of accomplishing this redefinition, and even after his efforts, the inclination to treat language as a system has consis- tently hypostatized the process, frequently under the rationale that this is the only way to treat it systematically, objectively, or "scientifically." Again, Saussure's work exemplifies this tendency. He acknowledged distinctions among human language–ability (*langage*), the system of language (*lan- gue*), and speech (*parole*) and noted that historically, the actuality of *pa- role* always comes first. But he also insisted that linguists concentrate on *langue*, the system of language. One reason Saussure focused on language as a system is that he wanted to emphasize how each linguistic unit is meaningful only in relation to the other units making up its system. As noted earlier, this insight was one of his primary contributions to modern linguistics and laid the foundation for structuralist theories of language and culture. But Saussure also restricted linguistics to the study of *langue* because, he claimed, it was the only phenomenon that was orderly enough and accessible enough to be studied scientifically. This move perpetuated a subject-object relationship between linguists and language, and it is this feature of commitment #4 that, I believe, has most distorted subsequent language study.

The reason the system commitment distorts language study is that it attempts to separate the analyst from the phenomenon being analyzed—language—even though the only way to analyze language (or any other topic)[41] is linguistically, discursively, communicatively, "in" language. This commitment, in other words, presupposes an impossible distinction between linguistically constituted beings and language, as if the human analyst could function as purely *res cogitans* examining and manipulating an equally pure *res extensa*—language. I argue more fully later in this chapter that although it may appear initially plausible to conceive of language as an object of study that is unproblematically accessible to investigation by human subjects, the pervasively linguistic nature of human being makes this subject-object approach to language ultimately incoherent.

Commitment #5: Tool

The tool commitment makes this subject-object focus explicit. Adherence to this commitment emerged relatively late in the development of the symbol model. Virtually all classical authors acknowledged that language is used in various ways. But the contemporary emphasis on language as an instrumental tool reflects the Enlightenment proclivity for analyses that begin with the Cartesian *cogito* and the irreducible distinction between the subject and the objects that subjects allegedly encounter, construct, and manipulate. From the perspective of commitment #5, language is one of the more-or-less objectifiable tools that subjects use to accomplish their goals.

Historically, of course, the primary use of the language tool has been viewed as the communication of thoughts or ideas. Among others, Locke underscored the importance of the communicative function of language, and the eighteenth-century theorist John Horne Tooke would not even grant "language" status to the solitary mental naming that some of his predecessors had analyzed. Horne Tooke argued that the fact that the purpose of language is "to communicate our thoughts" should "be kept singly in contemplation," but that unfortunately this fact "has missed all those who have reasoned on this subject."[42] As this commitment has been worked out, language has often been treated as an instrument uniquely available to humans and the primary reason for humans' superiority over other animals.

I emphatically do not mean to claim that any contemporary language scholar explicitly accepts the simplistic word-idea relationship that Aristotle or Locke outlined or, Kristeva's comment notwithstanding, the notion that there is a one-to-one correspondence between word and thing, idea, response, or meaning. As Cronkhite and others acknowledge, these simple referential versions of the symbol model have been fatally discredited by many modern and contemporary scholarly programs, including the analytic critiques of Wittgenstein, Ryle, Austin,[43] and Searle,[44] and the hermeneutic efforts of Heidegger, Gadamer, and other postmodernists. But as I noted in relation to Ryle's criticism of "the 'Fido'-Fido fallacy," the connection has not consistently been made between these discredited referential theories and the general practice of characterizing language as a semiotic system. In other words, many scholars appear not to recognize how some version of the symbol model inheres in every semiotic account of language or communication. This is because when language and communication scholars adopt "sign," "symbol," and "symbolizing" vocabulary, they are led by this vocabulary toward positions strikingly close to the discredited referential versions of the symbol model.

The Model's Primary Limitation: The Natural Language Problem

Despite the variety of critiques of representational views of language, few scholars have emphasized how difficult it is to apply the symbol model to the phenomena it purports to depict. Clearly any effort to define or characterize the nature of language should be informatively applicable to instances of language's natural occurrence. The theoretical formulation, in other words, should readily and fruitfully fit paradigmatic examples of its explanadum. It is equally clear that the paradigmatic instance of language is conversation, verbal-nonverbal exchange between humans in real time, either face-to-face or mediated by some electronic modality (e.g., telephone). This is the activity humans engage in characteristically, routinely, naturally, and constantly. Some version of it makes up the lion's share of most humans' personal and occupational lives. Unfortunately, this point appears to have been lost on many language theorists who concentrate instead on examples devised to support their arguments. Philosophers have typically generated armchair examples about the present king of France or the morning-and-evening star, and linguists and semioticians have speculated about whether green ideas sleep furiously and have attempted to analyze such pseudo-utterances as "Hello, Tom. This is Bill. I promise you that John will return the money." Artificial constructions such as these can often clarify their authors' claims, but they cannot test them. Like focusing on concrete nouns, the tendency to use only hypothetical examples has contributed to the persistence of the symbol model despite its manifest inapplicability.

But a group of researchers who call themselves conversation analysts do examine discourse much closer to actual conversation. They use audio and sometimes video recordings to create detailed transcripts that embody a much fuller sense of living language than do examples generated by even the most creative armchair theorist. These scholars employ a variety of print conventions to indicate such nonverbal features of spoken language as vocal emphasis, pause, and overlapped speech. For example, capital letters designate emphasis, one or more colons indicate a prolonged sound or syllable, brackets enclose overlapped talk, and pauses are marked by either a dot or a count of seconds in parentheses. Below is an excerpt from a conversation analyst's transcript of a naturally occurring interchange that should provide a reasonable test of the symbol model:

Example #1 Two College Students

1. John: So what do you THI::NK about the bicycles on campus?

2. Judy: I think they're terrible.

3. John: Sure is about a MIL:LION of 'em.

4. Judy: eh⌈he:h ⌉
5. John: ⌊Duzit⌋ SEEM da you: there's a lot more people this year?

6. Judy: The⌈re-⌉ ye:ah, for su:re
7. John: ⌊Go-⌋   GOD, there seems to be a mIL-lion people

8. Judy: Yeah. (1.0) YE:ah, there's: way too many. I can't- at tIMEs the

9.   bicycles get so bad I just got off mi⌐ne an   ⌐ hh .h
              and gi(h)ve up!

10. John: ⌊Oh riLleh⌋

11. John: I unno when I DODGE one then I have to DODGE another one 'n

12.   its an endless cycle.

13. Judy: Yeah (1.0) oh they're TERrible.

14. John: 'S so many people.

15. Judy: Um hmm[45]

As the reader no doubt can sense, this transcript captures something much closer to language as it actually occurs than the examples commonly used by philosophers, linguists, and semioticians. Of course, this is "informal" language, which means, among other things, that it functions only partly in the service of "propositional content" or "truth value." The interlocutors are as engaged in negotiating their respective identities as they are in making assertions. Questions are at least as important as answers, and pause, stress, rhythm, facial expression, proximity, gesture, movement, and various unmarked features of vocal intonation contribute significantly to conversational outcomes. But if one is interested in language as it is lived, this example is surely more paradigmatic than the hypotheticals typically discussed, and, as a relatively "spontaneous" and "natural" instance, it warrants close attention.

The reader may also sense what outcome will result from testing the symbol model by applying it here. But hopefully without belaboring the obvious, let us ask whether the language displayed here appears to fit the description of the nature of language offered by those who characterize it as a system of signs or symbols functioning representationally and instrumentally.

Several of the concrete nouns in these examples appear to be accurately described by the symbol model. "Bicycles," "campus," "people," and perhaps "year" could conceivably be thought of as language units that label, signify, represent, and in some cases even name objects or events in the interlocutors' nonlinguistic worlds. But to acknowledge that these words may be thought of as signs or symbols of things or concepts is still to leave unexplained the majority of the words and phrases in these examples. And it is much more difficult to generate coherent and useful insights by applying the symbol model to them.

For instance, consider just the first word of the first utterance—"So."[46] What might this unit of language signify or symbolize? If a theorist committed to the symbol model agreed that this were a suitable unit to analyze, he or she might argue that this word represents John's desire or intent to introduce his question with something like the equivalent of "hence" or "therefore." John begins his utterance this way in order to connect it with whatever preceded it, and he chooses the word "So" because of its informality. Thus the word symbolizes a "concept," "idea," or an aspect of the speaker's preceding emotional and mental state, and this state is specifiable, given the communicative context.

On its face, this account is plausible enough. But in order for it to be consistent with the two worlds commitment of the symbol model, the mental state must actually be specifiable and must be ontologically different from the word. Consider the first requirement: Is it specifiable? Could one describe a discrete mental state that actually could be said to precede the utterance of "So," and that would be signified by this specific utterance? Certainly this task would be difficult. One first wonders how to describe this specific a mental state. Some mental states can be easily, if a bit loosely, characterized as, for example, the state of "feeling worried," or "intending to be on time." But how might one go about describing the mental state signified by John's utterance of the word "So" in this context? Perhaps one could characterize it as one of informal-transitional-introductory-temporalizing, or as encouraging-tentative-inclusive-friendliness. But such abstract descriptions hardly satisfy the requirement to define the specific phenomenon that is the signified of this word. Notice, also, how the effort to describe this specific "intent," or "concept" depends on a model of the mind that is manifestly indefensible. To accommodate the commitment to two worlds, one has to view the mind as a container of some sort filled with entities of very puzzling ontological status. To develop this kind of model, cognitive functioning has to be hypostatized in ways that clearly conflict not only with the results of current cognitive psychology and artificial intelligence research but also with contemporary philosophical anthropology.[47] Today, virtually every schoolchild knows that the mind is not a container filled with the kinds of entities that are required by the symbol model.

What about the distinctiveness of this mental state? Is it different in kind from the utterance that allegedly signifies it? And can it coherently be said to precede the utterance of "So" in such a way that "So" can represent it? One way to test whether this is the case is to ask if the same mental state could occur in the absence of this word. Is the mental state that is the alleged signified of "So" the same or different from the one that would accompany John's utterance in this context of "Hence" or "Therefore"? On the one hand, the answer seems simple. Since "So" is more informal than either "Hence" or "Therefore," the mental states would obviously differ. On the other hand, in order to verify this response, one would have to be able to call up these mental states in the absence of these words or their synonyms and to assess their relative formality—and their other distinctive features. But it is extremely difficult to determine how one might call up the mental state of, for example, informal-transitional-introductory-temporalizing without the word "So," in order to see (hear?) whether it is identical to or different from a closely related mental state. In fact, the problem is even more basic: How does one go about calling up mental states in the first place? And if one can in fact perform this activity without using words, could a mental state that is "called up" for the purpose suggested here be identical to the mental state spontaneously experienced by John in this conversation? As "an example called up for purposes of analysis," wouldn't this mental state differ from the original one? It is difficult to tell how even to begin to respond to such questions, and yet they are necessarily raised by the theoretical commitments that make up the symbol model.

A version of this same analysis could be applied to virtually any of the other words that are not concrete nouns or pronouns in this example. In utterance #1 this list includes "what," "do," "THI::NK," "about," "the," and "on." There are at least an additional sixty-six words here that could be similarly analyzed.

But again, all this may seem a little silly. As I noted earlier, no contemporary scholar would seriously contend that one can specify any sort of one-to-one correspondence between specific signifier and specific signified. Surely the current understandings of language held by philosophers, linguists, semioticians, and communication theorists have progressed far beyond such a Lockean conceptualization. Contemporary scholars who subscribe to the symbol model might well argue that semiosis is basic to language, but they also insist that the process is much more complex and subtle than is implied by the simplistic analysis proposed and critiqued in the immediately preceding paragraphs.

For one thing, it is sometimes argued, individual words are not the units of signification in these examples. Phrases are, or idioms, or propositions, or sentences, or utterances. The signifier in line 1 is not the single word "So," but "So what do you THI::NK" or perhaps the entire utterance, "So what do you THI::NK about the bicycles on campus?" This move appears to avoid the worst difficulties created by word-by-word analyses. But it does not solve the problem, because these difficulties simply resurface at another point in the analysis. The shift from words to word or sound groups does not do away with the requirement to identify the ontological status of the signified. Assuming that it is nonlinguistic, one must again treat it as some sort of mental or cognitive state. And it is obviously just as difficult to specify the mental state signified by the phrase or sentence as it is to specify the mental state signified by a single word. It is also just as difficult to argue that the mental state signified by a phrase or sentence is distinct from the words that allegedly signify or symbolize it.

But what if it is not nonlinguistic? Can't this hoary ontological conundrum be dissolved by simply acknowledging that both signifier and signified are of the same ontological status? Saussure made exactly this move when he specified that "the two elements involved in the linguistic sign are both psychological,"[48] and when he emphasized that each linguistic unit is meaningful only in relation to the other units making up the circumscribed system. But there are two closely related reasons why the problem cannot be solved this way.

First, one cannot coherently abandon a commitment to there being an ontological difference between signifier and signified while maintaining that a representational relationship exists between the two. Representation, in other words, is a relationship that exists between two dissimilar phenomena. A symbol is something that stands for something *else*. A flag can represent a country; a graphic image—for example, a silhouette of a long-haired person wearing a skirt—can signify that a restroom is for women; an attorney can represent a client; and it can even be initially coherent to claim that a word signifies or symbolizes a thing, idea, or feeling. But a flag cannot *stand for* another flag, and a warning symbol cannot *signify* another warning symbol. Moreover, whenever one human represents another, he or she does so by virtue of the difference between them—one is elected and the other a constituent or one is professionally certified for the service and the other in need of it. And no morpheme, word, or phrase can coherently be said to stand for another morpheme, word, or phrase. Even synonyms are mutually substitutable but not representationally related. As a result, it cannot be coherent to claim both that two related phenomena are of the same ontological status and that the relationship between them is representational. If the purported relationship is a signifying or symbolizing one, then the phenomena need to be different in kind. This is why the two worlds commitment is so fundamental to the symbol model: This ontological difference is inherent in the meaning of "representation."

This coherency difficulty probably explains why theorists who claim at one point that signifier and signified are similar tend subsequently to treat them as ontologically distinct. And this is the second reason why the representational problem cannot be solved this way: This strategy presages a contradiction. Both Émile Benveniste and Kristeva make this point about the *Cours*. As Benveniste explains,

> Even though Saussure said that the idea of "sister" is not connected to the signifier *s-ö-r*, he was not thinking any the less of the *reality* of the notion. When he spoke of the difference between *b-ö-f* and *o-k-s*, he was referring, in spite of himself, to the fact that these two terms applied to the same *reality*. Here, then, is the *thing*, expressly excluded at first from the definition of the sign, now creeping into it by a detour, and *permanently installing a contradiction there* [italics added].[49]

Saussure appears to have noticed this permanent contradiction, that is, that he could not maintain both his claim that *signifiant* and *signifié* were

equally psychological and his commitment to there being a representational relationship between them. So later sections of his work acknowledge the necessity of the ontological difference. Eco's analysis cited earlier
contains the same contradiction. At one point Eco speaks of the two aspects representationally linked by the sign as different "portions of the
continuum," and subsequently he claims that one is linguistic and the
other is part of "the world" or "the pulp . . . of the matter."

In short, protests that the two worlds commitment of the symbol
model is no longer a part of serious language theorizing, and therefore
that any attempt to test it against living language is irrelevant or unfair,
can only be sustained if one ignores a substantial part of the significant
contemporary literature in philosophy, linguistics, semiotics, and communication theory. "*Up to the present time* (italics added)," Kristeva writes,
"every speaker is more or less conscious of the fact that . . . the elements
of the spoken chain . . . symbolize or *represent* real facts by *naming*
them." "Language," claims Osgood, functions "to *symbolize* (represent for
the organism) the non-necessarily-*here* and the not-necessarily-*now*." The
fact that symbols enable humans to distance themselves from "existence
here and now as a heap of matter" is "obvious," according to Elias. And
even as Eco resists the "trivial identification [of the sign] with the idea of
coded equivalence and identity," he develops an account that is dependent
on the same theoretical commitment that undergirds the "trivial" view he
resists; namely, that language essentially involves the occurrence in an
interpreting human being of a representational relationship between some
aliquid and some *aliquo*. These citations are only a sample of the expressions of the two worlds commitment that influential scholars in several
disciplines have made through the past decade. The ontological difference
basic to the symbol model is alive and well, and yet this feature of semiotic
characterizations of the nature of language cannot coherently be applied to
concrete instances of the phenomenon it purports to describe.

Before assessing the applicability of the remaining theoretical commitments, I want to underscore the hermeneutic approach to validity that
guides my analysis. A realistic or idealistic approach would argue that the
symbol model is "accurate" or "inaccurate," "true" or "false." It would do
so by identifying the independently existing, specifiable phenomena against
which one could juxtapose the model in order to determine how well the
model captured or corresponded to these realities. To test the symbol
model in this way, one would need a supply of words, representeds, and
manifest relations between them. But the process of testing the first commitment of the symbol model on these examples has clarified that the
model cannot be verified in this way because the signified is generally
unspecifiable. There is, in other words, a shortage of identifiable phenomena against which to test the model's correspondence, due primarily to

the impossibility of maintaining a subject-object relationship with one's language. As a result, I argue, one would be well-advised to give up the correspondence criterion and instead to ask how coherent, plausible, and applicable the symbol model is. These are the questions that guide a hermeneutic validity test. As Gadamer puts it, from this perspective the hermeneutic theorist is primarily interested in what a model comes to in its being worked out.[50] My primary argument is that the symbol model does not fare well as it is worked out and that the model has very limited applicability and equally limited plausibility and coherence. When those who propound it attempt systematically to trace out its implications and applications, they typically find themselves in one of several argumentative, theoretical, and/or philosophical cul-de-sacs similar to those just encountered in the attempted analysis of "So." And they are in good company; these intellectual and practical dead ends have been occupied by some of the West's most respected thinkers. The problem, I argue, is not a lack of rigor or imagination. The problem is the model: Language cannot be coherently, plausibly, and usefully described as a system of symbols.

Efforts to test the other commitments of the symbol model lead to a similar conclusion. As noted earlier, the atomism commitment pictures language as made up of identifiable units, often words. Leaving aside, for a moment, the difficulties of determining exactly what a word is, the bulk of the discourse in this example of conversation is both hearable and seeable as made up of grammatically identifiable individual units. But several utterances do not fit this pattern, for example "Duzit" (line 5), "unno" (1.11), and "'s" (1.14). How can the commitment to atomism be applied to elements that appear to be combinations of the basic units specified by the model? In addition, the brackets between lines 4–5, 6–7, and 9–10 indicate overlapped talk. Commitment #2 would indicate that Judy is simply saying "he:h" at the same time John is saying "Duzit" and is saying "-ne an" at the same time John is saying "Oh riLleh," and that one can appropriately understand this language by examining these individual words or individual sentences. But a conversation analyst would respond by repeating the argument outlined earlier against the efficacy of word-by-word or sentence-by-sentence analysis and for the claim that more is revealed in these instances of language by attending to the molar rather than the molecular units. Moreover, most conversation analysts would not treat the larger units as signifiers and thereby get caught in the search for signifieds. Instead, the claim might be made, for example, that the overlap as a whole is a notable unit, because all three talkovers are interruptions of the female by the male. Such analysis might also point out that Judy's "-hh.h and gi(h)ve up!" in turn 9 after John's overlap could be traceable in part to his overlap, not just to the previous words in her utterance or his locution

"Oh riLleh." These are some features of this exchange that any attempt to analyze these examples as made up of individual units would leave unexplained. And this is a central difficulty created by the atomism commitment of the symbol model.

Especially by way of commitments #4 and #5, the symbol model pictures language as a system existing over-against humans. According to this part of the model, persons manipulate the various language resources available to them to accomplish their conscious and unconscious goals. This approach foregrounds the construct of linguistic and communicative intent, which raises a welter of conceptual and empirical problems that have been widely discussed.[51] The central philosophical problem with these two commitments is that (along with several versions of the commitment to two worlds) they embody the Cartesian-Kantian, subject-object view of the nature of language noted earlier. This set of moves treats language as essentially a tool that humans employ strategically and tactically. But this picture has also been subjected to strong criticism. For example, Heidegger argued that subject-object analyses of humans begin one giant step too far into the problematic, because, prior to any operations as subjects over-against a more-or-less "objective" world, humans engage in a variety of everyday practices into which we are socialized but that we do not represent in our minds. Heidegger labeled this process being-in-the-world;[52] later, I call it *everyday coping*. The process consists primarily of the activities of interpretive involvement that constitute human existing. Sometimes humans experience themselves as conscious subjects relating to objects by way of intentional states, such as desires, beliefs, intentions, and goals, but Heidegger argued that this is a condition that presupposes the more fundamental being-in-the-world, which cannot be understood in subject-object terms. This line of thinking has led not only Heidegger but also many other authors to build a broad consensus that calls for serious rethinking of subject-object analyses of human being. As Thomas McCarthy puts it, for many postmodern writers,

> the epistemological and moral subject has been definitively decentered and the conception of reason linked to it irrevocably desublimated. Subjectivity and intentionality are not prior to but a function of forms of life and systems of language; they do not "constitute" the world but are themselves elements of a linguistically disclosed world.[53]

There are, in short, serious difficulties inherent in the claim that language is a semiotic system. One primary conceptual problem with this model of language is that it is impossible to develop and explicate while maintaining coherence. This task first requires one to distinguish between a linguistic and a nonlinguistic world so that symbols or signifiers can be shown to be related to their corresponding meanings or signifieds. But no theorist has yet been able satisfactorily to explain the ontological status of this alleged second world, the one made up of the entities that linguistic units supposedly represent. A similar coherence problem arises with respect to world$_1$. The model requires its user to identify discrete units of language, and each attempt to reduce an instance of conversation to individual morphemes, words, speech acts, or utterances distorts the amalgam of verbal and nonverbal features that make up living language. A third problem is that the model presupposes a subject-object relationship between language and the language analyst. In order to maintain this relationship, the analyst must disregard arguments made by some of the twentieth century's most influential thinkers, including the Wittgenstein of the *Philosophical Investigations*, Heidegger, Gadamer, and Rorty, and must maintain the fiction that language is an instrument or tool. These coherence problems lead directly to a fatal practical difficulty: The symbol model cannot be successfully applied to the naturally occurring language that makes up everyday conversation. No researcher I have read has yet been able to reduce a living conversation to its semiotic units and to identify unproblematically what the units represent. Finally, the symbol model creates a potential ethical problem by construing language as ancillary or secondary to the meanings, thoughts, concepts, or ideas that it allegedly codifies. The interactive events that engage humans so consistently and consequentially, in other words, are understood by this model to be derivative, in the service of more primary, private, internal acts of consciousness or thinking. As a result, speech communicating is devalued, decision making and identity development are treated as psychological rather than communicative processes, and the focus of philosophical anthropology stays on events "inside our skin." Fortunately, however, several writers have pointed toward a view of language that avoids the aporias of representational accounts. Their insights may be synthesized into a postsemiotic view of language as constitutive articulate contact.

Language as Constitutive Articulate Contact

The Human World

The distinction between two worlds in semiotic accounts of language alters the historical sense of the term, "world" as the *single* coherent sphere that humans inhabit. Historically, humanity's general and primary sense of "world" appears to have developed out of the varieties of the cosmological myth that arose in Babylonian, Egyptian, Chinese, and Andean civilizations.[54] John Angus Campbell argues that the Hebrew and then the Greek historical epochs were marked by significant substantive changes in "world pictures," that is, in the hierarchical, consubstantial, cyclical, and compact similarity-features that framed the understanding or sense-making of members of these cultures.[55] In Greece, philosophy began, as Aristotle noted, with "wonder" at the world being as it is. Such wondering led to the Greek concept of *cosmos*, which labeled the state into which human habitation changed the primordial chaos. When human involvement transformed chaos into cosmos, the result was a more or less ordered whole, a condition of coherence and a degree of harmony, accompanied by a further sense of wonder at the human's inhabiting it. This whole was labeled "world," and the term came to mean the coherent sphere or sphere of coherence that humans inhabit.

In the early twentieth century, the most influential account of this construct was Edmund Husserl's description of the *Lebenswelt* or "life-world," a "universe of what is indubitable in principle."[56] Husserl emphasized that because humans inhabit it, the life-world can never be completely objectified, and he maintained that the coherence of this indubitable universe is accepted and responded to, rather than being constructed or otherwise achieved.[57] Alfrede Schutz and Jean-Paul Sartre elaborated their own versions of this Husserlian "world," but Martin Buber and Hans-Georg Gadamer developed accounts most apposite to my emphasis here. Buber and Gadamer exploited the distinction made in German between the non-human's *Umwelt*—environment or surround—and the human's *Welt* or world. Buber held that,

> An animal . . . perceives only the things which concern it in the total situation available to it, and it is those things which make its *Umwelt*. . . . [But] It is only [the hu]man who replaces this unsteady conglomeration . . . by a unity which can be imagined or thought by him[/her] as existing for itself. . . . With [t]his human life, a world [*Welt*] exists.[58]

Buber also underscored that humans do not exist in a subject-object relationship with their world: the human inhabits this coherent sphere.[59]

Gadamer concurs with Buber that the human, "unlike all other living creatures, has a 'world,'" for other creatures are simply embedded in their environment and do not have a relationship to it. He also concurs that the human has an "orientation toward" this realm that enables one "to keep oneself so free from what one encounters . . . that one can present it to oneself as it is."[60] But both also argue that this presentation does not presuppose a subject-object relationship. Rather, the human's world frames or contextualizes his or her understanding, and although it is "oriented-toward" or "grasped" as a coherent whole, one's world cannot be reduced without remainder to an object of consciousness.

This general sense of the construct "world" has also been employed by scholars outside the ambit of philosophy. For example, John Shotter, the author of chapter 3, is one contemporary scholar who describes human understanding or sense-making in "worldly" terms. In 1984, Shotter argued that "we owe our being as we understand it" to "the world of our everyday social life," a world "consisting not only of socially constructed institutions, continually reproduced (and transformed) by the accountable activities occurring within them, but also of a larger social process out of which such institutions arise. . . ."[61] Shotter explicitly links understanding and world when he argues that people do not typically explain their actions by reference to their ideas, knowledge, or "to anything in their heads," but by reference to the contents of their worlds, and that "these are the terms in which the people themselves would account for their actions if pressed to justify them."[62] This is another expression of the point that one inhabits a world that frames understanding.

In short, Buber, Gadamer, Shotter, and others clarify that part of what it means to be a human is to dwell in a more-or-less coherent sphere describable as a "world." To say this sphere is "coherent" is just to say that it is understood or understandable, that it hangs together in a relatively unified complex into which all the parts more or less completely fit. Even claims that the human world is chaotic, incoherent, or "ineffable" characterize it as to some degree understandable and hence describable. Thus this sphere frames or contextualizes all human understanding or sense-making. Everything experienced as meaningful is experienced as part of this world. Importantly, humans do not construct this world individually; we experience much of it as a given, an ordinarily taken-for-granted sphere into which we are born and acculturated and that we inhabit. Although some questions are being raised in research with primates, dolphins, and whales, most theorists currently believe that humans are the only beings whose existence could be said to be "worldly" in this sense. Other animals exist in an "environment" or "surround," which lacks the sense of wholeness and coherence that routinely characterizes the human world.

Because "world," thus understood, is the sphere that humans inhabit, there can be nothing outside of it. The human world consists of everything that affects us and everything we affect. Humans cannot depart from their "worlds" or even project themselves into ontological outer space. All human activity and experience is historical (to employ a temporal frame), situated (to employ a spatial frame), thematic (to employ a topical frame), and relational (to employ a cultural, social, interpersonal frame), and the resulting multidimensional sphere is our "world." Thus there cannot be two worlds. "World" is the Ur-structure, the irreducibly primary site of human being.[63]

Language and World

This understanding of the construct "world" significantly alters the symbol model's account of the relationship between language and world. Semiotic perspectives postulate that persons (subjects) use units of language to signify, symbolize, or somehow represent aspects of the (objective) world. But, as I have already noted, almost seventy years ago, Heidegger demonstrated how this kind of subject-object analysis of humans overlooks a more primordial kind of human understanding. As Herbert Dreyfus explains,

> Since Descartes, philosophers have been stuck with the *epistemological* problem of explaining how the ideas in our mind can be true of the external world. Heidegger shows that this subject/object epistemology *presupposes a background of everyday practices into which we are socialized but that we do not represent in our minds* [italics added]. Since he calls this more fundamental way of making sense of things our understanding of being, he claims that he is doing *ontology*, that is, asking about the nature of this understanding of being that we do not *know*— that is not a representation in the mind corresponding to the world—but that we simply *are*.[64]

In other words, Heidegger noticed something that humans "are" before they operate as subjects on objects. He observed that humans are continuously immersed in what might be called everyday coping: For the most part "without thinking," we make our way about, grooming and eating, operating vehicles and machinery, avoiding or connecting with people around us, engaging in personal and professional transactions. These are all examples of our being-in-the-world. As a result of acculturation and upbringing, we more or less successfully, and yet in large part "mindlessly," accomplish this everyday coping. Heidegger explains the distinction between such a derivative and intermittent condition as "knowing" and the more primary being-in-the-world in these words:

> Knowing is now not a comportment that would be added to an entity which does not yet "have" a world, which is free from any relation to its world [i.e., a Cartesian *cogito*]. Rather, knowing is always a mode of being of Dasein on the basis of its already being involved with the world. The basic defect of epistemology is just that it fails to regard what it means by

knowing in its *original* [italics added] phenomenal datum as a way of
being of Dasein, as a way of its in-being, and to take from this basic
consideration all the questions which now begin to arise on this ground.[65]

So from Heidegger's perspective, the person is not first and foremost a
cogito employing reason to connect and disconnect with objects around it,
but is first and foremost a situated interpreter, understander, or sense-
maker engaged in everyday coping.

Importantly, this understander does not cope alone; Dasein is thoroughly relational not individual, social not psychological. As Heidegger put
it, "As being-in-the-world, Dasein is at the same time being with one another—more rigorously, 'being-with.'"[66] He emphasized that this human
quality of being-in-the-social-world is irreducible. It is not that humans
first "are" and then "behave in relation to" or "respond to" the people and
things around them. Instead, as Heidegger explained:

> The phenomenological statement, "Dasein as being-in-the-world is a be-
> ing-with with others," has an existential-ontological sense and does not
> intend to establish that I in fact do not turn out to be alone and still
> other entities of my kind are on hand. If this were the intention of the
> stipulation, then I would be speaking of my Dasein as if it were an envi-
> ronmental thing on hand. . . . Being-with signifies a character of being of
> Dasein as such which is co-original with being-in-the-world. . . . This
> character of being-with defines the Dasein even when another Dasein is
> in fact not being addressed and cannot be perceived as on hand. Even
> Dasein's being-alone is only a deficiency of being-with. . . .[67]

The specific relationship between language and world becomes evident when one recognizes that the paradigmatic site of everyday coping is
language. This is the primary point of Heidegger's often-quoted claim that
"Language is the house of Being."[68] Clearly Heidegger does not mean by
"language" the system that the symbol model highlights. Richard Rorty
agrees with Heidegger that approaches that reduce language to the status
of a system reify the living process.[69] They need to be replaced, Rorty argues, with the recognition that, as philosopher Donald Davidson puts it,
"there is no such thing as a language, not if a language is anything like
what philosophers . . . have supposed. . . . *We must give up the idea of a
clearly defined shared structure which language users master and then
apply to cases*" (italics added).[70] Rorty shows how Heidegger and the Wittgenstein of the *Philosophical Investigations* basically agree on this point.
When Heidegger claims that "language" is the paradigmatic site of everyday coping and self-interpretation, he means that Dasein accomplishes

these projects in events of speech communicating. In Heidegger's words, "Discourse as a mode of being of Dasein qua being-with is essentially *communication.*" Moreover, as understood in this formulation, communication is emphatically "not a matter of transporting information and experiences from the interior of one subject to the interior of the other one. It is rather a matter of being-with-one-another becoming manifest in the world, specifically by way of the discovered world, which itself becomes manifest in speaking with one another."[71]

Mikhail Bakhtin affirmed a closely related view of the irreducibly speech-communicative nature of language that has been sketched by Heidegger, Wittgenstein, Davidson, and Rorty. Bakhtin insisted that any philosophy of language must begin from the recognition that its subject matter is not an abstract system, because "language is realized in the form of individual concrete utterances (oral and written) by participants in the various areas of human activity."[72] When language is acknowledged to be this kind of phenomenon, Bakhtin argued, it becomes clear why it cannot be reduced to a system of signs or symbols and thus cannot be described or defined using the terms and methods of linguistics or semiotics. Bakhtin described the connections between one's world and concrete events of verbal/nonverbal speech communicating especially poignantly when he wrote:

> Everything that pertains to me [i.e., my world] enters my consciousness, beginning with my name . . . through the mouths of others (my mother, and so forth), with their *intonation,* in their emotional and value-assigning *tonality* [italics added]. I realize myself initially through others; from them I receive words, forms, and tonalities for the formation of my initial idea of myself. . . . Just as the body is formed initially in the mother's womb (body), *a person's consciousness awakens wrapped in another's consciousness*[73] [italics added].

Thus these authors describe how human worlds are collaboratively constructed (modified, developed, razed, reconstructed) in speech communicating. This is not to say that interlocutors usually or even typically agree or concur in their world-constructing. Conflict is obviously pervasive and significant. But it takes two (or more) to disagree, and thus conflict, too, is necessarily relational, mutual, and, in this sense, collaborative. Even humans working at cross-purposes—Arabs and Israelis, liberals and conservatives, Democrats and Republicans, plaintiffs and defendants—are collaborating. Humans naturally and characteristically accomplish everyday coping in collaborative speech communicating. In an effort to remove any vestiges of a subject-object orientation, this dynamic might be termed "worlding," a process that happens in address-and-response, in speaking-and-listening, that is, in verbal/nonverbal talk. The locution "worlding in talk" is admittedly awkward, but it does point toward the ontological, relational, mundane, and speech communicative characteristics of these relational events.

The view of the relationship between person and world sketched by these thinkers is especially well-articulated in Gadamer's works. The thoroughly postsemiotic quality of Gadamer's perspective was noted as early as 1969 when Richard Palmer wrote, "Fundamental to Gadamer's conception of language is the rejection of the 'sign' theory of the nature of language."[74] Gadamer's writings verify Palmer's early observation. From Gadamer's perspective, semiotic, subject-object analyses of language are inherently distorted, because "Language is not just one of [the hu]man's possessions in the world; rather, on it depends the fact that [the hu]man has a *world* at all." Humans are the only creatures for whom "the world as world exists," and this world depends on language.[75] Gadamer explains the connection between everyday coping or worlding and dialogue or conversation as follows:[76]

> . . . language has its true being only in dialogue, in *coming to an understanding*. This is not to be understood as if that were the purpose of language. Coming to an understanding is not a mere action, a purposeful activity, a setting up of signs through which I transmit my will to others. Coming to an understanding as such, rather, does not need any tools, in the proper sense of the word. *It is a life process in which a community of life is lived out* [italics added]. . . . for language is by nature the language of conversation; it fully realizes itself only in the process of coming to an understanding.[77]

In response to a question during a philosophy seminar at Boston College, Gadamer emphasized how this quality of language was focal for Plato and Aristotle in that they both studied the *logoi*, which means, as Gadamer put it, "colloquial life as such. How in life things are shared. Life. *Speech*."[78] Thus, from Gadamer's vantage, to be human is to engage in the life processes of coming to an understanding (everyday coping), processes that paradigmatically occur in conversation and are also carried out in reading and writing. Even when engaged in intractable conflict, humans are collaboratively constructing or negotiating their worlds in verbal/nonverbal address-and-response.

There is a clear distinction between this account of the relationship between language and world and the account present in the symbol model. This view emphasizes that understanding is a mode of being manifested in concrete events of conversing, and that ultimately these *events* are what the term "language" labels. Thus the traditional distinction between language and communication is materially altered, or even effaced. No longer is the former simply an instrument used to accomplish the latter. In other words, language is no longer understood simply to be an abstract system of semiotic units instrumentally employed by humans pursuing the goal of communicating. Instead, it is acknowledged that humans engage in understanding ("worlding") linguistically, and that this verbal-and-nonverbal languag*ing* is synonymous with the complex process that some philosophers and many theorists call interpersonal communication or communicating.[79] As a result, efforts to analyze syntactic or semantic aspects of what has been viewed as the "system" of language need to be broadened to acknowledge both the indivisible connections between the verbal and the nonverbal and the inherently relational nature of events of articulate contact.

Importantly, this view of the relationship between language and world is incommensurable with the claim that language functions by connecting individual phonetic, morphemic, syntactic, or semantic units with the thoughts, things, ideas, or meanings they represent. Why incommensurable? Could not a pluralist or eclectic perspective embrace aspects of both this view and the symbol model? Especially if one is working from a generally postmodern and, hence, polysemic perspective, what is problematic about the claim, for example, that "partially constituted" humans periodically make instrumental use of language?[80] Or, to put the challenge differently, cannot one's language be simultaneously representational and constitutive? As one critic put it, cannot one's home also be used as an office? When, for example, I wrote earlier in this chapter, "There cannot be two worlds,"[81] was I not making a statement *about* something nonlinguistic and *using* language to *represent*?

The first problem with these rejoinders is that they embody an equivocal sense of "language" that is ultimately fatal for coherence. From the perspective being developed here, language (read "events of languaging") is (are) constitutive, which, as P. Christopher Smith puts it, means that "What is, is there first *in* an ever spreading, ever self-transforming speaking of it."[82] On this view, features of human worlds do not first exist and then get spoken or written of; they come into being in talk. Of course, no human initiates this process; each of us is born into a family, which, in the context of its culture and speech community, bequeaths us a world that, as we mature, we more- or less-substantively alter. As adults, we carry this tradition into each encounter. Thus human worlds are not constituted *de novo*, but from what we inherit.

But humans—even stubborn and narrow-minded ones—do not simply repeat and reproduce these inherited worlds. To be alive is in part to be engaged in some degree of change. Each communicative transaction (instance of languaging) is constitutive in that it makes present-tense sense or meaning. And it is centrally important to recognize that the same phenomenon or event cannot be understood to be both constitutive and representational or instrumental. Language cannot be coherently treated as simultaneously a world-constituting, characteristically human way of being, and as a system that is instrumentally employed by already-constituted humans to represent aspects of their worlds and accomplish other goals.[83] The constitutive and respresentational-instrumental views are incommensurable, in other words, because the former treats languaging as a primary human event and the latter treats it as a secondary or derived undertaking. Insofar as languaging is a way of being, humanity gets accomplished in or by way of this complex of events. Human worlds get, as it were, verbally and nonverbally spoken-and-listened-into-being. But the claim that language instrumentally represents, assumes the prior existence of humans who are already-constituted and capable of intending and representing. It also presupposes the prior existence of worlds that are objectively given and thus capable of being intended and represented. The critic's question, "Can't my [language] home also be used as an office?" presumes the very subject-object ("using") relationship with language that this perspective denies. So the response is that one's "home" (language) cannot be "used" in *any* way, because it is not an instrument. From this constitutive perspective, in other words, language comes ontologically first, and from the representational-instrumental view, world$_2$ comes first and language reflects, signifies, or symbolizes that primary reality. Thus, one may argue either that humans come-into-being linguistically or that they are already "in being" and then subsequently "use" language. But both claims cannot be part of one coherent view of the nature of language.

Thus if one views language as a constitutive mode of being, then it must continue to be this kind of phenomenon at those moments when humans are allegedly "making instrumental use of it." When a speaker says, for example, "Please hand me that book," it certainly appears that she is simply *using* individual words to "make a request" and "refer to an object." For the scholar or student interested in the nature of language, it would seem to follow that the phenomenon under scrutinty could indeed be said to be a representational system. But when one is interrogating the nature of language, what seems plausible in this case turns out to be indefensible. One primary reason is that, "Please hand me that book" is, as Bakhtin emphasized, a *response* to elements of the discourse that frames it, and its discursive antecedents and consequents make up some small part of a world-constituting conversation or dialogue. The thinker interested in how the nature of language is evident in these discursive events cannot coherently focus only on the single utterance and argue that at the moment of this utterance language is systematic and representational and at some other moment in the dialogue it is constitutive. The claims are incommensurable, because *one cannot make instrumental use of the constitutive mode of one's being-in-the-world.* Such an undertaking would involve a process analogous to lifting oneself by one's bootstraps. It would require one to treat in a subject-object way that which one inhabits. It would require language to be at the same time both constitutive and representational, and this is an equivocation fatal for coherence.

Thus, it is clear why Gadamer concludes that, "if we stick to what takes place in speech," we recognize that "it is obvious that an instrumentalist theory of signs which sees words and concepts as handy tools has missed the point of the hermeneutical phenomenon."[84] As he explains this is one of the primary inadequacies of "the *concept of language* that modern linguistics and philosophy of language take as their starting point." And, he argues, this is also the specific problem with Cassirer's account of language as "symbolic form."[85] Accounts such as Cassirer's fundamentally misconstrue the relationship humans have to their language. As Gadamer elaborates,

> Language is by no means simply[86] an instrument, a tool. For it is in the nature of the tool that we master its use, which is to say we take it in hand and lay it aside when it has done its service. That is not the same as when we take the words of a language, lying ready in the mouth, and with their use let them sink back into the general store of words over which we dispose. Such an analogy is false because we never find ourselves as consciousness over against the world and, as it wore [sic], grasp after a tool of understanding in a wordless condition. Rather, in all our knowledge of ourselves and in all knowledge of the world, we are always already encompassed by the language that is our own.[87]

In other words, one cannot be in a subject-object relationship with the very feature that characterizes one as human.

What, then, can be said to be happening when I write, "There cannot be two worlds"? Why isn't such a sentence a representational, referential statement about something nonlinguistic? When I write such sentences, aren't I using language to refer or represent, the very activity I claim language does not or cannot do? I would respond in two ways. First, notice that this question asks, in effect, "What is 'actually,' 'really,' or 'objectively' happening here?" Such a question presupposes a naturalistic or objectivist metaphysics, an idealist epistemology, and a concomitant correspondence view of truth. The question asks whether my sentence is in fact a sentence of a certain type, that is, whether the sentence fits or corresponds with a specified category of referential or representational sentences. If my sentence ("There cannot be two worlds.") corresponds with this objectively definable category of sentence types, then the answer to the question is "Yes." If it does not fit within this category, then the answer is "No."

But the objectivist presuppositions that are taken-for-granted in this question can be problematized by contrasting it with a question growing from a similar inquiry motive but presupposing a hermeneutic orientation. From a hermeneutic perspective, the question would be, "How might this sentence be understood?" or "Can this sentence ('There cannot be two worlds.') coherently and usefully be viewed as a referential, representational statement about something nonlinguistic?" Then the suggestion embedded in the question can be followed—or the challenge taken up—and it can be shown what happens when one attempts to do this, that is, to view the sentence as a representation of something nonlinguistic. One can fairly confidently predict that the effort to analyze this sentence semiotically will fare no better than earlier examples. The analyst who wishes to view it as representational will be required to specify the semiotic units that make up this sentence—the morphemes, individual words, phrases, the utterance, or the speech act. Then it will be necessary to specify what each unit represents. And if experience is any indicator, the effort will soon fail because of the manifest inapplicability of the symbol model.

On the other hand, one could ask, "Might this sentence be viewed as part of an instance of constitutive articulate contact?" Then, as this option is pursued, the communicative event made up in part by this sentence might be usefully elucidated. One might, following Bakhtin, identify the elements of the discourse that this sentence responds to and how its discursive antecedents and consequents make up part of a world-constituting conversation or dialogue. The sentence might also be interpreted as a move in a conversation-like transaction between writer and reader in which they are negotiating sense or understanding. The relatively formal grammatical structure of the sentence, "There cannot be two worlds," might be understood as a strategic contribution to the writer's effort to define himself in relation to his reader. And so on.

The point is, theories or models are perspectives that can most appropriately be evaluated not by their accuracy (read "correspondence with the real") but by their coherence, usefulness, and applicability. Many works more erudite than this chapter have demonstrated how the symbol model has historically failed tests of coherence, usefulness, and applicability. I am proposing an alternative model that can, I believe, fare better. So my direct response to the question, "Isn't such a sentence a representational, referential statement about something nonlinguistic?" is this: One could view the sentence this way. But if one does, trouble lies ahead. As an alternative, I propose to view the sentence as an instance of constitutive articulate contact in order to see what is revealed about the nature of language.

In sum, I am arguing that the constitutive and representational-instrumental views of the nature of language are incommensurable for two reasons. First, one phenomenon—even as complex a phenomenon as language (languaging)—cannot coherently be understood to be both constitutive (ontologically primary) and representational (ontologically secondary or derivative). Second, if one construes representational-sounding sentences as signs or symbols of something else and one is asked to develop or work out the implications of this construal, one will end up in one or more of the conceptual and practical cul-de-sacs that have trapped language theorists for centuries.

Language as Constitutive

I titled this alternative to the symbol model "Constitutive Articulate Contact." My rationale for the first term, "constitutive" emerges from the connections I have outlined between and among world, understanding, language, and human being. First, to constitute is to produce rather than to reproduce or represent; to compose, form, or establish. As I noted, language-as-speech-communication functions constitutively, not *de novo*, but in the context of what is inherited. Thus, languaging is the way humans "do" understanding and, in the process collaboratively "build," "remake," or "modify" worlds.[88] To be a human is to be an understander, which is to engage in processes of coherence-building or sense-making, processes that occur communicatively and that enable humans to constitute, maintain, and develop the worlds we inhabit.

No human understanding occurs outside this dynamic; this is the implication of Gadamer's claim that *"Being that can be understood is language."*[89] On the one hand, this formulation simply restates the argument that has already been made about the relationship between language and world: "that which comes into language is not something that is pregiven before language; rather, the word gives it its own determinateness."[90] In other words, language, as Rorty or Davidson might put it, does not mirror reality; it constitutes it.

On the other hand, Gadamer's insight also underscores the fact that linguisticality pervades the human world, that all human understanding is linguistic or speech-communicative. This is a more consequential position to embrace. How can it be said that the entire rainbow of human emotions, for example, or the overwhelming presence of some works of art or dance are linguistic? Don't these phenomena transcend the boundaries of language? Certainly emotions and aesthetic experiences often seem not to be describable in words. So what could it mean to say that they are "linguistic"? What kind of new nominalism is being proposed here?

Gadamer responds to this line of questioning by reminding his reader that the human world is a world not of things but of meaning. No one but the solipsist denies *that* there is something separate from the human perception of it. But *what* the human world is taken to be is thoroughly a matter of interpretation. One's neighborhood, for example, is what it is (means what it means) not simply because of its number-of-persons-per-block but because of one's comfort or discomfort, preference or resistance, enjoyment or distress with its population density. *That* it is populated in such a way is undeniable, but this part of a human *world* consists of *what* those features of population are taken to *mean*. Similarly, one's occupation is what it is (means what it means) not just because of the number of hours worked, pay scale, number of days vacation, or ethnicity of one's superior or subordinate but because of one's satisfaction or dissatisfaction, pride or disappointment, security or insecurity with hours worked, dollars earned, and so on. The same can be said about all dimensions of our lives, from our relationships with our parents and children to what it means for us to wear a certain pair of shoes. Humans live in worlds of meaning.

The sense or meaning we make of things grows, in turn, out of our cultural, social, and interpersonal experiences—the values into which we are socialized as infants and children, the preferences we develop as we mature, the criteria we learn to apply. These cultural, social, and interpersonal experiences are what constitute linguisticality, because, in Gadamer's words, "language has its true being only in dialogue, in *coming to an understanding*."[91] In short, (a) our fundamental work as humans is the work of understanding, (b) this work is accomplished in-concert-with-others, that is communicatively, and (c) this communicative coming-to-understanding is, as noted earlier, what is meant by "language." Thus, although one may not be able satisfactorily to label an emotion or to capture an aesthetic experience in a sentence or paragraph, linguisticality nonetheless pervades these experiences of meaning. The fact that one identifies a given state of being as "a feeling," or an object as "a work of art" and a response to it as "overwhelming" or "ineffable," all reflect cultural categories and criteria of understandability that one has learned communicatively. Thus, these features of one's "wordless" experience are *linguistic*. The sense, "I can't put this into words" is a linguistic sense, and the conviction that one's inability constitutes a "failure"—or perhaps a "success"—is also accomplished or negotiated linguistically. Similarly, one can only determine that his or her available vocabulary choices are insufficient descriptors by applying criteria one has learned communicatively, so this feature of "nonverbal" experience is also linguistic. And this account could be extended: One's basic categories of sense-making develop in communicative life, and this is what it means to say that they are linguistic. This is way, as Gadamer puts it, "Language always forestalls any objection to its jurisdiction. Its universality keeps pace with the universality of reason," and "there is no point of view outside the experience of the world in language from which it could become an object."[92]

Importantly, however, this account of the universality of linguisticality is neither nominalist nor relativist. For one thing, the human's world is not relative in the sense that there is some absolute "world in itself" against which it could be compared, in order that, in Gadamer's words, "the right view from some possible position outside the human, linguistic world could discover it in its being-in-itself.[93] As was noted, mundane understanding acknowledges that mountains, trees, walls, and furniture are not simply "made of language." Every view of "world" but the solipsist's includes the affirmation of facticity or existence separate from the viewer. But each worldview includes this as an acknowledgement or affirmation, as an element of the meaningful world being affirmed. Facticity is a common feature of all worldviews save that of the solipsist, but it is not itself a "fact" separate from any view of the world. Whatever truth the affirmation of facticity enjoys is due to coherence and consensus not correspondence. There is no archimedean observation post available to render "relative" all worldviews that are allegedly dependent on other, less secure vantage points.

Equally importantly, this account is not relativist, because humans do not have free rein to constitute whatever world they prefer. As was also already noted, the reason is that just as we do not have a subject-object relationship with language, we also do not live in such a relationship with our world. We are subject to it as much as we intentionally construct it, or, in Gadamer's words, *"That language and world are related in a fundamental way does not mean, then, that world becomes the object of language."*[94] To say we inherit and inhabit the world is to say in part that we are constrained by it to at least as great a degree as we constrain it. The "it," which constrains us and which we constrain, however, is *world* not "reality" or "brute data,"[95] and this is to say that "it" is linguistic in the sense already explained (that is, it is communicative).

Heidegger used the phrase "undergoing an experience" to describe this dynamic. "When we talk of 'undergoing' an experience," he wrote, "we mean specifically that the experience is not of our own making; to undergo here means that we endure it, suffer it, receive it as it strikes us and submit to it. It is this something itself that comes to pass, happens."[96]

Gadamer fleshes out this sense of experience when he contrasts the German terms *Erlebnis* and *Erfahrung*. Both are translated "experience," but the former labels an experience one "has" of something. This notion, he claims, dominated classical and romantic aesthetic theory and led to the treatment of aesthetic experience as a grasping of "the infinite whole."[97] *Erfahrung*, on the other hand, is the term for experience as something one undergoes or is subject to. This kind of experience cannot be repeated or replicated, because we cannot reconstruct all the conditions surrounding an event we do not control. It follows that this kind of experience "is experience of human finitude." The person with this experience knows that he or she is "master neither of time nor the future. . . . Real experience is that whereby [the hu]man becomes aware of his[/her] finiteness."[98]

Conversation is one common event which is characterized by this dynamic of play as *Erfahrung*. In Gadamer's words:

> We say that we 'conduct' a conversation, but the more genuine a conversation is, the less its conduct lies within the will of either partner. . . . Rather, it is generally more correct to say that we fall into conversation, or even that we become involved in it. . . . Understanding or its failure is like an event that happens to us.[99]

In a parallel way, the dynamic of worlding is constrained—and sometimes even determined—by the forces of culture, tradition, and context. Worlding in talk is not an entirely relative event, because cultural, ethnic, and family history help to define available meaning-options, and individual experience helps frame interpretation. Thus there is a continuing tension between the repeated and the unrepeatable, between law and surprise. But this dynamic is nonetheless constitutive. Understanding is the human's way of being, and language is our way of understanding. By engaging both proactively and responsively in the play of language events, humans participate in the constituting of the coherent spheres we inhabit. And the paradigm form of this dynamic is conversation.

Language as Paradigmatically Articulate Contact

The "Articulate Contact" part of the label for the view of the nature of language I am proposing highlights the two central features of the constitutive linguistic events I have just described. First, they are events of contact, which is to say that they are dialogic not monologic, communicative not psychological, social not individual. This feature echoes Heidegger's, Gadamer's, Bakhtin's and Buber's views. Gadamer, for example, observes that dialogue is "the original phenomenon of language,"[100] that "language has its true being only in dialogue,"[101] and even more simply, that "Language, for me, is always simply that which we speak with others and to others."[102] Of course, Gadamer's primary interest as a hermeneutician is in the contact between interpreter and text, but since he recognizes that "the hermeneutical problem is basically the same for oral and written discourse,"[103] his account of the fundamentally dialogic nature of language is apposite here.

Gadamer emphasizes that when one focuses on dialogue, one leaves behind "any starting point in the subjectivity of the subject, and especially in the meaning-directed intentions of the speaker."[104] Interpersonal speech communicating does not merely produce a "reification of intended meaning;" rather, one becomes involved in a process of collaborative construction. One's prejudices are put at risk, in part by the mere presence of the other. One enters what Gadamer terms "the midworld (*Zwischenwelt*) of language," the event of collaborative coherence-construction or understanding that results in the text being a *Zwischenprodukt*.[105] This dynamically collaborative dimension of language and of the text, writes Gadamer, is inaccessible to the methodology of the linguist, who wants to "shed light upon the functioning of language as such," but who does not "enter into the discussion of the topic that is spoken of in the text."[106] But every case of understanding "remains dependent upon communicative conditions that, as such, reach beyond the merely codified meaning-content of what is said."[107] In short, it is crucially significant for Gadamer that human language occurs *between* understanders, in their contact.

Discussions of the nature of language produced by members of the Bakhtin circle focus on this same definitive feature of contact. As was noted, a central claim Bakhtin and his followers made is that language is irreducibly responsive, that every instance of language, each linguistic phenomenon, somehow responds to the language that frames it. In Volosinov's words, "Any utterance—the finished, written utterance not excepted—makes response to something and is calculated to be responded to in turn."[108] Word, he wrote, "is precisely *the product of the reciprocal relationship between speaker and listener, addresser and addressee*" (p. 86). Because of this defining feature, he insisted,

> the actual reality of language-speech is not the abstract system of linguistic forms, not the isolated monologic utterance, and not the psychophysiological act of its implementation, but the social event of verbal interaction implemented in an utterance or utterances. Thus, verbal interaction is the basic reality of language. (p. 94).

On the grounds of this claim, Volosinov labeled "fundamentally erroneous" the theory of understanding "that underlies . . . the whole of European semasiology" because "its entire position on word meaning . . . excludes active response in advance and on principle" (p. 73).

Buber echoed these claims about language as contact. In *I and Thou* Buber identified the human world as "twofold in accordance with the two basic words [humans] can speak," words that are relational in that they are "not single . . . but word pairs": I-It and I-Thou.[109] In a subsequent essay, Buber's point about the relational quality of language was stated even more explicitly:

> The fundamental fact of human existence is neither the individual as such nor the aggregate as such. Each, considered by itself, is a mighty abstraction. . . . The fundamental fact of human existence is [hu]man with [hu]man. . . . It is rooted in one being turning to another as another, as this particular other being, in order to communicate with it in a sphere which is common to them but which reaches out beyond the special sphere of each.[110]

These authors and others elaborate the truism that the human is a social animal by clarifying how the paradigmatic event of uniquely human understanding is the event of *contact*—Gadamer's "conversation," Volosinov's "social event of verbal interaction," Bakhtin's "speech communication," and Buber's dialogue occurring in spokenness between persons. Any adequate account of the nature of language must affirm this defining feature: language happens in the human nexus.

Again, this is clearly not to say that all events of contact are friendly or that they all lead to agreement. Articulate contact is hostile as often as it is welcoming; Gadamerian conversation includes conflict; Bakhtin's speech communication incorporates critique, and Buber's dialogue often occurs between opponents. The point is not that there is always a friendly resolution of differences but that meanings are collaboratively co-constructed.

The contact that characterizes all these language events is *articulate* in two senses. First, it is differentiated rather than compact. According to philosopher of history Eric Voegelin, the central direction of the development of human consciousness, both phylogenetically and ontogenetically, is from the compact "primary experience of the cosmos" to the "differentiated experience of existence."[111] This is the distinction between the contact of a hug or caress and the contact of a conversation; the former is compact and the latter differentiated. Human understanding centrally involves depicting differentiations, making distinctions, or categorizing; in fact, according to George Lakoff, contemporary cognitive science views this process "as the main way that we make sense of experience."[112] As Lakoff and others show, one approach to describing the unique power of human understanding is by tracing how such categories or distinctions as temporality, spatiality, family resemblance, polysemy, generativity, and metonymy turn the "blooming, buzzing confusion" we would experience without language into something articulate.

The second sense in which the events of contact that constitute language are "articulate" is that they are paradigmatically oral-aural. To articulate in this sense means to pronounce clearly and distinctly, to speak in ways that enhance understanding. Humboldt linked these two senses of "articulate" when he wrote:

> *Articulation* rests upon the power of mind over the vocal organs, to compel them to deal with sound in accordance with the form of its own working. The point at which form and articulation meet, as in a binding medium, is that both divide their domains into *basic parts* [categories] whose assembly does nothing but form such wholes as bear within them the striving to become parts of new wholes. *Thinking*, furthermore, demands collection of the *manifold into unity*. The necessary marks of the *articulated sound* are therefore a sharply apprehensible unity, and a character that can enter into specific relationship with any and every other articulated sound imaginable" (p. 66).

This view of the centrality of articulated sound is supported by studies of human development that indicate that the human's first senses through which contact normally occurs are sound and touch. After only twenty weeks in utero, the auditory apparatus of the normal human fetus is structurally comparable to that of an adult, and responses to sound are clearly part of normal fetal behavior.[113] Before the maturation of visual contact, the normal infant can recognize the sounds of its mother's and caregivers' voices, and as the infant matures, sound develops as its most economical and flexible contact modality.

Studies of orality indicate that this aspect of human development is one in which ontogeny recapitulates phylogeny. For example, Eric Havelock describes the significance of the development of human culture from sound-focused primary orality to sight-focused literacy:

> . . . in primary orality, relationships between human beings are governed exclusively by acoustics (supplemented by visual perception of bodily behavior). The psychology of such relationships is also acoustic. The relation between an individual and his[/her] society is acoustic, between [the individual's] traditions . . . law . . . government. . . . Recognition, response, thought itself, occur when we hear linguistic sounds and melo-

dies and ourselves respond to them, as we utter a variant set of sounds to amend or amplify or negate what we have heard.[114]

Walter Ong, Adam Parry, Marshall McLuhan, and Alexander Luria have also fruitfully elaborated on the fact that humans distinctively accomplish contact oral-aurally. Ong offers especially thorough descriptions of the distinctive acoustic features of orality. For example, in primarily oral cultures, "language is a mode of action and not simply a countersign of thought," and these oral peoples "consider words to have great power. Sound cannot be sounding without the use of power."[115] Orality also makes language essentially communicative: "An interlocutor is virtually essential: It is hard to talk to yourself for hours on end. Sustained thought in an oral culture is tied to communication."[116] Ong and other scholars describe how education in primary oral cultures exploits the biologically based power of rhythm and how new information is taught by inserting it into an ongoing repetitive acoustic pattern. It now appears that sound is a more prominent feature of human worlding than the visual bias of much of Western scholarship has heretofore acknowledge.

Extending this view, I am arguing, in short, that *to characterize language as articulate contact is both to affirm that languaging* (participating in language events as just described) *accomplishes the differentiated understanding that characterizes developed human being and to note that oral-aural sound is the paradigmatic modality of languaging.* Deaf people are not excluded from this analysis. Recent research on Sign, the language of the deaf, demonstrates that it too can be accurately characterized as constitutive articulate contact. Both conceptual and empirical studies conclude that contact is clearly the primary raison d'être for Sign and thus that Sign cannot be adequately described as simply a system of symbols.[117] Moreover, this research concludes that Sign fully qualifies as a language in its own right and that, although it exploits sight rather than sound as its primary modality, it uses time in ways that are parallel to oral-aural speech communicating.[118]

To summarize, this account of language as constitutive articulate contact affirms that: (a) language should be treated first and foremost as event, not system (as "languaging"); (b) this event embodies the distinctive dynamic of human being, which is understanding; (c) this ongoing process of understanding-via-languaging is the human's way of constituting world ("world-building-and-rebuilding" or simply "worlding"); (d) this understanding occurs in contact between persons, which is to say that the event is irreducibly dialogic or interpersonal; and (e) this understanding-in-contact is articulate, which means both that it accomplishes differentiation or categorization and that it occurs paradigmatically as oral-aural contact.

The Two Accounts Compared

The differences between the symbol model and the view that language is constitutive articulate contact can now be clarified by briefly contrasting the theoretical commitments embodied in each. First, the symbol model begins from the basic claim that there is a distinction between two realms or worlds, generally the "linguistic" and the "nonlinguistic." The post-semiotic view of the nature of language, which is outlined here, begins from the claim that there is only one kind of human world, a pervasively languaged kind. Importantly, this is not to say that one sits on, drinks coffee from, or drives "language." As has been noted, all but solipsists acknowledge the existence of facticity separate from human perception and interpretation. But this facticity, as such, is not a part of any *world*. As Charles Taylor puts it, there are no "brute data," if by "brute data" one means "data whose validity cannot be questioned by offering another interpretation or reading, data whose credibility cannot be confounded or undermined by further reasoning."[119] Data are encountered or experienced as situated, related to other data making up a world. This is to say that they are always interpreted, which means they are languaged. World, the Ur-structure of understanding, emerges from human contact, contact both with facticity and with other humans.[120] Each nonsolipsistic affirmation of facticity occurs as an acknowledgement that makes up part of the world being affirmed. And this affirmation is cultural, social, and interpersonal because it is anchored in the speaker's or writer's linguistic tradition and more or less responsive to his or her interlocutor(s). To put the point in other words, world is always world-for, and the beings "for" whom it is, are relational beings, ones formed, as Bahktin put it, "wrapped" in others. This one relational world of meaning is the irreducibly primary site of human being.

Second, the symbol model treats language as composed of identifiable units or elements, while the postsemiotic alternative focuses more holistically. This account of language as constitutive articulate contact is premised on the conviction that synthesis can contribute at least as much to an understanding of language as can analysis. Minimally, discourse critiques should move as the traditional hermeneutic circle prescribed, from whole to part and back again to the whole. There is little purpose served by focusing one's explicative energy exclusively on reducing language to its atoms. Of course, distinctions are still useful and important, but they can be made, for example, among types or functions of events rather than between individual elements. The anchor for understanding languaging should be the contact event as its participants live it.

Third, the symbol model embraces a representationalism rooted in the Cartesian-Kantian distinction between subject and object. This post-semiotic alternative treats language as constitutive or productive of (partial, tentative, and changing) ways of understanding rather than reproductive of cognitive states, things, or other units of language. This means that language is primary rather than secondary, that speech communicating is a principal not a surrogational dynamic. Friendly and hostile talk, conversation, address-and-response, and dialogue produce worlds; they do not simply reproduce or represent them.

The ethical implications of this point are obvious: Language (understood as worlding in talk) is considerably more consequential than the symbol model acknowledges.[121] Meaning-making does not just happen privately, to be expressed later in speaking or writing; rather, meanings are coconstructed in articulate contact. Worlds are not simply inherited from one's culture and family of origin; rather, they are expanded, contracted, and otherwise altered in verbal-nonverbal address and response. Selves or identities are not simply determined by socioeconomic, ethnic, and educational decree; rather, they are negotiated interpersonally. This means that how we talk and listen materially affects who we are. Communication is important not just because it reflects, expresses, symbolizes, or otherwise represents more fundamental or primary "realities" but because it is primary; it brings these realities into being.[122]

Fourth, the symbol model treats language as a system, whereas the alternative described here treats language as event. Insofar as language is viewed as constitutive articulate contact, it is more fruitful for theorists and researchers interested in human communication—a category that includes most of those in the human sciences—to concentrate on "languaging," "interacting," or "transacting"[123] rather than on the system communicators are allegedly employing. This focus is preferable, especially because the so-called system of language cannot coherently be conceived as existing separate from, and in an object-to-subject relationship with, humans communicating. As was noted, one implication of this concentration on event is that the traditional distinction between language and communication is significantly altered. Although it is still clearly useful to talk about individual languages, the term in such phrases as "the nature of language," or "language is a distinctive feature of humans" becomes synonymous with *communication* (or better, communicat*ing*). Thus questions like, "How is language operating here?" or "What features of the speaker's/writer's language contributed to this outcome?" call for responses that clarify how interlocutors collaboratively constructed meaning in their verbal-nonverbal discourse.

Finally, the symbol model treats language as a tool or instrument humans use to accomplish their goals. This account of language as constitutive articulate contact, on the other hand, is predicated on the conviction that such an instrumental view is incomplete and misleading, primarily because humans cannot live in the subject-object relationship with language that the tool analogy requires. It seems to me that Gadamer is profoundly correct to remind us that we do not engage in speech communication essentially—or even partially—by taking the words of a language that are lying ready in our mouths, uttering them, and then letting them sink back into the general store of words in our linguistic armentarium. "Rather, in all our knowledge of ourselves and in all knowledge of the world, we are always already encompassed by the language that is our own."[124] Thus it is most fruitful to treat language as the primary way humans accomplish who we are, and as a dynamic we are subject-to or used-by at least as much as we "manipulate" or "use." Here the view of language comes full circle. Insofar as world is linguistic, we *inhabit* or live in our language; we do not simply use it as a tool.

Conclusion

I argued earlier that the symbol model breaks down when applied to living language. The reader might legitimately ask for a demonstration that the proposed alternative fares better. How might this account of language as constitutive articulate contact inform, for example, an understanding of the brief excerpt from the dialogue between two college students about bicycles on campus? Recall that the partial text of this conversation looked like this:

Example #1 Two College Students

1.	John:	So what do you THI::NK about the bicycles on campus?
2.	Judy:	I think they're terrible.
3.	John:	Sure is about a MIL:LION of 'em.
4.	Judy:	eh ⌈he:h ⌉
5.	John:	⌊Duzit⌋ SEEM da you: there's a lot more people this year?
6.	Judy:	The ⌈re- ⌉ ye:ah, for su:re
7.	John:	⌊Go-⌋ GOD, there seems to be a mILlion people
8.	Judy:	Yeah. (1.0) YE:ah, there's: way too many. I can't- at tIMEs the

9.		bicycles get so bad I just got off mi ⌐ne an ⌐ hh .h and gi(h)ve up!
10.	John:	⌊Oh riLleh⌋
11.	John:	I unno when I DODGE one then I have to DODGE another one'n
12.		its an endless cycle.
13.	Judy:	Yeah (1.0) oh they're TERrible.
14.	John:	'S so many people.
15.	Judy:	Um hmm[125]

Douglas W. Maynard, the conversation analyst who cites this example of talk, finds in it several features of John's and Judy's articulate contact that would not be apparent if he were to treat this language simply as the systematic use of symbols. Maynard focuses on the operation of a strategy he calls a "perspective-display sequence." Conversation partners use this strategy, he argues, to adapt a personal opinion to their listener's frame of reference. The strategy consists of first soliciting the other's opinion and then producing one's own report in a way that takes the other's opinion into account. In the first three lines of the example, John provides a "perspective-display invitation," to which Judy replies, and then John offers his opinion as supportive of the perspective he has already elicited from her. Maynard argues that this conversational strategy can enhance the amount of agreement or consensus expressed in a conversation, and it is especially "pertinent to situations where cautiousness in giving reports and opinions seems warranted."[126]

Maynard points out that this excerpt includes a second perspective display sequence that builds upon the first. It begins at line 5 and ends at line 7. Subsequently, Judy produces a brief personal narrative at lines 8–9 telling how bicycles—the topic of the conversation—affect her. Then John's second story at lines 11–12 runs parallel with Judy's. He too has had to avoid bicycles to escape being a victim. Thus, "the kind of character that the teller of the first story is in hers is the same that second narrator is in his."[127] Maynard also notes that the stories work even though (because?) they are generic rather than specific. They both use such framing devices as "at times" and "when" to mark the experiences they narrate as typical rather than unique.

Finally, Maynard underscores the significance of the fact that John and Judy produce parallel second stories. The two could demonstrate understanding and agreement with statements of appreciation or approval. But a second story of the kind produced here *exhibits* a similar experience.

"And," Maynard continues, "to the degree that coparticipants orient to a shared experience (of 'victimization,' for instance), it is relationally significant, in that it constitutes an accomplished 'intimacy,' if only momentary, that is a product of participants systematically pursuing talk that reveals their similarity.[128] But John and Judy handle their victimization differently. Judy gets off her bike and "gives up," while John keeps dodging bikes in an "endless cycle." So John and Judy smoothly, subtly, but nonetheless poignantly display in this brief exchange both how they are different and how they are alike.

Clearly Maynard is able to develop several insights from outside the symbol model. In this brief excerpt, he finds evidence about the relationship displayed between the individual and the social, the dynamics of narrative collaboration, the discursive development of subject matter ("bicycles"), and the achievement of intimacy, without getting caught up in any effort to analyze "signifiers" and "signifieds." In fact, I would argue that he notices what he does in this discourse *because* he recognizes that these interlocutors are co-constructing the world they share in their aural-oral contact. John and Judy both produce bicycle stories that are "wrapped in" the other's parallel story, a clear example of collaborative construction. The complementary crescendo-decrescendo of the emphasized words that I noted earlier reveals another level of the interlocutors' intimacy, one embedded in the aural-oral dimensions of intonation, emphasis, and facial expression. Each speaker displays a world open to the other's participation, and both positively affirm the other's involvement in their worlds. In short, the symbol model collapsed in the attempt to use it to explicate the first word in turn 1, while aspects of the postsemiotic account prove useful for elucidating several ways this talk is operating syntactically, semantically, and pragmatically.

Of course, the symbol theorist might not be interested in the relationship between the individual and the social, the dynamics of narrative collaboration, the discursive development of subject matter, or the conversational achievement of intimacy. There are dozens of other questions that could be asked about this discourse, and many of them focus on phonemes, morphemes, or phrases; on syntactic structures; or on individual word choices. One might wonder why semiotic and postsemiotic language scholars cannot just agree to coexist, with those committed to the symbol model using it to pursue their questions and those who view language as constitutive articulate contact applying their own perspective.

On the one hand, continued coexistence is the most likely scenario. I recognize that, even taken together, this chapter, the book that elaborates and applies the perspective outlined here,[129] and the essays that make up this volume are not likely to alter the scholarly practices of most of those committed to the symbol model. On the other hand, I am less than fully satisfied by the eclecticism featured in this scenario. I would respond to the question about coexistence by appealing to the same criterion applied to the symbol model. Any account of language, if it is to be judged coherent and useful, should be informatively applicable to paradigm cases of the phenomenon it is designed to elucidate. Even most symbol theorists agree that language occurs paradigmatically as speech communication. But the symbol model cannot be informatively applied to these events. This is one reason why I am skeptical about coexistence, eclecticism, or theoretical pluralism when what is at issue is the understanding of the basic nature of language itself.

Another reason for not embracing both the symbol model and this postsemiotic alternative is that the fundamental assumptions grounding the former have been thoroughly questioned in a wide range of contemporary scholarly works by some of the twentieth century's most influential thinkers. In light of several of these critiques, for example, one simply cannot responsibly maintain a commitment to Cartesian-Kantian epistemology and its concomitant representationalism. It is no longer possible simply to affirm that philosophical language—or some other type—does, after all, "mirror nature." Similarly, after the philosophical work of Gadamer and Bakhtin and the anthropological studies of Dell Hymes,[130] Clifford Geertz,[131] John Gumperz,[132] and others, one can no longer affirm that language is simply a tool. It is clear that humans live in something other than a simple subject-object relationship with our language. And to the degree we inhabit it, it cannot be a tool. This is another argument against coexistence or theoretical pluralism.

Thus this chapter has argued initially that it is conceptually and practically useful to treat language first and foremost not as a system but as a kind of human event, as "languaging" or speech communicating. Second, this kind of event is the site of human being, the dynamic that distinguishes us as understanders from even our closest primate, whale, and dolphin cousins. Third, this ongoing, collaborative engagement in understanding-via-languaging is the human's way of constituting world ("world-building-and-rebuilding" or simply "worlding"), when "world" is understood as the sphere of coherence that we inhabit. Fourth, this understanding is negotiated; it occurs in contact between persons, which is to say that these events are irreducibly dialogic or interpersonal. Finally, this understanding-in-contact is articulate, which means both that it accomplishes differentiation or categorization and that it occurs paradigmatically as oral-aural contact.

The chapters that follow contain an interdisciplinary collection of responses to the general problematic outlined in this introduction. Some trace the history of semiotic and postsemiotic accounts of the nature of language. Some offer parallel or complementary views of language from the perspectives of philosophy, linguistics, semiotics, pragmatics, or communication theory. Others challenge the assumption that one can construct a coherent "postsemiotic" account of the nature of language. Some focus on individual figures, and others survey multiple authors. Some are written from philosophical or critical perspectives and others from more social scientific ones. But each chapter contributes to the ongoing conversation about how best to understand human languaging.

Notes

1. Richard Rorty, *Philosophy and the Mirror of Nature* (Princeton, NJ: Princeton University Press, 1979), p. 3.

2. Rorty, pp. 368, 371.

3. Richard J. Bernstein, *Beyond Objectivism and Relativism* (Philadelphia: University of Pennsylvania Press, 1985), pp. 16–20.

4. Bernstein, p. 229.

5. Martin Heidegger, "Letter on Humanism," in *Basic Writings*, ed. David Ferrell Krell (New York: Harper & Row, 1977), p. 193.

6. Martin Heidegger, *On the Way to Language*, trans. Peter D. Hertz (New York: Harper & Row, 1971), p. 97.

7. Heidegger, 1971, p. 123.

8. Heidegger, 1971, p. 96.

9. Heidegger, 1971, p. 123.

10. Hans-George Gadamer, *Truth and Method*, 2nd rev. ed., trans. Joel Weinsheimer and D. G. Marshall (New York: Crossroads, 1989), pp. 403–4.

11. Hans-Georg Gadamer, "The Hermeneutics of Suspicion," *Hermeneutics: Questions and Prospects* (Amherst: University of Massachusetts Press, 1984), p. 63.

12. Hans-Georg Gadamer, *Philosophical Hermeneutics*, trans. David Linge (Berkeley: University of California Press, 1976), p. 76.

13. Gadamer, 1989, pp. 445–56.

14. See, e.g., Kenneth Baynes, James Bohman, and Thomas McCarthy, eds., *After Philosophy: End or Transformation?* (Cambridge, MA: MIT Press, 1987); Stephen Best and Douglas Kellner, *Postmodern Theory: Critical Interrogations* (New York: Guilford Press, 1991); Jacques Derrida, *Of Grammatology*, trans. Gayatri

Chakravorty Spivak (Baltimore: Johns Hopkins University Press, 1974); Gary B. Madison, *The Hermeneutics of Postmodernity: Figures and Themes* (Bloomington: Indiana University Press, 1990); Calvin O. Schrag, *The Resources of Rationality: A Response to the Postmodern Challenge* (Bloomington: Indiana University Press, 1992).

15. Julia Kristeva, *Language: The Unknown*, trans. A. M. Menke (New York: Columbia University Press, 1989), p. 12.

16. Kristeva, p. 17.

17. Norbert Elias, *The Symbol Theory* (London: Sage, 1991), p. 2.

18. Elias, p. 4.

19. Charles E. Osgood, "What is a Language?" *The Signifying Animal*, ed. I. Rauch and G. F. Carr (Bloomington: Indiana University Press, 1980), p. 12.

20. Gary Cronkhite, "On the Focus, Scope, and Coherence of the Study of Human Symbolic Activity," *Quarterly Journal of Speech, 72* (1986), 232, 233.

21. Cronkhite, 233.

22. Michael T. Motley, "On Whether One Can(not) Not Communicate: An Examination via Traditional Communication Postulates," *Western Journal of Speech Communication, 54* (1990), 1.

23. Motley, 2–3.

24. Umberto Eco, *Semiotics and the Philosophy of Language* (Bloomington: Indiana University Press, 1984), p. 7.

25. Eco, p. 130.

26. Eco, p. 20.

27. Eco, p. 44.

28. Eco, p. 45.

29. Charles Sanders Peirce, *Collected Papers of Charles Sanders Peirce*, ed. C. Hartshorne and P. Weiss, 8 vols. (Cambridge, MA: Harvard University Press, 1960). Also see Ernst Cassirer, *Philosophy of Symbolic Forms*, 3 vols., trans. R. Manheim (New Haven, CT: Yale University Press, 1953–1957); D. S. Clarke, Jr., *Principles of Semiotic* (Boston: Routledge and Kegan Paul, 1987); Charles Morris, *Foundations of the Theory of Signs* (Chicago: University of Chicago Press, 1938); and Saussure, 1983.

30. Kenneth Burke, "(Nonsymbolic) Motion / (Symbolic) Action," *Critical Inquiry, 4* (1978), 809.

31. Stephen Ullmann, *The Principles of Semantics*, 2nd ed. (Oxford: Basil Blackwell, 1957).

32. In places, some important writers—e.g., Saussure and Eco—argue that linguistic or psychological units signify or represent other linguistic or psychological units. I address this issue later.

33. Roy Harris and Talbot J. Taylor, *Landmarks in Linguistic Thought: The Western Tradition from Socrates to Saussure* (London: Routledge, 1989); John Stewart, *Language as Articulate Contact: Toward a Post-Semiotic Philosophy of Communication* (Albany: State University of New York Press, 1995), chs. 2–3.

34. Aristotle, *De Interpretatione, The Basic Works of Aristotle*, ed. Richard McKeon (New York: Random House, 1941), 16a.

35. John Locke, *Essay Concerning Human Understanding* (London: Elizabeth Holt for Thomas Basset, 1690); Ludwig Wittgenstein, *Tractatus Logico-Philosophicus*, trans. D. F. Pears and B. F. McGuinness (London: Routledge and Kegan Paul, 1961).

36. Saussure, pp. 69–70.

37. Saussure, pp. 12, 15, 67–68, 71, 112. For a fuller development of this argument, see Stewart, *Language as Articulate Contact*, pp. 81–87.

38. Locke, III.8.5.

39. Gilbert Ryle, *Collected Papers, I* London: Hutchinson, p. 49.

40. Wilhelm von Humboldt, *On Language*, trans. Peter Heath (Cambridge: Cambridge University Press, 1988).

41. But can't one study mathematics without any recourse to words? No, I would argue, for at least two reasons. First, mathematical proofs depend centrally on such fulcrum terms as "Let," and "then." More importantly, the world of coherence within which mathematical reasoning is understandable and understood is a discursive world, a world of structure, topicality, definitions, and rules that are negotiated communicatively.

42. John Horne Tooke, *The Diversions of Purley*, 2nd ed. facsimile reprint (Menston, England: Scolar Press, 1968).

43. J. L. Austin, *How to Do Things With Words*, ed. J. O. Urmson (Oxford: Oxford University Press, 1962); *Philosophical Papers* (Oxford: Clarendon, 1961).

44. John Searle, *Speech Acts: An Essay on the Philosophy of Language* (London: Cambridge University Press, 1969).

45. Example from Douglas W. Maynard, "Perspective-Display Sequences in Conversation," *Western Journal of Speech Communication*, 53 (1989): 107.

46. In Chapter 9, John Wilson offers what he terms a symbol model analysis of utterances like "So."

47. Terry Winograd and Fernando Flores, *Understanding Computers and Cog-*

nition: A New Foundation for Design (Reading, MA: Addison-Wesley, 1986); W. Ramsey, S. P. Stich, and D. E. Rummelhart, eds., *Philosophy and Connectionist Theory* (Hillsdale, NJ: Lawrence Erlbaum, 1991).

48. Saussure, 1983, p. 66.

49. Émile Benveniste, *Problems in General Linguistics*, trans. M. E. Meek (Coral Gables, FL: University of Miami Press, 1977), pp. 44; Kristeva, 1989, p. 16.

50. Gadamer, 1989, p. 267.

51. See, e.g., Stewart, *Language as Articulate Contact*, pp. 24–27; Glen H. Stamp and Mark L. Knapp, "The Construct of Intent in Interpersonal Communication," *Quarterly Journal of Speech, 76* (1990): 282–99; Janet Beavin Bavelas, "Behaving and Communicating: A Reply to Motley," *Western Journal of Speech Communication, 54* (1990): 593–602; and Janet Beavin Bavelas and Linda Coates, "How Do We Account for the Mindfulness of Face-to-Face Dialogue?" *Communication Monographs, 59* (1992): 301–5.

52. Martin Heidegger, *Being and Time*, trans. J. Macquarrie and E. Robinson (New York: Harper & Row, 1962).

53. Thomas A. McCarthy, "General Introduction," *After Philosophy: End or Transformation?* ed. K. Baynes, J. Bohman, and T. McCarthy (Cambridge, MA: MIT Press, 1987), p. 4.

54. Mircea Eliade, *Cosmos and History* (New York: Praeger, 1959).

55. John Angus Campbell, "A Rhetorical Interpretation of History," *Rhetorica*, 2 (1984):236–237.

56. Edmund Husserl, *The Crisis of European Sciences and Transcendental Phenomenology*, trans. David Carr (Evanston, IL: Northwestern University Press, 1970) 127.

57. Husserl, p. 381.

58. Martin Buber, "Distance and Relation," *The Knowledge of Man*, ed. Maurice Friedman, trans. Maurice Friedman and Ronald G. Smith (New York: Harper & Row, 1965) 60–61.

59. Buber, p. 61.

60. Gadamer, *Truth and Method*, pp. 443–44.

61. John Shotter, *Social Accountability and Selfhood* (Oxford: Blackwell, 1984) x.

62. Shotter, p. 103.

63. Heidegger's analysis of "fore-meanings" in *Being and Time* underscores the ways that agendas, culture, and context continually constrain communicating. Gadamer's description of "prejudice" in *Truth and Method* makes this same point.

64. Herbert Dreyfus, *Being-In-The-World: A Commentary on Heidegger's Being and Time, Division I* (Cambridge, MA: MIT Press, 1991) 3.

65. Martin Heidegger, *History of the Concept of Time*, trans., T. Kisiel (Bloomington: Indiana University Press, 1985) 161.

66. Heidegger, *History*, p. 238.

67. Heidegger, *History*, p. 238.

68. Martin Heidegger, "Letter on Humanism," *Basic Writings*, ed. David F. Krell (New York: Harper & Row) 193.

69. Richard Rorty, *Essays on Heidegger and Others* (Cambridge: Cambridge University Press, 1991) 116.

70. Donald Davison, "A Nice Derangement of Epitaphs," *Truth and Interpretation: Perspectives on the Philosophy of Donald Davison*, ed. Ernest LePore (Oxford: Blackwell, 1986), 446.

71. Heidegger, *History*, p. 263.

72. Mikhail Bakhtin, "The Problem of Speech Genres," *Speech Genres and Other Late Essays*, trans. Vern W. McGee (Austin: University of Texas Press, 1986) 60.

73. Bakhtin, "Notes," p. 138.

74. Richard Palmer, *Hermeneutics: Interpretation Theory in Schleiermacher, Dilthey, Heidegger, and Gadamer* (Evanston, IL: Northwestern University Press, 1969) 201.

75. Gadamer, *Truth and Method*, p. 443.

76. It should be clear that for Gadamer, "dialogue" has a different meaning than it had for Martin Buber. See John Stewart, "Speech and Human Being: A Complement to Semiotics," *Quarterly Journal of Speech*, 72 (1986): 55–73.

77. Gadamer, *Truth and Method* p. 446. Occasionally, Gadamer seems to claim that Plato's texts are examples of "living dialogue." See, e.g., "Text and Interpretation," in *Dialogue and Deconstruction: The Gadamer-Derrida Encounter*, ed., Diane P. Michelfelder and Richard E. Palmer (Albany: State University of New York Press, 1989) 23. But Gadamer seems more often to have in mind spontaneous, natural conversation rather than the assertively agenda-driven and manipulative exchanges between Socrates and his interlocutors. P. Christopher Smith discusses this and broader issues in "Plato as Impulse and Obstacle in Gadamer's Development of a Hermeneutical Theory," *Gadamer and Hermeneutics*, ed. Hugh J. Silverman (New York: Routledge, 1991) 23–41.

78. Hans-Georg Gadamer, "Heidegger's relationship to the Greeks," unpubl. classroom notes by the author, Boston College Philosophy Department, October 15, 1984.

79. One recent persuasive argument for the inseparability of the verbal and the nonverbal is David McNeill's *Hand and Mind: What Gestures Reveal about Thought* (Chicago: University of Chicago Press, 1992). McNeill and his colleagues conclude from their exhaustive analysis of videotapes of individuals engaged in narrative discourse that "the whole concept of language must be altered" to take into account the results of their research. Unfortunately, however, McNeill's conception of communication is drastically oversimplified. He treats gestures as a means of "transferring mental images to visible forms" and "conveying ideas that language cannot always express," echoing John Locke's picture of the relationship between language and thought.

80. This question was raised by Professor Mark Alfino, department of philosophy, Gonzaga University.

81. p. 33.

82. Smith, "Plato as Impulse and Obstacle," p. 32.

83. In chapter 9, John Wilson takes issue with this claim.

84. Gadamer, *Truth and Method*, p. 403.

85. Gadamer, *Truth and Method*, pp. 403–4.

86. Two reviewers have claimed that the term, "simply" here indicates that Gadamer does not see the two views as incommensurable, but that for him, language is both instrument or tool and world-constitutive. This reading is only coherent if one ignores many other parts of Gadamer's corpus. First, later in this quotation Gadamer notes ". . . we *never* [italics added] find ourselves as consciousness over against the world. . . ." Other comments in this same essay echo this position, e.g., "In truth, we are *always* [italics added] already at home in language just as much as we are in the world" (p. 63). Several sections of Part III of *Truth and Method* also argue against subject-object conceptions of language in general and the symbol model in particular, e.g., pp. 401–5, 410–18, 433–38, and 443–56. On p. 417 of *Truth and Method*, for example, Gadamer writes, "A word is not a sign that one selects, nor is it a sign that one makes or gives to another. . . ." All this is why Richard Palmer concluded over twenty-five years ago that "Fundamental to Gadamer's conception of language is the rejection of the 'sign' theory of the nature of language" (p. 201). My argument for incommensurability, in short, is supported by Gadamer's corpus, just as it is by Heidegger—"The essential being of language is Saying as Showing [and] its showing character is not based on signs of any kind" (see note 7)—and Rorty—"we have to understand speech not only as not the externalizing of inner representations, but as not a representation at all" (see note 2).

87. Gadamer, *Philosophical Hermeneutics*, p. 62.

88. The scare quotes mark these verbs as subject-object terms enlisted to help limn a non-subject-opbject dynamic.

89. Gadamer, *Truth and Method*, p. 474.

90. Gadamer, *Truth and Method*, p. 475.

91. Gadamer, *Truth and Method*, p. 446.

92. Gadamer, *Truth and Method*, pp. 401, 452.

93. Gadamer, *Truth and Method*, p. 447.

94. Gadamer, *Truth and Method*, p. 450.

95. Charles Taylor, "Interpretation and the Sciences of Man," *Review of Metaphysics* 25 (1971): 3–51.

96. Heidegger, *On the Way to Language*, p. 57.

97. Gadamer, *Truth and Method*, p. 70.

98. Gadamer, *Truth and Method*, p. 357.

99. Gadamer, *Truth and Method*, p. 383.

100. Gadamer, "Text and Interpretation," p. 23.

101. Gadamer, *Truth and Method*, p. 446.

102. Hans-Georg Gadamer, "Letter to Dallmayr," *Dialogue and Deconstruction*, p. 98.

103. Gadamer, "Text and Interpretation," p. 36.

104. Gadamer, "Text and Interpretation," p. 26.

105. Gadamer, "Text and Interpretation," pp. 29, 31.

106. Gadamer, "Text and Interpretation," p. 31.

107. Gadamer, "Text and Interpretation," p. 33.

108. V. N. Volosinov, *Marxism and the Philosophy of Language*, trans. Ladislav Matejka and I. R. Titunik (Cambridge, MA: Harvard University Press, 1973) 72. In chapter 7 of *Language as Articulate Contact* I explore the tension between the clearly semiotic and the equally clearly postsemiotic dimensions of Volosinov's work. I also explain my rationale for attributing this work to Volosinov rather than Bakhtin.

109. Martin Buber, *I and Thou*, trans. Walter Kaufmann (New York: Charles Scribner's Sons, 1970) 53.

110. Martin Buber, *Between Man and Man*, ed. Maurice Friedman, trans. Maurice Friedman and R. G. Smith (New York: Macmillan, 1965) 203.

111. Eric V. Voegelin, "Immortality: Experience and Symbol," *Harvard Theological Review*, 60 (1967): 272.

112. George Lakoff, *Women, Fire, and Dangerous Things: What Categories Reveal About the Mind* (Chicago: University of Chicago Press, 1987) xi.

113. D. B. Chamberlain, "Consciousness at Birth: The Range of Empirical Evidence," in T. R. Verney, ed., *Pre- and Perinatal Psychology: An Introduction* (New York: Human Sciences Press, 1987) 70–86.

114. Eric A. Havelock, *The Muse Learns to Write* (New Haven CT: Yale University Press, 1986) 65–66.

115. Ong, p. 32.

116. Ong, p. 34.

117. See, e.g., Harlan Lane *The Mask of Benevolence: Disabling the Deaf Community* (New York: Alfred A. Knopf, 1992); Ursula Bellugi, "Clues from the Similarities between Signed and Spoken Language," in *Signed and Spoken Language: Biological Constraints on Linguistic Form*, ed. U. Bellugi and M. Studdert-Kennedy (Weinheim and Deerfield Beach, FL: Verlag Chemie, 1980); William C. Stokoe, *Sign Language Structure* (Silver Spring, MD: Linstok, 1960); and William C. Stokoe, "Sign Writing Systems," in *Gallaudet Encyclopedia of Deaf People*, ed. John Van Cleve (New York: McGraw-Hill, 1987).

118. For a review of these materials, see Oliver Sacks, *Seeing Voices: A Journey into the World of the Deaf* (Berkeley: University of California Press, 1989).

119. Charles Taylor, *Philosophy and the Human Sciences: Philosophical Papers*, vol 2 (New York: Cambridge University Press, 1985) 19.

120. In *I and Thou* and other works, Martin Buber argued that world emerges from contact not only with facticity and other humans but also with the Infinite, which he calls the Eternal Thou. I think he's right. A more complete account of articulate contact would include consideration of the spiritual dimension of communication. See Craig R. Smith, "Finding the Spiritual Dimension in Rhetoric," *Western Journal of Communication*, 57 (1993): 266–71.

121. Stuart J. Sigmand, ed., *The Consequentiality of Communication* (Hillsdale, NJ: Lawrence Erlbaum, 1995).

122. Feminist epistemology and communication theory elaborate this point, as does Michel Foucault's entire corpus—among many other postmodern writings. See, e.g., Lana F. Rakow, ed., *Women Making Meaning: New Feminist Directions in Communication* (New York: Routledge, 1992); Sandra Harding, *Whose Science? Whose Knowledge? Thinking from Women's Lives* (Ithaca, NY: Cornell University Press, 1991); Mary Margared Fonow and Judith A. Cook, eds., *Beyond Methodology: Feminist Scholarship as Lived Research* (Bloomington: Indiana University Press, 1991); Michel Foucault, *Power / Knowledge: Selected Interviews and Other Writings, 1972–1977*, ed., Colin Gordon (New York: Pantheon, 1980).

123. I clarify the distinction between "interaction" and "transaction" and ar-

gue for the appropriateness of the latter term in "A Postmodern Look at Traditional Communication Postulates," *Western Journal of Speech Communication,* 55 (1991): 354–79.

124. Gadamer, *Philosophical Hermeneutics* 62.

125. Maynard, p. 107.

126. Maynard, p. 91.

127. Maynard, p. 107.

128. Maynard, p. 107.

129. Stewart, 1995.

130. E.g., Dell Hymes, "Linguistic Theory and Functions in Speech," *Foundations in Sociolinguistics: An Ethnographic Approach* (Philadelphia: University of Pennsylvania Press, 1974) 145–78.

131. E.g., Clifford Geertz, *Local Knowledge: Further Essays in Interpretive Anthropology* (New York: Basic Books, 1983).

132. E.g., John J. Gumperz, and Dell Humes, eds., *Directions in Sociolinguistics: The Ethnography of Communication* (New York: Holt, Rinehart & Winston, 1972); John J. Gumperz, ed., *Language and Social Identity* (New York: Cambridge University Press, 1982).

Editor's Introduction

In this essay, Toronto philosopher Gary Madison develops his own "postsemiological" account of language, one very friendly to that developed in chapter 1. He too traces the identification of language and semiosis to Plato and Aristotle and finds evidence of its persistence in important twentieth-century philosophical works. He affirms that certain postmodern works contain both decisive critiques of this perspective and alternative conceptualizations. Madison insists that "any philosophy of language is inevitably (if only implicitly) a philosophy of human existence," and that "the basic task of the philosophy of language is thus that of clarifying the relation among language, experience, and world." He acknowledges Heidegger's and Gadamer's contributions to this line of thinking but finds some of the most promising insights in the writings of Maurice Merleau-Ponty and Paul Ricoeur. Madison also shows how a postsemiological account of language need not be caught up in the nihilistic excesses of the postmodernisms of Jacques Derrida and Jean Baudrillard.

One contribution this chapter makes is to situate Derrida in this conversation about the representational nature of language. Madison argues that Saussure proposed an antireferential theory of meaning anchored in the conviction "that it is not the (external) relations that words have to things (reference) that determines their meaning; what determines the meaning ('value') of words is only the (internal) relations they bear to all the other words in the language in question." In other words, according to Madison, Saussure rejected the two worlds commitment of the symbol model. Derrida pushed the limit of Saussure's claim that "in *la langue* there are only differences" to the metaphysical thesis, "*Il n'y a pas de hors-texte;*" all there is, is *différance*, "the infinite referral of signifier to signifier." This move, claims Madison, effectively undermined semiologism by deconstructing its metaphysical ground—the existence or reality of the signified. But it also deconstructed meaning itself, "a classic case of throwing the baby out with the bathwater." This led Derrida "directly to *nihil-*

ism, a joyful nihilism perhaps, but nihilism nonetheless." Thus the need continues for a postsemiological theory of language "able to furnish a *positive* alternative to the traditional semiological or metaphysical view of language." Madison's primary goal is to sketch such an alternative.

My gloss of Derrida would differ slightly from Madison's. I do not believe that Derrida ultimately undermined semiologism, and that this is precisely what led to his nihilism. Even Derrida's late works are laced with semiotic vocabulary, a manifestation of his continued commitment to the belief that units of language are meaningful insofar as they *relate,* albeit not to "things" (referentialism), but to other "signifiers." Thus Derrida's residual semiologism left him with the need for two worlds but the willingness only to affirm one. It is a short step from a closed system (world) of interdependent signifiers to metaphysical indeterminacy or nihilism. But one can avoid this step by simply avoiding the claims that language is made up of units and that these units somehow "signify." This approach can open the door to precisely the kind of communicative account of language that Madison develops with the help of Merleau-Ponty and Ricoeur.

I would also emphasize more strongly than Madison the dialogic quality of this postsemiological account of language. Merleau-Ponty's is a phenomenology of *speaking* more than a phenomenology of *communicating.* His and Madison's appropriations of Brentano's and Husserl's accounts of intentionality sometimes drift into a view of language as the expression of intent, for example when the claim is made that "language genuinely exists only in its use" and that "the most primordial usage of language is that of *narrative.*" Here one may understand Madison—and Ricoeur—to be claiming that language is the "tool" humans use to tell stories. In addition, although Madison acknowledges that language is not a "what," he is more wedded than he might ideally be to the decision to discuss language as "word" and "words." The *practice* Madison ultimately sketches here is communication and communicating.

Importantly, however, Madison also affirms that "language is nothing other than reality as we experience or live it," that "language is not a 'thing' but a *way of being,*" that as a result it is impossible to say, "with any acceptable degree of literalness, what language is in itself," and that "speaking together" constitutes "an overarching form of life or being-in-the-world." He also underscores perhaps the most important immediate consequence of a postsemiotic theory of language, which is that it is necessary to give up correspondence tests of the truth-value of stories. But, contra Baudrillard and Derrida, Madison notes that we continue to have at our disposal tests that are both rigorous and reassuring because they are the tests of practice. The truth of any particular way of speaking must be assessed "with an overriding view to its practical consequences, that is, its implications as to the 'quality of life' it either promotes or diminishes." And "in the last analysis," Madison concludes, "the most important story (theory) we can tell about our own being-in-the-world is the story of our ability, which is to say, our *freedom* to tell various kinds of stories about it."

2

Being and Speaking

Gary Madison

Is not language more the language of things than the language of man?

—————H.-G. Gadamer[1]

The most pernicious of ideas are often those that are seemingly the most self-evident. Precisely because they are so "self-evident," they are often very long-lived. Francis Bacon referred to them as *idola tribus*, idols of the tribe, errors ingrained in human nature (given, in the case of human reality, the ambiguous relation between Nature and Culture, they are also what Bacon called *idola fori*, idols of the marketplace, i.e., errors due to the influence of language). As with some kind of Freudian hang-up, it is often exceedingly difficult to free oneself from their spell (indeed, even to realize that they are something from which one ought to free oneself). So it is with the idea that words are nothing more than signs. Let us call this the "semiotic" theory of language (from the Greek *semeion* = "sign").

Words are signs. What could be more self-evident? Has not modern, post-Fregean logic taught us that, as Bertrand Russell put it in a disarmingly succinct way in his preface to Wittgenstein's *Tractatus*, "the essential business of language is to assert or deny facts."[2] In other words, as Russell also said, the essence of language is to refer to "facts," to "things" in the world (the "external world," as moderns called it). Whence Wittgenstein's "picture theory of language" (presupposing a "mirror" theory of mind, the mind as the great mirror of nature). This is what elsewhere I have referred to as "referentialist representationalism," a term which can conveniently serve to designate the essence of the metaphysics of modernity.[3] For moderns language was of an essentially "epistemological" nature, that is, it was held to be a "representation" of reality (reality itself being conceived of in a metaphysically atomistic way as essentially nothing more than isolated bits of matter in perpetual motion). In his role as leading logician, Russell was the expert to whom all right-thinking intellectuals deferred. Thus, for example, in deference to this referentialist, semiotic theory of language, we find the great anthropologist, E. E. Evans-Pritchard, remarking, in a philosophical aside:

> Terms are only labels which help us to sort out facts of the same kind from facts which are different, or are in some respect different. If the labels do not prove helpful we can discard them. The facts will be the same without their labels.[4]

(It may be noted, however, that, precisely because he was a great anthropologist [and thus, by necessity, a hermeneut], Evans-Pritchard ignored this theoretical point in his ethnographic practice; the meaning of words, he instinctively knew, is determined not epistemologically [by what the "facts" are] but existentially [by how people live their world]).

Words are only labels, signs pointing to things ("facts"). Such is the semiotic theory of language. *Signum est aliquid qui stat pro aliquo.* Words are signs, things which stand for other things. When a word ("name," as the medievals would have said) is used correctly, it "sticks" to the thing in question. Language has adhesive power; it enables us to get a grip on things. To put it another way, language is essentially but a tool; the nature of language is instrumental or utilitarian—"*Signa instrumentalia sunt,*" as the seventeenth-century semiotician, John Poinsot, put it. Language, so conceived, is what enables us humans (the "tool-using animal," as physical anthropologists have a certain proclivity for saying) to manipulate ("dominate," as Descartes would say) the world in which we live (cf. Merleau-Ponty's remark: "*La science manipule les choses et renonce à les habiter*").[5] Call a thing by its proper (correct) name, and, like an obedient dog, it will do your bidding. This instrumentalist view of language informs modern science and, is far too ingrained in our inherited view of things (and in our speech patterns) to be resolutely abandoned.

And yet writers like John Stewart should not be deterred from doing their best to overturn the semiotic model. It is possible, on rare occasions, for a David to slay a Goliath. The timing though, as Machiavelli would say, is all-important. And perhaps now, finally, the timing is right. The Twilight of the Idols is perhaps finally at hand. Throughout our culture, ancient verities and long-standing "self-evident" truths are everywhere and in every regard being called into question. The generic name for this cataclysmic *mise en question* is "postmodernism." Postmodernism, it is true, comes in a bewildering array of differing versions, but it is not quite true that, as one quipster has remarked, "postmodernism is whatever you want it to be, provided you want it bad enough."[6] Philosophically speaking, postmodernism signifies a radical calling into question, not only of modernity, but of the entire 2,500-year-old tradition of Western thought—what Richard Rorty for one has referred to as "Platonism." At its best, postmodernism seeks not simply to take a Nietzschean hammer to the idols of the Tradition, deconstructing them for the sheer, infantile delight of tearing things down (as in the deconstruction practiced by, for instance, Jacques Derrida).[7] As exemplified in philosophical or phenomenological hermeneutics, postmodernism seeks not just to deconstruct, but, above all, to *re*construct many of the core ideas of Western thought—ideas such as "freedom," "reason," "humanity," "history"; it seeks to reconstruct them in a thoroughgoing and decisively non- or postmetaphysical fashion. That is to say, it seeks not to reject but rather to free notions such as those mentioned from their traditional metaphysical formulation (which it views as an instance of "false consciousness"). It goes without saying that this reconstructive project necessarily involves work of a "deconstructive" sort. As the hermeneuticist Paul Ricoeur has cogently remarked: "[C]onsciousness is first of all false consciousness, and it is always necessary to rise by means of a corrective critique from misunderstanding to understanding."[8] Such, most succinctly stated, is the hermeneutical position. Its implications, as regards language, are especially worthy of note.

We must rise, if I may paraphrase Ricoeur, turning him to my own immediate purposes, from a (semiotic) misunderstanding of language to a (postsemiotic) understanding of it. John Stewart's work is exemplary in this regard. But resistances (in the Freudian sense) are not so easily overcome until we know expressly what it is we are seeking to move beyond. One cannot really "get over" something (in this case, the semiotic view of language) until, as Freud would say, one has "worked through" it (cf. his notion of *Durcharbeit*). I am therefore obliged in what immediately follows to say something, however brief, about the history of the semiotic view of language (for a more detailed account of this history see Stewart's *Articulate Contact*). I simply wish, by means of what follows, to discern the outlines of that particular form of thought that a postsemiological theory of language must set itself the task of overcoming.

Let us then go back to the beginnings, to the most prepubescent, infantile origins of our current semiotic hang-up about language. *In principio erat verbum . . . Et verbum erat signum.* From its beginnings, Western thought was concerned with language, with the relation between words, thought, and reality, words being taken to be signs of the last two. Plato was the key figure here. Before Plato, in Homer for instance, words functioned in all sorts of undefinable and uncontrollable sorts of ways, just as before Plato (and after him, for that matter) sexuality itself functioned in all sorts of "polymorphous perverse" fashions. Given his rationalist temper, however, Plato could not tolerate this sort of sexual/linguistic polymorphous or pluralist, liberal "anarchy"; like rationalists ever since, he harbored a deep-seated dread of *the protean* and was obsessed with nailing things down—decisively and definitively. This is what moved him (if one may surmise about a dead man's motives), to write the world's oldest and most influential book on language, the *Cratylus*. There were of course other books on language written around about the same time, by the Sophists or rhetoricians, and with quite other purposes in mind, but they were, in all likelihood, subsequently destroyed by Plato's pupils, and thus created no effective history.[9] Plato's work has therefore both defined a position and created a tradition. The tradition is that of the semiotic theory of language.

However much he might otherwise be indulgent towards Plato, Hans-Georg Gadamer has nevertheless exposed the Platonic presuppositions behind our inherited semiotic, instrumentalist view of language, helping thereby to call into question its "self-evidentness." In a noteworthy remark, he once observed how the Russelian (or Leibnizian) theory of language alluded to above has its origin in Plato's seminal discussion of the "correctness of names" (*orthotes onomata*) in the *Cratylus*. Speaking of how "Plato's discovery of the ideas ["essences"] conceals the true nature of language," Gadamer went on to say:

> Even where Plato, pointing forward to his dialectic, moves beyond the level of the discussion in the *Cratylus*, we find no other relation to language than that already discussed there: language is a tool, an image that is constructed and judged in terms of the original, the objects themselves. Thus even when he does not assign to the sphere of words (*onomata*) any independent cognitive function and calls for the transcending of this sphere, he keeps to the framework of reference within which the question of the "correctness" of the name presents itself. Even when (as in the context of the seventh *Letter*) he does not accept a natural correctness of names, he still retains resemblance (*homoion*) as the criterion: the image and the original constitute for him the metaphysical model with which he considers everything within the noetic sphere. Hence the critique of the correctness of names in the *Cratylus* is the first step in the direction at the end of which lies the modern instrumental theory of language and the ideal of a sign system of reason.[10]

In the *Cratylus* Plato was responding to the famous *nomos/physis* debate launched by the Sophists and was targeting those amongst them who had argued that the meaning of words is arbitrary (a matter of "cul-

ture" or "convention," *nomos*) and thus, as they said, has no correspondence to reality ("nature," *physis*). If such were the case, Truth, as Plato
conceived of it (the "correspondence" of our ideas with essential reality),[11]
would be a meaningless notion (as indeed Nietzsche proclaimed it to be
many centuries later when he said that the ancient metaphysical notion of
essential "being" was nothing but "the last fumes of evaporating reality").
Accordingly, Plato set forth in opposition to this his own metaphysical
theory of language. The basic tent of Plato's *doctrina signorum* was that
words are merely signs and are thus to be judged solely on the basis of their
relation ("resemblance") to things. Like logicians ever after, Plato insisted
that the meaning of words is (or ought to be) determined by reality itself
and that when a new word is coined it should be made to fit the concept it
is intended to express and should conform to the precise nature of the
thing talked about. To be sure, Plato was not ignorant of the fact that
different peoples speak quite dissimilar languages (all, however, grossly
inferior to Greek); nonetheless, despite their differing phonetic material,
they all express in their own way (to the degree that they are "correct") the
identical ideal form. Distinctions among words, in whatever language,
should correspond to natural (metaphysical) distinctions among things, to
"natural kinds." As Plato insisted, it is important "to put the true natural
name of each thing into sounds and syllables and to make and give all
names with a view to the ideal name."[12] The name, Plato said, anticipating
Wittgenstein and his picture theory of meaning, is the representation of a
thing; like all good portraits, it should be drawn with "correctness of representation" in mind. Words are nothing but mirror images of things (for
Plato the task of the philosopher or scientist was simply that of "holding a
mirror up to nature"); the essence of language is entirely epistemological.

The metaphysical assumptions underlying this semiotic theory of language were subsequently articulated by Plato's prize pupil, Aristotle (who,
in large part, made his fortune by spelling out in explicitly metaphysical
terms the prejudices of his teacher). In the opening lines of his immensely
influential *De Interpretatione*, the Philosopher stated in a superbly magis-
terial way:

> Spoken words are the symbols of mental experience and written words
> are the symbols of spoken words. Just as all men have not the same
> writing, so all men have not the same speech sounds, but the mental
> experiences, which these directly symbolize, are the same for all, as also
> are those things of which our experiences are the images.[13]

In other words, words, spoken or written, are nothing but external
signs of thoughts, possessing no significance in their own right, except

that which thought chooses to confer upon them. Thoughts, in turn, are but signs (of a rather diaphanous nature) of things, which, in turn, are the referential criteria of the meaningfulness of thought. All right-thinking people have the same thoughts (since, as Aristotle the metaphysician argued, reality or "being" is by nature one and the self-same), though because of the multiplicity of natural languages they express them in different ways. In a Platonically ideal world (or, at least, as Aristotle said, when one is doing science—"geometry"), everyone would, however, speak the same language: to the "oneness" of being would correspond a univocity of speech. This is what, in Aristotle's wake, modern logicians such as Russell referred to as "a logically perfect language." Ideally, as Russell said, words, like mathematical symbols, should have single, definite meanings ("uniqueness of reference"). The ideal of a semiologically ideal language is as old as main line philosophy itself.

The writings of Plato and Aristotle on language are canonical. They are indeed the canonical texts par excellence.[14] Like all canonical texts they inaugurate a tradition and establish an orthodoxy. They set an agenda. As with any orthodoxy, different individuals down through the Tradition may object to this or that aspect of the core idea and may seek to articulate it differently; these attempts at "revisionism" notwithstanding, the idea, and the agenda, remain basically the same. *Plus ça change.* . . . Thus, despite the logical precision it brought to the discussion of language or "symbolism," the much vaunted "linguistic turn" in philosophy earlier in this century in no way constituted a revolution in our thinking about language— unless "revolution" is understood in the old sense, as an orbiting return to an originary state of affairs. The new "philosophy of symbolism" may have been "philosophy in a new key," but the tunes it rehearsed were pretty much the old ones of the Tradition.[15] One may hope that this particular "revolution" did at least signal the completion of one great cycle in human thinking and that we may now be in a position to explore new horizons.

If a revolution in the approach to language did occur earlier on in our century, it was effected not by the logicians and philosophers of the symbol but by a linguist, Ferdinand de Saussure. Saussure's radically innovative approach to language was dictated by his desire to make of linguistics a genuine science. For language to figure as a scientific object in its own right, Saussure in effect (and quite correctly) reasoned, one must, as with all scientific objects, be able to treat it as a kind of closed system. This means that speech (*la parole*) and the speaking subject (*le sujet parlant*) must be excluded from the science of linguistics, whose sole object can only be language conceived of as a self-contained system of signs (*la langue*), as a kind of impersonal and abstract code existing independently of the uses (or misuses) that speaking individuals might make of it.[16] Now when language is conceived of in this way, that is, in Saussure's words, as "a system in which all the terms are interdependent and in which the value of each results only from the simultaneous presence of the others,"[17] it follows that the meaning of words (signs) is determined not "referentially" but "diacritically." That is to say, it becomes obvious (counterintuitive as it might at first appear) that it is not the (external) relations that words have to things (reference) that determines their meaning; what determines the meaning ("value") of words is only the (internal) relations they bear to all the other words in the language in question. In other words, the meaning of words is *arbitrary* and *differential;* no word has meaning "in itself" but only as a function of its relation to, which is to say, difference from, all others. (In saying this, Saussure effectively demolished what I. A. Richards called the Proper Meaning Superstition, an *idolum fori* dating back to Aristotle.) As Merleau-Ponty was later to say:

> What we have learned from Saussure is that, taken singly, signs do not signify anything, and that each one of them does not so much express a meaning as mark a divergence of meaning between itself and other signs. Since the same can be said for all other signs, we may conclude that language is made of differences without terms; or more exactly, that the terms of language are engendered only by the differences which appear among them.[18]

Unlike the structuralists who came after him, Merleau-Ponty was nevertheless not a Saussurian; he simply took from Saussure what he found useful (indeed, his reading of Saussure was rather idiosyncratic). Merleau-Ponty differed from Saussure in that his interests were not of a scientific but of a philosophical nature; as a phenomenologist he was interested primarily not in Saussure's *langue* but in the speaking subject Saussure had explicitly set aside in his attempt to make of linguistics a science. Merleau-Ponty's focal point was not language as an abstract system but rather the human subject who "lives his language." He in fact maintained that language lives only in speech,[19] and he was interested in the vital role that language plays in our experience of the world. This was a major theme in his *Phenomenology of Perception* where, in opposition to the Tradition, he had argued that the relation between language and thought is not external but internal (words *are* thoughts). Merleau-Ponty did not believe in the basic principles of referentialist-representationalism, he did not believe that words are copies of thoughts or that thoughts are copies of things, and he no doubt thought that Saussure's linguistics afforded additional reason for contesting these age-old precepts of semioticism.

The case is otherwise with a hyperstructuralist such as Jacques Derrida. Derrida looks to Saussure not as an ally in formulating a renewed theory of linguistic meaning but as a tool to be exploited in "deconstructing" the notion of meaning altogether. In, as it were, willful ignorance of the intrinsic limits of any methodological construct of a scientific nature (such as, precisely, Saussure's *langue*), Derrida seeks to push to the limit Saussure's postulate as to the arbitrariness of signs. Taking up Saussure's statement to the effect that *"in language [la langue]* there are only differences,"[20] Derrida, ignoring Saussure's qualification ("in language . . ."), generalizes Saussure's observation into an overarching metaphysical thesis: There is nothing but language (*"Il n'y a pas de hors-texte"*), and language is nothing but a differential system of slippage and dissemination. All there is, *überhaupt*, is *différance*, "the indefinite referral of signifier to signifier."[21] Language is simply not "about" anything at all—experience, existence, the world, reality, whatever. Language refers only to itself, and the meaning of what it says to itself by way of *auto-affection* is forever deferred.

Derrida's hyperstructuralist stratagem effectively undermines semiologism in that it deconstructs its metaphysical ground (what Derrida refers to as the "metaphysics of presence"), that is, Platonic essences and Aristotle's Proper Meaning Superstition. Unfortunately (depending on how you look at it), it also, in the process, deconstructs "meaning" itself. A classic case of throwing the baby out with the bathwater. For if, as Derrida would have it, meaning ("decidability") is forever deferred, this means that never, at any time, do we ever experience a meaningful world by means of language. In spite of Derrida's customary (and no doubt prudent) reluctance to draw conclusions, the consequence is that our lives ("existence") are themselves meaningless—"absurd," as the existentialists used to say. Derrida, of course, prefers to put it another, more positive-sounding, way. For him the demise of metaphysical seriousness signals the advent of play. Play, for him, is "the Nietzschean affirmation, that is the joyous affirmation of the play of the world and of the innocence of becoming, the affirmation of a world of signs without fault, without truth, and without origin which is offered to an active [anything goes] interpretation."[22] Derrida's Nietzschean play is a form of play which is both pointless, that is, without goal, and meaningless. As with Nietzsche, Derrida's critique of the Tradition leads directly to *nihilism*, a joyful nihilism perhaps, but nihilism nonetheless. Derrida's remedy for the excesses of semiologism is thus not so much an antidote as a poison which kills off the patient along with the disease.

Perhaps the greatest drawback to Derrida's way of contesting the Tradition is that it is such as to "scare off" those who otherwise might be receptive to a genuinely postsemiological theory of language. It needlessly provokes an inordinate amount of "resistance" in them, what Richard J.

Bernstein has aptly referred to as "Cartesian Anxiety," that is, the great horror that if the meaning of words is not rigidly nailed down by reference to immutable Truth, everything degenerates into chaos and flux.[23] The upshot is relativism, the total demise of meaning and truth. Or so it is thought. Thus, for instance, one horrified traditionalist, in speculating about whether or not postmodernism (of the sort defended in this paper) offers a promising future or is simply a dead end, exclaims in a fit of overreactive defensiveness: "[T]he postmodern turn is worse than a dead end."[24]

What this suggests is that a successful postsemiological theory of language must be able to furnish a positive alternative to the traditional semiological or metaphysical view of language. The lessons of recent times would seem to indicate that the task of a genuinely postsemiological theory of language is twofold: On the one hand, it must eschew the "sterile formalism" (as Merleau-Ponty referred to it) of the logicist approach to language characteristic of twentieth-century analytic philosophy, which reduces words to mere "symbols," while, on the other hand, doing its best not to land in the quicksand (*abîme*, as Derrida would say) of meaninglessness laid bare by post-Nietzschean deconstructionism.

I have titled this paper "Being and Speaking" since, in the case of human being, to be and to speak are one and the same. The human, as Isocrates said, is the "speaking animal."[25] The human being is that being which possesses the *logos* (*zoon logon ekon*). Reason (*ratio, logos*) is the "faculty" or ability to speak, of being able, by means of language (*logos*), to persuade and to be persuaded. "Reason" is the ability humans have of finding common ways of speaking (cf. Heraclitus),[26] which is to say, common ways of viewing the world, of coming to an understanding of it (this is what is called "truth"). What is called "reasonableness" is the ability to listen to the speech of others and to respond to these others by means of civil discourse rather than brute force. Language is what enables humans to be human; it is what enables them to have specifically human emotions; it is what enables them to behave humanely, to be truly political or social animals (*zoon politikon*).[27]

This is by way of saying that any philosophy of language is inevitably (if only implicitly) a philosophy of human existence. The central task of a philosophy of human existence which is aware of itself as such must accordingly be that of clarifying the relation between language and existence. For humans to be is to be in a world, and a world is something that gets constituted by language. The basic task of the philosophy of language is thus that of clarifying the relation among language, experience, and world.

Given the metaphysical and epistemological underpinnings of the received, semiological view of language, a postsemiological philosophy of language must be postmodern as well. That is, it must be able to formulate a theory of language free of the underlying presuppositions of semioticism as they came to be embodied in modern thought. The chief trait of modern semioticism is its epistemological doctrine of "representationalism." Under the influence of Descartes above all, modern philosophy grafted onto classical referentialism—the belief that words are signs of thoughts which in turn are signs of things—the belief that thoughts are only indirectly signs of things—mere re-presentations of things, not direct images of them. Between the "subjective" (the mind) and the "objective" (the world), modern philosophy instituted a fundamental, and ultimately unbridgeable, cleavage.[28] Ever since Descartes, modern philosophers have accordingly busied themselves with inventing "proofs for the existence of the world" (the "external" world), that is, they have attempted to come up with *methods* capable of guaranteeing reasonable certainty that our "ideas" "correspond" with "reality." All their heroic efforts went into bridging the gap between the subjective and the objective, thought and reality. No one of them ever succeeded in this endeavor, however, nor could they ever so succeed. The problem is quite simply intractable, given its underlying postulates.[29] Modern semioticism has not brought us any closer to "reality" but has succeeded only in widening the gap between not only thought and reality but between words and thoughts as well (by, as in Leibniz's *ars combinatoria* and its twentieth-century imitations, reducing words to mere conventional signs of thoughts existing independently of them). The end of modernism is the "sterile formalism" of the analytic "philosophy of language," which, in Merleau-Ponty's words, views words "only as the clothing of a consciousness, a facing on thought"[30]—as well as the nihilism of antisemiological deconstructionism that deconstructs consciousness or thought altogether leaving in its place nothing more than the free-play of meaningless signifiers.

A bold step is therefore called for if we are ever to get beyond the endless aporias of modern philosophy. Merleau-Ponty made just such a step when he proclaimed: "We must not, therefore, wonder whether we really perceive a world, we must instead say: the world is what we perceive."[31] In saying this, Merleau-Ponty was summing up what he perceived to be the lesson of Husserl's celebrated "phenomenological reduction." As Merleau-Ponty was quick to realize, Husserl's phenomenology represented a major frontal assault on the presuppositions of modern referentialist-representationalism. Husserl's "reduction" was in fact a deconstruction of the basic problematic of modern philosophy.[32] As such, it was a crucial first step in the direction of a decisively postmodern form of thought.

What above all the reduction serves to reveal is the intentionality of consciousness. Once the reduction is put into play ("bracketing" or "setting aside" the presuppositions of modern philosophy), it becomes apparent that consciousness is not one thing (*res cogitans*) standing alongside or over against another thing called the "world" (*res extensa*), such that to be conscious would mean (as moderns thought that it meant) that one was conscious only of one's own consciousness ("ideas," sense impressions, etc.) and not of the world of which one was conscious. As Sartre pointed out, the essence of consciousness is that it is consciousness-*of*-its object, *of*-the world. Consciousness is inseparable from that-of-which it is conscious, the "object" of consciousness, that is, the world.

As Sartre also pointed out, consciousness is intentional through and through; there is nothing "substantial" in it.[33] The whole "essence" of consciousness is to "intend" or "mean" (*meinen*) various "objectivities," the most encompassing of which is the world itself. The world is, ultimately, what consciousness "means," which is to say that it is, "in itself," as something meant, *a certain kind of meaning*. By means, therefore, of its notion of intentionality, phenomenology effectively overcomes the most fundamental of modern dichotomies, that of mind versus world. "Meaning" is not a mere mentalistic category, phenomenology insists; it is above all a worldly one.

The history of the phenomenological movement after Husserl, from Heidegger and Merleau-Ponty through Gadamer and Ricoeur, has amounted to an attempt to exploit to the utmost the nonoppositional, postmetaphysical possibilities for thought latent in Husserl's phenomenological deconstruction of the epistemological problematic. In particular, it has been an attempt to overcome the last vestiges of the "philosophy of consciousness" that Husserl had inherited from his modern forebears. Thus, in his "existentializing" of phenomenology, Heidegger abandoned all talk of "consciousness," preferring to speak instead of that unitary phenomenon he referred to as *Dasein* or being-in-the-world (what might colloquially be called "the whole human being"). In opposition to the mentalism which persists in analytic philosophy, Heidegger insisted that the primary locus of meaning or truth is not the judgment or proposition ("S is P") but our prepredicative or prereflective existence conceived of as being-in-the-world. As he stated in *Being and Time*:

> [A] '*commercium*' of the subject with a world does not get *created* for the first time by knowing, nor does it *arise* from some way in which the world acts upon a subject. Knowing is a mode of Dasein founded upon Being-in-the-world.[34]

There exists an awareness of the world more basic than what analytic philosophers call "knowing" the world. Meaning and truth are not in the first instance logical or epistemological (theoretical) categories but rather existential (practical) ones.

In his reflections on the human bodily subject (*corps propre*), Merleau-Ponty was to go even further in this attempt at overcoming the oppositional thought of modern philosophy.[35] The main theme of his major work, *Phenomenology of Perception,* was, as the title indicates, perception itself. Pursuing the phenomenological attack on mentalism, Merleau-Ponty argued here that the "knowing subject" is in the first instance a perceiving, bodily subject. Not only is consciousness not to be opposed to world (subject to object), but intellection is not to be opposed to perception (mind to body). "Experience" was for Merleau-Ponty a category that transcends the dichotomies of subject and object, mind and body; experience is in the first instance a bodily-experience-of-the-world, from which all intellectual knowing derives. The phenomenological world, the world in which we find ourselves as existing beings, is, as he said, "that world which precedes knowledge, of which knowledge always *speaks*, and in relation to which every scientific schematism is an abstract and derivative sign-language, as is geography in relation to the countryside in which we have learnt beforehand what a forest, a prairie or a river is."[36]

The language of science and logic may be a kind of "sign language," but, being derivative in regard to our bodily experience of the world, it is not paradigmatic of language itself. It is in fact parasitical on what is called natural language, and the latter is none other than that in which the speaking subject articulates his or her bodily contact with the perceived world. "Expressive significance" is more basic than "sign significance."[37] Language, Merleau-Ponty says, is a way our body has of "singing the world." The speaking subject is none other than the bodily subject; speech is not a power of the mind or intellect, an "operation of knowledge," but an existential function of the lived body. Merleau-Ponty effectively breaks with the tool conception of language when he argues that language is not merely a means of *communicating* our thoughts (the "post office" model of language) but, more importantly, of *thinking* them. Thinking and speaking are inseparable: "The meaning is not on the phrase like the butter on the bread, like a second layer of 'psychic reality' spread over the sound; it is the totality of what is said, the integral of all the differentiations of the verbal chain; it is given with the words for those who have ears to hear."[38] Thinking is nothing other than a matter of finding the right words for what one "wants to say," that is, means (*veut dire*). *Parole parlante* and *pensée pensante* are one and the same. Words *are* what they "signify"; they are not just signs but are rather the living flesh of thought itself—emblems of being.

Merleau-Ponty summed up his own postsemiotic, postmodern approach to language in the following way:

[S]peech is not the 'sign' of thought, if by this we understand a phenomenon which heralds another as smoke betrays fire. Speech and thought
would admit of this external relation only if they were both thematically
given, whereas in fact they are intervolved, the sense being held within
the word, and the word being the external existence of the sense. Nor can
we concede, as is commonly done, that speech is a mere means of fixation
[Plato's thesis], nor yet that it is the envelope and clothing of thought.
Why should it be easier to recall words or phrases than thoughts, if the
alleged verbal images need to be reconstructed on every occasion? And
why should thought seek to duplicate itself or clothe itself in a succession
of utterances, if the latter do not carry and contain within themselves
their own meaning? Words cannot be 'strongholds of thought,' nor can
thought seek expression, unless words are in themselves a comprehen-
sible text, and unless speech possesses a power of signification entirely its
own. The word and speech must somehow cease to be a way of designating [*désigner—déSIGNEr*] things or thoughts, and become the presence
of that thought in the phenomenal world, and, moreover, not its clothing
but its token [*emblème*] or its body.[39]

In his attempt at overcoming metaphysical oppositions, Merleau-
Ponty fully linked together in an unfragmented circular fashion what, at
the beginning of the metaphysical tradition, Aristotle, in the interests of
logic, had rigorously separated: words, thoughts, and things.[40] He thereby
effected a revolution of sorts, bringing us full circle and putting us in a
position to make a new beginning.

What lessons might one draw from phenomenological postmodernism
as regards the make-up of a genuinely postsemiotic theory of language?
The most obvious lesson is of an epistemological-ontological sort: We must
cease opposing language to thought or, more generally, experience, and
must cease also opposing experience to reality. We must, in other words,
rethink what we mean when we say that language is "about" something—
if, that is, we wish, unlike the deconstructionists, to retain in some way
the notions of "meaning" and "truth," avoiding thereby the nihilism that
follows from their denial.

The basic postulate of a postsemiotic theory of language is that, as
Gadamer puts it, "language is something other than a mere sign system to
denote the totality of objects. The word is not a sign."[41] Now, it is true that
if words are not signs, it is also true that they do not "refer" to or "denote"
anything whatsoever. This does not mean, however, that they are without
meaning. They mean exactly what they say, namely: thoughts, experiences,
things.

When the postsemiotician asserts that words are not signs, it is only natural to want to ask in return, "If words are not signs, just what are they then?" We should, however, resist this temptation, since it may well be a seriously misleading sort of question to ask. For it may be the case that language is not a "what" at all, that is, devoid of "essence."[42] Indeed, a postsemiotic theory of language calls for an overcoming of essentialist ways of thinking in general and of various metaphysical oppositions in particular. Thus, with the phenomenological notion of intentionality (the inseparability of mind and world) in mind as well as the phenomenological insistence on the inseparability of thought and language, we should perhaps say that words do not denote things but rather *intend* them; in other words, words are nothing other than *things themselves as-they-are-meant.* Or as Gadamer expresses the matter in speaking of "the inner unity of thinking and speaking to oneself," when we think of a thing "the word is not expressing the mind, but the intended object."[43] Between word and thing there is, as Gadamer says, a mutual belonging (*un rapport mutuel,* in phenomenological terms). Language (in the normal course of events)[44] is not about itself; it is about the world of which it speaks. As Gadamer states in a properly phenomenological fashion:

> Language is not just one of man's possessions in the world, but on it depends the fact that man has a world at all. For man the world exists as world in a way that no other being in the world experiences. But this world is linguistic in nature. . . . [L]anguage has no independent life apart from the world that comes to language within it. Not only is the world 'world' only insofar as it comes into language, but language, too, has its real being only in the fact that the world is presented in it.[45]

Since the world is what language *means* (intends), it is not something other than language to which language merely "refers" but is, rather, *the very meaning of language itself.*

To put it another way, language is the way in which we, as humans, the "speaking animals," experience what we call reality; that is, it is the way in which reality exists for us. Thus, as Gadamer says: "Reality does not happen 'behind the back' of language; . . . reality happens precisely *within* language."[46] Just as language and experience "belong" together,[47] so also do spoken experience and reality. The language that we speak is neither, as the structuralists would have it, a system of pure "signs," closed in upon itself and expressing nothing other than itself, nor is it, as the analysts maintain, simply a means of "referring" to things (or "propositions") that are what they are independently of it. What language means is the world or, more precisely, this or that way of being-in-the-world; the meaning of language is existential-ontological. Language is nothing other than reality as we experience or live it. This is why Gadamer says that "the nature of things" and "the language of things" are "two common expressions that for all intents and purposes mean the same thing."[48] Or as Merleau-Ponty said, referring to Valéry: "[I]n a sense . . . language is everything, since it is the voice of no one, since it is the very voice of the things, the waves, and the forests."[49]

If we wish in this way to maintain that it is the case that language neither merely "expresses itself" nor that it merely "refers" to an "extra"-linguistic reality, we must abandon also the traditional inside/outside opposition. It is their common adherence to this age-old dichotomy which leads both analysts and deconstructionists to maintain that words are, in one way or another, meaningless. They are meaningless in their own right for the analysts, since for them the meaning of words resides outside of them in the things they supposedly refer to (thoughts or things). They are meaningless for the deconstructionists, since for them language has no "outside" to begin with (and thus is not "about" anything). This leads some of them to assert that, since there is nothing but language, language is a kind of prison (or, as Derrida might say, a "padded cell").[50]

To be sure, Gadamer asserts on a number of occasions that "being that can be understood is language." Speaking as he is from a post-semiological standpoint, he does not mean thereby that language is all there is (what might be called "semiological reductionism")[51] but rather—and this is something quite different—that all that is and can be for us *is* by means of language. To put it another way, language must be viewed not as a finite system of sign-symbols but as an infinite medium of possible meaningfulness. Unlike artificial (logistic) sign-languages, which are of necessity closed or finite (cf. Gödel's theorem), natural, spoken languages are infinite in that they have no outer limits. Natural languages are not closed systems in which speakers are imprisoned and which determine in advance what can and what cannot meaningfully be said. There is, in other words, nothing that, with sufficient ingenuity, speaking subjects cannot make their language say: "[E]very language, despite its difference from other languages, is able to say everything it wants."[52]

Language, the "medium" of experience or consciousness ("there is no [human] experience without speech"[53]), must be viewed in the way phenomenology views consciousness itself. Being intentional through and through, consciousness does not exist in the mode of substance (a "substance" is that which exists *in se,* closed in upon itself). Unlike the material things of which it is conscious, consciousness itself has no inside strictly speaking, since its "inside" is, as Sartre observed, nothing other than what is "outside" of it. Unlike the material things of which it speaks, language also has no inside. Far from being a system of signs closed in upon itself (a finite object), language opens us to the infinity of what is and what can be thought. As Gadamer remarks, like consciousness itself ("understanding," in his words), language is never "simply an object, but comprises everything that can ever be an object."[54] Language is not a "thing" but a way of being,[55] and the way of being of humans, qua humans, is one which is not limited to any particular environment (*Umwelt*) but one which intends, with limited means, an unlimited reality (*Welt*).[56]

The name for this mode of being is reason. To be, as the human being is, a rational being is, as I mentioned earlier, to be a speaking being, for as Gadamer observes:

> [L]anguage always forestalls any objection to its jurisdiction. Its universality keeps pace with the universality of reason. . . . [I]f there are basically no bounds set to understanding, then the linguistic form which the interpretation of this understanding finds must contain within it an infinite dimension that transcends all bounds. Language is the language of reason itself.[57]

To say, as I did a moment ago, that language is not a "thing" should not, however, mislead us into thinking that it is something purely "spiritual" (in the sense in which the mind was customarily taken to be something "spiritual" and thus alien to the material body). A postsemiological theory of language must also avoid as best it can the ancient matter/spirit dichotomy. Words are, of course, and manifestly so, something material. Spoken words, after all, consist of modulations of physical air waves and are produced by the physical organs of mouth and throat; written words, too, are material in that to exist at all they must be inscribed in or on a material substance (paper, stone, etc.) by some material means (pen and ink, brush and paint, chisel and stone, etc.); even the electricity in which postmodern words are written is a material substance, albeit a highly ethereal and rather "ghostly" one.

And yet words are not things in any ordinary sense. They are most definitely not material things in the "materialist" (e.g., "vulgar" Marxist or nineteenth century) sense of the term. The materiality of the word does not stand opposed to the ideality of its meaning: There is "no gap between its appearance to the senses and its meaning"; "the ideality of the meaning lies in the word itself."[58] Traditionally, material things are said to be those things that are limited in their existence to the physical space they occupy, whereas spiritual or ideal entities transcend the limitations of space and time (whence the notion that they are "eternally true" or that an infinite number of angels can dance on the head of a pin). The word possess a unique mode of being in that it is both material and ideal, both temporal and "eternal." Although words (ideas) are always historical (localized) in origin, the unique thing about them is that they can always be detached from their place of origin (a particular form of life) and be transferred ("applied") to any other place and time.[59]

The ideality of the word is confirmed by the fact that the words of one natural language can always be translated into those of another (although this may oftentimes prove to be a daunting task). Anyone who has ever been forced to translate what he or she has said or written into another language knows that bilingual dictionaries are of limited usefulness in this task. Translation from one spoken language to another can never be *mot à mot*. This contrasts with the case of formal sign languages (which are never, properly speaking, spoken) where, once equivalences have been set up, translation can proceed automatically (indeed, no human translator is required, only a properly programed computer). In the case of translation from one natural language to another something more than a table of equivalences is required; one needs to know something about the way of being-in-the-world of the people in question. Universality in the ideality of meaning is achievable here, but this is not the homogeneous universality of formal sign languages but a kind of "transversal" universality (to borrow an expression from Calvin Schrag), a sameness within difference. What a successful translation realizes is an *analogical* commonality between different forms of life.

It must be admitted, parenthetically, that oftentimes the difficulties of translation are so severe that one simply transfers, without more ado, a foreign word bodily into another language. Thus, for instance, the postmodern French word, *écriture*, becomes, in Japanese, *ekrituru*. This sort of thing is a universal phenomenon in the case of natural languages. And it reveals something very important about languages as people speak or live them: They are amazingly permeable. Any language which is permeable in this way is open-ended and thus, unlike formal sign languages, infinite in its own resources—being open as it is to the resources of every other language, and to the ways of life (the "traditions," as Gadamer would say) embodied in them.[62]

Since words are always translatable, they are never mere markers or labels whose meaning would be nothing more than a function of the particular and unique thing they are attached to by stipulatory fiat. Indeed, for a word even to *be* a word, it, unlike individual physical things that are the particular individual things they are and nothing more, must possess a kind of intrinsic generality. Just as, as Sartre says, consciousness is not what it is and is what it is not, so likewise a word is not what it is and is what it is not (i.e., it is not what it is, a material thing, but is what it means). For a word to count as a word in the first place, it must (as Derrida well knows) be (re)iterable, indefinitely and without limit and without regard to predetermined context.[61] If you cannot take a word out of its original context and shift it around at your creative urgings, generating more meaning in the process, then what you are dealing with is not a word at all. (In other words, if words cannot be legitimately used as metaphors, then they are not words but mere signs or symbols.)

If, as I have asserted, words are not what they are (particular material things) but are what they are not, that is, the very things they mean, then it is not at all surprising that when we attempt to say what words truly are we should invariably be forced to have recourse to metaphor (the unique thing about metaphors is that they tell us what something is by saying what it is not).[62] Thus, we say that words are not signs or instruments but rather (as Gadamer for instance metaphorically says) "events," "processes," "images," or "appearances" (of the thing itself).

Words are not signs. Exactly what they are is something that cannot (literally) be said. Words are what they do, which is: to enable us to be the kind of beings we are, that is, beings who live not only in an environment but in a world. If theory is understood as a statement of what something is (even if only in a hypothetical mode), then it follows from what has been said that, strictly speaking, there can be no such thing as a postsemiotic theory of language, since language is not a "what." The best that any theorizing, that is, speaking, about language can do is to keep us from taking it to be something it is not, for example, a tool. It is no more possible to say, with any acceptable degree of literalness, what language is in itself than it is to say what being is in itself. The best we can do in our speaking about language is, as Heidegger might say, to let it freely be.

In any event, the "iterability" of the word (i.e., something of a "process" rather than a "substance" nature) is what constitutes the generality of the word, and thus its ideality, and thus also its universality. It is what, as Gadamer says, makes it be that language (any human language) is the language of universal reason itself. In the case of the word, it is, to paraphrase Merleau-Ponty, as though the flesh of this world emigrated into another, less heavy and more transparent flesh, a kind of universal flesh of the world which is that of language.[63] Language is what gives flesh to our experience of the world.

It is thus perhaps evident now why, in the case of human reality, being and speaking are one and the same. As Merleau-Ponty once said, anticipating those present-day postmodernists of a relativist and communitarian bent who extol "localism" and "particularity" and who spare no effort to debunk the universalist claims of reason, human beings are not trees, each proliferating in his or her own native country, oblivious to others, in other places and times.[64] Thanks to language, and thanks also to the new medium of global electronic communication, humans can, and increasingly do, communicate without limit (realizing thereby, as it were, Jaspers's idea of "boundless communication"). Because of the intrinsic generality of the word, they can translate or transport (*translatio, transferre*) themselves into other human (linguistic) contexts. This speaking together, when conducted in good will, amounts to a reasoning together. Through it, an overarching form of life or being-in-the-world gets constituted, which is itself that of a universal concept, that of "humanity." To speak like Hegel, it is language which confers on this concept real existence. Descartes, the archmodernist, said (to himself): "I think, therefore I am." To this the postmodern postsemiotician must retort: Not so! We speak (together), therefore we are (together, each and every unique one of us, as members of a single self-conscious humanity). If we did not speak together, we could not even say "I" to ourselves.[65]

No theory is without its appropriate practice. Indeed, what a given theory truly "means" is nothing other than the practice to which it gives rise or of which it is the expression.[66] What then is the practical meaning of the postsemiotic theory of language defended in this paper? In order to tackle this question a few preliminary points need first to be made.

The basic point stressed by phenomenologists or hermeneuticists such as Merleau-Ponty and Gadamer is that language genuinely exists only in its use (i.e., as speech or dialogue rather than as *langue*). Now it could be argued, as in fact Paul Ricoeur does,[67] that the most primordial usage of language is that of narrative (*récit*). It is, as Ricoeur says, through narrative emplotment that we achieve (to the degree that we do) meaning in our lives; the meaning of life (that of an individual just as much as that of a community) consists in the way in which what otherwise might be viewed as a haphazard series of events are strung together in the form of a coherent story. "Man," the speaking animal, is also the storytelling animal. Since as Heidegger pointed out, the "essence" of human being is "care" (*Sorge*), humans, ever since they have been human, have sat around the campfire telling and listening to stories about themselves. Speech (*Sprache, Sagen*) exists most fully in the form of story (*Saga*). It is speech qua narrative that makes of our lives *texts* to be read and understood (by ourselves or our biographers, by psychoanalysts or cultural anthropologists). As one commentator of Ricoeur's has remarked: "Hermeneutics is concerned with the interpretation of any expression of existence which can be preserved in a structure analogous to the structure of a text. . . . Taking

it to the limit, the entirety of human existence becomes a text to be interpreted."[68]

As Gadamer would say, understanding is not merely a reproductive
activity but is always of a transformational nature (scientific statements
are true to the degree that they allow us to intervene in the natural course
of events in such a way as to change them). Self-understanding is thus a
matter of self-transformation.[69] This is where narrative comes in. By re-
counting our lives to ourselves and others in novel (and novelesque) ways,
we are enabled thereby to become more the kind of person we want to
become. As Ricoeur has observed: "What would we know of love and hate,
of moral feelings and, in general, of all that we call the *self*, if these had
not been brought to language and articulated by literature?"[70] In exposing
ourselves to texts, we undergo "imaginative variations" (as Husserl would
have said) of our egos and receive in this way from the text "an enlarged
self."[71]

What this all comes down to is that, since the meaning of our lives
gets constituted by the way in which we speak them in the form of a story,
the kind of stories we tell about ourselves is a crucially important matter.
And since, moreover, as Heidegger emphasized, the "world" is a part of the
all-inclusive phenomenon of being-in-the-world, the kind of stories we tell
about the world is an issue of equally crucial importance, since the way we
view (speak about) the world determines the way we view ourselves.[72] In
this regard, it must be noted that the postsemiological rejection of referentialist-representationalism raises anew the fundamental issue as to the criteria to be used in assessing the worth (truth-value) of the stories we tell
about ourselves and the world.

The immediate consequence of a postsemiotic theory of language is
that we can no longer pretend to assess the truth-value of our stories by
the degree to which they "correspond" to "reality." In fact, the very notion
that there exists an "in-itself" reality, unconnected to our ways of speaking
about it and that can serve as the ultimate criterion of the truth or falsity
of what we say about it, becomes thoroughly meaningless. This should not
be taken to mean that, as the deconstructionists would maintain, in a
postmodern era language becomes nothing more than a disconnected en-
semble of free-floating signifiers devoid of all truth-value because devoid of
all reference to "reality." The realm, as Baudrillard would say, of "hyper-
reality" and *simulacra* (or, as Derrida would say, "a bottomless chess-
board"). It means, instead, that the notions of truth and falsity must be
viewed not as theoretical but as *practical* concepts. That is to say, the
criterion of truth, which is to say, of the appropriateness of our various
ways of speaking about the world (there are always a number of them), can

only be the function of the worthiness of the particular way of being-in-the-world that they both bring into being and serve to legitimate. Truth in thinking is a matter of rightness in acting.

Thus, for example, we can say that the sign language of science-technology is "true" to the degree that, as a most ingenious tool, it enables us (as Descartes said) to control and dominate nature. The truth-value of this way of speaking about the world is, therefore, not "epistemological" (having to do with a "correspondance" with an in-itself reality) but rather *practical*, meaning, in this case, *technological*. The truth-value of the sign language of modern science lies entirely in its technological use-value. Science is "true" to the degree that, as Nietzsche might say, it enables us to build better bridges.[73] And that is about as far as it goes. (Which is not to say that science-technology is not a very important, indeed, an indispensable way of talking about and relating to the world; without decent bridges we could not easily get about and communicate with others.)

When, however, as is generally the case, this particular form of language is held up to be *the* correct way of speaking about and thus relating to the world, the consequences are potentially disastrous. In fact, not only potentially, but actually so, as we are now coming increasingly to realize. Nature itself is beginning to speak back to us and our "control and domination" way of speaking about it. I refer of course to the growing ecological crisis that we have precipitated thanks to our single-minded, scientific-technological (instrumental) approach to our earthly habitat. The point that I want to emphasize is that the truth-value of any particular way of speaking about nature and our place in it is always limited and must always be assessed with an overriding view to its practical consequences, that is, its implications as to the "quality of life" it either promotes or diminishes. In the case of science-technology, it must be said that this particular mode of discourse is quite simply false—to the degree, that is, that it is taken to be the supreme (and only truly correct) way of speaking about the world. The proof of this is entirely practical: The single-minded, and mindless, pursuit to exploit nature to the hilt can only result in the destruction not only of a life worth living but of life itself on this planet.

Theories (ways of speaking about things) must always be assessed in terms of the practice (ways of being) that they both generate and seek to justify. The important thing about the stories we tell ourselves about ourselves is not that they be "factual" rather than "fictional"—for the distinction between the factual and the fictional does not overlap with the distinction between the true and the false. As Aristotle rightly observed, a good story (drama) can afford as good if not better an insight into the "nature of things" than can an empirical history.

In the last analysis, the most important story (theory) we can tell about our own being-in-the-world is the story of our ability, which is to say, our freedom, to tell various kinds of stories about it.

This is something that Hegel (much maligned though he now be by postmodern opponents of any "grand narrative" whatsoever) fully realized when he declared that the history (*histoire, récit*) of the world is nothing other than the history of the progress of the consciousness of freedom. To tell to ourselves the story of freedom and liberation (as, for instance, the Jewish people do on the occasion of Passover and the Americans on the Fourth of July) is the most important story we can tell ourselves, since it is what enables us, as speaking, storytelling animals, freely to develop new stories, and thus to become, in the process, more fully human, more what we in fact are. In what does the supreme value (truth) of freedom lie? Not in any particular, instrumental purpose, to be sure; if freedom is a value, it is not because it enables us, instrumental-wise, to achieve this or that particular goal, but simply because it enables us to be the kind of person we not only want, at any given moment, as a matter of fact, to be, but because it is the necessary condition for becoming the altogether different kind of person we might in the unforeseeable future just possibly might want to become. This is simply to say that freedom is an "end in itself." Anything which is such is, by definition, a supreme value. Now since freedom (of speech) is the necessary condition for creation of any and every value whatsoever ("values" are what are created by various kinds of storytelling), it is necessarily the supreme value. No one can deny their freedom or the freedom of others without thereby denying their humanity. To be a human, a speaking, storytelling animal, is to be free. The freedom to speak and tell stories is the supreme "human right." Not to be free in this sense, not to possess and enjoy this "right," is to be not fully human.

Any story (such as a materialist one) that explicitly, or even implicitly, denies this freedom is, *eo ipso*, false, a "school of slander," as Nietzsche might say[74] (which is not to say that it may not have some technological use-value in this or that regard). The Q.E.D. of a theory lies always in the practice of which it is the articulation. When all is said and done, the practice of freedom is the only truth there is.[75]

Notes

1. Hans-Georg Gadamer, "The Nature of Things and the Language of Things" in *Philosophical Hermeneutics*, ed. David E. Linge (Berkeley: University of California Press, 1976), p. 77.

2. Bertrand Russell, Introduction to L. Wittgenstein, *Tractatus Logico-Philosophicus* (London: Routledge, 1961), p. ix.

3. See my *The Hermeneutics of Postmodernity: Figures and Themes* (Bloomington: Indiana University Press, 1988), ch. 11: "The Philosophic Centrality of the Imagination."

4. E. E. Evans-Pritchard, *Witchcraft, Oracles and Magic among the Azande* (Oxford: Oxford University Press, 1937), p. 11.

5. Maurice Merleau-Ponty, *L'Oeil et l'esprit* (Paris: Gallimard, 1964), p. 9.

6. For a treatment of postmodernism from a philosophical point of view, see my "Postmodern Philosophy?," *Critical Review* 2 (Spring/Summer 1988); for a discussion of the issue from a political point of view, see my "The Politics of Postmodernity," *Critical Review* 5 (Winter 1991).

7. Derrida, like a number of other playful figures in these uncertain times of ours, draws much of his inspiration from "Nietzsche's child"—the child who symbolizes the "innocence of becoming," who in his playfulness "constructs and destroys, all in innocence," who "builds towers of sand . . . at the seashore, piles them up and tramples them down . . . in innocent becoming" (see Nietzsche, *Philosophy in the Tragic Age of the Greeks*, trans. M. Cowan [Chicago: Henry Regnery, 1962], p. 62).

8. Paul Ricoeur, *The Conflict of Interpretations*, ed. Don Ihde (Evanston, IL: Northwestern University Press, 1974), p. 18.

9. For an alternative, non-Traditional account of the "sophistic" or rhetorical movement, see my "The New Philosophy of Rhetoric," *Texte: Revue de Critique et de théorie littéraire* (Toronto), vol. 8/9 (1989). See also in this regard my *Understanding: A Phenomenological-Pragmatic Analysis* (Westport, CT: Greenwood Press, 1982).

10. Gadamer, *Truth and Method* (New York: Seabury Press, 1975), p. 378.

11. See the argument to this effect in Heidegger's *Platons Lehre von der Wahrheit*.

12. Plato, *Cratylus*, Jowett trans., 389d.

13. Aristotle, *De Interpretatione*, Edghill trans., 16a3–8.

14. Heidegger referred to the text of Aristotle quoted above as "the classical passage" in the sign-theory of language that "has remained the standard for all later considerations of language, although with numerous modifications" ("The Nature of Language" in *On the Way to Language*, trans. Peter D. Hertz [New York: Harper & Row, 1971], p. 97).

15. See Susanne K. Langer, *Philosophy in a New Key: A Study of the Symbolism of Reason, Rite, and Art* (Cambridge, MA: Harvard University Press, 1942).

16. "La langue," Saussure says, "n'est pas une fonction du sujet parlant" (*Cours de linguistique générale* [Paris: Payot, 1964], p. 30). Elsewhere Saussure compares language to a symphony and says that what the symphony "actually is" is something completely independent of its performance (and of the mistakes that musicians might make in executing it). As we shall see presently, this is not the way phenomenology-hermeneutics views the matter. For a comparison of the Saussurian or structuralist approach to language with the phenomenological approach and a discussion of the "challenge" that the former poses for the latter, see Paul Ricoeur, "The Question of the Subject: The Challenge of Semiology" in *The Conflict of Interpretations: Essays in Hermeneutics*, ed. Don Ihde (Evanston, IL: Northwestern University Press, 1974), pp. 256–61.

17. Saussure, *Cours* p. 159: ". . . la langue est un système dont tous les termes sont solidaires et où la valeur de l'un ne résulte que de la présence simultanée des autres . . ."

18. Maurice Merleau-Ponty, *Signs*, trans. R. C. McCleary (Evanston, IL: Northwestern University Press, 1964), p. 39.

19. This is what he called "operative language" (cf. *The Visible and the Invisible*, trans. Alphonso Lingis [Evanston, IL: Northwestern University Press, 1968], p. 153). In his *Wahrheit und Methode*, which appeared some fifteen years after Merleau-Ponty's *Phénoménologie de la perception*, Gadamer similarly viewed the word primarily in regard to its "performance," i.e., speech—dialogue or "conversation" in particular..

20. Saussure, *Cours*, p. 166, emphasis added.

21. Jacques Derrida, *Writing and Difference*, trans. Alan Bass (Chicago: University of Chicago Press, 1978), p. 25.

22. Ibid., p. 292.

23. There are, to be sure, some who welcome this turn of events and adore the "flux," and Derrida as well. See, for instance, John D. Caputo, *Radical Hermeneutics: Repetition, Deconstruction, and the Hermeneutic Project* (Bloomington: Indiana University Press, 1987).

24. Jeffrey Friedman, "Postmodernism vs. Postlibertarianism," *Critical Review* 5, no. 2 (Spring 1991), p. 150.

25. See, in particular, Isocrates, *Nicoles*, 5–10, *Panegyricus*, 48–51, *Antidosis*, 257, 294.

26. "Although the Logos is common [to all] the many live as though they had a private understanding" (fr. 198, Kirk and Raven).

27. For a good statement of the "linguistic" theory of reason, see Roger Scruton, *A Dictionary of Political Thought* (New York: Harper & Row, 1982), "rational":

> The rational being: a being who thinks and acts for reasons. Some philosophers argue that such a being must possess language, and that the pos-

session of symbolism and reasoning powers is not an isolated capacity that can be thought of simply as an addition to the mental repertoire of a living being. On the contrary, reason permeates and transforms every element of the life of the being that possess it [this was a point much insisted upon by Merleau-Ponty]. A rational being acquires intentions (in addition to desires), self-consciousness (in addition to consciousness), remorse and regret (in addition to disappointment), hope and determination (in addition to expectation), values and ends (in addition to preferences and means). In short, it is argued that a rational being is a being of a different kind from a nonrational being, and this is often presented as a ground for the views that only rational beings have rights (p. 392).

28. See my *The Hermeneutics of Postmodernity*, pp. 178–79. One of the best accounts of the origin of the modern problematic and the distinction between the subjective and the objective is Heidegger's "The Age of the World Picture" in *The Question of Technology and Other Essays*, trans. William Lovitt (New York: Harper, 1977).

29. Heidegger, following up on clues afforded by Husserl, was one of the first explicitly to denounce this overriding problematic of modern philosophy. As he wrote in *Being and Time*, trans. John Macquarrie and Edward Robinson (New York: Harper & Row, 1962):

> The question of whether there is a world at all and whether its Being can be proved, makes no sense if it is raised by *Dasein* as Being-in-the-world; and who else would raise it? . . . [T]he world is disclosed essentially *along with the* Being of Dasein. . . . The "scandal of philosophy" [Heidegger is here alluding to Kant's remark to the effect that it was a scandal that philosophy had not yet come up with a decent proof for the "existence of the world"] is not that this proof has yet to be given, but that *such proofs are expected and attempted again and again*" (pp. 246–49).

30. Merleau-Ponty, *Consciousness and the Acquisition of Language*, trans. Hugh J. Silverman (Evanston, IL: Northwestern University Press), p. 4.

31. Merleau-Ponty, *Phenomenology of Perception*, trans. Colin Smith (London: Routledge and Kegan Paul, 1962), p. xvi.

32. See above all in this regard Husserl's 1907 lectures on "The Idea of Phenomenology," where the overriding aim is to overcome what the French translator of this work, ALexandre Lowit, refers to as "la situation phénoménale du clivage"— the subject-object, mind-word split instituted by Descartes.

33. See Jean-Paul Sartre, "Une idée fondamentale de la phénoménologie de Husserl: l'intentionnalité" in *La Transcendance de l'ego* (Paris: Librairie philosophique J. Vrin, 1966). Sartre says here that there is nothing "inside of [consciousness] apart from a movement to escape from itself, a slipping outside itself. . . . [C]onsciousness has no 'inside.' It is nothing other than the outside of itself."

Heidegger had already remarked: "When Dasein directs itself towards something and grasps it, it does not somehow first get out of an inner sphere in which it has been proximally encapsulated, but its primary kind of Being is such that it is always 'outside' alongside entities which it encounters and which belong to a world already discovered" (*Being and Time*, p. 89).

34. Heidegger, *Being and Time*, p. 90.

35. In speaking of Merleau-Ponty's project in relation to that of Heidegger, Alphonse de Waelhens remarked:

> It must be admitted, nevertheless, that the authors most resolved to equate existence and being-in-the-world have most frequently neglected or avoided describing for us this mixture which is human consciousness. Heidegger always situates himself at a level of complexity which permits imagining that the problem which concerns us here is resolved. For it is at the level of perception and the sensible that this problem must receive its decisive treatment. But the projects which, according to *Being and Time*, engender the intelligibility of the real for us already presuppose that the subject of daily existence raises his arm, since he hammers and builds; that he directs his gaze, since he consults his watch; that he orients himself, since he drives an automobile. That a human existent can accomplish these different tasks raises no difficulty once his capacity to act and move his body, once his faculty of perceiving, has been judged "evident." Tracking down the "evidences" of common sense is a never-ending task; and the reader of Heidegger realizes too late that the minute acuity manifested by the author has had as a counterpart a total negligence of the world which for us is "always-already-there." . . . [I]n *Being and Time* one does not find thirty lines concerning the problem of perception; one does not find ten concerning the body" (in Merleau-Ponty, *The Structure of Behavior*, trans. Alden L. Fisher [Boston: Beacon Press, 1963], pp. xviii–xix.

36. *Phenomenology of Perception*, p. ix.

37. See ibid., p. 291.

38. Merleau-Ponty, *The Visible and the Invisible*, p. 155.

39. *Phenomenology of Perception*, pp. 181–82. Gadamer makes the same point in his *Truth and Method* when he argues that the word is not a sign but more like an "image" (in that it belongs to what it "reflects") (p. 377).

40. For a detailed discussion of the "circularities of existence" as Merleau-Ponty describes them, see my *The Phenomenology of Merleau-Ponty* (Athens: Ohio University Press, 1981), ch. 1. Like Merleau-Ponty, Gadamer also insists upon the "intimate unity of language and thought" and "the intimate unity of word and object" (*Truth and Method*, 364–65). It should be remembered that Aristotle's *De*

Interpretatione (Peri hermeneias), from which I quoted earlier, was not a treatise in which much later (the seventeenth century) came to be called "hermeneutics" but in apophantic logic.

41. Gadamer, *Truth and Method*, p. 377. Gadamer goes on to say:

> Language and thinking about objects are so bound together that it is an abstraction to conceive of the system of truths as a pre-given system of possibilities of being, with which the signs at the disposal of the signifying subject are associated. A word is not a sign for which one reaches, nor is it a sign that one makes or gives to another, it is not an existent thing which one takes up and to which one accords the ideality of meaning in order to make something else visible through it.

42. To paraphrase the ninth-century philosopher-theologian, Scotus Erigena, who said that you cannot say what God is, since He is not a "what," i.e., God is not a "thing" (*res*, substance); He has no essence, is "above essence."

43. Gadamer, *Truth and Method*, pp. 385–86.

44. One of the most favored tactics of Derrida's deconstructionism is to focus in on exceptional and abnormal instances of language use, and to hold up these cases as paradigmatic of language in general.

45. *Truth and Method*, p. 401 (translation corrected).

46. Gadamer, "On the Scope and Function of Hermeneutical Reflection" in *Philosophical Hermeneutics*, trans. David E. Linge (Berkeley: University of California Press, 1976), p. 35.

47. Cf. Merleau-Ponty, *Signs*, p. 18: "There is not *thought and language*. . . . There is an inarticulate thought . . . and an accomplished thought, which suddenly and unaware discovers itself surrounded by words. Expressive operations take place between thinking language and speaking thought; not, as we thoughtlessly say, between thought and language. It is not because they are parallel that we speak; it is because we speak that they are parallel." Comp. Gadamer: "The experience is not wordless to begin with. . . . [I]t is part of experience itself that it seeks and finds words that express it. We seek for the right word, i.e., the word that really belongs to the object, so that in it the object comes into language" (*Truth and Method*, p. 377).

48. Gadamer, "The Nature of Things and the Language of Things" in *Philosophical Hermeneutics*, p. 69.

49. Merleau-Ponty, *The Visible and the Invisible*, p. 155.

50. In his *Positions*, trans. Alan Bass (Chicago: University of Chicago Press, 1981), Derrida speaks of "the padded interior of the 'symbolic'" (p. 86).

51. See M. C. Dillon, *Semiological Reductionism: A Critique of the Decon-*

structionist Movement in Postmodern Thought (Albany: State University of New York Press, 1995).

52. Gadamer, *Truth and Method*, p. 363.

53. Merleau-Ponty, *Phenomenology of Perception*, p. 337.

54. Gadamer, *Truth and Method*, p. 365.

55. To speak in grammatical terms, language is not, ultimately, something substantive (a *system* of signs) but something verbal (a way of *being*). This is perhaps why the later Heidegger says, quite simply: *Die Sprache spricht.*

56. Nonspeaking animals, in contrast, live only in an environment and do not intend a world.

57. Gadamer, *Truth and Method*, p. 363.

58. Ibid., pp. 371, 377.

59. For a discussion of the hermeneutical notion of "application," i.e., universality as hermeneutics conceives of it, see my "Hermeneutics: Gadamer and Ricoeur" in *The Routledge History of Philosophy* (London: Routledge, 1993), vol. 8, ch. 9.

60. That certain countries, such as France, worry a great deal about the incorporation of foreign (in this case, American) words into their language and react with measures designed to keep their language "pure" simply confirms the fact that what a language basically is is a particular form of life. Attempts to preserve a language "intact" are attempts to preserve "inviolate" a way of life. Given the "communicative" nature of human being and speaking, however, such attempts generally always meet with only limited success. No human, no culture, no language is an island.

61. See Derrida, "Signature Event Context" in *Margins of Philosophy*, trans. Alan Bass (Chicago: University of Chicago Press, 1982).

62. For a detailed discussion of metaphor, see my *Understanding*.

63. See *The Visible and the Invisible*, p. 182.

64. See *Signs*, p. 336.

65. As the French linguist Emile Benveniste points out:

Consciousness of self is only possible if it is experienced by contrast. I use *I* only when I am speaking to someone who will be a *you* in my address. It is this condition of dialogue that is constitutive of *person*, for it implies that reciprocally *I* becomes *you* in the address of the one who in his turn designates himself as *I* ("Subjectivity in Language" in *Problems in General Linguistics*, trans. M. Meck [Coral Gables, FL: University of Miami Press, 1971], pp. 224– 25).

66. For a discussion of the relation between theory and practice as post-modern hermeneutics views it, see my "The Practice of Theory, the Theory of Practice," *Critical Review* 5, no. 2 (Spring 1991).

69. See Ricoeur's three volume, *Time and Narrative* (Chicago: University of Chicago Press, 1984, 1985, 1988). For a succinct account of Ricoeur's views on narrative, see his "History as Narrative and Practice," interview with Peter Kemp, *Philosophy Today* (Fall 1985).

68. David Pellauer, "The Significance of the Text in Paul Ricoeur's Hermeneutical Theory" in *Studies in the Philosophy of Paul Ricoeur*, Charles E. Reagan, ed. (Athens: Ohio University Press, 1979), pp. 112, 109.

69. See my "Hermeneutics: Gadamer and Ricoeur," pp. 317–18.

70. Ricoeur, *Hermeneutics and the Human Sciences*, trans. J. B. Thompson (Cambridge: Cambridge University Press, 1981), p. 143.

71. See ibid., p. 189.

72. See my "Kuviteltu Luonto/Nature Imagined" in *Strata* (Helsinki: The Museum of Contemporary Art, 1992).

73. That pinnacle of twentieth-century science, quantum mechanics, illustrates very well the sense in which scientific statements can be said to be true. It is scientific dogma that a "good" (read: true) theory is one that can generate accurate predictions; predictions are what "verify" theories and hypotheses. Now quantum mechanics is supremely adept at making useful predictions. And yet quantum physicists have accepted (reluctantly, perhaps) the fact that their discipline doesn't tell them anything about "reality," in the metaphysical sense of the term. As one writer remarks, speaking of the supporters of the standard ("Copenhagen") interpretation of quantum mechanics:

> They . . . claim that the very precise formalism of the theory is not to be taken seriously as a picture of actual "reality." They often assert, accordingly, that the whole question of quantum reality is a non-question. One should not think of the theory as providing us with a picture of actuality, they argue, but merely as giving us a calculational procedure that accurately provides the correct mathematical probabilities for the different possible outcomes of experiments. This, they say, is all that we should ask of a theory and not ask questions about "reality." We do not need an understanding of the "actual" nature of the world; it is amply sufficient for our theory to make accurate "predictions"—something that quantum mechanics is indeed supremely good at (Roger Penrose, "The Biggest Enigma," *New York Review of Books*, March 28, 1991).

74. See Friedrich Nietzsche, *The Will to Power*, trans. Walter Kaufmann and R. J. Hollingdale (New York; Vintage Books, 1968), p. 253 (#461).

75. There may exist supernatural, revealed truths, but, as a philosopher, I am not in a position to say anything about them. All I know is that, if there are such truths, they can in no way contradict the truths available to natural reason, the *lumen naturale*.

Editor's Introduction

As chapters 1 and 2 have already indicated, several influential twentieth-century authors working from diverse perspectives have challenged representational accounts of language and meaning. Here psychologist John Shotter draws on Vygotsky, Bakhtin/Volosinov, Billig, and especially Wittgenstein to argue that representational accounts of meaning and communication should be replaced by a study of "how, by interweaving our talk in with our other actions and activities, we can develop and sustain between ourselves different, particular, situated, living ways of relating ourselves to each other."

Representational accounts depend, emphasizes Shotter, on the fiction that humans are "only 'spectators' of [their world], set at a distance over against it, separated from any direct contact with the events they must merely look at." But because humans are involved, engaged, or as Heidegger put it, "thrown" into prereflective and reflective worlds of meaning, our linguistic and communicative actions are inherently "joint," because they are *responsive* to the humanly-inhabited situations that frame them. Wittgenstein underscored this point in his discussions of "forms of life" and "language-games." Shotter claims, along with Wittgenstein, that all claims about "things" as such are grounded within these relational ways of acting and talking—"and nothing more!"

Primarily because theory, Shotter argues, is representational discourse *par excellence*, one implication of his perspective is that human scientists should "turn away from our theoretical ways of talking (at least for a while)" in order to "attend to other more practical or 'instructive' forms of talk—those we actually use in our everyday conversations with each other, prior to any theorizing that we might do." Wittgenstein believed that the language-games such a scientist might study begin not with ratiocination but with a responsive contact with another in which one is "*struck* or *arrested*" by events, and, Shotter writes, "it is to an understanding of such moments that this chapter is devoted."

Understanding these events does not develop either what Gilbert Ryle called "knowing-that"—theoretical, representational knowledge—or "knowing how"—technical knowledge of a skill or craft. Rather, such understanding constitutes what Shotter calls "knowledge of a third kind," from *within* the social situations that frame it. This knowledge "has primarily to do with us—even when all alone—relating ourselves to each other, and with us primarily coordinating our actions together as members of a community." One aspect of the "strange nature" of this kind of knowledge is that it cannot exist as an object, system, or framework; "it only ever makes its moment-by-moment changing appearance between us, in the process of our talk as it temporally unfolds." A new and growing movement in the human sciences and humanities known as social constructionism studies precisely these phenomena and this kind of knowledge.

In the second half of the chapter, Shotter outlines the basis for evaluating this kind of knowing, how it may be studied, and where it might be located. The *basis*, he argues, can be found in "the different embodied *sensibilities* associated with the different 'realities' or 'forms of life' we establish and sustain between ourselves in our everyday conversation itself." We live out meaning, in other words, in conversational practices. The *method* for studying such claims is fundamentally *poetic*, in the sense of *poiesis*, as a making. Forms of talk "gesture" or "point" toward something in our circumstances in such a way that we relate ourselves to these circumstances differently; thus these forms of talk function as "re-minders," or "'mind-making' remarks." Such talk does not represent any hidden reality; "words in their speaking are just different 'means' or 'devices' that we can use in our making of meanings." "In other words, it is in the actual, living interplay of responses and reactions in everyday concrete circumstances—not in the play of signifiers within an abstract system in a person's head or anywhere else—that practical meanings are made."

The site of this "joint action" is what Shotter calls "the interactive moment," the moment described in chapter 1 as "articulate contact." One implication of this claim is that our understanding of human agency shifts from the individual subject (as Kant envisioned) or already-existing discourse (as in Foucault) to "the voices at work in an interactive moment." This realization focuses the analyst's attention on the crucial ethico-political dimensions of these joint-actions. One practical outcome of this shift in focus is that groups can grasp how not to "have forms of life constructed by elite-others imposed on us."

The chapter concludes with a list of some important properties of the dialogic space that professional academics can, and Shotter believes, should create. These spaces can enable academics to understand "those moments when, in the interplay of voices, our voice can count," and, more importantly, can "increase our grasp of [as Foucault put it] what *what-we-do* does."

As I noted, one significant feature of Shotter's rhetorical-responsive version of social constructionism is that it clarifies how Wittgenstein's thinking about language and communication complements the insights appropriated in chapters 1 and 2 from philosophers on the other side of the Channel, especially Heidegger, Gadamer, Merleau-Ponty, and Ricoeur. In addition, Shotter fruitfully synthesizes the psychologist's fundamental interest in understanding human behavior with the speech communication scholar's focus on actual, mundane, conversational contact.

Although I share Shotter's discomfort with the most egregiously representational features of traditional social scientific *theory*, I do not believe that one can write about language and communication as do this book's authors without engaging in *theorizing*. In fact, this is obviously one feature of Shotter's own work; both his *Conversational Realities: Constructing Life Through Language* (London: Sage, 1993) and his *Cultural Politics of Everyday Life: Social Constructionism, Rhetoric, and Knowing of the Third Kind* (Toronto: Toronto University Press, 1993) advance our conceptual and theoretical understanding of discursive identity-management and the cultural politics of conversation. Shotter cites Wittgenstein, Garfinkel, and Vico partly because they all focus on mundane, situated conversation, but also because, like Shotter, they make important *general* claims about the conservative, poetic, and political dimensions of this discourse.

Notwithstanding this difference in emphasis, however, Shotter's social constructionism offers another alternative to representational, semiotic accounts of language and communication.

3

Before Theory and after Representationalism: Understanding Meaning 'from within' a Dialogical Practice

John Shotter

"'the matter talked about' [was] a developing and developed event over the course of action that produced it, as both the process and product were known *from within* this development by both parties, each for himself [sic] as well as on behalf of the other" (Garfinkel, 1967, p. 40).

"For someone broken up by love an explanatory hypothesis won't help much.—It will not bring peace" (Wittgenstein, 1979, p. 3).

"Truth is not born nor is it to be found inside the head of an individual person, it is born *between people* collectively searching for truth, in the process of their dialogic interaction" (Bakhtin, 1984, p. 110).

"As opposed to being the primary locus of understanding, representations prove to be nothing more than islands in the vast sea of our unformulated practical grasp on the world" (Taylor, 1992, p. 173).

"People know what they do; they frequently know why they do what they do; but what they don't know is what what they do does" (Foucault, in Dreyfus and Rabinow, 1986, p. 187).

Communicating in practice is strange. Few of the properties we have assigned to communication in our theories about it seem to be relevant to the doing of it in practice. In studying people's communicative practices, we are interested in their practical behavior out in the world, with how they 'go on' with each other in their everyday, social activities, with how in fact they make sense both *of* their surroundings, and *to* the others around them, in practice, not in theory. What in practice (not theory) is meaning in practice? In our theorizing about communication, we have usually taken it, that central the problem of meaning is the problem of how people *represent* their world both to themselves and to others—as if they are only 'spectators' of it, set at a distance over against it, separated from any direct contact with the events they must merely look at. But this is to assume that our fundamental way of being in the world is as monological individuals, essentially unresponsive in any immediate way to the others around us, who in their turn are also unresponsive to what we are doing and saying. To understand each other, we must both await the end of each other's sayings and doings, and then 'work out' (or 'compute'), so to speak, *what* was said or done. However, influenced by Bakhtin's (1984, 1986), Volosinov's (1973, 1976), Vygotsky's (1978, 1986), and Billig's (1987; Billig et al., 1988) emphasis on the *dialogical* and *responsive* character of our nature as living human beings, as well as by Wittgenstein's (1953) more indirect approach to these matters, I want to argue that instead of beginning with a study of people's inner mental representations, i.e., via the testing of theories as to their supposed nature, we should begin in a quite different way: By first studying how, by interweaving our talk in with our other actions and activities, we can develop and sustain between ourselves, different, particular, situated, living ways of relating ourselves to each other.[1]

Our Dialogical, Responsive Forms of Life

We must first study, I suggest, how we construct what Wittgenstein calls our different shared "forms of life" along with the associated "language-games" that are intertwined within them—where "the term 'language-game'," he says, "is meant to bring into prominence the fact that the speaking of language is part of an activity, or a form of life" (1953, no. 23). And only then, once we have a grasp of the general character of our practical, embodied, talk-entwined (normative) relations with each other, and with our surroundings—when we have grasped what Wittgenstein (1953) calls their different "logical grammars"—should we then turn to a study of how, as distinct individuals, we can 'reach out' from within such forms of life, so to speak, to make the many other different kinds of further contact with our surroundings, through the various ways of making sense of such contacts, that these forms of life provide. In other words, in a dialogical, relational approach to knowing, we must treat people as attempting to make sense of everything they do from within different conversationally mediated and sustained relationships (actual or imagined), and we must study how they form and re-form such relationships by the use of certain practical 'ways of talking'. As individuals, it is only from within such already formed (and often still forming) relationships that we can 'link' our words to our surroundings in ways already intelligible to the others who share those ways of taking with us. In fact, what I want to claim along with Wittgenstein is that all our claims about 'things' as such, are always grounded within certain of our relational ways of acting and talking, and nothing more! That is, they are not grounded in presuppositions, nor in supposedly true theories, nor in the nature of the 'world' itself, but solely—although it may be next to impossible to accept this—in certain of our living, conversationally structured, ways of relating ourselves to each other, ways that are in themselves ungrounded![2] Hence, much of the talk of theory and theories, depicting events underlying or beyond our ways of acting, in which we as individuals indulge in the human sciences—though it may come as a surprise to hear it said—is both after the fact and beside the point. For it hides from us, not only the form or character of the relationships from within which our talk can make sense (whether they are, for instance, relationships of an equal, a hierarchical, an official, or of a personal kind), but also, the kinds of (essentially ethical and political) activities involved in their formation. To invert some terms of Garfinkel's (1967), the very ways in which we linguistically conduct ourselves in the human sciences, our linguistic practices, work to render much of what is important to us rationally-invisible, or, unaccountable,[3] i.e., they divert our attention from such matters to such an extent that, not only do some of their important features go unnoticed, but if we do try to draw attention to their nature, there are few appropriate terms in which to do so.

What is crucially rendered invisible to us in our current individualistic and scientistic forms of talk, is the fact that—although we talk of ourselves as the authors of our own actions—we hardly ever act independently of each other. For when a second living human being responds to the acts of a first, and thus acts in a way that *depends on* their acts, then the activities of the second person cannot be accounted as *wholly their own*. As responses to the first, the second person's must be partly shaped by the first's. In such circumstances as these, instead of me acting individually and independently of *you* (in, for instance, in me writing this book chapter with you as a reader), to an extent at least, *we* are acting jointly. For what *I* write now depends on what, overall, *we* (as some kind of social group, academic or otherwise) are doing. Thus what *I* do is a 'mixture', so to speak—a complex mixture—of influences from within myself and elsewhere. This is why our nature as dialogical beings is so strange and requires of us some new kinds of understanding.

Indeed, if we are to grasp the character of our practical, everyday, dialogical dealings with each other, and the indefinitely many different ways of relating ourselves to each other they make available to us, then we must turn away from our theoretical ways of talking (at least for a while). We must attend to other more practical or 'instructive' forms of talk— those we actually use in our everyday conversations with each other, prior to any theorizing that we might do. For, if it is true that theorizing as such can only be conducted from within, i.e., 'grounded' within, a well established language-game, and publicly intelligible 'contacts' with our surroundings made through the established ways of making sense it provides, then we cannot intelligibly turn such theoretical talk itself around to make sense of its own grounds. We must come to a grasp of our own activities in some other way. We must come to a grasp of our practices in our practicing of them! We must draw attention to certain of the crucially important features of our conversational activities from within the activities themselves, features that would otherwise escape our notice. In particular, we must attend to the power of the human voice to 'move' us and 'position' us in certain ways, to influence our wants and desires, and what we expect and what we anticipate.

It is this living, reactive, responsive, function of our talk that has been ignored in our representational, mechanistic approaches to meaning. Yet, unlike computers and other machines, as living, embodied beings, we cannot continuously react to the world around us; we cannot be indifferent to it. Our surroundings 'call out' responses from us, spontaneously, whether we like it or not; and we mostly 'answer to' such calls directly and immediately, without having 'to work them out'. In so doing, we necessarily relate and connect ourselves to our surroundings in one way or another. We are always in a living relation to our circumstances; this spontaneous, living, responsive activity constitutes the background to all our later activities. It is this kind of spontaneous, responsive, dialogical understanding that Bakhtin (1986) emphasizes as being central to our practical relations to each other: "All real and integral understanding [of our utterances in their speaking] is actively responsive, and constitutes nothing other than the initial preparatory stage of a response (in whatever form it may be actualized). And the speaker himself [sic] is oriented precisely toward such an actively responsive understanding. He does not expect passive understanding that, so to speak, only duplicates his own idea in someone else's mind. Rather he expects response, agreement, sympathy, objection, execution and so forth (various speech genres presuppose various integral orientations and speech plans on the part of speakers and writers)" (p.69). Indeed, our unique understandings in unique practical contexts are of an indefinite multiplicity and complexity, always open to yet further specification—hence, the impossibility of definitively finishing any dialogue. About the nature of our understanding in such circumstances, Taylor (1992) remarks that: "To situate our understanding in practices is to see it as implicit in our activity, and hence as irreducible to representations. It is not a matter of claiming that we do not frame representations, for [as individuals] we do indeed explicitly formulate what our world is like, what we aim at, and what we are doing. At the same time, however, much of our intelligent action in the world is carried on unformulated. It flows from an understanding that is largely inarticulate" (p.173).

Of special importance in our responsive contacts with each other are those contacts in which we are, so to speak, *struck* or *arrested* by events that call out from us new or previously unnoticed reactions, *ways of responding* that can on occasion function as the origin of entirely new language-games. And it is these fleeting, often unremarked but nonetheless 'striking' responses that occur in the momentary gaps between people as they react to each other, which I want to emphasize as the primary focus for our studies here. For it is in these momentary reactions that people express to each other what *their world* (their individual 'inner life') is for them. And it is these kind of contacts—in which one is struck by something—that are of special importance in Wittgenstein's thought. For, as he sees it, "language did not emerge from some kind of ratiocination" (1969, no. 475). "The origin and primitive form of the language game is a reaction; only from this can more complicated forms develop. Language—I want to say—is a refinement, 'in the beginning was the deed'"[4] he says (1980, p.31). Thus, we can start new language-games anywhere, anytime. For example: "'At these words *he* occurred to me'.—What is the primitive reaction with which the language-game begins—which can then be translated into these words?," he asks. "The primitive reaction may have been a glance or a gesture, but it may also have been a word" (1953, p. 218). On some occasions, the mere flicker of an eyebrow at an appropriate moment is all that is needed to 'speak volumes'. It is only such moments as these, I shall argue, that make our theoretical talk and the establishment of disciplinary discourses possible at all. And it is to an understanding of such moments that this chapter is devoted.

In the Thrall of the 'Way of Theory'

Before turning to that task, however, I would like to discuss the special and limited nature of theoretical talk: As academics, we find talk of *theory* and of *theoretical* investigations very familiar, and feel that we know how to make sense of and to evaluate talk of that kind. It is what we have been trained in. However, as I have indicated above, I think that there is something very wrong in us attempting to grasp our basic nature as conversational beings through the activity of us each, as individuals, constructing theories and then debating them between ourselves—as if one day, sooner or later, the rest of us are bound to account one of us correct. To begin with, it is not just that the social and historical conditions making such an activity possible remain unacknowledged, but something else of great importance about the nature of these conditions is obscured: as Billig et al. (1988) argue, "even the main forms of 'post-structuralist' theory have, in their attacks on dominant methodological tendencies, only produced new *theoretical monologues*, not displaced them with a perspective in which [a] truly dialogic principle and its necessary conditions are a prime concern" (pp. 149–150, my emphasis). For the move to a dialogic principle (i.e., a move, in effect, to the relational stance discussed above) is literally unthinkable; we do not know how to delineate its implications; it is radically alien to us.

For instance, at the moment, it is only too easy for us to think that when we talk of such things as 'society', 'the individual', 'the person', 'the self', 'identity', 'thought', 'speech', 'language', 'motivation', 'perception', 'desire', our 'biology', etc., that such things exist, and that were we to plan a research project into any one of them, we would all know perfectly well what 'it' is that we were researching. We find it unthinkable that 'objects' such as these are not already 'out there' in the world in some primordial, naturalistic sense, awaiting our study of them. The idea that stable reference to such objects is only possible from within an agreed language-game, does not occur to us—let alone the possibility that, like a good piece of science fiction, our mere talk of them can create an illusory sense of their reality in us. The idea that such concepts are "essentially contested concepts" (Gallie, 1962), and that they only literally come to 'make sense' as we develop them in living out the discourse into which they are interwoven in practice, and do not at first have a distinctive existence as such at all, is, to say the least, something of an unusual notion. This is what is so hard for us to imagine, for us to envision: we do not know how to think and to talk about that aspect of our speaking in which we can 'call out', or simply 'say', new forms of human life—with their associated human 'ways of being' with their 'worlds'—into existence between us; we do not know how to grasp the nature of the social processes within which we jointly construct the 'realities' within which we find ourselves 'placed' as individuals, and *into* which, and *out of* which, we situate our talk and actions.

Why is this? Why are we so blind to these processes? How do we continually fail to notice our own hand in our creation of our own worlds? What is at work in our current textual and argumentative practices in academe reinforcing this tendency? Currently, it is not putting it too strongly to say that we are 'in the thrall' of, or 'bewitched' by what might be called 'the way of theory': the desire to survey a whole set of (essentially historical) events retrospectively and reflectively—as if they are all 'already-finished' events—with the overarching aim of placing them all within a framework or system, thus to create a single, fixed, stable, coherent, and intelligible unitary order amongst them that can be intellectually grasped by an individual. Such a project manifests a dream that has come down to us, through the Enlightenment, from the ancient Greeks, the dream of being able to 'see' into the inner workings of things so well (as if with a God's eye view) as to be able to 'play' through possibly important sequences of events, ahead of time, thus to be ready for them in some way when they occur—a desire for certainty. It is a dream, of course, which is still implicit in almost all our work in the social sciences. As yet, however (as we are reminded in every moment of our lives), it remains unfulfilled. This is, I suggest, because it is in fact riven with a number of unrecognized tensions in conflict with each other, between, among many others, whether our arguments should come to an end in a kind of 'seeing' on our part, as individuals, or whether the 'truth' of our claims should be played out in practice, collectively between us.

If we turn to Wittgenstein on this particular point, we find him claiming that: "Giving grounds, however, justifying the evidence, comes to an end;—but the end is not certain propositions striking us immediately as true, i.e., it is not a kind of seeing on our part; it is our acting, which lies at the bottom of the language-game" (no. 204). That might seem to settle the matter. However, in the thrall the 'way of theory', it still seems to me possible for us to fail to grasp what this actually means for us in practice. For, even though we might accept the limited adequacy of true statements, i.e., that they are only true within a 'way of talking' or a 'language-game', and accept that, because of this, our search must be for a fitting or appropriate practices, we can still be puzzled as to how we might go on, in practice, to carry out that search. We can still be tempted into a wholly theoretical way of talking, into searching for a basis, a foundation for our claims to truth beyond our own relations to each other, beyond our own human histories, as if we can have a special access to a reality 'in itself' merely in a system of talk—as in the theoretical monologues produced by post–structuralists, mentioned above.

To explore the nature of this particular tension further, let us consider, say, the claims made about human phenomena in the epigraphs to this chapter: (i) First, as claims about ourselves or our activities, in the thrall of the 'way of theory', it is only too easy for us to be urged to see such claims as these, as theoretical propositions, and to be drawn into argument over whether they are in fact true or not. Outside of the thrall of the 'way of theory', however, such utterances can, of course, be heard and responded to in many other ways.[5] (ii) But nonetheless, if we are inclined to see them as claims to truth, we will also be inclined to agree that they must ultimately be put to test in practice. But here, we run into another tension, for we are unclear as to what, in practice, this means for us. For we still tend to feel that to be convinced of the truth of something entails us, as individual academics, seeing something special that we had not seen before: how questionable claims can be derived from a set of seemingly unquestionable principles. Thus we are still tempted into thinking that, in every case, we *must* seek something that "lies *beneath* the surface. Something that lies within, which we see when we look *into* the thing, and which analysis digs out" (Wittgenstein, 1953, no. 92). We must discover a hidden order underlying the seemingly chaotic array of observable linguistic phenomena and must account for its existence in terms of an explanatory theory; we seem to desire certain agreed 'final' propositions upon which to base our actions. In other words, although we agree that our claims should be tested in practice, in the thrall of the 'way of theory', the ultimate appeal in our practice, paradoxically, is to us each individually, simply 'seeing' something to be true.

Because I think it is impossible to overemphasize the pervasiveness of this tendency—as I mentioned in endnote 1 above, even great physicists fall victim to it—let me illustrate the nature of the paradoxical tensions and inclinations confronting us here, by noting Garfinkel's (1967) remarks on the "'reflexive', or 'incarnate' character of [our everyday] accounting practices" (p. 1), and our inability to take what he says seriously. As he sees it, what makes our ordinary, everyday talk special, is that the many, changing 'ways' we use for making sense of another person's words, moment by moment, are at work 'there', embedded in the very situation in which the words are being uttered. As the other speaks, their words 'call out' in us various responses, and it is in relation to these responses that we reply, repeating ourselves or correcting each other if we fail to 'follow' appropriately. Thus, our everyday talk is "an endless, ongoing, contingent accomplishment" (Garfinkel, 1967, p. 1), something people work out how to accomplish between them as they go along, i.e., in the course of accomplishing it. Our difficulty in taking him seriously shows up, for instance, in those of our studies in which we seek to find any supposedly fixed 'things' underlying our talk, be they 'accounting strategies or devices', 'linguistic repertoires or resources', or whatever. For, if he is correct, then we cannot turn the contingent nature of our everyday, conversational talk around, to understand it in terms of anything (any 'thing') supposedly *underlying* it[6] —whether the entities in question are rules, conventions, representations, or theories. Indeed (although it is pointless to remark upon it in this way), without any way of discussing such entities conversationally, we would have no way of justifying to each other that we were indeed formulating and applying our claims about them aright in our studies. Because of this, because no stable, uncontested meaning can be attached to their nature, clearly, no such entities can form the fixed, underlying basis or grounds, supposedly required to make our conversational talk with others possible; rather, they can only themselves be formed and fixed, i.e., invented, as a consequence of the possibility of such talk between us. In other words, it is something other than rules, conventions, representations, or theories, that make our conversational talk possible. We shall explore what that 'something other' is below.

Talk Leading to a Practical Knowing of the Third Kind

What we need, I want to claim, is not the kind of knowledge supposedly enshrined in theoretical representations, but a knowing of a very different, much more practical kind—derived, in fact, from the more everyday forms of conversational talk already available to us in our daily lives. What makes this kind of talk very different to theoretical talk, to repeat, is that it can work to 'call out', both from ourselves and others, various responses and reactions. Thus it is the kind of talk that, on being interwoven into our everyday, spontaneous ways of acting in the world, will enable us to gain a more deliberate control over them. Thus my concern in what follows is with the nature of the social relations between us that might enable us to make a more disciplined use of such forms of talk in our academic practices; I want to grasp what might be involved in fashioning a more dialogical and involved, a less monological and distanced stance toward our own construction of our own abilities. Thus the kind of talk in which I am interested, is very closely related to the kind of talk that 'floats' around, so to speak, in an uncertain way within the everyday conversational background to our more institutional and disciplinary lives. It exists on the boundaries of, or zones in between, our separate disciplines and orderly discourses. Its use gives rise to a special kind of knowing that—although it has been more properly recognized and identified in the past—has in more recent times been forgotten.

Elsewhere, I have related it to Vico's (1968) notion of *sensus communis*, or common sense, which, as he says, is a means of "judgment without reflection, shared by . . . an entire people" (para. 142). Richard Bernstein (1983) has called it, "practical-moral knowledge," and related it to Aristotle's notion of phronesis, which, as Bernstein puts it (following Gadamer, 1975), is a kind of "knowledge not detached from our being but determinative of what we are" (Bernstein, 1992, p. 25). Since it is continuous with, and determinative of who and what we are, rather than 'in our minds' it is more properly called embodied knowledge—a linguistically structured way of 'calling out', both from others, and from ourselves, various ways of attending to, and acting in, the 'world' of a language-game.

Consider the ways in which we can 'instruct' both others and ourselves: We can 'point things out to them' ("Look at this!"); 'change their perspective' ("Look at it like this"); give an 'order' to their actions ("Look at the model first, then at the puzzle pieces"); 'shape' their actions ("Turn it over, then it will fit"); 'remind' them ("Think what you did last time," "What do you already know that's relevant?"); 'encourage' them ("Try again"); 'restrain' them ("Don't be too hasty"); 'evaluate' circumstances for them ("That's not right," "Don't do that, that's greedy"); 'set their goals' ("Try to put these pieces together to match that [pointing at a model]"); 'count' ("How many will it take?"); make 'measurements' ("Will that fit properly?" "Just compare"); make them 'check' their descriptions ("Is that right?" "Who else says so?" "What's the reason for your belief?"); and so on, and so on, in countless ways. Indeed, we can form such instructions into sequences, to construct step-by-step programs of perception and action: First: "survey," then "choose," then "act," then "survey again," and so on. These are the means Vygotsky has in mind when he says (Vygotsky, 1986, p. 102, my emphasis) that "the main question about the process of concept formation—or, about any goal–directed activity—is the question of the means by which the operation is accomplished. . . . To explain the higher forms of human behavior, we must uncover the means by which man [sic] learns to organize and direct his behavior." And, "our experimental study proved that it was the functional use of the word, or any other sign, as means of focussing one's attention, selecting distinctive features and analyzing and synthesizing them, that plays a central role in concept formation" (ibid, p.106). "Learning to direct one's own mental processes with the aid of words or signs is an integral part of the process of concept formation" (ibid, p.108). That is, in Vygotsky's terms, in learning to think conceptually, one is not learning to compare the configuration of a supposed mental representation with the configuration of a state of affairs in reality, but something else much more complicated: One is learning how to organize and to assemble in a socially intelligible way, i.e., a way which makes sense to the others around one, bits and pieces of information dispersed in space and time in accordance with 'instructions' they (the others around one) at first provided, and which now a supposed 'concept' provides.

In being a common *sense*, such knowledge is not present to us as an inner representation—indeed, it is not knowledge about any 'thing' as such at all; to repeat, as Taylor (1992) puts it, it is inarticulate and unformulated: It has to do with the possible ways of responding to our surroundings available to us from within particular forms of life; as such, it has to do with the 'shape' of the (socially sharable) feelings of anticipation and expectation that we have at any one moment in time in social situations, the sense of the possible reactions we might have to what is occurring around us. In how we respond and react, we 'make' connections or relations between, not only aspects of our present situation, but between it and other such possible situations also.[7] However, to the extent that it is knowledge to do with us constructing one or another kind of relationship with others and with our circumstances, and to the extent that talk by individuals referring to 'things', as such, is only possible from within such relationships, it is impossible for us as individuals to characterize it or to linguistically formulate it in any clear way. Hence, it cannot be captured in knowledge of a theoretical kind (a "knowing-that" in Ryle's 1949, terminology), for it is not a kind of knowledge that can be stated by individuals, but is only present to us in our everyday social practices. Although we cannot 'say' its nature, in Wittgenstein's terms, we can 'show' it in our practices (see Volosinov's example in endnote 6). It cannot, however, be simply a technical knowledge of a skill or craft (a "knowing-how") either. For although we cannot as individuals state its nature, this is because it is a joint kind of practical–moral knowledge, a knowledge–held–in–common with others, and *judged by them* as such in the process of its use. If we transgress its *ethics*, we can be made to 'feel bad' (Shotter, 1995).

Thus, it is its own, third kind of knowledge, *sui generis*, irreducible to either of the other two. Rather than to do with us representing our surroundings, it has primarily to do with us—even when all alone—relating ourselves to each other, and with us primarily coordinating our actions together as members of a community. So, although we may 'reach out' from within it, to make a contact with other aspects of our surroundings, besides the other people around us, if we want to act in ways intelligible to them, we must do so in its terms. It is thus a kind of knowledge one has only *from within* relationships with *others*, whether the relationship is actual or imagined. We might thus call the kind of knowing involved, a "knowing-from-within," for it determines what at any one moment, prospectively, we *anticipate* or *expect* will happen next from within any situation in which we are involved: It has to do with not just what will surprise us and what we and others will merely find familiar, but also what we and they will find disgusting, frightening, as well as delightful and want to celebrate, what we all will count as objective and what subjective, what real and what unreal, what ordinary and what extraordinary, and so on— as well as with what we fail to notice altogether, with what is rationally invisible to us. While the other two forms of knowledge can be said to be disciplined and orderly, and sustained by systematic discourses, conversational knowing seems by contrast to be disorderly and undisciplined.

Furthermore, it is unlike the other two forms of knowledge in other important ways. In them, we experience ourselves as individuals standing over our surroundings, as separate from them, as uninvolved, thinking and perceiving subjects observing them objectively. In this third kind of knowing, we experience ourselves as involved 'in' a 'situation', a 'circumstance', or whatever, and we are affected by, or responsive to, what goes on within that 'situation'. We find that 'it' seems to 'call out' or to 'demand' various activities of us; we are as much a part of 'it' as 'it' is a part of us. Indeed, 'it' is as if it is a third agent on the scene, to which you and I, and all the rest of us, must be responsive—responsible, even.[8]

However, I cannot emphasize enough the strange nature of this kind of knowledge, the difficulties involved in focusing upon its workings, or the elusiveness of its existence. For to repeat, the other kinds of knowledge familiar to us—theoretical "knowing-that," and technical "knowing-how"—are manifested in people relating themselves to their surroundings as individuals. Thus, to the extent that these forms of knowledge exist 'in their heads', they can be theorized and studied as objects, as systems. Knowing-from-within cannot exist as an object, system, or framework; it only ever makes its moment-by-moment changing appearance between us, in the process of our talk as it temporally unfolds. Our 'ways' of talking' do not exist as isolable, temporally constant 'things'; they cannot be arranged and rearranged like building blocks in external relations to each other. They can, perhaps, be (partially) thought of as like 'implements' through which we can make contact with each other and our circumstances, like blind people make contact with their surroundings through their sticks and through echoes they hear. But if they are spoken of in this way, it can only be as relational 'things', as 'things' that owe their nature at any one moment to their internal or intentional relations to the rest of our living activities at that moment—that is, to their relations both to our earlier activities, and, to what we expect our activities to become. Their being as a 'tool' is thus somewhat transitory, to say the least.

It is the nature of this kind of sensuous, embodied knowledge—and the moment-by-moment task we face of making use of it in bridging 'gaps' between our utterances as we connect them to those of others in our conversational activities—that we must explore.

But how might we study this really peculiar kind of knowledge? This is the task of a new and growing movement in the human sciences and humanities, known as social constructionism (Berger and Luckman, 1966; Coulter, 1979, 1989; Gergen, 1985, 1991; Harre', 1983, 1986; Shotter, 1975, 1984, 1993a&b). The version of it that I explore further below, is a version influenced very much, as I have already mentioned, by Wittgenstein, Bakhtin, Volosinov, Vygotsky, and Billig—that focuses upon the operation of this third kind of knowing in the conversational background to our everyday social lives together. In particular, I want to outline (i) a basis in terms of which we might evaluate claims as to its nature; (ii) a method for its study; as well as (iii) a site or focus for its investigation.

Interweaving 'Instructive Ways of Talking' into Our Acting

Basis

The basis, I shall claim, can be found in the different embodied *sensibilities* associated with the different 'realities' or 'forms of life' we establish and sustain between ourselves in our everyday conversation itself. Thus, not just any 'way' of talking will do. For, it is in our use of words that we arouse (in others and in ourselves) certain feelings of anticipation and expectation, a sense, as to the possible nature of our future conduct—how we will relate what we do both to the others around us, and, to the rest of our circumstances. It is this sense that 'shapes' how it is felt appropriate to respond. And what Wittgenstein realized was, that although we cannot say what these feelings of tendency, of expectation and anticipation 'are', to the extent that they do shape our conduct—what we do and what we say—then they are *shown* in the temporal unfolding of our conduct in quite precise ways. We 'live out' their meaning in our practices. In relating ourselves both to our own circumstances, and, to the others around us, we 'show' the 'movement' of our minds (so to speak), in the pitch, pacing, pausing, and intonation of our speech. And if, as Volosinov (1973) puts it, "meaning belongs to a word in its position between speakers [at the moment of its utterance]; that is, meaning is realized only in the process of active, responsive understanding" (p.102), then the tone in which a word is uttered is, the way it is 'shaped' in its speaking, is a part of the constructing of the relation between speaker and listener: whether the relation demands submission ('just listen'), invites collaboration ('is this so?'), requests refutation ('please say I'm wrong), etc. It also expresses our relation to our own position, our confidence, happiness, uncertainty, and so on. And others—although they may not in any way be conscious of the fact—sense the tendencies toward which a speaker's words gesture.

This 'gestural meaning' of our words (to use a term of Merleau-Ponty's (1964, p.89)[9]—although Wittgenstein (1980, p. 52) talks of our utterances as being like gestures too—is shown in the fact that such and such an utterance 'feels' an appropriate thing to say, while so and so evokes feelings of surprise and awkwardness. For instance, saying: "From what he says, that seems to be his intention, but I doubt it," raises no problems. Whereas, if I myself say: "From what I say, that seems to be my intention, but I doubt it," is decidedly odd. We are struck by its senseless nature. We do not know how to respond to it, how to anticipate the behavior of the person who says such a thing, how to coordinate our actions in with theirs. If some one says to us: "I really mean every word I say, but please don't take me seriously," the anticipations raised by the first part of the utterance are dashed by the second. It is its *logical grammar* that is all wrong. For, in knowing of the third kind, it is not our relations as already constructed individuals to our already constructed 'worlds' that is at issue, but the character of the practical constructing that is to 'go on' between us—the kinds of relationships that will be permitted to develop further between us, in practice, and those that will be refused. This is how our claims will be judged: not in terms of truth or falsity in relation to already existing facts, but in terms of the forms of life their speaking anticipates or projects, and whether that form of life will, literally, be 'allowed' by the others around us, where the 'allowing' is not a merely cognitive matter, but a practical matter, involving both ethical and political issues.

Thus, to repeat again Wittgenstein's (1969) remark about what it is that brings our claims to an end: "Giving grounds . . . comes to an end;— but the end is not certain propositions striking us immediately as true, i.e., it is not a kind of *seeing* on our part; it is our acting, which lies at the bottom of the language-game" (no. 204). In other words, for us, our historically developing and developed, linguistically structured and sustained forms of life, are foundational. They are determinative of not only who and what we are, but also of what counts for us as our *world* or *worlds*, as well as of everything else that can count for us in some way. Let me hasten to add, in case this is interpreted to mean that we must always seek out the already existing language-games, *already existing* rules, conventions, or customs of talk, or current *usages*, if we want to grasp what is possible for us, that this is not the case at all: For that would be, yet again, to fall into the thrall of the 'way of theory', to think that there was some 'thing' (rules, conventions, or customs) underlying and limiting our practices.

Method

> "philosophy ought really to be written only as a *poetic composition*" (Wittgenstein, 1980, p.24).

To turn now to the question of method: If we cannot work in terms of theories, in terms of representations, what can we do? Well, the stance toward words I suggested above—that we can think of the gestural meaning of our words-in-their-speaking as ordinarily working to draw our attention to the connections between our utterances and their circumstances—suggests that they can also be used extraordinarily, in a *poetic* fashion, to draw our attention to how we do in fact make such connections. The way in which we can use certain ways of talking as like psychological tools,[10] as instruments or implements through which to responsively influence both our own behavior as well as that of others, can give us a clue. For these *instructive* forms of talk can 'move' us, in practice, to do something we would not otherwise do. In 'gesturing' or 'pointing' toward something in our circumstances, they can cause us *to relate ourselves to our circumstances* in a different way. It is the 'poetic', 'gestural' function of these 'instructive' forms of talk that is their key feature, that gives them their 'life', that gives them their function 'within' our lives. He calls the remarks he uses to draw our attention to what is, in fact, already know to us, "reminders:" For, "something that we know when no one asks us, but no longer know when we are supposed to give an account of it [cf. Augustine], is something we need to *remind* ourselves of" (Wittgenstein, 1953, no. 89), he says. Their function as 're-minders', as 'mind-making' remarks, gives us some further set of clues as to his 'striking', 'poetic methods'.

They work, first: (1) To *arrest* or *interrupt* (or 'deconstruct') the spontaneous, unself-conscious flow of our ongoing activity, and to give "prominence to distinctions which our ordinary forms of language easily make us overlook" (1953, no. 132). Thus his talk is full of such expressions as "Think of . . .," "Imagine . . .," "It is like . . .," "So one might say . . .," "Suppose . . .," and so on, all designed "to draw someone's attention to the fact that he [sic] is capable of imagining [something]" (1953, no. 144). They show us other possibilities present in a circumstance, where, in imagining something new, a person is "now . . . inclined to regard a given case differently: that is, to compare it with *this* rather than *that* set of pictures. I have changed his *way of looking at thing*" (Wittgenstein, 1953, no. 144), he says. In other words, prospectively, he draws our attention to the fact that, from our position of involvement in things, there are always other possibilities available to us, other possible ways of 'going on'.[11]

This suggests to us a second aspect of his methodology that is sometimes important: (2) By the careful use of selected images, similes, analogies, metaphors, or 'pictures', he also suggests *new ways of talking* that not only orient us toward sensing otherwise unnoticed distinctions and relations for the first time, but which also suggest new connections and relations with the rest of our proceedings. Here, his notion of a "perspicuous representation" (*übersichlichte Darstellung*)" is central: "A main source of our failure to understand is that we do not *command a clear view* of our use of words.—Our grammar is lacking in this sort of perspicuity. A perspicuous representation produces just that understanding which consists in 'seeing connections'," he says (Wittgenstein, 1953, no. 122). The kind of understanding he is after here is again a practical understanding, an understanding that allows one to 'go on' in practice with one's activities. "Try not to think of understanding as a 'mental process' at all.—For *that* is the expression which confuses you," he says (Wittgenstein, 1953). "But ask yourself: in what sort of case, in which circumstances, do we say, 'Now I know how to go on' . . ." (no. 154). It is as if our task is to move about within a particular landscape of possibilities. A "perspicuous presentation" is a presentation in which "problems are solved, not by giving new information, but by arranging what we have always known" (Wittgenstein, 1953, no. 109) so we can move easily from one part of a landscape of possibilities to another. Thus, if we are 'to find our way about' inside our own linguistic forms of life, we need to grasp, to sense, their inner 'landscape', their 'grammatical geographies', so to speak.

This brings us to a third aspect of his methodology: (3) By the use of various kinds of *objects of comparison*, e.g., other possible ways of talking, other "language games" both actual and invented, etc., he tries "to throw light on the facts of our language by way of not only similarities, but also dissimilarities" (1953, no. 130). For, by noticing how what occurs differs in a distinctive way from what we otherwise would expect, such comparisons can work, he notes, to establish "an order in our knowledge of the use of language: an order with a particular end in view; one of many possible orders; not *the* order" (1953, no. 132). Again, the goal is to achieve a kind of understanding that is useful in the 'going on' of a practice, the overcoming of a 'disorientation', of 'not knowing one's way about'.

Such metaphors cannot represent any already fixed orders in our use of language, for, by their very nature, in being open to determination in the context of their occurrence, they do not belong to any such orders. But what such invented concepts do for us—in artificially creating an order where none before existed—is to make aspects of our situated use of language publicly discussable and accountable. They provide a practical resource: a way of talking that works to draw our attention, in different ways in different contexts, to what otherwise we would not know how to attend. Other ways of talking, other relational stances, will function to bring out other connections. One can imagine many different aims. Though what is at stake in them all, is not so much the grasp by isolated individuals, of an inner 'mental picture' of a state of affairs, but a grasp of the actual, practical connections between aspects of our own communicative activities, influences that are present and at work in 'shaping' what we say in a particular circumstance.

Lacking the appropriate sensibility to notice these relational phenomena, we have felt in the past that they require explanation in terms of special, mysterious, hidden factors, already existing either within us somewhere, or, within our circumstances—hence, our tendency to seek theories, and to search for something beyond our own human forms of life. But, suggests Wittgenstein (1953): "The aspects of things that are most important for us are hidden because of their simplicity and familiarity. (One is unable to notice something—because it is always before one's eyes.). The real foundations of his [sic] enquiry do not strike a man at all. Unless *that* fact has at some time struck him.—And this means: we fail to be struck by what, once seen, is most striking and most powerful" (no. 129). However, we do not need theories to explain these phenomena, to explain our meaning in our talk, for there is nothing to be explained, because there is nothing hidden or concealed. "How do sentences do it?" Wittgenstein (1953) asks rhetorically. And he answers: "Don't you know? For nothing is hidden." (no. 435). For, in his view, words do not in themselves have a hidden meaning underlying them. Words in their speaking are just different 'means' or 'devices' that we can use in our making of meanings, with different words (like different tools) making available a range of different possible uses. Or better: We can use our words in their speaking in further specifying, in refining or making a difference to, the meanings already present in any circumstance in which people are in each other's living presence. The words we use draw their power, their ability to change the whole character of the living flow of language–entwined activity between us, very little from the words themselves. They merely function to make a crucial difference at a crucial moment, a moment that arises due to what we count as the history of its flow so far.

In other words, it is in the actual, living interplay of responses and reactions in everyday concrete circumstance—not in the play of signifiers within an abstract system in a person's head or anywhere else—that practical meanings are made. They are made in terms of how, in any living dialogue, "we have this interplay going on with the gestures [or the gestural meaning of words] serving their functions, calling out the responses of the others, these responses becoming themselves stimuli for readjustment, until the final social act itself can be carried out" (Mead, 1934, p. 44, my emphases). Thus in practice, meanings are made by the way in which an utterance of a second person is not only 'linked' or 'connected' as a response to an utterance of a first, but also 'linked' or 'connected' in some way with the circumstances of its utterance. To repeat my Wittgensteinian formulation above, although we cannot say what these links and connections are, to the extent that they shape our conduct, they are *shown* in its temporal unfolding, i.e., in its 'movement', in quite precise ways.

Thus, Wittgenstein breaks away from explanatory theories, and turns

to the use of striking metaphors and similes, not because he wants different or better models or idealizations than those so far used (as the usual
preliminary to the production of a rigorous theory), but for another reason
altogether: His concern is to draw our attention to the relations, links, or
interconnections between our speaking and the circumstances surrounding them, that we would otherwise not notice. In other words, for him, the
meaning of a spoken word—everything of import to its practical–moral
meaning for us: its demeaning, insulting nature; its demand to be answered; its tangled, puzzling meaning—is not to be found in a mental
representation in a person's head, nor within a system of signifiers or conventions of meaning. It can only be found in its particular use, in a particular context; it is there that their meaning is to be found. Thus it is to
these circumstances that we must now attend.

The 'Site' of 'Joint Action': the 'Interactive Moment'

The crucial 'site' upon which such investigations should focus, is that
moment of uncertainty, that 'interactive moment', when a 'gap' or a
'space' is opened up by a change in speaking subjects, when one embodied
person stops speaking and another responds to them—the place where
what elsewhere I have called "joint action" occurs (Shotter, 1980, 1984,
1993a&b, 1995). For no matter how mechanical, rule–governed, or systematic the speech of each may be while speaking, there are no rules or
principles for bridging this gap: a unique, relation–creating, dialogical response is required. The response produced will be influenced by the factors
at work at that moment, in that space, and the speaker's response to them
will be manifested in the 'shape', the 'style' and the 'tone' of their utterance (again see endnote 6). A listener, perhaps, sensing it as unjustifia-
bly angry, wimpishly feeble, or cunningly misleading, rather than simply
fitted appropriately to its circumstances, replies to it accordingly. As Volosinov (1986) puts it, "in point of fact, word is a two-sided act. It is determined equally by whose word it is and for whom it is meant. . . . Each and
every word expresses the 'one' in relation to the 'other' . . . . A word is
territory shared both by addresser and addressee, by speaker and his [or
her] interlocutor" (p. 86). The focus upon living, embodied, dialogical utterances is crucial: Utterances are relational things; they exist only in the
interactive space between speakers and listeners; they do not exist 'in the
minds' of either; neither do they exist in disembodied discourses. It is in
the dialogical interplay of voices that meanings are developed and negotiated, finalized for a moment, and then, perhaps, as a new voice enters the
dialogue, answerable for a new position in reality not before noticed, again
destabilized.

Here, then, we have a new focus for human agency and the site of its operations: in the voices at work in an interactive moment. In the past, we have attempted to locate human agency either in 'the individual subject' (Kant, for instance), or in recent times, in a 'discourse'. For example, as Foucault (1986) claims: "The author function is [a] characteristic of the mode of existence, circulation, and functioning of certain discourses within a society" (in Rabinow, 1986, p. 108)—as if it is only in already existing discourses of a certain kind, that authorship is possible. Both these ways of talking seem to me to be equally 'blind' (or 'deaf'?) to the fact that theorist's talk is never a matter of innocent description: as if now, instead attending to 'subjects', we should attend to 'discourses'. Both ways of talking are the product of quite peculiar kinds of disciplinary discourses, with their own cultural, ethico–political, and historical dimensions. Indeed, they are both exclusionary, professional ways of talking that have been carved out (not without violence, let it be said) of the ordinary, everyday conversational background to our lives. They both work, in fact, to render what I have called 'the interactive moment' rationally invisible. And they claim to be justified in this, for they are revealing something 'hidden' that is worth revealing. However, instead of placing the real social and historical processes at the center of our attention, they seduce us—like a good piece of science fiction writing—into talking to each other (as a professional elite) about supposed theoretical events occurring within an abstract framework.[12]

Here, then, is precisely what I think is at stake in Wittgenstein's method of continually drawing our attention to what is actually occurring in the circumstances of our talk, but lack the sensibility to notice. For in attempting to make up that lack by theorizing, we open the door to all kinds of claims by elite groups who want to claim, ahead of time, that certain of our words must already have a well-defined meaning; that a monologue can be instituted to replace a living dialogue. Concerned with the enormity of what is happening here—the promotion of deafness to the interplay of everyday voices, and the devaluation of its interactive moments—he 'shouts' at us: "Don't think, but look!" (Wittgenstein, 1953, no. 66). Make use of your ways of talking in whatever ways you can, to *look through* your current ways of talking, to notice in these situations what it is that we are connecting with what, what it is that we are doing to ourselves. For, as he puts it, "a main source of our failure to understand is that we do not command a clear view of our use of our words . . ." (Wittgenstein, 1953, no. 122). But this is a handicap that can be overcome. For certain of our ways of talking can change our sensibilities—help us notice the 'coin' or 'currency', the 'means' of our transactions—thus to focus upon what, what–we–do does (Foucault), and to avoid not just misleading ourselves, but entrapping and imprisoning ourselves in inhuman forms of life of our own devising.

In shifting to a concern with the nature of conversational realities then, this has been my concern: To move away from those forms of talk that divert our attention away from what is important to us, that exclude us (or a great number of us) from those moments in which we as ordinary people can participate in the constructing of our own realities—so that we do not have forms of life constructed by elite others imposed upon us. And to explore what is involved in opening up new spaces, new possibilities for being human, between us. As professional academics, we really must move away from what can only go on within individual persons (within us), to what goes on within relationships—even if it means giving up the theories we can each get inside our own heads. For only then, can we help create a truly dialogic 'space' within which everyone can participate in the interplay of voices.

Conclusions

Above, I have gestured toward what I think are a number of the properties of that 'space', and toward the conditions making it possible. They are, I think, as follows:

- 'Voices' become the loci of linguistic agency; and problems of agency—who is responsible for what—become problems of whose voice is being heard and taken seriously.

- Subjects (and objects) are not ontologically prior to people's linguistic activities; indeed, no such 'things' are, or can be prior. For although we may say that our surroundings stay materially the same from one moment to the next, that is a way of talking, and no way of talking is ever an innocent matter of mere description: All our 'ways of talking' are the product of quite peculiar kinds of disciplinary discourses, with their own cultural, ethico–political, and historical dimensions.

- Thus, the instability of a word's meaning is not to be found in the 'free play of signifiers', but in the free ethico–political interplay of voices in the different circumstances of life.

- Instabilities are decided in practice, however. And it is just at that moment of uncertainty—in 'joint action' at the 'interactive moment'—that a politics of ethics (to do with whose being is respected, and whose form of life is to go on), is at its most intense.

- Indeed, to the extent that our 'inner' lives are not a matter of tranquil, private calculation within already decided systems of meanings, but reflect in their functioning the same ethico–political and rhetorical considerations as those influencing our transactions with others out in the world, they too are not exempt from the same conflicts and struggles.

- Thus, the center of gravity, so to speak, of what we talk of as our *thinking*, is not to be found deep within us, at the center of our being, but at its boundaries. The way in which we are a responsive addresser of others (actual or imagined), 'shapes' how we 'answer' for our sense of our own position in our relations to those others.

- Thus in this sense, our use of psychological terms does not work by reference to an already existing inner state, but, as Mills (1940) put it so long ago, as an indicator of possible future actions, as a gesture toward the future that allows others (or not) to coordinate their actions in with ours.

- But, "monologism, at its extreme, denies the existence outside itself of another consciousness with equal rights and equal responsibilities, another I with equal rights (thou). With a monologic approach (in its extreme form) another person remains wholly and merely an object of consciousness. Monologue is finalized and deaf to the other's response, does not expect it and does not acknowledge in it any decisive force" (Bakhtin, 1984, pp. 292–93). In the past, it has been the task of professional elites to produce such monologues (Bauman, 1987). But now our task is changing.

- "The single adequate form of verbally expressing authentic human life is the open-ended dialogue. Life by its very nature is dialogic. To live means to participate in dialogue: to ask questions, to heed, to respond, to agree, and so forth. In this dialogue a person participates wholly and throughout his whole life: with his or her eyes, lips, hands, soul, spirit, and with his or her whole body and deeds" (Bakhtin, 1984, p. 293).

- The institution of a dialogic practice entails a new focus (upon the 'interactive moment'), a new method (Wittgenstein's *poetic* methods for directing our attention), a new basis (in the conversational realities of everyday life), and a new politics (in the interplay of voices). A detailed, worked example can be found in Katz and Shotter (in press).

- For, in our talk, we are concerned (i) to be responsive to what has gone before; (ii) to appropriately address those around us; but also (iii) to be answerable for our own unique position in the world, and to have it make a difference in the world we share with others. These are just some of the conditions necessary, it seems to me, if we all are going to be able to participate in the collective search for truth, "in the process of their dialogic interaction" (Bakhtin, 1984, p. 110).

In setting out these properties, rather than attending to language considered in terms of previously existing patterns or systems, formed from 'already spoken words', I have focused upon the *formative uses* to which 'words in their speaking' can be put. My concern has been with the nature of the relationships and relational situations thus created between those in communicative contact with each other in their speakings. Such a focus attends precisely to the ethical and the political influences at work in deciding the form of connections and contacts made, the possibilities and tendencies they open up, and those they close down. Within systems of already spoken words (in what one might call already-decided-forms-of-talk), these tense moments of uncertainty and instability—when the constructing of which possibilities are to be realized and which passed over is decided— are ignored. As individual 'spectators', we study only what has been done. But in so doing, we exclude ourselves from the originary interplay of voices that decided the system. However, if we want actively to enter into the constructing of our own forms of life, then we must both: locate those sites, those moments when, in the interplay of voices, our voice can count; and, increase our grasp of what *what-we-do* does (with apologies to Foucault, 1982, p.187). Thus my concern here has been with the ways of talking, the practical means appropriate to a more dialogical way for us, still as professional academics, of conducting our affairs that is not so exclusive of all the others around us.

Notes

1. We cannot, of course, *prove* by evidence that our testing of our theories by the doing of experiments, is in fact a test of our theories. The testing of theories by the doing of experiments is simply an accepted human practice; it cannot in itself be proved, so to be speak, to be a 'correct' practice. As Wittgenstein (1969) remarks: "What *counts* as its [an empirical proposition's] test?—'But is this an adequate test? And, if so, must it not be recognizable as such in logic?'—As if giving grounds did not come to an end sometime. But the end is not an ungrounded presupposition: it is an ungrounded way of acting" (no. 110).

2. It is just as hard for great physicists to accept this as it is for us mortals. In a recent book on the myth of a unified theory in Physics, Lindley (1993) points out: (i) that physicists now realize that to want to know what an electron 'really is', is to ask for an understanding of it "beyond the scope of physical experimentation" (p.75); (ii) yet nonetheless, the great physicist Heisenberg, "with his revived Aristotelian 'potentia', was trying to explain the quantum world in terms of the [now abandoned] classical, trying to invent an underlying reality when no such thing exists" (p. 76). In other words, even great physicists find it hard to accept that the only true 'contacts' with the physical world available to them, are contacts made by 'reaching out', so to speak, *from within* the confines of a particular language-game. There is no truth beyond one's ways of relating oneself to others.

3. Garfinkel (1967) talks of people's everyday activities as reflexively containing within themselves "methods [i.e., "ethno-methods"] for making those same activities visibly-rational-and-reportable-for-all-practical-purposes, i.e., 'accountable', as organizations of commonplace everyday activities" (p.vii). By the same token, these self-same ethno-methods, in failing to render other aspects of our everyday activities 'accountable', render them *rationally-invisible*, i.e., inaccessible to easy rational discussion.

4. Here he quotes from Goethe's *Faust*, Part I (In the Study).

5. In wanting truth, we want, of course, some 'foundations', a 'basis', in terms of which to proceed with our acting. Later in the chapter I will argue that this is precisely what such statements or claims provide. For, although they do not function as propositional statements from which one can derive any empirically provable theoretical claims, in 'calling out' certain responses from those who read/ hear them, they are 'foundational' for what Wittgenstein calls a *language-game*, and what I have called simply a 'way' of talking.

6. Garfinkel (1967) talks of events in conversations as being "open with respect to internal relationships, relationships to other events, and relationships to retrospective and prospective events" (p. 41). Retrospectively, as a spectator, looking back on already existing outcomes, we might see what has occurred as finished and complete, and as possibly falling into a well known category, while prospectively, as a participant in the action, looking forward, we may see what is occurring as open to an indefinite number of possible continuations. In practice, we clearly oscillate between a retrospective and a prospective sense of our circumstances. The categorical claims we make, the boundaries we draw, the re-opening of past issues we perform, and so on, are all up to us, a matter of our judgment as to what is appropriate for us to do in the circumstances.

7. Volosinov (1976) gives a very nice example of how the utterance of a single word, the word "Well!", can in the 'shaping' of its utterance, come to be 'full' of a whole interconnected set of circumstances: "At the time the colloquy took place, both interlocutors *looked up* at the window and *saw* that it had begun to snow; *both knew* that it was already May and that it was high time for spring to come; finally, *both* were *sick and tired* of the protracted winter—*they both were looking forward* to spring and *both were bitterly disappointed* by the late snowfall. On this 'jointly seen' (snowflakes outside the window), 'jointly know' (the time of year— May) and 'unanimously evaluated' (winter wearied of, spring looked forward to)— on this the utterance *directly depends*, all this is seized in its actual, living import—is its very sustenance. And yet all this remains without verbal specification or articulation. The snowflakes remain outside the window; the date, on the page of the calendar; the evaluation, in the psyche of the speaker; and nevertheless, all this is *assumed* in the word *well*" (p. 99).

8. Goffman (1967) studies our deep sense of both our own and other's involvements in dialogue and what happens when we fail to honor such "involvements obligations." "Joint spontaneous involvement," he says, "is a *unio mystico*, a

socialized trance. We must also see that a conversation has a life of its own and makes demands on its own behalf. It is a little social system with its own boundary-maintaining tendencies; it is a little patch of commitment and loyalty with its own heroes and its own villains" (pp. 113–114).

9. "Speech is comparable to a gesture because what it is charged with express-ing will be in the same relation to it as the goal is to the gesture which intends it . . ." (Merleau-Ponty, 1964, p.89).

10. The idea of words being like 'tools' able to shape an activity into a struc-ture, is, of course, primarily Vygotsky's (1978, p. 58; 1986). But Mead (1934) also says, regarding gestures: "They became the *tools* through which the other forms responded" (p. 44, my emphasis).

11. Again, taking a much more practical stance than usual, Wittgenstein (1953) suggests that "a philosophical problem has the form: 'I don't know my way about'" (no.123). In practice, to understand something simply means being able to continue in the practice, irrespective of anything that might be happening in one's head or not.

12. Indeed, in this connection, it is worth remarking that Derrida's (1981) way of talking also, is a product of the self-same theoretical individualism or monolog-ism (that invents *analytic concepts* to represent otherwise hidden entities or pro-cesses), that he seeks in his 'deconstructions', to undo. For instance, in his talk of the mysterious movement of *différance*, he says: "Since there is no presence before and outside semiological *différance*, one can extend to the system of signs in gen-eral what Saussure says about language. . . . [But] there is a circle here, for if one rigorously distinguishes language and speech, code and message, schema and us-age, etc, and if one wishes to do justice to the two postulates thus enunciated, one does not know where to begin, nor how something can begin in general, be it language or speech. Therefore, one has to admit, before any dissociation of lan-guage and speech, code and message, etc. . . . a systematic production of differ-ences, the *production* of a system of differences—a *différance*—within whose ef-fects one eventually, by abstraction and according to determined motivations, will be able to demarcate a linguistics of language and a linguistics of speech, etc." (p.28). Clearly, whatever else Derrida is doing, he is talking *about* a something—"différance"—that he suggests has all kinds of properties (that eventually one will be able to demarcate), and is at work within a system of signs. But to talk in this way, of mysterious processes going on behind the backs of those involved in them, is to reinstate the very metaphysical hierarchy that privileges already existing codes, systems, and forms over social life, dialogue, and the creation of new mean-ings, that he claims to be displacing. As I remarked in the main text, Derrida also leaves us (unstably) fixated, either within a disciplinary, imaginary textual-world, or, unclear as to what it is that we are doing in our talk.

References

Bakhtin, M.M. 1984. *Problems of Dostoevsky's Poetics.* Edited and trans. by Caryl Emerson. Minneapolis: University of Michigan Press.

———. 1986. *Speech Genres and Other Late Essays.* Translated by Vern W. McGee, edited by Caryl Emerson and Michael Holquist. Austin, TX: University of Texas Press.

Bauman, Z. 1987. *Intellectuals: Legislators or Interpreters.* Oxford: Polity Press.

Berger, P. and Luckman, T. 1966. *The Social Construction of Reality.* New York: Doubleday and Co.

Bernstein, R.J. 1983. *Beyond Objectivism and Relativism.* Oxford: Blackwell.

———. 1992. *The New Constellation.* Cambridge, MA: MIT Press.

Billig, M. 1987. *Arguing and Thinking: a Rhetorical Approach to Social Psychology.* Cambridge: Cambridge University Press.

Billig, M., Condor, S., Edwards, D., Gane, M., Middleton, D. and Radley, R. 1988. *Ideological Dilemmas.* London: Sage Publications.

Coulter, J. 1979. *The Social Construction of Mind.* London and Basingstoke: Macmillan.

———. 1983. *Rethinking Cognitive Psychology.* London and Basingstoke: Macmillan.

Derrida, J. 1981. *Positions.* Translated and annotated by Alan Bass. Chicago, Ill: University of Chicago Press.

Dreyfus, H.L. and Rabinow, P. 1986. *Michel Foucault: Beyond Structuralism and Hermeneutics.* London: Harvester.

Gallie, W.B. 1962. Essentially contested concepts. In M. Black, ed., *The Importance of Language.* New Jersey: Prentice Hall.

Garfinkel, H. 1976. *Studies in Enthnomethodology.* Englewood Cliffs, NY: Prentice-Hall.

Gergen, K.J. 1985. The social constructionist movement in modern psychology. *American Psychologist, 40.* pp. 266–75.

———. 1991. *The Saturated Self: Dilemmas of Identity in Contemporary Life.* New York: Basic Books.

Goffman, E. 1967. *Interaction Ritual.* Harmondsworth: Penguin Books.

Harré, R. 1983. *Personal Being: a Theory for Individual Psychology.* Oxford: Blackwell.

Harré, R., ed. 1986. *The Social Construction of Emotions.* Oxford: Basil Blackwell.

Katz, A. M. and Shotter, J. (in press). Hearing the patient's voice: toward a social poetics in diagnostic interviews. *Social Science and Medicine*.

Lindley, D. 1993. *The End of Physics: the Myth of a Unified Theory*. New York, NY: Basic Books.

Mead, G.H. 1934. *Mind, Self and Society*. Chicago: University of Chicago Press.

Merleau-Ponty, M. 1964. *Signs*. Translated with an introduction by Richard C. Mc-Cleary. Boston, MA: Northwestern University Press.

Mills, C.W. 1940/1975. Situated actions and vocabularies of motive. In D. Brisset and C. Edgley, eds., *Life as Theater: a Dramaturgical Sourcebook*. Chicago; Aldine Publishing Company.

Rabinow, P. ed. 1986. *The Foucault Reader*. Harmondsworth: Penguin Books.

Ryle, G. 1949. *The Concept of Mind*. London: Methuen.

Shotter, J. 1993b. *Conversational Realities: Constructing Life through Language*. London: Sage.

———. 1993a. *Cultural Politics of Everyday Life: Social Constructionism, Rhetoric, and Knowing of the Third Kind*. Milton Keynes: Open University Press. Toronto: Toronto University Press.

———. 1984. *Social Accountability and Selfhood*. Oxford: Blackwell.

———. 1980. Action, joint action, and intentionality. M. Brenner, ed., *The Structure of Action*. Oxford: Blackwell.

———. 1995. In conversation: joint action, shared intentionality, and ethics. *Theory and Psychology*, 5, 49–73.

Taylor, C. 1992. Following a rule. In M. Hjort, ed., *Rules and Conventions: Literature, Philosophy, Social Theory*. Baltimore, MD: Johns Hopkins Press.

Vico, G. 1968. *The New Science of Giambattista Vico*. Ed. and trans. by T.G. Bergin and M.H. Fisch. Ithaca, N.Y.: Cornell University Press.

Volosinov, V.N. 1973. *Marxism and the Philosophy of Language*. Trans. by L. Matejka and I.R. Titunik. Cambridge, MA: Harvard University Press.

———. 1976. *Freudianism: a Critical Sketch*. Bloomington and Indianapolis: Indiana University Press.

Vygotsky, L.S. 1978. *Mind in Society: the Development of Higher Psychological Processes*. M. Cole, V. John-Steiner, S. Scribner, and E. Souberman, eds. Cambridge, MA: Harvard University Press.

———. 1986. *Thought and Language*. Translation newly revised by Alex Kozulin. Cambridge, MA: MIT Press.

Wittgenstein, L. 1953. *Philosophical Investigations*. Oxford: Blackwell.

———. 1969. *On Certainty*. Oxford: Blackwell.

———. 1979. *Remarks on Frazer's 'Golden Bough'*. Edited by Rush Rhees. Atlantic Highlands, NJ: Humanities Press.

———. 1980. *Culture and Value*. Chicago: University of Chicago Press.

Editor's Introduction

Gillian Roberts and Janet Bavelas study verbal and nonverbal communicating in Bavelas's laboratories at the Department of Psychology of the University of Victoria, British Columbia. Since Bavelas' 1967 collaboration on the classic *Pragmatics of Human Communication*,[1] she has studied manifest communicative behavior and observable communicative effects, but always within the broader context of what she and her coauthors call an "interactional" understanding of communication. Gillian Roberts recognized that both the general interactional view and the specific approach developed by the Victoria research team call into question several psychological and linguistic models of meaning. Roberts and Bavelas argue here that the theoretical and conceptual issues addressed in *Beyond the Symbol Model* can best be studied empirically; in their words, "the nature of language (and meaning) can only truly be elucidated through analysis of communicative acts." Thus this chapter reviews some weaknesses of earlier conceptions of meaning and sketches an alternative grounded in the authors' empirical communication research. The primary contribution of this discussion is that it outlines an observationally-anchored, social psychological approach to some of the same issues that are addressed in other chapters by philosophers, semioticians, communication theorists, and linguists.

Roberts and Bavelas begin by briefly demonstrating some problems that are inherent in the claims that meaning resides in words, that it can be identified by analyzing words-plus-context, and that it is a function of speaker intent. These problems and close observations of actual communicating lead the authors to "propose that the meaning of an utterance depends on both the speaker and the addressee; it exists only 'in' their interaction." This collaborative approach to meaning echoes aspects of the treatment of articulate contact in Chapter 1, Madison's discussion of being and speaking, and Shotter's discussion of Wittgenstein.

Roberts and Bavelas analyze a paradigm case of communicating from earlier research to demonstrate that neither words, nor context, nor speaker's intention can provide sufficient explanations of meaning, especially if one affirms the co-existence of both "insider" and "outsider" perspectives. Meaning negotiation in these situations requires three elements: A presents an utterance for B to consider, B accepts the utterance, *and* A accepts that B accepts the utterance. The authors focus, in other words, on what they call the *effective meaning* of an utterance, which can be known to an outsider only "by observing a process of *semantic collaboration* that consists of three steps in a fixed order: (1) Utterance (2) Reaction (3) Confirmation."

In communication, Roberts and Bavelas argue, "only effective meaning matters;" other translations of utterances could be imposed linguistically, but they "have no intrinsic communicative status." Even successful irony appears to illustrate the efficacy of their analysis. Irony occurs in natural dialogue, they explain, as "interlocutors actually collaborate on one effective meaning, which is an inversion of the usual meaning."

Roberts and Bavelas acknowledge that consequential mental or "internal" events accompany observable communication behaviors. But, they argue, cognitive or psycholinguistic perspectives cannot provide adequate analyses of actual, as contrasted with armchair examples, of communication. They do not quarrel with the characterizations in linguistics of the "standard dictionary" and "mental lexicon," but they insist that language and communication researchers must also acknowledge the existence and importance of a *communicative dictionary* that "reflects the effective meanings accomplished through semantic collaboration."

The final major section of the chapter analyzes nine examples of actual communication to illustrate *implicit* semantic collaboration, *explicit* semantic collaboration, and *problematic* semantic collaboration. In all cases, the authors demonstrate the importance of considering the contributions of both verbal and nonverbal cues to effective meaning. The first three examples are of successful communicative events where "the discourse flows smoothly, as if there were nothing to negotiate." Analysis reveals, however, that even this success depends on coordination among utterance, reaction, and confirmation. The following two examples show how interlocutors sometimes explicitly negotiate utterance meaning, again, both verbally and nonverbally. Roberts and Bavelas' final four examples illustrate how misinterpretation and manipulation can result when utterance, reaction, and confirmation are not adequately aligned.

The authors emphasize at the end of the chapter that unsuccessful semantic collaboration often arises because of intractable or unchallenged power imbalances. They argue that "politically correct" language evolved only when it became possible to negotiate mutually acceptable terms.

One implication of this perspective that Roberts and Bavelas mention without developing is that linear causal analyses of communication events are inherently flawed because, in their words, "interlocutors must actively co-operate and share responsibility for the success or failure of communication." This means that the everyday tendency to assign unilateral "fault" or "blame" for a problematic interpersonal or social event manifests an incomplete understanding of effective meaning. Since interlocutors routinely *collaborate* on meaning, misunderstanding is never simply one person's "fault." The presence of confusion, misinterpretation, or misconception demonstrates a breakdown in the *three* part process of utterance, reaction, and confirmation. Thus the most fruitful response to a misunderstanding is not, "Who's to blame?" but "What can the interlocutors do (together) next?"

Each of the chapters in this section argues against oversimplified analyses of language and linguistic meaning. All resist the historical tendency to treat language simply or even primarily as a representational tool that humans use to realize their intentions or achieve their goals. These authors affirm in widely different ways the importance, when considering the nature of language, of attending to practice, to language as it occurs, as it is lived by interlocutors. This means that they recognize how thoroughly a conception or theory of language must be a conception or theory of communicating.

Note

1. Paul Watzlawick, Janet Beavin Bavelas, and Donald D. Jackson, *Pragmatics of Human Communication* (New York: Norton, 1967).

4

The Communicative Dictionary:
A Collaborative Theory of Meaning[1]

Gillian L. Roberts and Janet Beavin Bavelas

If a word exists in the forest, and no one is there to hear it, does it have meaning? Our answer is No. Language does not exist in a vacuum and does not occur independently of its users. In this chapter, we will outline a theory that casts meaning as a collaborative creation of interlocutors. First, we will briefly summarize existing theories of meaning, with an emphasis on their limitations for actual language use. Then we will present and illustrate our collaborative theory, concluding with implications for the manipulation of meaning.

Previous Approaches to Meaning[2]

Meaning is "In" Words

In response to the question, "How do we know what a word means?" most people would probably suggest looking it up in a dictionary. That is, words "have" meanings accessible to us through dictionaries. This intuitive notion is reflected in traditional semantic approaches, which have been realized by reduction to "the study of the semantic *properties* of natural languages" (Crystal, 1991, p. 310; italics added). That is, meaning has been described as metaphorically "contained" in linguistic structure (Lakoff & Johnson, 1980, p. 206; Reddy, 1979). Since Aristotle defined words as the smallest significant units of speech (Kess, 1992, p. 196), many linguists and language philosophers have shared the belief that meaning is "in" words (e.g., Jackson, 1990, p. 3; O'Grady & Dobrovolsky, 1992, p. 229; Tough, 1977, p. 31). Nelson (1985, p. 8) summarized this perspective:

Psychological and linguistic models have usually been based on the assumption that words have enduring and conversational meanings that can be represented in static structures. . . .

Plausible as this view is, it has some serious limitations. As Yule (1985, p. 91) pointed out,

we cannot assume that there is some God-given, meaningful connection between a word in a language and an object in the world [because] in order to hold that view, you would be forced to claim that God is an English speaker.

Another problem is that, even within one language, a word can have more than one dictionary definition, which creates potential lexical ambiguity; for example, "We were surprised to see a crane in the empty lot." The polysemic nature of words such as "crane" presents a challenge because all of the possible meanings would have to be "in" the word, and yet there is no way to determine the appropriate meaning by looking at the word in isolation.

In our view, the "meaning in words" approach also fails because it focuses on the abstract nature of language, independent of its use and users. First, far from being the passive consumers of dictionary meanings, language users constantly change word meanings, creating new words and constructing entirely new meanings for old words (which is one reason dictionaries periodically require new editions). The relationship between dictionary users and dictionary editors is a reciprocal rather than unilateral one. Second, there is an implicit assumption in this and most other approaches that we always speak "properly," only using words with accepted meanings in an explicit manner within grammatically constructed sentences. However, anyone who transcribes actual conversation encounters a great deal of what Chomsky called "degenerate speech" (Ellis, 1985, p. 130), such as poor word choices, ungrammatical or incomplete sentences, and even non sequiturs—all of which the interlocutors nonetheless understand and build upon.

Meaning is "In" Words and Their Context

As a result of some of the problems mentioned earlier, there are theories that widen the word container and treat meaning as "in" the word plus its context (cf. Kess, 1992; Yule, 1985). *Linguistic* context refers to the text surrounding the word of interest and can resolve many instances of lexical ambiguity. Thus, in the sentence "I will light the fire," the linguistic context makes it evident that "light" is being used as a verb and therefore does not mean "illumination" (noun) or "of little weight" (adjective). However, linguistic context will not help clarify the meaning of "Visiting relatives can be boring," in which "visiting" illustrates syntactic ambiguity. Presented on its own, this sentence could equally mean "the act of going to visit relatives is boring" or "relatives who come to visit are boring." One way to resolve the meaning would be to invoke the situational context (e.g., the speaker's in-laws are arriving). *Situational* context includes

> the total non-linguistic background to a text or utterance, including the immediate situation in which it is used, and the awareness by speaker and hearer of what has been said earlier and of any relevant external beliefs or presuppositions. (Crystal, 1991, p. 79)

One immediate problem is that "total non-linguistic background" excludes almost nothing and is therefore useful mostly as a post hoc explanation. Situational context may narrow the possibilities somewhat, but in many cases we could always find something in the situational context that would "explain" virtually any meaning.

A deeper problem is that at least two distinct kinds of situational context are being blurred together: (a) *static* features of the previous text or physical situation in which a word occurs (e.g., when standing on a ski slope, the word "cat" is likely to mean the machine that grooms the hill), and (b) *dynamic, social* features created within the dialogue by the interlocutors; the latter are central to our theory. The failure to distinguish between these illustrates what Linell (1982) called the "written language bias" in linguistics, which casts language as static and monologic, with an explicit context. Spoken language, in contrast, is dynamic, dialogic, and inherently interactive; we will propose that the participants constantly create, draw upon, and update their own context, on-line.

Meaning is "In" the Speaker's Intention

Do words mean or do people mean? (Nelson, 1985. p. 9)

A third approach, grounded in spoken language, radically relocates meaning as "in" the speaker's intentions (Grice, 1989). That is, knowing what the speaker meant to say is sufficient to determine the meaning of an utterance.

> "When I use a word," Humpty Dumpty said in a rather scornful tone, "it means what I choose it to mean—neither more nor less." (Lewis Carroll; from Yule, 1985, p. 92)

This approach solves not only lexical but also syntactic ambiguity without invoking context because, even if an utterance has two possible interpretations, there can only be one intended meaning.[3] The speaker knows what he or she meant, and that determines the utterance's meaning.

Speech act theory proposes that messages carry not only content but also intent (Austin, 1962; Searle, 1969). That is, meaning is equated with *illocutionary force*, which is what the speaker intends to say with an utterance, regardless of the particular words he or she chooses. In the classic example of "Can you reach the salt?" the speaker is not asking for information about the hearer's arm length but is politely requesting that the hearer pass the salt shaker.

Austin (1962) briefly mentioned *perlocutionary* force, which is what the speaker hopes the effect of the utterance will be on the hearer; however, this notion has received little attention in linguistics (J. Kess, personal communication, 1992). Our criticism is that the hearer, while acknowledged, is still definitely a minor player who simply catches (or misses) the ball that is thrown. Suppose, for example, the hearer responded to "Can you reach the salt?" by answering "Yes" without passing the salt. Presumably, this hearer would be seen as incompetent, and the speaker would have to become explicit about his or her intentions (e.g., "No, I mean please pass me the salt"). Suppose, however, that the speaker's request was not well formed (e.g., one might simply say "Salt?" in an informal dialogue); the hearer might still pass the salt. Who gets credit in this case?

Meaning is Created By and For the Interlocutors

> Our talk exchanges do not normally consist of a succession of disconnected remarks, and would not be rational if they did. They are characteristically, to some degree at least, cooperative efforts. . . . (Grice, 1975, p. 45)

Clearly, the change from "meaning-in-words" to "meaning-in-speakers" is a major step from language in the abstract to language in use, but speech act theory implies that the main language user is the speaker. We will take one further step to include the *interlocutor* as well, treating both participants as an inseparable unit. In brief, we will propose that the meaning of an utterance depends on both the speaker and the addressee; it exists only "in" their interaction. Meaning cannot be explained by the illocutionary force or perlocutionary force of an utterance but by what we might call *interlocutionary* or *interactional* force.

One possibility of such an approach began with experimental research by Clark and his colleagues. Rather than casting addressees as "mute and invisible" (Clark & Wilkes-Gibbs, 1986, p. 3), they proposed that "speakers and their addressees . . . collaborate with each other moment by moment to try to ensure that what is said is also understood" (Schober & Clark, 1989, p. 211).

In their first experiment, Clark and Wilkes-Gibbs (1986) asked dyads (who were visually separated by a partition) to work together on a task requiring that the speaker be able to refer unambiguously to the odd geometric figures they had to talk about. Over a series of trials with the same figures, the dyads used fewer words and fewer turns to identify each figure. The change in number of turns is particularly important: While the dyad initially took several steps to agree on how to refer to a figure, later they could just use this agreed-upon term to expedite their reference. For example,

> Speaker: Okay, and the next one is the person that looks like they're carrying something and it's sticking out to the left. It looks like a hat that's upside down.
>
> Addressee: The guy that's pointing to the left again?
>
> Speaker: Yeah, pointing to the left, that's it. (laughs)
>
> Addressee: Okay. (p. 23)

Later, the speaker could say simply "the guy pointing left." Notice the contributions of both people as the dyad collaboratively created a term to refer to this figure.

In the next phase, Schober and Clark (1989) used the same task to investigate how well third parties would understand the dyad's collaboration. They identified two kinds of listeners: the *addressee*, or interlocutor with whom the speaker is actually talking, and the *overhearer*, or outsider who hears this conversation. As before, the addressees achieved virtually 100 percent accuracy working with the speaker. Each of Schober and Clark's overhearers listened, live or on audiotape, to the dialogue of one speaker and addressee. Some overhearers were in the same room behind another partition, and others had exactly the same information from an audiotape and even the advantage of being able to pause the tape when they wished. However, their average accuracy was significantly less than the addressees achieved. Being present in the room or being able to pause the tape had no benefit, but coming in late (i.e., hearing only the second half of the trials) was much worse (88 to 68%).

There are two crucial empirical findings here: First, words, context, and speaker's intention are not sufficient explanations because these were identical for both addressees and overhearers, yet overhearers did not understand the meaning of all of the references. There was a significant advantage to being in the original dyad, that is, to having been part of the collaborating pair who tailored the meanings for themselves. Second, the accuracy that overhearers did achieve depended on their access to this collaboration. They did fairly well if they heard it all, but if they missed the actual collaboration in the first few trials, they understood much less of what the speaker was talking about.

Thus, in these two experiments, Clark, Schober, and Wilkes-Gibbs were able to capture evidence of the process of collaboration. They looked closely at how dyads actually performed meaning and found evidence not consistent with previous theories. They showed, both in the dyad's communication over time and in the problem of the overhearers, that unique meaning was being created that could only be attributed to the moment-by-moment interaction.

Clark and Schaefer (1987) identified a unit of conversation they called a *contribution,* which is accomplished by speaker and addressee together, a process that consists of a minimum of three parts:

(a) A presents u for B to consider.
(b) B accepts u.
(c) A accepts that B accepts u.
During the presentation phase, A places her utterance u into consideration.
During the acceptance phase, B needs to accept u in a *unilateral* acceptance.
For *mutual* acceptance, however, A must accept that B has actually understood. (p. 127)

As will be seen, we will apply these three steps to the establishment of meaning.

Summary of Previous Research: Perspectives on Meaning

We view this historical sequence of theories as a refinement of perspective on how meaning exists and for whom. To say that words or words-in-context "contain" meaning is to take what we call an entirely *outsider* perspective. Everyone stands outside the words (and their context), which have encapsulated meanings completely independent of their users. We are all outsiders who observe or manipulate these containers. The shift to speaker's intention creates the speaker as an *insider* with special authority on what the meaning is. Words are not independent, preexisting capsules; the speaker determines what they mean. The rest of us, including the addressee, remain outsiders, who must figure out (and defer to) the speaker's intended meaning. The work of Clark's group clearly demonstrates that both the speaker and addressee are insiders, creating their meanings together, and the rest of us (as overhearers) are always outsiders.

We propose that the insider and outsider perspectives always coexist, that both are valid, and both are common in our everyday experiences. We speak with others, and we overhear others speaking. When conversing in a group, we can actively take part in a dialogue (as an insider) and then be a third party to one (an outsider). As interlocutors, we are the insiders, and the ultimate criterion for the meaning of our words and actions is our understanding and use of them; it cannot be imposed from outside. When we are talking with another person, the meaning we create and accept together *is* the meaning of our words and actions. When we are outsiders observing or overhearing people talk, our best chance at inferring their meaning is by observing their exchanges. In the next section, we propose that an outsider must observe at least three utterances by speaker and addressee to understand their meaning. Later, we will return to the insider perspective.

Semantic Collaboration

Suppose we observe the following exchange between a couple at dinner:

A: [looking up] Uhhh, salt?

At this point, the question could have several plausible meanings: A is unsure that he wants salt; he wonders if B thinks that salt is needed; he is asking whether any salt is available; he is offering her salt; he is asking whether the substance available is indeed salt or whether the name for the substance (in English) is salt. A speech-act theorist might hypothesize a request for salt, albeit a poorly formed one. As outsiders, we must be officially undecided, based on the data available. The next utterance is:

B: Here [passing salt shaker].

The interlocutor reacts as if A had requested salt, ignoring all other meanings. As outsiders, the array of possible meanings has been considerably narrowed for us. We can now be fairly sure that A meant "Please pass me the salt." It is vital to note that we are inferring this meaning retroactively and from B's reaction as much as from A's utterance. We also need the next step:

A: [taking it] Thanks.

The speaker's word and action confirm that he had indeed meant to request that B pass the salt. If this were not the case, A would have said something like "No, I meant you should add some salt" or "No, I wondered whether you think this needs salt?" or the like. Because of these possibilities, the third step is essential for us, as overhearers, to be reasonably sure we have understood.

Thus, the *effective meaning* of an utterance is only known to us by observing a process of *semantic collaboration* that consists of three steps in a fixed order:

1. Utterance

2. Reaction

3. Confirmation

Step 1 is A's utterance, of which we wish to know the meaning. Utterances can be defined in the linguistic sense as "a stretch of speech about which no assumptions have been made in terms of linguistic theory" (Crystal, 1991, p. 367) or simply as "things spoken" (Swannell, 1986, p. 622). In addition to this broad linguistic definition, we will also include all nonverbal communicative acts (i.e., excluding adaptors). Thus we include such communicative acts as gestures, facial displays, eye contact, intonation, and so on (Bavelas & Chovil, 1993), including those that occur without words. In step 1, Interlocutor A offers the utterance.

Step 2 is B's reaction to the utterance. Any utterance of A's, regardless of its form, has a range of possible interpretations. Even putting aside unintelligible, disordered, or obstructed speech (for which clarification might be requested), it is probably impossible to utter anything in conversation that has only one interpretation. The possible interpretations include one or more literal meanings that a dictionary would permit and could be multiplied by the range of interpretations that each listener could imagine. Interlocutor B responds (verbally and/or nonverbally), and this reaction reflects one of the possible interpretations. It may consist of a request for clarification, a formulation or reformulation (Davis, 1986, p. 47), or other explicit comment, but most often it will simply be appropriate continuation. That is, B goes on as if there were one clear meaning, usually building on A's utterance. However, considering the range of possible interpretations and therefore reactions, there is also a powerful potential for misinterpretation at this point. How do we know their communication was successful? Was the reaction appropriate?

In step 3, Interlocutor A confirms (verbally and/or nonverbally) the appropriateness or inappropriateness of Interlocutor B's reaction to A's original utterance. Confirmation may be explicit or, more commonly, may also be exhibited by appropriate continuation, in which no objection is offered to the reaction. A builds on B's reaction, and dialogue proceeds smoothly and on track. The observer now understands what is meant. For the insiders, the steps of the "salt" exchange may easily have passed unnoticed, with no mystery or plausible alternatives. Still, step 3 was crucial to their semantic collaboration and their accomplishment of effective meaning because both A and B must give observable evidence ("mutual acceptance") of a shared meaning. The process of semantic collaboration is illustrated in Figure 1. When all three of these steps are in alignment, the effective meaning of the utterance has been accomplished, and communication is thus deemed successful.

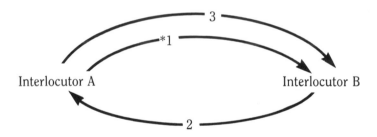

Figure 1. The process of semantic collaboration

The earlier description of semantic collaboration has several corollaries that should be made explicit:

1. All utterances are subject to semantic collaboration to establish their effective meaning.

2. In communication, only effective meaning matters: literal translations of utterances could be imposed linguistically but have no intrinsic communicative status.

3. Our ability to use or to understand a wide variety of figurative, indirect, and colloquial forms of language (metaphor, humour, polite requests, etc.) depends on the process of semantic collaboration.

4. When the collaboration is successful, there will be only one effective meaning for that utterance (at that time). An apparent exception is irony, but Coates (1993) has shown that, in natural dialogue, the interlocutors actually collaborate on one effective meaning, which is an inversion of the usual meaning.

5. Violation of steps 2 or 3 of semantic collaboration interferes with the accomplishment of effective meaning. We deem this unsuccessful communication because there is no agreed-upon meaning. Utterances presented under these conditions are prone to misinterpretation and even manipulation.

The reader may have noticed that, with its inclusion of the addressee, the collaborative theory also becomes potentially more behavioral than earlier approaches. That is, to include both speaker and addressee requires either that we jump from one mind to the other or that we step outside to describe the observable manifestations of their communication. We will take the latter approach, which contrasts with an intrapsychic approach as follows:

Observable Process (outsider view)	Inferred Mental Cause (insider view)
1. Utterance	1. Speaker's intended meaning
2. Reaction	2. Addressee's interpretation of the underlying meaning
3. Confirmation	3. Speaker's interpretation of addressee's understanding

Although the focus of our theory is on observable social interactions, it neither precludes the reality of the internal processing of language nor the validity of the effects that such workings have on our use of language. Indeed, these two approaches (observable and inferred) can be seen as compatible and even complementary. However, to focus solely on a cognitive or psycholinguistic perspective can be problematic when analysing actual communication. Often the fact that communication is inherently social and observable is forgotten or ignored. For example, the speaker's intended meaning often has primacy in traditional approaches, but it is not an observable process. Unless one is a mind-reader, there are only two ways to know the intended meaning of an utterance; one is either (a) the speaker or (b) an observer or participant in the process of semantic collaboration. As we pointed out in the "Uhhh, salt?" example at the beginning of this section, we have a better chance of inferring A's meaning from B's reaction and A's confirmation than we would from speculating about A's initial utterance in isolation.

To summarize this section, our title suggests a new conception of *dictionary*, which challenges the primacy of a dictionary in its standard form as a reference for use in everyday communication. There are classically two ways to characterize dictionaries in linguistics: The *standard dictionary* is a bound, alphabetized collection of words that constitute a language, with their individual definitions and grammatical properties; it may also include examples of applications for each word. The *mental lexicon* (according to psycholinguists) is the cognitive form of the standard dictionary. This is the theoretical dictionary in each person's mind that "contains" the words and images (cognitions) of his or her experience.

The *communicative dictionary* reflects the effective meanings accomplished through semantic collaboration. This metaphorical dictionary is both variable and transient; that is, it may be different for every dyad and may even disappear as soon as they have finished a conversation. The process of semantic collaboration creates a communicative dictionary, but the "definitions" in this metaphorical dictionary are written in disappearing ink, which will fade with the life of the interaction but can be revived by reuse. Therefore, the communicative dictionary is always being created and recreated by dyads within the contexts of infinite interactions. Common ground (Clark & Marshall, 1981) between interlocuters may consist of expedited (re)collaboration of effective meaning during subsequent interactions.

As we suggested earlier, standard dictionaries can be thought of as part of the process we are describing. Consider that people were speaking English long before the first formal dictionaries in the eighteenth century. These dictionaries simply documented the meanings of words as they were being used at that time. However, people kept using words and, in the process, changing meanings as well as creating new words, which constantly necessitated new editions and even new kinds of dictionaries. This is a larger-scale version of the same process we are describing, in which people collaboratively change and even create the meanings of words. Dictionaries may eventually record some of these changes. Thus, compiling a standard dictionary is like taking still photographs of each of the major scenes in a moving picture. These photographs would not include how the movie got from one scene to the next (nor any of the minor scenes). Useful as they are, standard dictionaries are always limited to describing what a meaning has become after a sufficient number of people have used it for a sufficient amount of time (necessarily an outsider perspective). They never attempt to capture the innumerable transient and idiosyncratic uses in all of the conversations that occur at any given moment. Our metaphor of a communicative dictionary is an attempt to legitimate these "insider" usages and especially to draw attention to the process that creates them.

To summarize, "language" is an abstraction; it is realized only in its actual and dynamic form, communication. Indeed, the nature of language (and meaning) can only truly be elucidated through analysis of communicative acts. The collaborative theory of meaning proposes that *effective meaning is accomplished by interlocutors through the process of semantic collaboration, and this mutually accepted effective meaning exists within the life of the interaction.* Their interaction is therefore the necessary context in which interlocutors accomplish the effective meaning of communication. Although we can attempt to communicate in the absence of this process, mutually agreed-upon (and therefore useful) meaning can only be established when the conditions of semantic collaboration are satisfied in their entirety.

Empirical Examples of the Model

This section illustrates, specifies, and expands the collaborative theory with examples from naturalistic observation and from the media; the only restriction was that examples could not be hypothetical. There are three groups of examples, illustrating *implicit* semantic collaboration, *explicit* semantic collaboration, and *problematic* semantic collaboration. For the sake of simplicity, A's first utterance (marked *A:) will always be the focus, that is, the one whose effective meaning is being negotiated. However, we want to emphasize our view that this process is actually continuous and overlapping throughout an interaction; that is, reactions and confirmations are also utterances and equally subject to semantic collaboration.

In reading these examples, the reader can either follow the step-by-step annotations or first scan the three-part sequence (in bold face) and then go back to the annotations. The first approach emphasizes the outsider view and the inadequacy of a "meaning in words" approach, while the second shows how easily meaning is accomplished in practice because the reader will usually understand the effective meaning from the entire sequence.

Case A: Implicit Semantic Collaboration

These cases represent the natural, easy flow of communication in which effective meaning is negotiated or accomplished implicitly, without the need for explicit expansion or explanation of the utterance. Reaction and confirmation are often simply appropriate continuations in the form of another utterance; mutual understanding can be inferred by the absence of an objection. Successive utterances commonly proceed in this manner, as effective meanings are continually negotiated throughout the life of the interaction. The discourse flows smoothly, as if there were nothing to negotiate:

1. Two students entered a university computer lab where, in contrast to its usual state of occupancy, there were few students working:

   *A: Wow, there's no one here!

The literal translation of this utterance is an exclamation that there are no other people present in the room, and A is surprised at this uncharacteristic state. From a quick observation, it is evident that there are in fact some people in the room; therefore A's literal utterance is untrue.

   B: Well, it's Friday.

B's reaction appears to be a non sequitur; it has no relation to A's initial utterance. If B had taken A's utterance literally, the reaction would have been something like "Can't you see that person?" or "How can you say that? There are five people in here!" Instead, B may be treating A's utterance as hyperbole and surprise at the *relative* emptiness of the room and offering a possible explanation for this.[4]

   A: Yeah, I guess everyone's started the weekend already.

A confirms the appropriateness of B's reaction by accepting and elaborating B's explanation that the impending weekend is responsible for the occupancy rate. Therefore, the effective meaning of "Wow, there's no one here!" = *"Isn't it surprising that there are so few people here working as opposed to the usual rate of occupancy, and I wonder what is responsible for this difference?"*

2. According to Bavelas, Black, Chovil, and Mullett (1990) equivocation is purposefully ambiguous language. These authors proposed that

> equivocation may blunt the impact of a message, but we do not expect it to change the denotative meaning. Like any other indirect speech act . . . the meaning of an equivocal message should be clear to competent speakers of the language. (p. 137)

However, the method used by Bavelas et al. (1990) focused only on an initial question and the equivocal response, which we would consider the *utterance* whose effective meaning is being negotiated. They did not study real dyads, which would have included B's reaction and A's confirmation, so it is not possible to know which of the interpretations was confirmed by the speaker. We would modify their proposal to say that the effective meaning of an equivocation is clear only if it is accomplished through semantic collaboration. An example of equivocation in an exchange between siblings will illustrate this process:

> B: Does my hair really need help?
>
> *A: Oh, it's not that bad.

The literal meaning of A's utterance is that something ("it") cannot be described as bad in comparison with something else. Given that "it" refers to B's hair, an appropriate response to this literal translation would be for B to express pleasure that his hair is good or to thank A for the compliment.

> B: Not THAT bad? Oh, damn! (goes to wash it)

B reacts as if A had said that his hair does *not* look good because he curses and goes off to remedy the situation.

> A: Well, yah, you might want to fix it. (laughs)

A confirms this interpretation by agreeing that he should wash his hair after all. Therefore, the effective meaning of "Oh, it's not that bad" = *"You could get by without washing your hair, but it looks like it needs it."* Her original utterance was equivocal and ambiguous, that is, "not bad" does not equal "good" and "not THAT bad" is an ambiguous contrast point. B reacted to A's utterance as if it meant that he should fix his hair, that is, it was in fact "bad," so we can see that this example follows the definition of equivocation given earlier.

3. Two friends were outside a professor's office, and one was checking her posted grade. When she located her score, she said:

> *A: Oh, I'm dead meat!

The literal meaning is that A has suddenly proclaimed that she is the flesh of a carcass. This is obviously not a logical statement in this or any context. Even treated as an idiom, the phrase simply means she is not in a good state; it does not say exactly how or why.

B: Did you at least pass?

B reacts to A's utterance as if it were a statement regarding A's academic performance in the course, that is, the metaphor *"my performance in the course has killed me!"* because B asks A about the grade.

A: I needed to do a lot better than that.

A confirms B's reaction to this metaphor by adding relevant information. Therefore, the effective meaning of "Oh, I'm dead meat!" = *"I am in trouble because my grade reflects that I have performed poorly in this course when I needed to do well."* This example contrasts directly with example 4, later, of explicit semantic collaboration on the metaphorical use of "dead."

Space limits preclude our illustrating implicit semantic collaboration of nonverbal acts, but an example can be found in Bavelas and Coates (1992, pp. 302–3) and another in Bavelas, Chovil, Coates, and Roe (in press, pp. 9–10).

Case B: Explicit Semantic Collaboration

Sometimes the effective meaning of an utterance is not accomplished implicitly. Instead, B's reaction is to request explicit clarification of A's utterance or parts of it, for example, with "What does that mean?" "What do you mean (to say) by that?" or "I'm sorry, I don't follow you." In these cases, we have access to an insider's view.

4. The following example illustrates explicit semantic collaboration about different metaphorical uses of the word "dead." The dyad negotiated the effective meaning using a five-step sequence. The setting was outside a classroom where students were waiting to write an exam. Two friends were talking, and one who appeared to be either anxious or tired (or both) began the exchange:

A: Oh, I am so dead!

The literal meaning of this statement is that A is no longer alive, which is obviously not true because A is present and talking to B.

B: You're dead?

This reaction indicates that B understands that A did not literally mean that she is dead (because B did not say "What do you mean? You're alive!"), but B also communicates through use of rising intonation (question) that it is unclear to her which metaphorical translation of "dead" is appropriate in this situation.

A: Totally dead.

A reiterates her original statement and appears not to realize that B needs further clarification of this term.

B: Are you DEAD for this exam or are you DEAD tired?

B takes the initiative and explicitly asks A to clarify the meaning of her utterance.

A: Well, both, but for this exam mostly.

A indicates that both of B's reactions to "dead" are appropriate (that is, very tired *and* likely to do poorly on the exam) but that the latter reaction is most appropriate.

B: Oh, don't worry, I'm sure you'll do fine.

Having accomplished the effective meaning of "dead" as "Oh, I'm so dead!" = *"I'm going to perform poorly in writing this exam!"* B proceeds appropriately.

5. A father (B) and a daughter (A) were sitting in a public place and starting to eat their ice cream cones:

*A: (loudly) Daddy, don't beat me!

The most obvious literal meaning of A's utterance is that B is imploring her father not to hit her.

B: (looking around nervously) WHAT, honey?!

B reacts as if he interprets the literal meaning and fears that others around them might similarly interpret A's remark. However, A's utterance does not make sense to him, so he asks for clarification (perhaps not only for himself but for those around him, too).

A: You always beat me!

A reiterates and emphasizes her first statement. She apparently does not understand that B needs clarification and interprets "WHAT, honey?!" as a request for a simple paraphrase of her initial statement.

B: What do you mean?

B still does not appear to understand what A means to say and becomes very explicit to get the information he needs from his daughter.

A: You always finish your ice cream cone first!

A responds to his request to explain what she means and finally explicates her initial utterance.

B: Oh! (displays relief)

B reacts to A's explanation as if he understands what A meant, and he indicates that he is relieved that he had initially interpreted her utterance in an inappropriate way.

A: (smiles, eats ice cream)

A confirms that B has now interpreted her utterance appropriately because she continues in her goal of finishing her ice cream faster than her father. Therefore, the effective meaning of "Daddy, don't beat me!" = *"Daddy, eat your ice cream cone slowly so that you don't finish before me."*

Case C: Problematic Semantic Collaboration

Cases that lack the alignment of the three steps of semantic collaboration are problematic because there is no clear negotiation of an utterance, and therefore effective meaning is not accomplished. Furthermore, when the three steps cannot be aligned because the setting is noncollaborative—for example, when utterances are presented through unilateral (monologic) media or in situations where power differences prevent collaboration—then misinterpretations and even manipulation may occur. These are situations where one person is "kept at bay." The following examples illustrate the inconclusive nature of utterances for which effective meaning has not been mutually accomplished, as a result of an interference with or violation of semantic collaboration.

6. This example is from an actual interaction between a pilot (B) and co-pilot (A) just prior to a fatal commercial plane crash (Goguen & Linde, 1981). The dialogue was recorded on the "black box" and was recovered at the crash site. Both A and B realized that they were lost and in trouble, and the co-pilot was trying to ascertain the plane's location:

*A: Do you have any idea of what the frequency of the Paris VOR is?

The literal meaning of A's utterance is a request for specfic information about B's knowledge of the VOR (a ground radar system that would help establish the plane's location). It can be hypothesized that A is indirectly suggesting that they use the VOR. An appropriate response to the indirect request would be for B to give A the frequency or even to tune into the VOR himself. Instead, he responded:

B: Nope, don't really give a [expletive deleted].

B reacts to the literal meaning of A's utterance, that is, he indicates that he does not have the information about the VOR. Indeed, he reacts as if the co-pilot has also asked whether he *cared* about knowing the VOR frequency.

A: (silence)

Perhaps because of their difference in power and authority in the cockpit, A does not confirm B's reaction as inappropriate, nor does he initiate explicit negotiation. In fact, A's dropping the subject could be interpreted as a confirmation that B's reaction was appropriate and that A has received the information he was seeking. Therefore, the effective meaning of "Do you know what the frequency of the Paris VOR is?" was left tragically unresolved.

7. Television is a medium that particularly interferes with the process of semantic collaboration because it does not permit step 3 (A's confirmation of B's reaction) to occur. B was watching a newscast about a local businessman who was charged with murder. The accused's business partner (A) was being interviewed:

*A: He was a conscientious, fair, honest businessman on most of the business deals that he handled.

The literal meaning of A's utterance is that the accused possessed honourable qualities as a businessman most of the time. However, the construction of his praise is odd because A implies that the accused was not necessarily honourable in all of his business deals. This construction may have been used in order to defend the accused while still telling the truth (i.e., an equivocation). Alternatively, it may simply be that A does not have information on all of his partner's business deals, so he is being very precise in what he says.

> B: (Viewing at home) Oh, MOST of the deals he handled!

B seems to notice that A may have been "waffling," and she focuses on that possible meaning, that is, that the accused was dishonest in some of his business dealings. Because the medium precludes reciprocal communication, A is not aware of B's reaction. Therefore, he is unable to confirm B's reaction as appropriate or inappropriate, and they could not accomplish an effective meaning.

8. Politicians are notorious for manipulating language for their own benefit. One means of accomplishing this goal is to place themselves in situations where communication is inherently problematic, that is, where the steps of semantic collaboration are violated. The following is an example of an interaction between then–Prime Minister Brian Mulroney (A) and a reporter (B) about his planned ceremonial trip to the United States at a time when he had major problems in Canada:

> B: Why are you going to the signing of the NAFTA agreement when you are not required to be there?
>
> *A: Would you have me deny an invitation from the president of the most important country in the world?

The literal meaning of A's question is to ask whether B would feel it appropriate for the prime minister to turn down an invitation from the president of the most important country in the world (referring to George Bush and the United States). Note, however, that this utterance is not only an equivocation (i.e., A answers B's question with a question), but it also manipulates the issue by inventing an offense to George Bush and placing responsibility for this squarely on the reporter. Finally, A clearly implies that Canada (and its people) are less important than the United States (and its people). However, because of the setting, which made challenging the person holding the press conference difficult, steps 2 and 3 did not occur. Not only the reporter but also the audience viewing on television (a "collective B") were unable to react effectively to A's utterance, so A did not have to confirm any of their possible reactions. In a sense, A "got away with" his statement because there was no opportunity for semantic collaboration; he avoided taking responsibility for the negative implications of his utterance. We propose that many politicians are able to manipulate language so astutely in part because they recognize the power of using ambiguous language in contexts where they will not have to answer directly for their comments, that is, when semantic collaboration is not possible.

9. A final example of problematic semantic collaboration expands on the ability of politicians to manipulate language to avoid responsibility for their statements. Former federal cabinet minister John Crosbie quipped, in a 1990 after-dinner speech in Victoria, that Sheila Copps's Liberal leadership bid reminded him of a song that goes:

*A: "Pass me the tequila, Sheila, and lie down and love me again."

The literal meaning of A's utterance is that Crosbie is having an affair with Copps and wants her to give him some tequila and to have sexual intercourse with him again. Among the reasons that this is an egregiously offensive and inappropriate comment are that (a) Crosbie and Copps are not in an intimate relationship, so his insinuation is slanderous; (b) he insults her abilities as a possible candidate by casting her in an inferior role (servant, concubine) to him; and (c) he is implying, metaphorically, that because Copps is a woman, her worth is based on her ability to satisfy a man sexually, and she should not waste her time vying for a leadership position. It is crucial to our point that the context in which the utterance was made (an after-dinner speech at which Copps was not present) and then the medium in which it was subsequently reported (newspaper) did not permit a direct reaction to A's utterance. Had he made the remark in the House of Commons, Copps would certainly have let him know her reaction, as she had done with considerable wit on similar past occasions. When Crosbie was later confronted with the widespread reaction that his remark was offensive and inappropriate, he offered the following explanation (renegotiation or confirmation):

A: I was only joking!

That is, he indicated that the collective B reaction was inappropriate. This is a case where those who choose not to believe Crosbie's explanation refuse to collaborate on the effective meaning of his initial utterance; that is, we can never agree on its meaning. The opportunity for successful collaboration reached an impasse and was abandoned.

All of these examples demonstrate the importance of semantic collaboration for accomplishing the effective meaning of utterances in successful communication. Whereas the implicit and explicit examples of semantic collaboration illustrate the complete process, the problematic examples highlight the importance of alignment of all three steps and how misinterpretation and manipulation can result when this condition is not met. Indeed, these were the instances that originally led to our interest in the problem of meaning and to the development of this theory. The remainder of this chapter is devoted to consideration of problematic semantic collaboration in many forms of communication.

Imposing Meaning

An important feature of examples 6 to 9 is that one person's reaction was, effectively, enforced silence. In each case, we would argue, this was because that person (usually B) was denied the opportunity to collaborate, for one (or both) of two important reasons: hierarchical power or the medium of communication. The pilot's authority silenced the co-pilot; the reporter's status in a press conference made it difficult to object to the prime minister's statements; the medium of television made it obviously impossible for the viewer to negotiate the meaning of "most of his deals"; and the social setting of John Crosbie's speech operated in the same way, to exclude the listeners' reaction.[5]

If meaning were "in" words, contexts, or speaker's intentions, the reason for the silence would be irrelevent because A's utterance would have an intrinsic meaning independent of B's reaction, opinion, or even presence. However, in our view, B's right to participate in the collaboration is vital. If B's reaction is precluded, then the sequence can become:

1. Utterance

2. *Imposed* reaction

3. *Pseudo*-confirmation

all of which are controlled by A. When B is silenced, A controls the entire process and is imposing meaning rather than collaborating on meaning, making an inherently social process unilateral.

Propaganda is an important instance of this imposition of meaning. A recent example was the apparently innocuous choice of name for the organization that the federal government established to advocate support for the "Yes" side in the 1992 constitutional referendum; they called themselves the "Canada Committee." This name equated a "yes" vote with Canada itself, thereby implying that a person who voted "no" on the referendum was not a (real) Canadian. The other implication was that a "yes" vote would keep Canada together as one country, while a "no" vote was a vote against the country—rather than a vote against a particular set of constitutional amendments. This is a case of a subtly imposed meaning, which there was no opportunity to reject or even challenge.

Certain forms of communication are inherently problematic because they are unilateral in nature: Television, radio, newspapers, books and articles, even art—in brief, "the media"—all eliminate the opportunity for the listener to respond immediately or effectively. The individual Bs are limited to letters to the editor, call-in programs, or reliance on a like-minded editorial commentator to challenge the original utterance. Even if these reactions eventually reach an audible threshold of collective B reaction (i.e., objection), A always has a "back door" to retreat through: "I was just joking!" or "You misunderstood me." Once the listener's reaction has been precluded, the collaborative process is fractionated, and meaning becomes instead an individual interpretive process. When the process can no longer be collaborative, the potential for manipulation of interpretations is omnipresent.

For example, advertising slogans can sculpt meanings not only about the product but about people and the world around them; for example, "Be young, have fun, drink Pepsi!" or "Don't hate me because I'm beautiful!" Notice that these ads do not characterize the product (a soft drink and a shampoo) at all. Rather they impose a link between use of the product and qualities that people might gain by using them (youth, happiness, beauty). Moreover, they imply that these particular personal qualities are everyone's ultimate goal; why not "Be mature, be serious, drink Pepsi"? And suppose, instead of a unilateral ad, a stranger said to you in person, "Don't hate me because I'm beautiful." You as B might have a variety of reactions, including explicit semantic collaboration, such as

> So, are you saying that you're beautiful, I'm not, and that I am so superficial, insecure, and completely lacking in integrity as to be concerned only with your appearance? Do I look like I care? And, by the way, who invited you?

Or, simply,

> Why would I, when there are clearly so many other reasons to?

When semantic collaboration is precluded, these kinds of advertising slogans and their connotations can become accepted as true because no one has or takes the opportunity to question the validity or basis of their claims; acceptance is inferred from the listeners' imposed silence and taken as acceptance or appropriate continuation. We view this use of the media to impose views on people and to regulate both the information they receive and their ability to respond as an extension of what Chomsky (1992) called "manufacturing consent."

Our final application concerns the evolution of "politically correct" language. For example, the term "man" was long accepted (or imposed) as meaning "humans" or "people," both male and female. At some point, this usage was questioned; were women collectively being excluded, subsumed, or treated as an exception to the male norm? Clearly, any members of a group (based on gender, race, handicap, sexual orientation, etc.) who are being described have a legitimate desire and right to collaborate on the terms used to describe them. For example, in the United States, there has been a change from "Coloreds" to "Negroes" to "Blacks" to "Afro-Americans" to "African Americans." People are still in the process of negotiating mutually acceptable terms for referring to each other; is the solution to impose a "politically correct" alternative?

To us, it is important and fascinating that people sometimes call themselves "niggers," "fags," or "bitches"—all terms they would presumably object to an outsider using for them. This apparent contradiction derives from the false idea that the term itself "has" an offensive meaning. That is, to see these terms as *intrinsically* offensive is the same as saying that they "contain" offensive meanings. Our alternative view is that their meaning is and will remain open to collaboration. For example, if the person chooses to use such a term in reference to himself or herself among friends, with appropriate reaction and confirmation that the term is not being used for the purpose of degradation, then the effective meaning is *not* offensive and indeed is quite different from the effective meaning of the same term in another interaction. This state of affairs may bother those who wish to legislate for or against specific, literal terms, but to us that goal is futile. We can only work together within interactions, focusing on mutual understanding as the desired goal of communication.

The ultimate goal of communication is the exchange of meaningful messages. However, when semantic collaboration is problematic, regardless of the reasons, communication serves to divide people instead of bringing them together. This collaborative theory of meaning not only redefines how meaning is accomplished in communication but highlights the interlocutors' actual, immediate interaction as the process by which language has meaning. There are no right or wrong terms or constructions in communication, simply a need to collaborate. It is neither the speaker's sole responsibility to speak clearly and explicitly nor is it the addressee's sole responsibility to read the speaker's mind in order to interpret utterances appropriately. Instead, both are responsible for ensuring that collaboration occurs. The collaborative approach proposes that interlocutors must actively cooperate and share responsibility for the success or failure of communication.

Notes

1. This chapter is adapted from Roberts (1993). We are grateful to Dr. Herbert H. Clark for his detailed comments on our penultimate version.

2. The literature on meaning is obviously an extensive one, whereas our review will select only certain features. For a similar review, in more detail, see Kess (1992); for an analysis of the need to move past individually based theories of meaning, see Clark (1992).

3. With the possible exception of puns and double entendres.

4. We should re-emphasize here that we are not describing or speculating about the cognitive process whereby B came to this interpretation; our interest is the observable process of collaboration.

5. Enforced silence in these situations is fundamentally different from other kinds of silence in natural dialogue. For example, spontaneous silence can be a form of appropriate continuation, indicating acceptance because both people have had the opportunity to object or negotiate. Alternatively, spontaneous silence after an explicit request for a reply (e.g., "Do you forgive me?") can be an equivocation (Bavelas et al., 1990, p. 168). We are focusing here on situations that *constrain* the other person(s) to silence.

References

Austin, J. L. (1962). *How to do things with words*. New York: Oxford University Press.

Bavelas, J. B., A. Black, N. Chovil, and J. Mullett (1990). *Equivocal communication*. Newbury Park, CA: Sage.

Bavelas, J. B., and N. Chovil (1993). *Redefining language. An integrated message model of language in face-to-face interaction*. Unpubl. ms., Department of Psychology, University of Victoria.

Bavelas, J. B., Chovil, N., Coates, L., and Roe, L (1995). Gestures specialized for dialogue. *Personality and Social Psychology Bulletin*, 21, 394–405.

Bavelas, J. B., and Coates, L. (1992). How do we account for the mindfulness of face-to-face dialogue? *Communication Monographs*, 59, 301–5.

Chomsky, N. (1992). *Manufacturing consent: Noam Chomsky and the media*. (Videorecording). Montreal: Necessary Illusions.

Clark, H. H. (1992). *Arenas of language use*. Chicago: University of Chicago Press.

Clark, H. H., and C. R. Marshall (1981). Definite reference and mutual knowledge. In A. K. Joshi, B. L. Webber, and I. A. Sag (Eds.), *Elements of discourse understanding* (pp. 10–63). Cambridge: Cambridge University Press.

Clark, H. H., and E. F. Schaefer (1987). Collaborating on contributions to conversations. *Language and Cognitive Processes*, 2, 19–41.

Clark, H. H., and D. Wilkes-Gibbs (1986). Referring as a collaborative process. *Cognition*, 22, 1–39.

Coates, L. (1991). *A collaborative theory of inversion: Irony in dialogue*. Unpublished master's thesis, Department of Psychology, University of Victoria.

Crystal, D. (1991). *A dictionary of linguistics and phonetics (3rd ed.)*. Oxford: Basil Blackwood.

Davis, K. (1986). The process of problem (re)formulation in pschotherapy. *Sociology of Health and Illness*, 8, 44–74.

Ellis, R. (1985). *Understanding second language acquisition*. Oxford: Oxford University Press.

Goguen, J., and C. Linde (1981). *Linguistic methodology for the analysis of aviation accidents*. (Contract no. NAS2-11052). Palo Alto, CA: Ames Research Centre, National Aeronautics and Space Administration.

Grice, H. P. (1975). Logic and conversation. In P. Cole and J. L. Morgan (eds.), *Syntax and semantics: Speech acts* (Vol. 3, pp. 225–42). New York: Academic Press.

———. (1989). *Studies in the way of words*. Cambridge, MA: Harvard University Press.

Jackson, H. (1990). *Grammar and meaning. A semantic approach to English grammar*. London: Longman.

Kess, J. (1992). *Psycholinguistics. Psychology, linguistics, and the study of natural language*. Amsterdam: Benjamins.

Lakoff, G., and M. Johnson (1980). *Metaphors we live by*. Chicago: University of Chicago Press.

Linell, P. (1982). *The written language bias in linguistics*. Linkoping, Sweden: Department of Communication Studies, University of Linkoping.

Nelson, K. (1985). *Making sense. The acquisition of shared meaning*. Orlando: Academic Press.

O'Grady, W., and M. Dobrovolsky (1992). *Contemporary linguistic analysis. An Introduction (2nd ed.)*. Toronto: Copp Clark Pitman.

Reddy, M. (1979). The conduit metaphor—a case of frame conflict in our language about language. In A. Ortony (ed.), *Metaphor and thought* (pp. 284–324). Cambridge: Cambridge University Press.

Roberts, G. L. (1993). *The communicative dictionary: A collaborative theory of meaning*. Unpublished honour's thesis, Department of Psychology, University of Victoria.

Saussure, F. (1959). *Course in general linguistics*. New York: McGraw-Hill.

Schober, M., and H. H. Clark (1989). Understanding by addressees and overhearers. *Cognitive Psychology*, 21, 211–32.

Searle, J. R. (1969). *Speech acts*. London: Cambridge University Press.

———. (1975). Indirect Speech Acts. In P. Cole & J. L. Morgan (eds.), *Syntax and semantics: Speech acts* (Vol. 3, pp. 59–82). New York: Academic Press.

Swannell, J. (1986). *The little Oxford dictionary (6th ed.)*. Oxford: Clarendon.

Tough, J. (1977). *The development of meaning. A study of children's use of language*. New York: Wiley.

Yule, G. (1985). *The study of language*. Cambridge: Cambridge University Press.

Part II

Postmodern Rediscoveries

Editor's Introduction

The two chapters in this section reflect on the representational nature of language by attending closely to the works of two seminal thinkers, Friedrich Nietzsche and Jean-François Lyotard. Each has contributed significantly to the loosely related complex of perspectives called "postmodernism." Nietzsche is arguably the progenitor of the entire postmodern impetus in philosophy. His approach and his writings are focal, in different ways, for Heidegger, Derrida, Foucault, Deleuze, Baudrillard, Lyotard, and other prominent critical theorists. Lyotard's proscription of grand theorizing is accepted by most postmodern writers, and he also authored a putatively postsemiotic account of designation and signification.

In this chapter, Ernst Behler, professor of comparative literature, argues that, although "it would not make much sense to compile a coherent theory of language from [Nietzsche's] various fragmentary statements," there is in Nietzsche's corpus "a fundamental reflection on language, in a continuous process of questioning the problems of expression and communication in a basic manner." Behler demonstrates how all but a few scholars have overlooked the centrality of rhetoric to the view of language Nietzsche developed especially in *On Truth and Lie in a Nonmoral Sense*. This insight enables Behler to reveal the close conceptual link between Nietzsche's account of language and his critiques of metaphysics and reason. Since the pre-socratics, rhetoric has focused on the historicity, occasionality, finitude, temporality, and human variability of discursive life. All these features were present in Nietzsche's discussions of language, and they were echoed in the critiques Nietzsche offered of "fundamental reality," "universal reason," and "ultimate truth."

Behler begins with a biographical sketch that shows how "the theme of a philosophy of language was indeed fundamentally rooted in [Nietzsche's] existence and education." He distinguishes between works written during and after Nietzsche's university associations, which he terminated in 1878 at the age of thirty-four because of ill health. Behler also reminds readers of the unreliability of the pseudo-Nietzsche *The Will to Power*.

163

Behler argues that Nietzsche's early writings on language were part of his "relentless self-critique of philosophy, and attempt at overcoming the metaphysical binds of a theory of language." Nietzsche first considerd language as a "product of instinct," an art to be contrasted with music because it is marked by an "infinitely deficient symbolism." He was also caught up with Rosseau, Herder, and others in speculations about the origin of language, and argued against the notion that the ground of language was consciousness. Instead, he saw language and consciousness as coexistent; as Behler puts it, there was for Nietzsche "no zone free of language in consciousness."

The Birth of Tragedy characterized music "as a kind of primordial language, even before poetry," which was "capable of representing and expressing the Primordial One in an immediate, i.e., unmediated manner." But shortly thereafter, "Nietzsche's early theory of lanaguage begins to dissolve and that nonrepresentative, rhetorical conception of art and language emerges, which is fully articulated in *On Truth and Lie in a Nonmoral Sense.*" In this work Nietzsche confronted the central problem of Neoplatonism, "which is to explain the transition from unity (of being) into plurality and the world of appearances." This fundamental problem of representation moved Nietzsche to "the position according to which everything is language and there is no privileged language having direct access to being." In his later writings, Nietzsche described this phase of his intellectual development "as a process of liberation and emancipation."

The next phase in the development of his theory of language occurred as he undertook an intensive study of rhetoric in preparation for his lectures on rhetoric at the University of Basel during the winter semester of 1872–73. As rhetoric, language does not present itself as an expression of truth but as a coping with pragmatic exigence, whether in deliberative, forensic, or epideictic discourse, poetry, drama, or prose. This realization led Nietzsche to interrogate what chapters 1, 2, and 3 of this work discuss as the philosophical commitment to two worlds. As Behler puts it, "under the impact of this rhetorical thinking . . . everything non-linguistic that had served only to safeguard language had to be removed from the philosophy of language to reveal language as merely language, as a rhetorical means." In this move, Behler notes, Nietzsche was especially influenced by Gustav Gerber's text *Language as Art*, which argued for the inherent tropical or metaphoric nature of all words. Nietzsche integrated "Gerber's critical observations on language into a comprehensive critical discourse directed against metaphysics and our metaphysical presuppositions in general. This discourse dominates Nietzsche's later writings and indicates that his early critical reflections on language were by no means a passing event, but of a lasting importance for the formation of his thought."

On Truth and Lie frames reason rhetorically. "With words," wrote Nietzsche, "it is never a question of truth, never a question of adequate expression. . . . [W]e possess nothing but metaphors for things—metaphors which correspond in no way to the original entities. . . ." In fact, "When someone hides something behind a bush and looks for it again in the same place and finds it there as well, there is not much to praise in such seeking and finding. Yet this is how matters stand regarding seeking and finding 'truth' within the realm of reason."

Philippe Lacoue-Labarthe argues that Nietzsche's study of rhetoric was decisive, because it convinced him "that everything, even music, is rhetorical and that which the Greeks, those exemplary human beings, produced as their 'highest' was not philosophy and poetry, but rhetoric." But, Behler notes, Lacoue-Labarthe sees Nietzsche's early auto-critique as a detour that could have been avoided had he studied rhetoric earlier. Paul de Man, says Behler, more effectively relates Nietzsche's rhetorically oriented theory of language to his entire oeuvre.

The crucial point, however, is that *On Truth and Lie* manifests Nietzsche's conviction that "language does not entitle us to a decision concerning the nature of things, but that we remain enclosed in the inner laws of language." But this "language" is not simply the technical system analyzed by many of Nietzsche's intellectual forebears in philosophy and linguistics. As a fundamentally rhetorical phenomenon, language is more event than substance or presence. Although Behler does not make this point here, this is surely one of the insights Heidegger took from Nietzsche.

Once more, the reader may note in this chapter how an account of the nature of language evolves when the centrality of communicating is affirmed. Behler demonstrates how the Nietzschean critiques of metaphysics and reason that help fuel contemporary postmodernism resonate strongly with Nietzsche's fundamentally rhetorical and communicative account of the nature of language.

5

Friedrich Nietzche's Theory of Language and Its Reception in Contemporary Thought

Ernst Behler

A brief look at Nietzsche's life and upbringing shows that the theme of a philosophy of language was indeed fundamentally rooted in his existence and education. He was born October 15, 1844, in Röcken near Lützen (eastern Germany) as the son of a family deriving from Protestant pastors on the side of his father as well as his mother.[1] After the early death of his father, Carl Ludwig Nietzsche (1813–49), the family moved to Naumburg, where Nietzsche obtained an excellent education, concentrating on the humanities, including music, under the guidance of his mother, Franziska Nietzsche, née Oehler. From 1858 to 1864, Nietzsche received his secondary education with a strong emphasis on Greek and Roman literature and philosophy at the School of Pforta, an elite school open only through competition. At the beginning of the winter semester of 1864, he took up his studies of theology and classical philology at the University of Bonn and became associated with the influential classical scholar Friedrich Ritschl. When Ritschl moved to the University of Leipzig in 1865, Nietzsche followed him, concentrating his studies exlusively on classical philology. In Leipzig, he entered upon an exciting intellectual life that acquainted him with the philosophy of Arthur Schopenhauer, from then on a major influence for his thought. He also distinguished himself as a student with independent publications on Diogenes Laertius, and Theognis. The period in Leipzig is additionally marked by Nietzsche's discovery of Richard Wagner and his complete "conversion" to him. Before even obtaining his Ph.D., Nietzsche, as a privileged disciple of Ritschl, was offered the position of an "extraordinary" (associate) professor of classical philology in 1869 at the University of Basel, Switzerland, and promoted to "ordinary" (full) professor in the same field by 1870. The University of Leipzig then gave him the doctoral diploma on the basis of what he had already published. Nietzsche began his academic activity at Basel with lectures on the history of Greek literature and Latin grammar. The last lecture of winter semester 1869–70 reveals his occupation with the philosophy of language for the first time in a coherent and prominent manner.

In Basel, Nietzsche maintained intellectual contacts with a number of colleagues, among them the historian Jakob Burchhardt and the Protestant theologian Franz Overbeck. Beginning with May 1869, he established a close personal relationship with Richard Wagner and Cosima von Bülow, whom Nietzsche frequently visited in their house in Tribschen near Lucerne. Delivering lectures and engaging in private writings in Basel from 1871 to 1872, Nietzsche produced his first major publication, *The Birth of Tragedy Out of the Spirit of Music*. Dedicated to Richard Wagner, the work is permeated by the philosophy of Schopenhauer. The brilliant text combines several discourses and makes it difficult to reduce it to a common denominator. At first glance, *The Birth of Tragedy* appears as a work of classical philology concentrating on the historical origins of Greek tragedy. The distinction between the Apollonian and Dionysian styles of art soon introduce an additional level of aesthetic theory, even of cultural anthropology. At about the middle of the text, the world of the Greeks is progressively abandoned, and attention shifts to the rebirth of the Dionysian spirit in the modern age through Wagner's universal work of art combining music, poetry, mythology, and stage setting in a modern equivalent of ancient Greek tragedy. Among these various themes, music is certainly the one most closely related to Nietzsche's theory of language. For the early Nietzsche, music is the most powerful medium of human expression, a protolanguage, which permits us not only to designate, represent, and imitate the essence of existence, what he called the "Primordial One," but to bring this ground of being to direct expression, an idea taken from Schopenhauer. Nietzsche's contemporaries in classical scholarship sharply rejected the views articulated in the *The Birth of Tragedy*, but today the book enjoys a fine reputation in that discipline, too.

During winter semester of 1872–73, Nietzsche offered a course on Greek and Roman rhetoric, which led him to an intensive study of the theory of language, not only with regard to the ancients but also in terms of modern times, especially following Herder and the period of romanticism. Nietzsche developed a predominantly rhetorical and metaphorical conception of language in these lectures, a view of "language as art," making language a highly unreliable organ for science and the search for truth. Nietzsche condensed this approach to language in his treatise *On Truth and Lie in a Nonmoral Sense*, which he wrote on the basis of his study of rhetoric during the summer of 1873 but never published. Here he articulated his critical views of language in the imposing thesis that our philosophical-scientific formation of concepts oriented toward truth is preceded by an artistic formation of images, metaphors, for which the abstract search for truth is irrelevant and which is dominated by an aesthetic interest instead. Still in Basel, Nietzsche published his *Unfashionable Considerations* from 1873 to 1876, four treatises critical of trends of his time: on David Friedrich Strauß and modern Bible exegesis, on historicism in the developing historical disciplines, on the philosophical ethos of Arthur Schopenhauer in contrast to other contemporary philosophers, and on the impact of Richard Wagner's music. None of these texts relates directly to themes of a theory of language, but from then on the topic of language is present in every Nietzschean text.

Nietzsche's next writing, *Human, All Too Human*, appeared in three parts (1878, 1879, 1880) with the subtitle *A Book for Free Spirits*. Although the first edition is dedicated to Voltaire, the designation "free spirit" is not to be understood as freethinker in the sense of the Enlightenment, but rather as becoming free, as separation and emancipation from tradition, which for Nietzsche meant from the German traditions of romanticism, idealism, Wagnerianism, but also from Christianity and Western metaphysics in a more general sense, that is, from "Platonism." All these phenomena are to be reduced to the "Human, All Too Human" according to the device: "where *you* see ideal things, *I* see—the human, alas the all too human" (EH [*Human, All Too Human*], Aph. 1; KSA 6, 322).[2] This certainly includes the idealized view of language as a perfect means of designation and communication. In Aphorism 11 of the First Part, Nietzsche ridicules the human belief "to really possess in language the knowledge of the world." From then on, and more so emphatically in the following writings, Nietzsche shifts his critique of language to something prior to and operative in language that controls it, something he calls grammar, logic, reason, knowledge, but also race, atavism, instinct, or simply the physiological conditions of the human being.

The texts of *Human, All Too Human* also differ from Nietzsche's previous writings in that they are no longer written in the form of a treatise or essay, but as short, polished aphorisms. This tendency is already noticeable in his earlier texts. If the notion of aphorism is at all applicable to these earlier writings, these aphorisms were longer, more coherent, and had the rhythm of a development of thought, whereas now they appear shorter, more precise, instantaneous, and less coherent. They now correspond to Nietzsche's conviction about the unrecognizability of the world through language, grammar, or reason, and attempt to render this conviction that is incommunicable through language and reason, by means of a rapid change in position, through "perspectivism," for which the aphoristic style is well suited.

The appearance of the First Part of *Human, All Too Human* marks the end of Nietzsche's friendship and intellectual relationship with Richard Wagner, the foundations of which had long since been shattered. At the time of the appearance of the Second Part, Nietzsche had left his professional association with the university, retiring at the age of thirty-four because of recurring and deteriorating fits of disease such as migraines, giddiness, and vomiting that he likened to the feeling of seasickness. On June 14, 1878, the president of the administrative region of Basel approved his request and granted him a pension for the following six years. From then on, Nietzsche lived without a permanent domicile, as a "fugitivus errans," in those regions of Switzerland and northern Italy agreeable to his state of health, that is, mostly in Sils-Maria in the Upper Engadin during the summer; in Genova, Rapallo, Nice, Portofino, and Venice during the following seasons; occasionally also in southern Italy (Sorrento) and Sicily (Taormina), but rarely in Germany. In the spring of 1888 he discovered Torino but toward the end of January 1889 he fell insane there, stricken by his fate.

During this interval, Nietzsche published one book after the other with most impressive titles and in a language overloaded with images, visions, and metaphors: *Dawn* (1881), *The Gay Science* (1882), *Thus Spoke Zarathustra* (1883, 1884, 1895), *Beyond Good and Evil* (1886), *On the Genealogy of Morals* (1887), *The Case of Wagner* (1888), *Twilight of the Idols* (1889), *The Antichrist* (1889), *Ecce Homo* (1889), *Dionysus Dithyrambs* (1889), *Nietzsche contra Wagner* (1889). In spite of some friendships he entertained during these years, Nietzsche, as far as communication is concerned, stood in a broken relationship with the world. He first communicated in monological fashion through the publication of his writings but was eventually to receive unsurpassed responses from the public in many parts of the world and from a variety of disciplines, such as art, science, literature, and philosophy, a reception with which no modern author can compete. With the exception of the *Dionysus Dithyrambs* and *Thus Spoke Zarathustra*, all of these writings are composed in aphoristic style. *Thus Spoke Zarathustra* takes the form of direct, prophetic communication ("O, my friends, I tell you"), but even this style contains so much parody, caricature, and irony that it is impossible to reduce the text to one single meaning. Some of the last writings refer in their notes or subtitles to a more comprehensive and coherent book project bearing the title "Revaluation of Values," but this endeavor to provide a more cohesive structure to his work soon evaporated, and Nietzsche continued to write in a manner typical for him since *Human, All Too Human*, namely, in an aphoristic, incoherent style.

At about that time, Nietzsche developed a project known under the title, "The Will to Power: Attempt at a Revaluation of all Values." This project occupied him from the autumn of 1884 to the summer of 1888 and is mainly concerned with his unpublished fragments. Nietzsche tried to establish systematic connections for these fragments, attempting to structure them according to a central principle constituting the core of his doctrine. In a most extreme contradiction to all idealism and Platonism, he conceived of this principle as a drive termed the will to power. Some sketches have been transmitted showing how Nietzsche had projected the arrangement of this book. In the summer of 1888, however, he dropped this plan that had proven to be unrealizable because of the resistance of his texts to such treatment.

This episode of Nietzsche's literary production would be of little significance, had it not been the occasion for Elisabeth Förster-Nietzsche, Nietzsche's sister and the curator of his writings, to produce such a work titled *The Will to Power* by compiling parts of the unpublished texts. She obviously felt that a central work of philosophy was lacking and wanted to correct this deficiency. This work, compiled by editors and certainly not really a text by Nietzsche himself, has nevertheless strongly influenced Nietzsche interpretation during the first half of this century. Today, however, it is no longer recognized as a Nietzsche text. The fragments of this compiled edition are now part of the section of all the unpublished fragments in the complete edition and arranged chronologically according to the years 1884 to 1889 but without the sensational title and claim to constituting the main work. When *The Will to Power* was constructed, Nietzsche was already in a state of deep mental derangement. On January 3, 1889, he collapsed mentally on the Piazza Carlo Alberto in Torino and from then on lived first in the care of his mother in Naumburg and then beginning in April 1897 with his sister in Weimar. During these years, Nietzsche's fame rose, and he died on August 25, 1900.

Nietzsche's early writings are of crucial importance for his theory of language.[3] Most fascinating in his early occupation with this theme is the progressive development, the dynamic movement of his thought from 1869 until the summer of 1873, when his text *On Truth and Lie in a Nonmoral Sense* originated. During this interval of only three to four years, Nietzsche traverses the most important philosophical systems of modern philosophy, as far as the theme of human language is concerned, those of Herder, Kant, Schelling, Schopenhauer, and Eduard von Hartmann, to name only the most important authors. The process of this movement has paradigmatic character for modern thought about language and can be characterized as a relentless self-critique of philosophy, an attempt at overcoming the metaphysical binds of a theory of language. The result of this process consists in the thesis of "Human, All too Human," which summarizes this overcoming of metaphysics in compact fashion. In his Prefaces to this text, Nietzsche emphasized how much self-discipline and self-restraint were needed to pursue this pathway of thought and how difficult it had been for him.[4]

If one turns to the early Nietzsche from the vantage-point of a self-critical development of his thought, interest in particular results or contents of knowledge recedes, even if these topics concern such prominent themes as the distinction of the Apollonian and Dionysian, the interpretation of the tragic and the chorus of Greek tragedy, the wedding of philology and philosophy, the occupation with classical rhetoric, or the outline of Greek literary history. These themes do not lose their importance, but appear from this point of view as examples, as manifestations, of a dramatic process of thought of larger dimensions, the overriding movement of which Nietzsche interpreted as emancipation, as self-liberation. This also applies to the theory of language of the early Nietzsche. It would not make much sense to compile a coherent theory of language from his various fragmentary statements on language of this time, which could be used as Nietzsche's contribution to a comparative history of the philosophy of language. The particular character of his thoughts on language consists in a fundamental reflection on language, in a continuous process of questioning the problems of expression and communication in a basic manner.

The theme of language is, furthermore, specifically linked to the writings of the early Nietzsche because he never again dealt with problems of language in such an intensified fashion. His earliest pronouncement on language can be found in a fragment of 1869–70 *On the Origin of Language* now considered to be part of his *Lectures on Latin Grammar* of the same time.[5] In this text he attempts to consider language "as a product of instinct, as with bees—the anthill, etc." (LG, 186). Instinct here is not a mechanism coming from outside, but as "the most proper accomplishment of an individual or of a group, derives from its character." To determine this type of a development of language more closely, Nietzsche refers to the "infinite purposiveness" or teleology in Kant's *Critique of Judgment*, which is a "purposiveness without purpose," or he refers to Schelling's notion of unconscious creation, which outdoes the conscious activity "by far." He thereby rejects all other derivations of language from "consensus," divine inspiration, feeling, or a "reflective activity of the mind." Kant related this teleological conception, according to which "something is purposeful without consciousness," not only to nature, however, but also to art (LG, 188). In this sense, Nietzsche describes music as an art "in which the effect of instinct is overwhelming" (KSA 7, 49), or as a language "which is capable of infinite elucidation" (KSA 7, 47), whereas language (not so much spoken, but written language) is marked by an "infinitely deficient symbolism" (KSA 7, 63). Language represents the "Apollonian" (KSA 7, 159), whereas music as a "Dionysian" art represents a type of art "which is not 'appearance of appearance', but 'appearance of being'" (KSA 7, 184). Nietzsche constantly emphasizes "how unnatural, even impossible the attempt is to produce music for a poem, that is, to want to illustrate a poem with music, perhaps even with the declared intention of symbolizing the conceptual representations of the poem through music and of providing music with a conceptual language" (KSA 7, 185). The "visions of the Primordial One," as "adequate mirrorings of Being," can only be expressed by a "genius" as the "highest peak of rapture in the world" (KSA 7, 199–200).

This origin of language from instinct or an unconscious teleology is characteristic for the early Nietzsche's thinking about language until far into his composition of *The Birth of Tragedy*. This approach is dominant in his *Lectures on Latin Grammar* of the winter semester of 1869–70 that also evidence how thoroughly familiar he was with the topic of language and the main representatives of a theory of language. The easiest, he maintains, is to determine "how the origin of language is *not* to be thought." Language is "neither the work of individuals nor of a majority," because every form of conscious thought is only possible through language (LG, 185).[6] Language and consciousness are coexistent, and there is no zone free of language in consciousness. The assumption of an animalistic language of sounds as a starting point for our language does not help either because the "marvelously thoughtful organism" of language already contains the "deepest philosophical knowledge" in a state of preparation. Kant, as far as this point is concerned, is right when he says: "a large part, perhaps the largest, of the activity of reason consists in the analysis of concepts which reason finds as already pregiven" (ib.).

The puzzle of language and the fact that its "origin cannot be proven through the nature of things" (LG, 187) is clearly demonstrated for Nietzsche in the history of various theories of language "from the Indians, the Greeks, to the most recent times" (LG, 185). The Greeks were already confronted by the question "whether language is θέδει or φύδει, that is, constituted by arbitrary production, contract and consensus, or by a conceptual content of the sounding substance" (LG, 186). These ancient positions were repeated in modern times when the mathematician Maupertius, for instance, maintained the theory of a "consensus as the basis" for language. Another question arising in this context is "whether language could have originated through merely human mental power or as a direct gift of God." The Old Testament is the only religious document that gives us information about the origin of language. Here God and man speak the same language, "not so as with the Greeks." God and man give names to things "that express the relationship of the thing to the human being." The giving of names to animals in the Old Testament, but also the "arbitrary giving of names" in Plato's *Cratylus*, however, presuppose "a language before language." About this "origin of language," the peoples remain silent: "they cannot imagine the world, the Gods, and human beings without it" (LG, 186–87).

Modern theories of language are also shipwrecked on this question. It was impossible according to Rousseau "that languages could originate by purely human means," whereas De Brosses maintains a "purely human origin." Monboddo assumes a "reflective activity of the mind" and relinquishes a "primitive language." For twenty-one years he worked on his theory, but the difficulties only increased. About one hundred years before Nietzsche's lectures, the Berlin Academy of Sciences called for a competition concerning the origin of language, in which Herder won the prize. He is the originator of the important idea that the human being is "born for language," which manifests itself in the impressive statement: "Therefore the genesis of language is such an inner urge as the urge of the embryo for birth at the moment of maturity." Like his predecessors, however, Herder maintains an origin of language from "expressive sounds" (LG, 187–88). Only with Kant's idea of a "teleology in nature" in the *Critique of Judgment* did the right insight emerge. Kant emphasized the "marvelous antinomy" according to which "something can be purposeful without consciousness." Nietzsche comments: "This the essence of instinct." To enforce this thought, he quotes Schelling, who in the Introduction to his *Philosophy of Mythology* had written:

> Since without language not only no philosophical, but also no human consciousness can be thought, the ground of language cannot be placed in consciousness; and moreover the more we penetrate language, the more precisely we discover that its depth by far surpasses the depth of the most consciously created product. It is with language as it is with organic beings; we believe to see them originate blindly and cannot deny the impenetrable intentionality of their formation down to the most detailed feature.[7]

As is obvious in his early approach to language, Nietzsche proceeds problematically by pointing out the insolubility of the problem in earlier theories and their mutual contradictions. He does not stop short at this sceptical position, however, but develops his own theory of an origin of language on the basis of the indeterminable purposiveness of instinct and writes:

Nothing remains, therefore, but to consider language as a product of instinct, as with bees—the anthill, etc. Instinct, however, is not the result
of conscious considerations, not the consequence of corporeal organization, not the result of a mechanism which has been placed in the brain,
not the effect of a mechanism coming from outside of the mind and alien
in its essence, but the most proper achievement of an individual or a
multitude, deriving from its character. Instinct is even one with the innermost kernel of an essence. This is the true problem of philosophy, the
infinite purposiveness of organisms and the unconsciousness of their origin (LG, 186).

The instinctual origin of language is still the basis for Nietzsche's
remarks on language in *The Birth of Tragedy* and closely related to his
emphatic statements about music as a language before language and the
capability of music to directly express the last ground of all beings, the
"Primordial One." The theory of language in this text thereby articulates
itself as a metaphysical theory of absolute representation because the human being is capable of representing and expressing the Primordial One in
an immediate, that is, unmediated manner. This is possible, however, not
through language, but only through art, more precisely, through music. In
the sixteenth section of this text, Nietzsche quotes the famous passage in
Schopenhauer's *The World as Will and Representation,* according to which
music is different from all the other arts "because, unlike them, it is not a
copy of the phenomenon, but an immediate copy of the will itself, and
therefore complements *everything physical in the world* and every phenomenon by representing *what is metaphysical,* the thing in itself" (KSA
1, 104). This is precisely Nietzsche's famous mythicizing of music as a kind
of primordial language, even before poetry.

At this point of transition from being to appearance, of a self-satisfac-
tion of being in appearance, of a transformation into representation and
language, however, Nietzsche's early theory of language begins to dissolve
and that nonrepresentative, rhetorical conception of art and language
emerges that is fully articulated in *On Truth and Lie in a Nonmoral Sense.*[8]
Several fragments from his unpublished manuscripts reveal this development. One fragment of spring 1871 titled "On the Relationship of Language and Music" is particularly significant for Nietzsche's critique of the
natural, instinctual theory of language that relates to art and music (KSA
7, 359–69). The decisive point of his earlier theory was the assumption of a
center, a ground of being, and the expressibility and representability of this
principle through art and particularly through music. This transition from
being into representation and thereby into language is the crucial point.
The difficulty Nietzsche is encountering here can perhaps best be illus-

trated by the central problem of Neoplatonism, which is to explain the transition from unity (of being) into plurality and the world of appearances. Neoplatonism, just like Nietzsche, introduces intermediary stages to explain this transition. In the Neoplatonic system the absolute auto-concentration of the One leads to the emanation of the nous, the world soul, and eventually, through a progressive process of emanation, the manifold world of individual and material things. Nietzsche's conception of the Primordial One, seen and perceived by the artistic genius and represented by him in art, shows a similar view of intermediary stages, best illustrated perhaps in the *The Birth of Tragedy* in his interpretation of Raphael's painting "The Transfiguration" (BT Aph. 4; KSA 1, 39). Mentioning the parallel between Neoplatonism and Nietzsche, one has, of course, to keep in mind that Neoplatonic thought relates to an ontological process, whereas Nietzsche's conception of transition or transformation is thought of in terms of transcendental philosophy and assumes an orientation toward the philosophy or metaphysics of art. Yet as for Schelling and Schopenhauer, art has the capability for the early Nietzsche to say the absolute and thereby is language in the most eminent sense of the word. We can refer briefly to Schelling in this context, who in his *System of Transcendental Idealism* says:

> For this very reason [unconscious and conscious productivity] art occupies the highest place for the philosopher, since it opens to him, as it were, the holy of holies where in eternal and primal union, as in a single flame, there burns what is sundered in nature and history and what must eternally flee from itself in life and action as in thought.[9]

These difficulties in explaining the transition from the Primordial One to the sphere of representation, signification, art, and language are not so obvious in *The Birth of Tragedy* because Nietzsche covered them up through his manner of writing, through rhetorical means, or with quotes from Schopenhauer. His unpublished fragments show with great clarity, however, that he was fully conscious of these difficulties and that he eventually recognized his solutions of the problem as metaphysical constructions that he subsequently dropped in favor of the position according to which everything is language and there is no privileged language having direct access to being. The fragment in question[10] develops the additional argument that while music is supposed to be a spontaneous, natural expression of the will, a kind of natural language in reality, only the highest, artistic, and elaborate forms of music would be capable of fulfilling this metaphysical task of representation. In his later writings, Nietzsche liked to describe this phase in his intellectual development, as has already been noted, as a process of liberation and emancipation. If we ask here what he sought to liberate himself from, the answer would be romanticism, including, of course, the intellectual worlds of German classicism (Goethe, Schiller) as well as idealistic philosophy (Schelling, Hegel).

The next step in the development of Nietzsche's theory of language consists in an intensive study of rhetoric that he undertook in preparation for his lectures on rhetoric at the University of Basel during the winter semester of 1872–73.[11] This study was not limited to ancient Greek and Roman rhetoric but also extended to modern views on rhetoric and language and included critical texts on ancient rhetoric and modern views of language.[12] Philippe Lacoue-Labarthe, who has investigated these studies,[13] assumes that the project of a critique of philosophy initiating from a theory of language and rhetoric originating at this time does not constitute a radical break, a turn, in Nietzsche's development, or an antiromantic tendency opposing *The Birth of Tragedy*. Rhetoric is for Nietzsche at that time rather a "further development of the artistic means comprised in language," but now "in the bright light of reason" (D, 88). This does no longer imply, however, that prior to the rhetorical or artistic language there had been a nonrhetorical, natural language that could serve as a reference point. No, an outside of language, an origin of language in this sense, is now unthinkable. Language itself is already "the result of purely rhetorical arts." For Nietzsche, this means rejecting all previous points of view that related to something originary. As rhetoric, for instance, language is no longer an expression of truth. Just as man's nature hardly consists in knowing, so can the original function of language hardly be seen as telling the truth (D, 89).

Under the impact of this rhetorical thinking, Nietzsche had to rethink his own earlier position concerning absolute expression in music and the outdoing of all other functions of communication through music. Everything nonlinguistic that had served only to safeguard language had to be removed from the philosophy of language to reveal language as merely language, as a rhetorical means (D, 93). Rhetoric now destroys the mythifying of language as a kind of original language, even before poetry. Now everything becomes language. This new thinking about language, however, also alters the notion of art. More precisely, Lacoue-Labarthe argues, one would have to say that rhetoric, as far as the themes of language and art are concerned, makes it unavoidable to think "art from the perspective of language, and not the other way—a movement which alters art as well as language and makes it possible for both to remain what they once were" (D, 99).

Dionysian art, Nietzsche had maintained in *The Birth of Tragedy*, always is capable of articulating nature "in its 'true voice', its 'undissimulated voice'," whereas Apollonian art covers up "pain in the basic features of nature" (D, 99). For Lacoue-Labarthe, the "monstrosity" of rhetoric in Nietzsche's early theory of art consists in the fact that from the point of view of language, such distinctions can no longer be maintained, that "the origin is not originary, and that representation precedes presence" (D, 100), so that language had always already been language. Rhetoric also eliminates the possibility "to have recourse to mythology." The unavoidable result of this critique is: "there is no new mythology, at least not a mythology which a philosophical discourse might think of as *prior* to itself" (D, 102). If there are reminiscences in Nietzsche of Friedrich Schlegel's theme of a new mythology, one would have to characterize them, as perhaps in the case of Schlegel, too, with formulations like: "the myth does not have a musical origin, the myth is rhetorical. The myth participates in the doxic duplicity of language which thereby does not articulate truth, but always believes to be the language of truth" (D, 103).

Of particular interest for Nietzsche's rhetorical turn is Gustav Gerber's text *Language as Art*, which had appeared from 1871 to 1872, shortly before Nietzsche's study of rhetoric.[14] Gerber belongs to a forgotten chapter in the philosophy of language of the second half of the nineteenth century, somewhere between Wilhelm von Humboldt and Frege, between Peirce and Wittgenstein. According to his sources, he represents the romantic tradition and quotes the most important figures of the romantic philosophy of language. The following quotation from Jean Paul, also cited by Nietzsche, can be seen as characteristic of his conception of language: "As in writing picture-writing was earlier than alphabetic writing, so in speaking the metaphor, because it designates relationships and not objects, was the *earlier* word and *had to gradually decolor to the proper expression*. The soul-giving and body-giving functions were still one because Ego and World still fused. Every language is therefore, as far as spiritual relations are concerned, a dictionary of faded metaphors" (SK I, 361).[15] Gerber was of crucial importance for Nietzsche's conception of tropes, which had already been an essential element of his earlier thinking about the purposeless, artistic, and poetic character of language in *The Birth of Tragedy* and the texts prior to this work. Now, however, Nietzsche formulates these statements in such a way that all words originally were tropes and that language, in its essence, is metaphorical. Gerber had said "that tropes approach words not now and then, but that it is the most proper nature of words to be tropical" (SK I, 386). Nietzsche reformulates this statement and says: "In sum: Tropes do not approach words now and then but form their innermost nature. There can be no question of a 'proper meaning' that could be translated in special cases."[16] Gerber intensified Nietzsche's approach to language from the point of view of rhetoric by providing him with a theory of tropes and metaphors. He simultaneously increased the romantic dimension in Nietzsche's thinking about language present in Gerber through his relationship to Wilhelm von Humboldt, the Schlegel brothers, and Jean Paul.

Gerber also develops the theory of a fixation of words by way of social conventions and the oblivion of these events during the process of a development of language. The sensual, metaphorical origin of language and the indissoluble connection of our concepts to this origin had motivated Gerber's critique of the use of abstract concepts in philosophical speculation, which he called "twaddle" and about which he said: *"Pure* thought is such a chimera as *pure* language would be, although nobody has as yet come to think of it" (SK i, 261). Gerber directs this critique of a hypostasis of abstract concepts in philosophical language mainly against Plato and Aristotle and views philosophers like Bacon, Hobbes, Locke, Leibniz, Hamann, Herder, and Jacobi as having prepared his own critique of language. To a large extent, Gerber's critique of language consists in making conscious the process of oblivion relating to the original formation of words and in illustrating the original character of words as synecdoche, metaphor, and metonymy through a broad range of examples.

Nietzsche took note of many of these examples for his lecture course on rhetoric. When during the following summer he composed the text *On Truth and Lie in a Nonmoral Sense* and articulated the thesis that the origin of language had not occurred in a logical but a poetical manner, he used Gerber's examples of the hardness of stone and the coiling of the snake. Gerber had tried to illustrate through these examples that language does not permit us a decision about the nature of things, but that we remain in this regard within the inner laws of language. Nietzsche interprets these examples as signs of the general undecidability of our philosophical and metaphysical position. "How far does this overstep the canon of certainty!" he says (TL, 82). In another instance, he writes: "What one-sided preferences, first for this, then for that property of a thing!" (ib.). He integrates Gerber's critical observations on language into a comprehensive critical discourse directed against metaphysics and our metaphysical presuppositions in general. This discourse dominates Nietzsche's later writings and indicates that his early critical reflections on language were by no means a passing event, but of a lasting importance for the formation of his thought.

Nietzsche dictated the text *On Truth and Lie in a Nonmoral Sense* during the summer of 1873, but never published it. The text relates to his fragments on language in previous years and has similarities with *On the Pathos of Truth*, which he composed for Cosima von Bülow on Christmas, 1872, together with four other writings. Among all the texts of this time and within the radius of *The Birth of Tradegy Out of the Spirit of Music*, this small writing appears as a skeptical monster, since it denies fundamentally and categorically our ability to make any truth-related statement about the world surrounding us. According to a later statement, he composed the text at a time when he was "already deep in the midst of moral scepticism and destructive analysis" and "already 'believed in nothing anymore', as the people put it, not even in Schopenhauer" (H II, Preface, Aph. 1). Nietzsche begins his text with a fabulous framing and writes:

> Once upon a time, in some out of the way corner of that universe which is dispersed into numberless twinkling solar systems, there was a star upon which clever beasts invented knowing. That was the most arrogant and mendacious minute of 'world history,' but nevertheless, it was only a minute. After nature had drawn a few breaths, the star cooled and congealed, and the clever beasts had to die (TL, 79; KSA 1, 875).

In the text *On the Pathos of Truth* this fable is told by a "heartless spirit" who does not think very highly of what we call by proud metaphors "world history," "truth," and "fame" and makes disdainful remarks about these themes. Upon the death of the clever beasts he remarks:

> The time had come so, for although they boasted of how much they had understood, in the end they discovered to their great annoyance that they had understood everything falsely. They died and in dying they cursed Truth. Such was the nature of these desperate beasts who invented knowing (PT, 61; KSA 1, 760).

In *On Truth and Lie*, Nietzsche attempts to show "how shadowy and transient, how aimless and arbitrary the human intellect looks within nature" (TL, 79; KSA 1, 875). Although this intellect was "allotted to these most unfortunate, delicate, and ephemeral beings merely as a device for detaining them a minute within existence," it always accomplishes to bring up "the most flattering estimation of the value of knowing." Dissimulation, even "deception, flattering, lying, deluding" appear as the true essence of the intellect which makes it hard to comprehend "how an honest and pure drive for truth could have arisen" among men (TL, 80; KSA 1, 876). This question is the focus of the text in its further development. With impressive arguments, interwoven with images and metaphors, Nietzsche describes how the human eyes, "deeply immersed in illusions and in dream images," glide "over the surface of things" and "engage in a groping game on the backs of things." Nature conceals almost everything from the human being, "even concerning his own body," and locks him "aloof from the coils of the bowels, the rapid flow of the blood stream, and the intricate quivering of the fibers," within his consciousness and "threw away the key." Woe to the one who would attempt "to peer out and down through a crack in the chamber of consciousness" and would realize "that man is sustained in the indifference of his ignorance by that which is pitiless, greedy, insatiable, and murderous—as if hanging in dreams on the back of a tiger." Considering this situation, Nietzsche asks: "where in the world could the drive for truth have come from?" (TL, 80; KSA 1, 877).

The first step in acquiring this enigmatic drive for truth consists, according to this text, in a convention, a "peace treaty," in this general warfare that fixes "*that* which shall count as 'truth' from now on." But only by means of "forgetfulness," could man "ever reach the point of fancying himself to possess a 'truth' of the grade just indicated" (TL, 81; KSA 1, 878). For the conventions of language are hardly products of knowledge, a congruent designation of things, an adequate expression of reality, but rather "illusions" and "empty husks." Only convention, not truth, had been decisive in the genesis of language. Properly speaking, we are not at all entitled to say "the stone is hard" because "hard" is only known to us as a "subjective stimulation." Just as little are we entitled to "separate things according to gender" and to designate the tree as masculine and the plant as feminine or to speak of a "snake," whose ability to twist itself could also refer to a worm. If we placed the various languages side by side, we would realize "that with words it is never a question of truth, never a question of adequate expression; otherwise, there would not be so many languages." The "thing in itself" is something toward which the "creator of language" is indifferent, something that for him is "not in the least worth striving for." He only "designates the relations of things to men, and for expressing these relations he lays hold of the boldest metaphors" (TL, 82; KSA 1, 879).

In describing this creation of language, Nietzsche uses a transformation theory that states that during the formation of language "each time there is a complete overleaping of one sphere, right into the middle of an entirely new and different one." He writes: "To begin with, a nerve stimulus is transferred into an image: first metaphor. The image, in turn, is imitated in a sound: second metaphor. Like someone who is totally deaf and by gazing with astonishment at Chladni's sound figure, believes to discover by the vibrations of the string what men mean by 'sound,' so we believe that we know something about the things themselves when we speak of trees, colors, snow, and flowers," although "we possess nothing but metaphors for things—metaphors which correspond in no way to the original entities" (TL, 83; KSA 1, 879). At any rate, the origin or genesis of language is not a logical procedure, "and all the material within and with which the man of truth, the scientist, and the philosopher later work and build, if not derived from never-never land is at least not derived from the essence of things." The inadequate relationship of [the hu]man to objects is further elucidated by Nietzsche's analysis of the transformation from metaphor to concept. This occurs when "the unique and entirely original experience" that leads to the origin of a word is relinquished in favor of the concept and now "has to fit countless more or less similar cases—which means, purely and simply, cases which are never equal and thus altogether unequal." Nietzsche writes: "Every concept arises from the equation of unequal things." As if there was something in nature that would correspond to our concepts of "leaf" or "honesty!" Only by overlooking "what is individual and actual" do we arrive at concepts, "whereas nature is acquainted with no forms and no concepts, and likewise with no species" (ib.).

As is obvious in these arguments, Nietzsche's critique of language is a critique of the language of philosophy and the claim to truth traditionally connected with this language. "What then is truth?" he asks and responds:

> A movable host of metaphors, metonymies, and anthropomorphisms: in short, a sum of human relations which have been poetically and rhetorically intensified, transferred, and embellished, and which, after long usage, seem to a people to be fixed, canonical, and binding. Truths are illusions which we have forgotten are illusions; they are metaphors that have become worn out and have been drained of sensuous force, coins which have lost their embossing and are now considered simply as metal and no longer as coins (TL, 84; KSA 1, 880–81).

The particular point in Nietzsche's argumentation, however, is that the philosophical formation of concepts that is related to "truth" is preceded by an artistic formation of metaphors, which is irrelevant for the finding of truth and in which the aesthetic aspect is predominant. A concept, Nietzsche maintains, "bony, foursquare, and transposable as a die," is merely "the residue of a metaphor," which in itself is the artistic transformation of a nerve stimulus into an image. Truth, in this philosophical game of dice, requires nothing but to use "every die in the designated manner, counting its spots accurately, fashioning the right categories, and never violating the order of caste and rank." Man is truly to be admired as the "genius of construction" of such "complicated domes of concepts" and indeed far above spiders and bees. But the question remains what is actually accomplished by this. Nietzsche writes: "When someone hides something behind a bush and looks for it again in the same place and finds it there as well, there is not much to praise in such seeking and finding. Yet this is how matters stand regarding seeking and finding 'truth' within the realm of reason" (TL, 85; KSA 1, 883).

Nietzsche illustrates this thought with numerous examples. When an investigator makes up the definition of a mammal and after the inspection of a camel says, "this is a mammal," he has of course "brought a truth to light in this way, but it is a truth of limited value" (ib.). This truth is "thoroughly anthropomorphic" and does not contain a single point that would be "universally valid apart from man." He behaves similarly to an astrologer who considers "the stars to be in man's service and connected with his happiness and sorrows." Such an investigator seeks "only the metamorphosis of the world into man." He considers "the entire universe in connection with man: the entire universe as the infinitely fractured echo of one original sound man; the entire universe as the infinitely multiplied copy of our original picture—man." Such an investigator forgets "that the original perceptual metaphors are metaphors and takes them to be things in themselves." Science originates only "by means of the petrification and coagulation of a mass of images which originally streamed from the primal faculty of human imagination like a fiery liquid," only by forgetting on the part of man "that he himself is an *artistically creating subject*." As soon as man could escape from this forgetting and step out "from the prior walls of his faith, his 'self-consciousness' would be immediately destroyed" (TL, 86; KSA 1, 883–84).

This sequential order and interrelationship of metaphorical and abstract language, art and science, poetry and philosophy is condensed into the compact statement that it is "originally *language* which works on the construction of concepts, a labor taken over in later ages by *science*." Science, working on the "great columbariun of concepts," is the "graveyard of perception." However, when the scientific investigator "builds his hut right next to the tower of science," he does this also out of fear and "to find shelter for himself beneath those bulwarks" of science. For there are powers of a more profound nature, "powers which oppose scientific 'truth' with completely different kinds of 'truths'" (TL, 88; KSA 1, 886). Now the sequential order of art and science is reversed, since at the height of the scientific formation of concepts, man's original need of art finds new and powerful expression. We know from Nietzsche's *The Birth of Tragedy* that the insatiable hunger for scientific knowledge, which appears in paradigmatic fashion in Socrates reaches a point where it suffers shipwreck and gazes into the incomprehensible and sees with "horror how logic coils up at these boundaries and finally bites its own tail." At this point, a "new form of insight breaks through, *tragic insight* which, merely to be en-

dured, needs art as a protection and remedy" (BT, Aph. 15; KSA 1, 101).
Nietzsche even maintains that this "metaphysical illusion," that is, "that
thought, using the thread of causality, can penetrate the deepest abysses of
being," accompanies science and leads "science again and again to its
limits at which it must turn into *art*—*which is really the aim of this
mechanism*" (BT, Aph. 15; KSA 1, 99).

In *On Truth and Lie*, he intensifies this transitory character of science
and its transition into art and derives science from a primordial metaphorical tendency of man. "The drive toward the formation of metaphors,"
he says, this "fundamental human drive" is not tamed and subdued by
science, but constantly present and always "seeks a new realm and another
channel for its activity." This is obvious in our dreams in the "desire to
refashion the world which presents itself to waking man," or becomes
manifest in the world of myth, for example, of the ancient Greeks, "which
more closely resembles a dream than it does the waking world of a scientifically disenchanted thinker" (TL, 89; KSA 1, 887).

At this point, Nietzsche's critique of science and philosophy seems to
turn toward the utopian ideal of a new age of art and myth. Indeed, German ideology critique has frequently read Nietzsche in this fashion.[17] That
this is a distortion of his text, however, is clearly evident in the concluding
passages of the text, which project not the opposite dominance of art over
science, but rather an interaction of art and science, an alternation of
metaphor and concept. In these concluding passages, Nietzsche confronts
mythical and artistic thought with scientific and philosophical thought,
characterizing the former as an irreducible form of knowledge that cannot
be suspended by science. When for the ancient Athenian "every tree can
suddenly speak as a nymph," or "when a god in the shape of a bull can
drag away maidens, when even the goddess Athena herself is suddenly seen
in the company of Peisistratus driving through the market place of Athens
with a beautiful team of horse," then, "as in a dream, anything is possible
at each moment, and all of nature swarms around man as if it were nothing but a masquerade of the gods, who were merely amusing themselves
by deceiving men in all these shapes" (TL, 89; KSA 1, 888). The human
being likes to be deceived in this manner, which is obvious "when the
rhapsodist tells him epic fables as if they were true, or when the actor in
the theater acts more royally than any real king." Here, the intellect is free
and "released from its former slavery." Now the intellect has thrown "the
token of bondage from itself" and can "wipe from its face the expression of
indigence." Here, the intellect can dissimulate without doing harm, and
"everything that it now does bears the mark of *dissimulation*, just as that
previous conduct did of *distortion*." Here too, the intellect imitates life, but
now "it considers this life to be something good and seems to be quite
satisfied with it" (TL, 90; KSA 1, 888). Nietzsche writes:

That immense framework and planking of concepts to which the needy man clings his whole life long in order to preserve himself is nothing but a scaffolding and toy for the most audacious feats of the liberated intellect. And when it smashes this framework to pieces, throws it into confusion, and puts it back together in an ironic fashion, pairing the most alien things and separating the closest, it is demonstrating that it has no need of these makeshifts of indigence and that it now will be guided by intuitions rather than concepts (ib.).

These intuitions are the opposite of the schemata and abstractions of scientific language. The one who has them either remains silent or speaks "in forbidden metaphors and in unheard-of-combinations of concepts" and does so "that by shattering and mocking the old conceptual barriers he may at least correspond creatively to the impression of the powerful present intuition." Again, this does not imply for Nietzsche an elimination of scientific language and thought in favor of artistic intuition. He projects a state "in which the rational man and the intuitive man stand side by side, the one in fear of intuition, the other with scorn for abstraction." The former attempts to satisfy the "needs" of life, the latter ignores these needs and counts as real only "that life which has been disguised as illusion and beauty." The rational man, guided by concepts, only wards off "misfortune," whereas the intuitive man "reaps from his intuition a harvest of continually flowing illumination, cheer, and redemption." When, however, the intuitive man comes to recognition, as perhaps in ancient Greece, "art's mastery over life can be established," and the manifestations of such a life will be "this dissimulation, this disavowal of indigence, this glitter of metaphorical intuitions," which are the mark of a culture impregnated by art (TL, 91; KSA 1, 889).

The essay *On Truth and Lie* constitutes a decisive and perhaps the most important step in the development of Nietzsche's theory of language. His earliest explanation of language as originating from an instinctual and teleological drive had been absorbed by his idea of absolute music in *The Birth of Tragedy*. Theory of language and aesthetics thereby came to a close relationship. In his critique of the habitual language, that of concepts and of written language, Nietzsche expressed himself as harshly as possible, even out doing the satires of the romantics in this regard. His critique of language of that time clearly shows a hierarchical order of rank. Written language is dead, the language of speech is sounding, has intervals, rhythms, tempi that "symbolize" a realm of feeling. The "largest amount of feeling," however, cannot be expressed in words, because the words merely designate, they are, as Nietzsche puts it, "the surface of the agitated sea, whereas deep down it storms" (KSA 7, 48). That is where the realm of music begins, the sphere of an absolute expression. Poetry, lyric poetry in particular, often is on "its way to music," especially when poetry seeks "the most tender concepts which make the coarsely material of the concept almost disappear" (ib.).

This entire metaphysical edifice collapsed, however, when Nietzsche assumed his study of rhetoric in 1872 and made the decisive discovery that before language as art (rhetoric), there can be no language of nature (music), because language in its entire nature is art, namely, rhetoric. Lacoue-Labarthe designates this effect of rhetoric upon Nietzsche as a "shock" and says:

> The reason for this is very simple: it is simply that rhetoric since the beginning of its appearance is eager to expel music and to take its place. Rhetoric destroys, at least partly, that which was not linguistic in language and had permitted its 'rescue': its originally musical nature and its sounding essence, in other words that which during speaking and through intonation preserves the original strength and provides expression (D, 93).

Recognizing that everything, even music, is rhetorical and that which the Greeks, those exemplary human beings, produced as their "highest" was not philosophy and poetry, but rhetoric, a "subterranean and hardly visible movement" is set in motion through which the "work" of the early Nietzsche, that is, his metaphysics "begins to crumble or, more precisely, to slide from the proper realm of the work and to get lost in what nevertheless is not the other of work," but its stubborn alternation, its "unrelenting exhaustion," its "un-working," its *"desoeuvrement"* (D, 82). Combined with this earthquake-like movement are a number of other events as, for instance, the breach with philology, the breach with Wagner, but especially a transformation of the concept of symbol, removing it from its Goethean-Schellingian connotation and aligning it more with a structure of metonymical cross-references. One could add that the movement in Nietzsche's thought initiated through rhetoric also leads to a displacement of the classical-romantic notion of nature into that of art and to a new understanding of art no longer in analogy to nature but purely and simply as art, as "l'art pour l'art," at least according to Nietzsche's intention.

On Truth and Lie, looked at from this perspective, appears as the resumé of this movement in Nietzsche's early thought. Lacoue-Labarthe undoubtedly has the merit to have shown this decisive reorientation on the part of the early Nietzsche and to have emphasized the importance of his study of rhetoric that he first put onto the agenda. Furthermore, his essay on Nietzsche and rhetoric and the effect of "desoeuvrement" initiated by these events certainly is one of the most accomplished pieces of a deconstructive reading of Nietzsche as well as a good model of deconstruction itself. The only blemish this text has, however, is its title, *Le détour, The Detour*. It automatically suggests that the laborious pathway of auto-critique and self-overcoming accomplished by the early Nietzsche had only been a regrettable detour and that he could have reached his goal, *On Truth and Lie in Nonmoral Sense*, much easier and faster if only he had studied rhetoric and had developed the position of "language as art" instead of writing *The Birth of Tragedy*. Furthermore, the word *detour* appears to be a most surprising formulation for a deconstructionist of the caliber of Lacoue-Labarthe because it seems to suggest that there is a right or straight way, a King's way. Lacoue-Labarthe also thinks that the earthquake-like movement in Nietzsche's early thought occurred "accidentally" (D, 80), when because of his Basel teaching obligations, he had to lecture on rhetoric and began his study of this topic. A sharp division between the Nietzsche of *The Birth of Tragedy* and the Nietzsche of *On Truth and Lie* is drawn and a breach is projected that appears to be so deep that one actually denies in respect to a theory of language, even to philosophy in general, what the other affirms.

It was Paul de Man who attempted to give Nietzsche's rhetorically oriented theory of language a broader meaning by relating it to his entire oeuvre and by approaching this goal from the interaction of philosophy and literature in his text.[18] Like Plato, Augustine, Montaigne, and Rousseau, Nietzsche obviously was one of those authors "whose work straddles the two activities of the human intellect that are both the closest and the most impenetrable to each other—literature and philosophy" (AR, 103). Nietzsche's study of the "rhetoric of tropes" is an important link for these two realms and permits a better understanding of their irrelationship. This rhetorical vocabulary almost vanishes with the appearance of *Human, All Too Human*, but nevertheless remains the key to his later critique of metaphysics. This critique is not simply, as one has maintained, a reversal of metaphysics or of Plato but "lies in the rhetorical model of the trope or, if one prefers to call it that way, in literature as the language most explicitly grounded in rhetoric" (AR, 109). *On Truth and Lie* is a capital text in this regard because it substitutes "a human-centered set of meanings that is reassuring his (man's) vanity for a set of meanings that reduces him to being a mere transitory accident in the cosmic order." That the text is self-contradictory in the "performative" sense is for de Man the most natural thing in the world because this text, "although it presents itself legitimately as a demystifying of literary rhetoric, remains entirely literary, rhetorical, and deceptive itself" (AR, 113). According to de Man's interpretation, this text makes literature the main topic of philosophy and the model for that type of truth after which philosophy is striving. In de Man's own words: "Philosophy turns out to be an endless reflection on its own destruction at the hands of literature" (AR, 115). This relentless reflection is intimately linked with the rhetorical structure of the text, since it cannot escape from the rhetorical dissimulation it denounces. More precisely and also more in the manner of de Man, this thought means that the self-destruction and self-consummation comprised in this intimate reflection is indefinitely postponed: "this self-destruction is infinitely displaced in a series of successive rhetorical reversals, which, by the endless repetition of the same figure, keep it suspended between truth and the death of this truth:"

> A threat of immediate destruction, stating itself as a figure of speech thus becomes the permanent repetition of this threat. Since this repetition is a temporal event, it can be narrated sequentially, but what it narrates, the subject matter of the story, is itself a mere figure. A non-referential repetitive text narrates the story of a literally destructive but nontragic linguistic event. We could call this rhetorical mode, which is that of the 'conte philosophique' *On Truth and Lie* and, by extension, of all philosophical discourse, an ironic allegory—but only if we understand 'irony' more in the sense of Friedrich Schlegel than of Thomas Mann. The place where we might recover some of this sense is in Nietzsche's own work, not in that of his assumed continuators (AR, 115–16).

A further point in de Man's reading of Nietzsche is neither to reduce Nietzsche's tendency toward a critique of language and metaphysics to a particular step in his development, nor to date this orientation to a particular event, for example, his study of rhetoric, but to relate it to the entirety of his oeuvre. A writing like *The Birth of Tragedy* should not be exempted from such a reading, although this text obviously pleads for the unmediated presence of the will and for a tragic, not ironical, form of art. What matters is to undermine, with the help of this rhetoric, all authoritative claims of the text with statements that are made in the text itself. *The Birth of Tragedy* is even an excellent subject for such a deconstructive reading if one thinks of the genesis of this text, the hasty compilation of the manuscript and the many unutilized parts of the previous drafts that no longer were fitting the progressively narrowing conception of the text. Yet de Man does not want to restrict deconstructive reading to individual texts but to extend it to every complex text of philosophy and literature, even to every linguistic expression. In this tendency, he follows Nietzsche according to whom language altogether is rhetorical and thereby only capable of expressing opinions, not truths. Examined from this point of view, Nietzsche's text resembles the gesticulation of an artist, who does not learn from experience and moves again and again into the same trap. De Man comments: "what seems to be most difficult to admit is that this allegory of errors is the very model of philosophical rigor" (AR, 118). What matters with regard to Nietzsche's early metaphysics is to explain the collapse of his early system from its own structure, to view the desoeuvrement not as occasioned from outside, the "accidental" reading of rhetorical texts, but to locate this process in his work itself, *The Birth of Tragedy*, and to apply deconstruction at a deeper level.

The critical analyses in *On Truth and Lie* had resulted in Nietzsche's conviction that language does not entitle us to a decision concerning the nature of things but that we remain enclosed in the inner laws of language. Nietzsche's critical reflections on language thereby become integrated and even transformed into a general discourse of critique of metaphysics. One of these transformations takes place in Aphorism 39 of *Human, All To Human* and relates the formation of our language to the genesis of our moral concepts. Nietzsche writes in this instance:

> First of all, one calls individual actions good or bad quite irrespective of their useful and harmful consequences. Soon, however, one forgets that origin of these designations and believes that the quality 'good' and 'evil' is inherent in the actions themselves, irrespective of their consequences: thus committing the same error as that by which language proclaims the stone itself as hard, the tree itself as green—that is to say, by taking for cause that which is effect (KSA 2, 62).

In a more fundamental manner, but also more removed from a critique of language, Nietzsche says in Aphorism 121 of *The Gay Science*:

> We have arranged for ourselves a world in which we can live—by positing bodies, lives, planes, causes and effects, motion and rest, form and content; without these articles of faith nobody now could endure life (KSA 3, 477–78).

The transformation of Nietzsche's theory of language is also noticeable when he extends the theme of language to realms that can be considered as preconditions of language, conditions of possibility, something previous to language, but also to something that develops from language as does, for instance, science. Language is interrelated with a great variety of phenomena in man's interaction with the world. This is obvious in Aphorism 11 of *Human, All To Human* where Nietzsche writes:

> The shapers of language were not so modest as to believe that they only gave designations to things, but instead they fancied that they expressed the highest knowledge of things with words; in fact, language is the first step of the struggle for science (KSA 2, 30–31).

Now it is "dawning on people that they have propagated a terrible error in their belief in language." Yet Nietzsche comments by making the reassuring statement: "Luckily it is too late for the development of reason that rests on that belief to be reversed (ib.).

Some examples from Nietzsche's later writings can illustrate this transformation. Aphorism 115 of *Dawn* deals with the "prejudices" on which our language is built and that hinder us "when we want to explain inner processes and drives." We have words "only for *superlative* degrees of these processes and drives" (anger, hatred, love, pity, desire, knowledge, joy, pain) but not for "the milder, middle degrees, not to speak of the lower degrees which are continually in play." Yet precisely these degrees "weave the web of our character and our destiny," whereas the others are "outbursts" and all too often "mislead the observer" (KSA 3, 107–8). This aphorism stresses the lack of words, whereas Aphorism 47 from *Dawn* has as its motto: "*Words lie in our way!*" and reads:

> Wherever primitive mankind set up a word, they believed they had made a discovery, [which leads to the result that now] with every piece of knowledge one has to stumble over dead, petrified words, and one will sooner break a leg than a word (KSA 3, 53).

An important text in this context is Aphorism 354, *On the 'genius of the species',* from *The Gay Science.* Nietzsche begins his argument with the observation that there are wide regions of life activities that never enter our consciousness and are operating "without this mirror effect." "*For what purpose, then, any consciousness at all when it is in the main superfluous?*" Nietzsche asks and develops the answer that this derives from man's "*capacity for communication,*" more precisely, from his "*need for communication,*" and that "*consciousness has developed only under the pressure of the need for communication.*" As the "most endangered animal," man needed "help and protection, he needed his peers, he had to learn to express his distress and to make himself understood," and for that he needed consciousness. The development of language and the development of consciousness "go hand in hand." As every living being, man thinks continually without knowing it. Thus "conscious thinking," the "thinking that rises to *consciousness* is only the smallest part of all this—the most superficial, the worst part." This origin of consciousness from "signs of communication" makes it obvious that "the world of which we can become conscious is only a surface—and sign—world, a world that is made common and meaner" (KSA 3, 590–93).

Beyond Good and Evil is a text that frequently approaches the topic of language from that of "grammar." Grammar, however, is not to be understood in a technical, linguistic sense but as that "unconscious domination and guidance by similar grammatical functions" that governs people of a similar family of languages, of the same "atavisms," as Nietzsche proposes in Aphorism 20 (KSA 5, 34–35). In the Preface to this text, he had referred to a "seduction by grammar" as a possible reason for the origin of philosophical systems (KSA 5, 11–12). In Aphorism 34, he equates the "faith in grammar" with the "faith in governesses" and asks" "but hasn't the time come for philosophy to renounces the faith in governesses?" (KSA 5, 54). And in Aphorism 54, he attempts to discredit the Christian belief in the soul as an outdated assumption, saying: "For, formerly, one believed in 'the soul' as one believed in grammar and the grammatical subject" (KSA 5, 73).

Many of these thoughts have parallels in Nietzsche's unpublished fragments. He relates language to reason and claims that language has provided reason with the "most naive prejudices." We read "problems and disharmonies into things because we think only in the form of language," and we would cease to think *"if we did not do it under the coercion of language."* These reflections lead up to Nietzsche's famous statement: *"Reasonable thinking is an interpretation according to a scheme we cannot throw off"* (KSA 12, 193–94). How Nietzsche thinks about language, grammar, and reason as a unity, is best noticeable in a tour de force of his critique of reason in *Twilight of the Idols*, one of his latest writings. In Aphorism 5 of the section "'Reason' in Philosophy," Nietzsche says that the question about the origin of language would bring us back into an "age of the most rudimentary form of psychology," and that we would find ourselves "in the midst of a rude fetishism when we call to mind the basic presuppositions of the metaphysics of language—that is to say, of *reason.*" Nietzsche concludes this aphorism with the exclamation: "'Reason' in language: oh what a deceitful old woman! I fear we are not getting rid of God because we still believe in grammar . . ." (KSA 6, 77–78).

The response to Nietzsche's thoughts on language focused mostly on these scattered statements and only recently took account of his more coherently developed theory in his early texts, especially in *On Truth and Lie*. The first reaction to Nietzsche's philosophy of language occurred al-

ready in 1890, when Fritz Mauthner, the Austrian writer, himself a prominent theorist of language of the time, saw an immediate link between the
critique of language and the critique of knowledge in Nietzsche's theory, in
that his critique of morality, for instance, proceeded primarily via a critical
analysis and dissolution of the traditional designations for "good" and
"evil."[19] Yet the result of all this was according to Mauthner only a "new
superstition of words," the attitude of a "trumpeter of immorality," of a
"moralist" who only wanted to set up "new tablets" and thereby manifested
a new belief in language.[20] Later interpretations, when they turned to
Nietzsche's theory of language at all, tended to interpret his view of language as relating to prior, more originary principles such as grammar,
reason, instinctual moves in the primordial self-preservation of the human
being. Nietzsche himself suggested such an interpretative scheme and often expressed it in his writings. In Aphorism 20 of *Beyond Good and Evil*,
for example, he writes: "the spell of certain grammatical functions is ultimately also the spell of *physiological* valuations and racial conditions"
(KSA 5, 35).

    More sophisticated views of Nietzsche's treatment of language as de-
veloped, for instance, by Foucault in the realm of communication and
indirect communication[21] are lacking in earlier Nietzsche interpretations,
and the first comprehensive study of this theme did not occur until 1988.[22]
Nietzsche's statements on language seemed to require a basic text for the
human being, a text in which instinctual drives, cruelty, and survival tech-
niques are the main features. Aphorism 230 of *Beyond Good and Evil*
clearly points in this direction. The task is to rediscover beneath all "flattering colors and make-up" the "frightful prototext *homo natura*," which
means: "To translate man back into nature; to become master over the
many vain and overly enthusiastic interpretations and connotations that
have so far been scrawled and painted over that eternal basic text of homo
natura" (KSA 5, 169). It was precisely Nietzsche's theory of language,
which in more recent interpretations led to a different view of his writing
that insisted on the ambiguity of his statements and the impossibility of
ascribing a definitive meaning to them. The discovery of the importance of
rhetoric for the formation of Nietzsche's philosophical discourse was the
main stimulus for this turn. This was primarily accomplished by Lacoue-
Labarthe, who focused on Nietzsche's lectures on rhetoric, and Paul de
Man, who extended this new approach to *The Birth of Tragedy* and other
Nietzsche texts.[23] Yet it was undoubtedly Derrida who established this new
reading of Nietzsche in the sense of a plurality of styles and a final undecidability of his statements.[24] Today, for many of us, Nietzsche's various
utterrances on language and communication appear to derive from a plurality of voices and texts and to configure to that type of complex, ambig-

uous text constituting the peculiar character of his philosophical discourse.

Notes

1. An account of Nietzsche's life is provided by Ronald Hayman, *Nietzsche* (Penguin Books, 1980). A more comprehensive and scholarly biography has been established by Curt Paul Janz, *Nietzsche*, 3 vols. (Munich: Hanser, 1978–79).

2. Nietzsche is quoted according to book titles and number of aphorisms. References are given in parenthesis in the text: A: *The Antichrist*; BT: *The Birth of Tragedy*; D: *Daybreak*; EH: *Ecce Homo*; GE: *Beyond Good and Evil*; GS: *The Gay Science*; H: *Human, All To Human*. The English translations refer to the following editions: Friedrich Nietzsche, *Twilight of the Idols/The Antichrist*, trans. R. J. Hollingdale (New York: Penguin Books, 1968); Friedrich Nietzsche, *The Birth of Tragedy* and *The Wagner Case*, trans. Walter Kaufmann, (New York: Vintage, 1967); Friedrich Nietzsche, *Daybreak*, trans. R. J. Hollingdale, (Cambridge: Cambridge University Press, 1982); Friedrich Nietzsche, *On the Genealogy of Morals/Ecce Homo*, trans. Walter Kaufmann; Friedrich Nietzsche, *The Gay Science*, trans. Walter Kaufmann, (New York: Vintage, 1974); Friedrich Nietzsche, *Human, All Too Human*, trans. R. J. Hollingdale, (Cambridge: Cambridge University Press, 1986).
Nietzsche's essays *On Truth and Lie* and *On the Pathos of Truth* are quoted from Friedrich Nietzsche, *Philosophy of Truth*, trans. Daniel Breazeale, (Highlands, NJ: Humanities Press, 1979) and referred to by abbreviated titles (TL and PT) and page number in parenthesis in the text. Nietzsche's lectures on rhetoric have appeared in the following edition: *Friedrich Nietzsche on Rhetoric and Language*, trans. Sander L. Gilman, Carole Blair, and David J. Parent (Oxford University Press, 1989).
I have also added references to the most recent German edition: Friedrich Nietzsche, *Kritische Studienausgabe*, eds. Giorgio Colli and Mazzino Montinari, 15 vols., Berlin: de Gruyter, 1980, and given these references according to an abbreviation (KSA), volume, and page number in parenthesis in the text.

3. This is obvious in the most comprehensive and important book on Nietzsche's theory of language that has appeared so far: Claudia Crawford, *The Beginnings of Nietzsche's Theory of Language* (Monographien und Texte zur Nietzsche-Forschung, Vol. 19, Berlin: de Gruyter, 1988).

4. See in particular the Preface to the Second Part of *Human, All Too Human*, which focuses on his self-liberation from romanticism.

5. This text had appeared earlier in several separate editions but is chapter 1 in the recent critical edition of his notes for *Vorlesungen über lateinische Grammatik (Winter Semester 1869–70)*, ed. Fritz Bornmann and Mario Carpitella in Friedrich Nietzsche, *Kritische Gesamtausgabe der Werke* II, 2 (Berlin: de Gruyter, 1993, 185–88). Translations are my own.

6. References to these lectures are given by page number of the edition quoted in footnote 5 and put in parenthesis in the text.

7. Friedrich Wilhelm Joseph Schelling, *Einleitung in die Philosophy der Mythologie*, in: *Sämtliche Werke* (Stuttgart, Germany: Cotta, 1856), Vol. 11.

8. See Diana Behler, "Nietzsches Versuch einer Artistenmetaphysik," *Kunst und Wissenschaft bei Nietzsche*, ed. Mihailo Djurić and Josef Simon, Würzburg, Germany: Königshausen und Neumann, 1986, 130–49.

9. Quoted from *Philosophy of German Idealism*, ed. Ernst Behler (New York: Continuum) p. 215.

10. *On the Relationship of Language to Music*: KSA 7, 359–69.

11. See the translation of the text quoted in footnote 2. The German original has not yet appeared in the critical edition and is quoted from Friedrich Nietzsche, *Rhetorik*, in: *Friedrich Nietzsche's Werke* Vol. 18: *Unveröffentlichtes zur Literaturgeschichte, Rhetorik und Rhythmik*, ed. Otto Crusius (Leipzig: Naumann, 1912).

12. Nietzsche studied in particular Richard Volkmann, *Die Rhetorik der Griechen und Römer in systematischer Übersicht dargestellt*, (Berlin, 1872) and Gustav Gerber, *Die Sprache als Kunst*, 2 Vols. (Bromberg, Poland: 1871–72).

13. Philippe Lacoue-Labarthe, "Le détour (Nietzsche et la rhétorique)," *Poétique* 2 (1971), 53–76. Quotes from this text are given in the text according to the abbreviation D and page number.

14. See the edition cited in footnote 12. References to this text are given in parentheses in the text according to SK and page number.

15. Nietzsche quotes this dictum in his *Rhetorik* (see footnote No. 12), 264–65.

16. *Rhetorik*, 250. See on this relationship Anthonie Meijers and Martin Stingelin, "Konkordanz zu den wörtlichen Abschriften und Übernahmen von Beispielen und Zitaten aus Gustav Gerber: Die Sprache als Kunst (Bromberg 1871) in Nietzsches Rhetorik-Vorlesungen und in 'Über Wahrheit und Lüge im außermoralischen Sinne,'" *Nietzsche-Studien* 27 (1988), 350–68.

17. E.g., Jürgen Habermas, *The Philosophical Discourse of Modernity*, trans. Frederick Lawrence (Cambridge, MA: MIT Press, 1987), 83–105.

18. Paul de Man, *Allegories of Reading* (New Haven, CT: Yale University Press, 1979), 103–18 ("Rhetoric of Tropes"), 119–34 ("Rhetoric of Persuasion"). In the following AR with page references in the text.

19. Especially in *On the Genealogy of Morals*.

20. Fritz Mauthner, Beiträge zu einer Kritik der Sprache, 3 vols. (Leipzig, Germany: 1901–2) 1: 366–69.

21. Michel Foucault, *The Order of Things. An Archeology of the Human Sciences* (New York: Random House, 1970), 303–7.

22. See the book quoted in footnote 3.

23. See the books quoted in footnotes 13 and 18.

24. Jacques Derrida, *Spurs: Nietzsche's Styles*, trans. Barbara Harlow (Chicago: Chicago University Press, 1978).

Editor's Introduction

This broad-ranging essay argues that Jean-François Lyotard's work develops a critique of Peircean semiotics that can politically inform communication research in general and ethnography of communication in particular. With Lyotard's guidance, Smith addresses two central problematics, one concerning the question of truth and the other the question of justice. Classical semiotics—which for Lyotard means Augustinian and, probably, Peircean semiotics—holds out the hope of adequate representation, discourse that is true because it corresponds with that which is. The two worlds commitment of the symbol model underlies this view, and it contributes to discourse theories that strive for certainty, closure, and control. Lyotard's discourse theory, by contrast, is agonistic; it foregrounds the untranslatability of the *differend*, the impossibility of conquering alterity with names that render uniqueness as the same. Thus Lyotard would characterize as naive the attempts by objectivist ethnographers to provide "accurate" or "true" descriptions of the cultures they encounter.

The second problematic surfaces because, although signification, in Smith's words, "has nothing to do with essential truth," it has "everything to do with the way justice is conceived and practiced." Semiotics is not only fallacious for Lyotard; it is also an accomplice of efforts to convert those who are different into versions of those in power. Augustinian semiotics is a semiotics of convertible beings, when, as Smith puts it, "to be converted is to lose one's alterity, to convert others is to save them from thing-ness by humanizing them with Christian names, and this humanity is defined by the signs and codes of the conqueror." Currently, ethnographers are one group of human scientists especially susceptible to this distortion. Some ethnographers whose academic homes are in both anthropology and communication have recognized the danger and are affirming versions of postmodern, performative, or critical ethnography. These scholars and those who characterize their ethnographies as "objectivist," Smith argues, could learn from Lyotard's critique of semiotics.

197

The first section of Smith's essay reviews the ways Lyotard contrasts sophistic or "pagan" sign theory with the theory developed by Augustine and codified by classical linguistics. Lyotard's central problem with Augustinian semiotics is that it "valorizes the language offices (*langue*) of those who conquer; structures the remoteness of the other according to political, economic, or academic expediency; and assimilates differences as a singular, immediate, and compelling event in order to construct a manageable 'message'." Protagoras, Georgias, and Antisthenes, on the other hand, preferred an agonistic sign theory, one that foregrounded ontological and axiological paradox. Georgias described paradoxes of existing and knowing, Antisthenes the paradoxical relation between designation and signification, and Protagoras the metacommunicational paradox that Bertrand Russell "solved" with his theory of logical types. Lyotard argues that these paradoxes are informative not when they are *resolved* but when they are embraced as reflective of the human condition and then extended to the point where they make *ethical* claims on the persons they implicate.

The second section of Smith's essay develops this tension between Augustinian and pagan semiotic theory in a dialogue between a follower of C. S. Peirce, who claims not to be an Augustinian, and a Lyotardian who, as Smith puts it, "is reluctant to accept a would-be Peircian *paganism.*" The two central problematics of truth and justice are worked in this dialogue about discourse theory, but, appropriately, no resolution is reached. Rather, the end of the conversation is "a differend, that is, an 'unstable state and instant of language wherein something which must be able to be put into phrases cannot yet be. . .' ."

The final section of the chapter addresses concerns of those researchers in anthropology and communication who are working out what might be termed the rights and responsibilities of communication ethnographers. Smith begins with the contention that "an objectivist ethnography is untenable," and hence that some version of critical ethnography needs to be fleshed out from the initial work of such anthropologists as James Clifford, Victor Turner, and Renato Rosaldo, and such communication scholars as Dwight Conquergood and Michael Huspek. Three pivotal concerns in this effort, Smith argues, are *linkage, embodiment,* and *power relations* between and among selves and others, and these hinge on views of the subject or subjects of discourse. Smith shows how Lyotard's deconstruction of the discourse subject contributes to the development of this emerging "ethnography of differends." He identifies six complex questions such an ethnographic project might address and proposes that "communication ethnography radicalize even further the notions of linkage, body and power such that new forms of expression and perception become possible and desirable even though these forms may not be replicable or verifiable according to the states of the cognitive genre of discourse. Living on the margins requires this type of break, if we are to follow the suggestions of Lyotard, especially."

Smith contributes to this volume by demonstrating how another prominent postmodernist works some of the central problems generated by the symbol model. Lyotard foregrounds crucially important political concerns that many works, including the first four chapters of this book, leave unaddressed and argues that these concerns are inescapably philosophical. Yet, some of Lyotard's concerns with Augustinian semiotics are the same as those that prompted, for example, my attempt to characterize language as constitutive articulate contact, and Lyotard and I would both resist efforts by Peirceans to dissociate themselves from the ontology of the symbol model. But Lyotard tries to develop his transformational account of language as a theory of *signs*, albeit one radically different from the classic view. I believe he would have succeeded even more completely than he did were he to articulate his discourse theory as not only postmodern but also postsemiotic.

6

Simple Signs, Indeterminate Events: Lyotard on Sophists and Semiotics

Andrew R. Smith

Let's take up this business of signs once more, you have not understood, you have remained rationalists, semioticians, Westerners, let's emphasize it again, it is the road toward *libidinal* currency that must be opened up by force. What the semioticians maintain as a hypothesis beneath their discourse is that the thing of which they speak may always be treated as a sign; and this sign in its turn is indeed thought within the network of concepts belonging to the theory of communication. . . . (Lyotard, 1993, 43)

Lyotard's polemic against semiotics takes aim at the logocentric presupposition that a system of linguistic and extralinguistic signs can be negotiated and codified to reflect the truth of some *thing*, and that this truth can be embodied in persuasive and revelatory ways. In contrast, Lyotard argues, not only can the thing never be known in itself, but any name is a provisional designation that bears no motivated relation to that which it *ostensibly* designates. Signification, it follows, has nothing to do with essential truth but everything to do with the way justice is conceived and practiced.

In this chapter I present Lyotard's attack on the Augustinian notion of the sign and his defense of the early Greek sophists' views of designation and signification. The question of the sign-object relation in modern semiotics, as developed by C. S. Peirce, is then addressed through an improvised dialogue between a Lyotardian and a Peircian. I conclude with a discussion of the import of Lyotard's views on communication research in general and communication ethnography in particular. Specifically, I argue that the pivotal notions of critical ethnography—that is, linkage, body, and power—should be revisited and extended in light of Lyotard's more pagan notions of the sign.

Augustinian and Pagan Signs

In Lyotard's most virulent critique (1993) he argues that semiotics has specific political and psychological agendas that emerge out of the Augustinian theory of the sign. These agendas center on how the other can be conceived as something convertible. The other has an exchange rate for semiotics, a value to be posited and used to assimilate and destroy its alterity, its *thing-ness*. Augustinian semiotics is a semiotics of convertible beings; a capitalization of sensibilities formed into a system of exchange based on the two-world model of inclusion and exclusion. It is a system of predictability with specific pedagogical intents. To be converted is to lose one's alterity, to convert others is to save them from thing-ness by humanizing them with Christian names, and this humanity is defined by the signs and codes of the conqueror.

Augustinian semiotics is structured according to an economy of messages that tends to ignore or deny legitimacy of differences, and so it becomes a generic practice that negates indeterminacy in favor of sameness. The indeterminacy of the other is unsettling, if not frightening, for the Augustinian, since it impinges upon self (and the Same) unpredictably in an immediacy that cannot be grasped or controlled. But the occurrence of the other must be grasped and controlled, in the Augustinian worldview, delicately and measurably, before it grasps us. To mitigate fear, potential violence, humiliation, or usurpation, a concerted effort is made to convert the other through a *currency* of, for example, salvation, good will, community, fellowship, redemption, and so on.

In a similar manner the ideology of communication exchange presupposes that everything real, and everything other, can and will be explained according to rational lights:

> Communication is the exchange of messages, exchange the communication of goods. The instances of communication like those of exchange are definable only in terms of property or propriety . . . the propriety of information, analogous to the propriety of uses. And just as the flow of uses can be controlled, so can the flow of information. As a perverse use is repressed, a dangerous bit of information is banned. As a need is diverted and a motivation created, an addressor is led to say something other than what he or she was going to say. (1988, 20)[1]

Such a communication ideology—one built on the creation and satisfaction of the dominant need for property and propriety—forgets the intensities and obligations associated with being damaged, wronged, susceptible, transgressive, or silenced. For semiotics (and communication theory) in the Augustinian tradition, feelings are transposed (*aufheben*) cognitively as messages in an already coded system. Reality is determined according to culture-specific verification procedures. The reality of the unverifiable or indeterminate is denied or suppressed. Difference is marked out in familiar signs and categories. The heathens are saved. The youth are educated to serve the authorities of a repressive system. Transgressors are suspended, banished, excommunicated, tortured, or killed. Suspected transgressors are watched, surveillance is internalized, and the threat presented by the other's difference is postponed if not eliminated.

In the broadest sense, then, Lyotard argues that privileging semiotics as a system of communication exchange valorizes the language offices (*langue*) of those who conquer; structures the remoteness of the other according to political, economic, or academic expediency; and assimilates difference as a singular, immediate, and compelling event in order to construct a manageable "message" (see 1993, 48). What is needed is a radically different notion of the sign, a notion that Lyotard defines as pagan.

Although Lyotard's development of the idea of paganism can be found in many of his works,[2] I am particularly interested in discussing how, in *The Differend: Phrases in Dispute*, he takes up the paganism of the early Greek sophists. Through *Notices* on Protagoras, Gorgias, and Antisthenes—as well as Plato and Aristotle—he addresses the problem of "bearing witness to differends,"[3] and the associated problem of signification, in ways that are particularly compelling for communication theorists.

The sophists, "the partisans of agonistics," were masters at constructing paradoxes that rendered the perception of taken-for-granted reality problematical, while the Greek philosophers, especially Plato, "the partisans of dialogue," were determined to get the better of signs, to show that the truth of the referent could be revealed through proper dialectical methods that would not allow the weaker argument to prevail over the stronger (see 1988, Plato Notice, pp. 19–26).

Lyotard, who believes that the weaker argument should, indeed, prevail over the stronger under certain conditions, takes up the following sophistic paradoxes: (1) if Being exists, then Not-Being must also exist, but how can there be both Being and Not-Being at the same time? (Gorgias Notice); (2) if signification is possible, then designation must be presumed, but how can one designate something (especially through naming) without first going through a process of signification? (Antisthenes Notice);

and (3) if there is a phrase "whose referent is all phrases" (e.g., I am lying), then, under what conditions can this phrase remain part of its referent? (Protagoras Notice). Each of these paradoxes raises the question of positing and knowing reality through signs—in slightly different ways.[4]

Gorgias

Gorgias argues that it is problematical to state that something exists, and even if it does exist, it is foolish to think that it can be known in signs. And if it can be known, "it cannot be revealed to others" (1988, Gorgias Notice, p. 14). Being—the essential nature of something—implies its opposite, Not-Being. Either something is or it is not. But if "Not-Being is Not-Being [. . .] just as much as the existent, then the non-existent would be: in fact, the non-existent is non-existent as the existent is existent, such that actual things (*ta pragmata*) are, no more than they are not [. . .] But then if Not-Being is, its opposite, Being, is not" (1988, Gorgias Notice, p. 15). When it comes to revealing the nature of reality, "it is possible to neither be nor not to be."

To neither be nor not to be results in an indeterminacy of the referent to the extent that the essence or Being of the thing—conceived as an object, event or other—cannot be presented and hence known. Rather (the sophists were the first deconstructionists) the "what" of the signified is contingent on the phrase universes that take it up *each time it is taken up*. That to which signs ostensibly refer is not some thing that can be represented positively or isomorphically; in fact, the thing itself suffers from a kind of negation through representation, a suffering that compels differends: "If nothing is therefore, then demonstrations say everything without exception" (Gorgias), to which Lyotard rejoins, "Reality [. . .] has to be 'demonstrated,' that is, argued and presented as a case, and, once established, it is a state of the referent for cognitive phrases. This state does not preclude, that, simply put, 'nothing is'" (1988, Gorgias Notice, p. 16).

The important distinction in this rejoinder is between "demonstration" and "cognitive phrases." Demonstration is understood not in the sense of revealing the essential nature of some thing—i.e., the *what* of the *quid*, which presumes an already situated referent that can be rendered in determinate signs; but in asking *Is it happening?*—i.e., the *whether* of the *quod*, which presumes that, simply put, an event is taking place that is summoning phrase universes to battle out its indeterminacy (1988, 131, 132). For Lyotard, the *whether* of demonstration links onto the differends implied by phrasing (broadly conceived, not just language, but also feeling, silence, etc.)[5] the occurrence of the thing, and the indeterminacy of that demonstration, its future orientation, the silences associated with the *quid*, are indeterminate, unknown, and silent precisely because the occurrence does *not* arrive already clothed in self-evident signs or ready-made truth. It is an "Is it happening?" that does not "need" human beings to realize "Being (or language)" (1988, 173) nor does it "obligate" addressees as genres obligate according to their stakes (1988, 174), but rather "summons humans to situate themselves in unknown phrase universes, even if they don't have the feeling that something has to be phrased" (1988, 263). The occurrence opens "passages" that agitate members of a community, or communities (1988, Kant Notice 4, p. 167), who come and take their places in its universe and do battle over how to link onto it. But how can we take our places if something is not designated or signified? This brings us to the paradox of naming associated with Antisthenes, to whom even Aristotle conceded ground, reluctantly (1988, Antisthenes Notice, pp. 35–37).

Antisthenes

The paradox of naming addresses the question: Which comes first, designation or signification? Lyotard states the problem as follows:

> What can be said about the referent? "Before" knowing whether what one says or will say about it is true or false, it is necessary to know what one is talking about. But how can it be known which referent one is talking about without attributing properties to it, that is, without already saying something about it? (1988, Antisthenes Notice, pp. 36–37)

How can I speak about that which has not been named? And if it is named, does that not presuppose some expressed knowledge about it? The way out of the paradox suggests, again, that demonstration is not grounded in a preconceived notion of the essence of "reality" per se; nor does it necessarily produce verifiable or replicable results; but is contingent, rather, on names and the relations of names, understood as *simple* signs that designate some reality as existing. Names become primary referents insofar as they are *taken* as designating some form of reality. They are not significations, however. They do not express a primary sense about a referent in the world (1988, 57–60), and they do not remain in place, so to speak, as invariant.

Following Antisthenes, then, "contradiction is impossible" as long as neither of us can speak the essence of the thing, but it is also impossible even if I could speak the essence and you cannot, for "how can not talking [about it] [*ho me legon*] contradict talking [about it]" (1988, Antisthenes Notice, pp. 35–36; see also 60; brackets in original). If I refer to a name which you recognize, then we are referring to the same "thing," even if we do not know its Being. If we argue about its denomination, then we are either arguing about its name or referring to different things. And if we argue about its essence, then we are arguing about different things, because if we each knew the essence of a common referent, there would be no argument and probably no need to talk (*ti legein*) at all. Contradiction, therefore, is impossible as long as only one name is linked to one referent in any singular event. This is not to valorize sign-object representationalism, nor a nascent nominalism. The name, Lyotard notes,

> fixes the referent, but that does not mean that the name is derived from or motivated by the named. This motivation cannot, in truth, be described, unless the essence of the named is already known independently of its name, which is an absurdity [. . .] Nomination is an active designation, a poiein [. . .] which isolates singularities in the "neither being nor Not-Being" (1988, Antisthenes Notice, p. 37).

Fixing the referent, however, does not last very long. A name and its ostensible referent have "to be affirmed 'each time'" [. . .] "that it actually acts as a linchpin and endows its referent with a reality, that at least remains contingent. That is why reality is never certain (its probability is never equal to 1)" (1988, 66; see also Caputo, 1993, 75–77, 267n23). In short, the name is not proprietary. In the singular event it works pragmatically as a linchpin as long as agreements can be reached concerning its designation. But this does not mean that denomination is intrinsically linked to the referent. It also does not mean that its senses cannot change in an instant.[6]

This notion can be broadened to designations other than pronouns and names. In Peircian terms, for example, just because a phrase resembles some singular aspect or aspects of its referent iconically (*buzzing bee*), is connected to it indexically (*my Chair was angry*), or represents it symbolically (*he's a sexual harasser*), does not mean that an essence is revealed by the name. It simply means that singularities have been isolated that suggest possibilities for designating an event, for the moment. The sound of a bee buzzing motivates the word *buzz* iconically, but that does not mean that the essence of the bee (its bee-ing) is a "buzz." Buzzing is one attribute that has taken on, anthropocentrically, the identity of the bee.

> The problem raised by Antisthenes, if it is retranscribed in Aristotelian terms, would be the following: one can perhaps say the "what its being was" of a referent, but this referent would first have to be named "before"

any predication is made about it. The simple or the elementary is not a component of the object, it is its name and it comes to be situated as referent in the universe of the definitional phrase. It is a simple—hence prelogical—logic which by itself is not pertinent with regard to the rules of truth (1988, Antisthenes Notice, p. 37).[7]

Since signification presupposes a contingent designation through names that is prior to knowledge of truth about the referent, then the "reality" of an occurrence can be demonstrated not simply by ostension (*There it is, the buzzing, that's a bee*); nor by some proprietary description of sense that holds absolutely between sign and object over time; but indeterminately by "networks of names [. . .] and by names of relations" (1988, 60) in the singular event. Names and relations become building blocks, however fallible and tentative, for the invention of idioms that attempt to put into phrases the differends marked or signaled by a *feeling* (see note 3). Recall that a feeling is not a differend, nor is it language, nor is it Being, but one possible phrase that signals a differend. If that feeling is named, it becomes a simple sign that is situated as a referent in a phrase universe that begins to battle over the indeterminate status of the event.

The difference, then, between the pagan and Augustinian notions of the sign should be clear. In the Augustinian worldview, the event is linked determinatively to other "signs" that signify, a priori, the truth of the event. Silence by addressees and addressors ipso facto signifies this truth. The name is not only a compound of the object, it stands for an essence in the "inner man," which does not vary. Signification is motivated by what is already known: *My name is Andrew; my brother's name is Philip; together we become apostles who piously serve the Lord through humble toil; let His Will be done, and so on, amen.* In a more contemporary sense: *We know what sexual harassment is; we have reason to believe that X harassed Y; therefore the case will have had features a, b, c, d, and so on, amen.*

Protagoras

The final paradox is actually the first discussed by Lyotard in *The Differend*. I have saved it for last because it brings the question of communication ethics into the indeterminacies of demonstration and signification. It is the most well known paradox, since it was taken up by Bateson and others as expressing the classic double bind (1972; see also PC). It was first attributed to Protagoras: *"I have not won a case!" cries the former pupil to the master, "but you guaranteed I would win if I followed your teaching! You must, therefore, refund my money or I will charge you*

*before the tribunal." To which the master responds, "Let us go before the
tribunal then. If you lose the case, I owe you nothing, and, if you win the
case, you will have won a case, and I still owe you nothing."*

As Lyotard notes, Russell "solves" the paradox with the theory of logical types:

> [A] proposition (here the verdict in the litigation between master and
> pupil) that refers to a totality of propositions (here, the set of prior ver-
> dicts) cannot be a part of the totality . . . the phrase whose referent is all
> phrases must not be part of its referent. Otherwise, it is 'poorly formed'
> and it is rejected by the logician. (This is the case for the Paradox of the
> Liar in the form of *I Lie*). The logician has nothing but scorn for the
> sophist who ignores this principle: but the sophist doesn't ignore it, he
> unveils it (and in laughter, while Ibanskian power makes one weep)
> (1988, Protagoras Notice, pp. 6–7; original emphasis).

In a pagan semiotics, where the "neither Being nor Not-Being" is the
modus for demonstration, where names are simple signs that do not signify truth, the phrase whose referent is all phrases, can, indeed, be part of
its referent—under conditions that are neither dogmatist (the logician)
nor empiricist (the physicist) (see 1988, Protagoras Notice, p. 7). First
condition: The phrase could *not* be framed within a cognitive genre of
discourse whose stakes are tied to the law of noncontradiction. The tribunal, thus, cannot accept it, the judges would simply be confused. But what
genre would allow it? Lyotard suggests that the "physics" of "generalized
relativity" would accept it, but this is empiricism. Certain forms of literature would accept it—witness Gertrude Stein's "prose" or e.e. cummings's
poetry—as would an everyday agonistics like "playing the dozens," for example (see Kochman, 1981). Other genres are possible. But the crucial
point is that the phrase can exist differentially prior to its assimilation or
qualification by any genre. Its possibility is an interdisciplinary event that
summons logicians, physicists, poets, philosophers, communicologists, and
others into its universe to battle over its sense.

Second condition: By allowing the phrase legitimacy, the referent is
rendered indeterminate, but it cannot be rendered as such merely to the
advantage of one "player," be it the master. The pupil is part of the same
relativized play of time and phrases as the master, and is given equal opportunity to express it: "If I lose (against you), I will have lost; if I win
(against you), even if I say I always lose, then I will still have lost" (1988,
Protagoras Notice, p. 8). Note the future perfect tense of the argument: *If
taking this case to the tribunal means that I still do not get my money
back, whether I win or lose, then I will have lost. Therefore, give me my*

money back! The stakes of the discourse depend on what is designated as winning and losing in the particular case, not simply on the logical status of the phrase. Perhaps something more is necessary, something other than a third party who can judge. A *third* condition, at least, is necessary, but it must be a *singular third*, and highly contingent.

Third condition: The problem remains whether the pupil should get his or her money back. Should the teacher be responsible for the pupil's lack of competence in arguing cases? The edifice of education would tumble if such an ethical or legal responsibility existed. Ethics, perhaps, should be problematized, as Caputo (1993) suggests. That is, the differend should not be *resolved* out of some necessity dictated by an absolute law, be it legal or ethical, but *extended* by a feeling of obligation to open up an agonistics that might find an idiom to express the wrong. A third party, in the sense of an absolute eyewitness, is not required (1988, 64, 88, 164); "[w]hat is absolutely required, on the contrary, is the contingency of the future. By this, not only the contingency of the 'events' should be understood but also the contingency of sense" (1988, 89).

To recognize this degree of indeterminacy is not, however, to abdicate responsibility. Responsibility is not the question. Obligation is the question. With regard to the paradox, we do not know what happens next, but we can guess at a scenario of mutual obligation: The master, having been equalized by that which he or she thought was proprietary discourse, would be obligated to acknowledge this equality. The pupil, having recognized the futility of litigation and been empowered by his or her discourse with the master, might pursue new cases with more confidence. Since they agree not to agree on the issue of money, they become obligated to pursue other projects together, albeit agonistically. Perhaps the master becomes the pupil's (unpaid?) consultant in court; or the pupil sits in on the master's seminars (tuition free?); or they meet and talk weekly, over coffee and bagels (at the master's expense?). The contingencies are endless.

The Agony of Semiotics

The following is a conversation between a Peircian, who claims *not* to be an Augustinian, and a Lyotardian, who is reluctant to accept a would-be Peircian *paganism*. Note that this is not a dialogue in the Platonic sense but an agonistics in the sophistic sense. The end of the conversation does not open onto a truth, but a differend, that is, an "unstable state and instant of language wherein something which must be able to be put into phrases cannot yet be . . . " (see note 3).

Peircian: When Lyotard states that the differend, the "Is it happen-

ing?" is not a sign, is he not suggesting, essentially, that it is general and/
or vague?

Lyotardian: Yes, if by "general or vague" you mean indeterminate. No,
if you mean that the differend can be known by a general rule of linkage. It
is, rather, a singularity that *seeks* rules for linkages that are currently
unknown.

Peircian: Then there are some commonalities between Peirce and
Lyotard that should be noted. For example, Peirce took up the problem of
the "neither being nor not-being" (see CP, 6.350–52)[8] and states: "There
are even realities, if we admit the reality of generals (which is, at least, not
to be refuted by mere definition), which are indeterminate in respect to
the applicability of many signs" (CP, 6.352). He defines the indeterminate
as that to which the principle of contradiction does not apply (CP, 5.447–
48) and that which opens up the possibility for interpretation through the
use of signs that might connect up to the indeterminate (CP, 5.505). This
seems much more a pagan than Augustinian position.

Lyotardian: But is not Peirce still bent on forming the indeterminate
in particular ways? In signs to be used for purposes of scientific progress,
for example? His take on the general may be a recognition of indeterminacy, but the general and the differend are not to be equivocated. The
general can be phrased according to existing idioms; the differend cannot.
Was his theory of signs not a way to reduce the indeterminacy of such an
event?

Peircian: His interest was to push thought to the most general, yes,
not necessarily as a way of assimilating all phenomena within his classification of signs, but in spilling off occurrences, so to speak. The theory of
signs enables interrogation and experimentation with what is currently
unknown and has not been assimilated into current scientific idioms. This
seems to resemble Lyotard's call for thought to be experimental and find
rules for linkage that are not currently given by one genre or another.

Lyotardian: But not by imposing a system of signs that mark them off
in ways that scientific practice—the cognitive genre—can smile upon and
verify with its particular set of verification procedures.

Peircian: Then this leads to some confusion in Lyotard's account of
designation and signification. By valorizing the differend, which he states
is neither "language nor Being," does Lyotard not depend on the "simple
sign" as a first step in making sense of that event or finding an idiom for
it? The differend becomes a phrase-event, does it not? Everything is a
phrase, whether it can be shown or known, or not. Even the *Idea* (in
Kantian sense) that there is something other than phrases, is a phrase.
Lyotard states, following Kant, that the feeling of the sublime is a *sign*. He
appears to use the terms "phrase" and "sign" interchangeably. Why, then,
does he discount the place of signs and codification?

Lyotardian: *I music you.*[9] This phrase is an event prior to its being signified. Do you know what it signifies? No, you do not, even if you think you do. Can I tell you what it signifies? No, I cannot, though I can describe its occurrence by linking onto it with these metalinguistic phrases. To presume that I can tell you, or you me, the *what* of its signification is to assume a being-in-itself that expresses itself through the occurrence of the phrase and holds over time and location. The phrase summons us to take our places in its universe. What does the noun *music* signify when it is used as a verb? What does "you" signify in this phrase? What does "I" signify? Is it *you?* Is it *I?* The "music," the "you" and the "I" emerge as the phrase arrives: "you [and I] are nothing but its advent (whether addressee or addressor or referent or sense even, or several of these instances together) in the universe presented by the phrase that happens. It wasn't waiting for you [or me]. You [and I] come when it arrives. The occurrence is not the Lord. The pagans know this and laugh over this edifying confusion" (1988, 173).

Peircian: Given the generality of the phrase *I music you,* it is, ipso facto, indeterminate. Generality (and vagueness) are useful for exploring possibility, but any single phrase-event like the one you just cited seeks through addressors and addressees some sense for its referential functions. The phrase is nothing if it does not stand to somebody in some respect or capacity, which is the very definition of a sign (CP, 2.228). *I music you* may stand in different respects and capacities to different addressees, and this vagueness does, indeed, define its indeterminacy. But those addressees become addressors, as you know very well, just as I, as an original addressee of the phrase, am becoming an addressor. Hence, as you also know, we give the phrase form by taking it up. The more we discuss it, form it, figure it, with an interest in reaching some agreement as to its sense and reference, the more we depend on communication and signification, do we not?

Lyotardian: The phrase is indeterminate precisely to the extent that, as an event, it stands in many possible respects and capacities to any number of addressees, who, then, in acknowledging its materiality, give it form by raising questions and becoming addressors. And yes, communication signifies the phrase, but not according to a preconceived rule of its occurrence—e.g., the author's intention—but in order to seek a rule that is not yet known. As an occurrence the phrase "presents" the possibility of many differends, many possible linkages (1988, Kant Notice 1, pp. 61–65). Discussing the phrase creates linkages among and through these differends, and thus *forms* the "neither being nor not-being," which creates further differends, ad infinitum. Just because we come to a recognition regarding its significance here and now, however, does not mean that a rule has been established for other cases. A consensus on its meaning should not be the "end" of the communication about its indeterminacy.

Peircian: Let me address the problem in slightly different terms. Form, from the Kantian point of view, takes hold (it seems we have agreed on this) at that moment when an addressee becomes an addressor and imbues the first addressor's phrase with a referential function (1988, Kant Notice 1, p. 62). There are many varieties of form that impinge upon signification (CP, 6.360), but the form of cognition is not simply one among others for Kant. Cognition is that which makes sense and reference possible, not to mention their speculative (dialectical) conflation, and renders to absurdity the attempt to know a thing-in-itself (CP, 6.362). Cognition, for Kant, creates the possibility for the syntheses of the imaginative and the intuitive, for the experience of the sublime, not to mention the previous phrase. This presupposes some form of communication, does it not? Which, in turn, presupposes signification, and so on. We have already agreed to discuss and perhaps disagree about the signification of the occurrence. Even if consensus is not reached, this does not mean we will not talk to each other again, and perhaps agree on some points and become clear on what we disagree on.

Lyotardian: You have stated the case well. To the extent that the cognitive is, for the Peircian, the genre of genres, so to speak, then it remains difficult if not impossible to link onto the occurrence without prejudging it. The pragmaticist still wants a community of scholars to recognize the reality of his or her insight and to conduct further experiments, or discussions, to replicate results, verify the truth, converge on definitions, and fixate belief—if it is scientific belief. Experimentation is accomplished in the cognitive genre, and if the reality of the referent cannot be substantiated through signification, then it loses its legitimacy as an occurrence and is perceived consensually as unreal to the extent that it remains indeterminate. Hence, the gas chambers at Auschwitz, since there were no survivors or witnesses, no third party to verify their existence, limited material evidence, and so on, may or may not exist for the Peircian. The differends associated with the sense of the event (gas chambers) for those who did not die at Auschwitz, would be suppressed, and consensus would take hold within the norms of a community that has decided not to acknowledge the legitimacy of that particular event.

Peircian: Peirce was neither a fascist nor a positivist, despite certain of his following. In fact, he suffered many damages, if not wrongs, at the hands of those who had power over his academic career. He was forced by circumstance to develop several careers, and was no stranger to uncertainty and indeterminacy, both personally and philosophically.[10] Through necessity and experience he learned how to be innovative, to take risks, and to think against the grain. He knew what it meant to search for a rule in conjunction with the contingencies of an occurrence . . .

Lyotardian: Peirce's agonies are a tribute to philosophy . . .

Peircian: The point, however, is, that he developed a prelogic—perhaps out of Aristotle's notes on Antisthenes—that is akin to that which Lyotard argues is necessary for the contingent designative function of simple signs. That is, abductive logic, which is a logic of feeling, guesswork, and experimentation (CP, 5.181), is integral to Peirce's theory of signs. It hinges on the fallibility of sign-object-interpretant relations, a fallibility that is crucial for insight into the occurrence, or, in Peirce's terms, the particular case (CP, 5.151–212; 5.587). Moreover, the classification of signs is not an explanatory model but a heuristic for putting into phrases that which appears as a startling case. Signification, for Peirce, takes up the challenge of the indeterminate and the other (see Colapietro, 1994). Peirce has provided an idiom for putting into phrases that which resists being phrased, which Lyotard claims is his own philosophical domain (see 1988, 22), for arguing and signifying the indeterminacy of the case, for seeking a rule currently unknown without presupposing a rule of one's own (see Shweder, 1991, 361n4; Lanigan, 1994).[11]

Lyotardian: But still, the whole thrust of pragmaticism is to name and agree on definitions in order to establish the truth of the referent, which is conceived as an object, event, or situation in the world. Is it not? What is signified is not the truth of the referent understood in this way, but the relative truth of the significations at a particular place and time, which must battle with other significations and create or suffuse differends. Peirce was interested in common ends, not differ-ends. Is this not correct?

Peircian: He was interested in both. Abduction and indeterminacy are the domain of differends, ethics and aesthetics the domain of common ends. Perhaps we can agree on this: The occurrence takes form, so to speak, through naming and signification. To the extent that the occurrence presents itself as other, but cannot be posited in itself, it evokes silent feeling on one hand and vociferous argument on the other. Thus it is ensconced in a landscape of signification. Peirce's classification of signs hinged on a recognition of feeling or "firstness" (CP, 1.304–22), which is not the differend but could be the sign of the differend; on the brute otherness of the other or "secondness" (CP, 1.322–42), which evokes shock and compels phrase universes of various sorts; and the linkages inherent in mediation or "thirdness" (CP, 1.343–53), which is a speculative *rhetoric* (not dialectic) that promotes argument as a precursor to the constitution of reality (see Langsdorf and Smith, 1994; cf. Rorty 1982, 160–61; 1991, 138–39). Please note that I am using Lyotard's language to define Peirce's terms in a wholly Peircian manner. It seems clear, then, that Lyotard, despite protestations to the contrary, is a Peircian!

Lyotardian: The alterity of the other (which includes Lyotard and his work) should remain manifest in the indeterminacy of linkages among phrases. Just because an event is phrased (or a person defined as such and such) does not mean that alterity has withdrawn from the scene or been assimilated into a result. This is, as you might say, a rhetorical problem. Damages are created from resolutions. Occurrences add up. Progress is tied to the sublimity of their recognition, the sublimity of the feeling, the simultaneous pain and joy of finding a provisional name or an idiom for that which resists being expressed. Although one may be justified in bringing a case before the tribunal, the end of that case is not necessarily the rendering of justice as an end but the smothering of a differend, on one hand, and, on the other, the creation of an occurrence, yet to be named, in the neither being nor not-being. This is where we end, in ongoing indeterminacy, with a dissensus rather than a consensus. You do not agree?

Peircian: Yes, I do not (laughter).

Lyotardian: Then let us bear witness to that (more laughter).

An Ethnography of Differends?

Lyotard's concerns with an Augustinian semiotics end in a theory of the *event*, and a theory of *phrasing of the event*, that renders false any "graphism" that pretends to represent the truth of something, or some other, in signs (1988, 171). Even the most nuanced description of an event is false to the extent that someone makes a claim to it being true. This does not mean that description is superfluous but simply that one description is always already in conflict with others, and this conflict of phrases rather than the "true" rendition of the event is the most fruitful site for critical inquiry.

The relativism of the "true" does not, however, lead to a relativism of the *just*. Lyotard's engagement of the problem of "simple signs" also makes possible a judicial phrasing of events that acknowledges the legitimacy of the "inflation of senses" attached to names and relations (1988, 75–84; see note 6) but links the possibility for "adducing proof" and thus circumscribing the equivocalities of unlimited semiosis (in the Peircian sense), not according to some "real" referent in the world (which is the bias of historical cognition) but according to a reflective judgment that presupposes a reflexive re-cognition of the ethical, aesthetic, and political stakes tied up with signifying practices. Lyotard does not *promote* an inflation of senses, he simply recognizes *that* reality and force but also the possibility for its judicial circumspection with regard to a singular event. Conflict is thus inevitable, and consensus is continually made problematical. Consensual descriptions that argue for a true picture of the event, or some essence of the other, however, beg the question of the critical judgments presupposed by any descriptive act. Lyotard's shift from the true to the just opens even the circumspect to a perpetual vigilance.

What, then, does such a vigilance portend for communication research? I address this question by focusing on a form of communication research that, in many ways, subsumes concerns about objectivism, on one hand, and rhetorical purport, on the other: communication ethnography, the attempt to articulate an identifiable culture as it is embodied in its communicating. Clearly, as many scholars have shown, an objectivist ethnography is untenable, and I do not intend to repeat those specific arguments here. I will restrict myself instead to how a critical ethnography of communication is being conceived and deployed and how Lyotard's notion of the differend might contribute to this deployment. Is an ethnography of differends possible and desirable? Or is this a mere contradiction in terms? Dwight Conquergood's work in the ethnography of performance (1991, 1992) and Michael Huspek's work in critical ethnography (1989/90, 1993, 1994) provide good points of reference for introducing the admittedly contradictory idea of an ethnography of differends.

Following anthropologists Clifford, Jackson, Rosaldo, Trinh, Turner, Tyler, and others, Conquergood charts how postmodern ethnography has moved away from the objectivist and normative positing of others (see Philipsen, 1992),[12] and toward an acknowledgement of the contingent and provisional constitution of self and other in intercultural contact. Ethnography should be conceived as a rhetoric of performance, or performance of rhetoric, argues Conquergood, that takes up a critical position on the margins of discourses where subjects are polysemic rather than autonomous, displaced rather than already assimilated into an existing system, and part of an ongoing social drama in which meaning is continually made problematical. Forms of dominance are recognized and subverted in an altogether sophistic manner (1992, 82–83) on these margins, and "subjects" should be thought of as "subjects in process/on trial," to use Kristeva's phrase (see 1984) and certainly not static and largely predictable products of insular and rigidly constituted rules and regulative forms. Indeed, the ethnographer is conceived as one of many subjects whose self-reflexive and self-reflective modalities become integral to a process of reversibility between self and other (see especially Huspek, 1994). Conquergood concentrates on how displaced people enter the public sphere as "counterpublics" and often subvert the normative modes of interaction in this so-called "public sphere" (1992, 92).

The ethnographic "expedition" (see Shweder, 1991), therefore, must become attuned to the conflicts, entanglements, and vulnerabilities engendered by those people who live on the borderlands. The ethnographer rec-

ognizes that he or she is part of the displacement observed and thus constitutes by his or her bodily presence an ongoing site of contestation. In
Conquergood's view, this and other "sites" can be reproduced through various performative modes, only one of which is scholarly writing. Reproduc-
tion through performance is less concerned with what others *mean* as a
matter of semantics, however, and more concerned with how linkages are
made syntactically between and among diverse cultural forms; with how
evocative (intonation, gesture) and expressive (music, dance, poetry, ritual)
forms *take form* as a matter of sustenance and survival (see especially
1991). Conquergood's fieldwork exemplifies the commitment and force of
critical ethnographic work. His various modes of presenting his material—
through video, performance, writing and speaking—reveal in stark terms
the conflicts and struggles of those who live on the borderlands, including
himself at times. His approach helps to unveil the dynamics of cultural
process, expose power relations, and challenge conventional modes of
scholarly representation.

In complementary fashion, Huspek, who productively links the often
dissensual work of Habermas, Gadamer, Winch, and Geertz, takes up the
problem of how culture/tradition contributes to and detracts from the possibility of knowing the other intersubjectively, and thus sharing in some
form of understanding, however provisional. He notes (1994, 58–59) that
critique hinges on the ethnographer's being able (1) to assume some perspective from the other point of view, (2) to recognize how his or her (the
ethnographer's) culture/tradition impinges upon the possibility of such a
perspective and thus frames the other and the possibility of taking on the
other, and (3) to reflect on how the perspective of oneself and one's tradition is changed by the experience of attempting to take on the perspective
of the other. For Huspek, the problem of "shared understanding" is a problem of translation and demonstration (in Lyotard's sense), not simply between languages but between and among subjectivities who variously embody one another's cultural world according to the normative assumption
that such mutual embodiment is possible, desirable, and empowering, if
not emancipatory.

It would seem, therefore, from both Conquergood's and Huspek's
points of view, that *linkage, embodiment*, and *power relations* between and
among selves and others constitute the pivotal concerns of a critical ethnography. And that these concerns hinge upon *a subject* or *subjects of
discourse* who embody—reflexively in the moment and reflectively over
time—culture(s), tradition(s), history(s), and so on. I will first summarize,
from Lyotard's view, the problem of clinging to the notion of a speaking-
subject of discourse, then conclude by extending the notions of linkage,
body, and power.

Yes, the subject (why hold onto this term?) of discourse is polysemic, a locus of many influences and power relations. But to the extent that the subject is defined as such, like a whorl or knot in the grain of wood through which any number of heterogeneous forms collide and recoil, it is no longer simply a subject of discourse that can be re-presented through language or performance. It is a multiplicity that, when phrased, becomes something else or something other depending upon the stakes (ethical, aesthetic, political) of the genre of discourse that wins the battle of appropriation (see Lyotard, 1988, 178–81).

The critical ethnographer should admit, then, that rendering the other, and/or rendering self-other interactions, no matter how marginal s/he (or they) may be, is a presentation of a presentation of an event—a meta–re–presentation, if you will—and certainly not a semblance of any single event or practice in itself. In such a re–presentation, one phrase universe wins the battle for supremacy and necessarily includes the prejudices and competencies of the ethnographer as well as the depicted language and practices of the other. The event is originally phrased according to the stakes of the genre or genres of discourse within which the ethnographer, and the other, are working, respectively, whether these be principally cognitive, ethical, aesthetic, political, or otherwise. Self-other understanding is contingent upon the degree to which the senses and references of phrases, as they become meaningful in one (self's or other's) genre, resonate with senses and references in the other's (self's or other's) analogous genre. This translation process is, again, not a matter of truth but a matter of justice, and thus a matter of agonistics (1988, 79). Senses and references, and hence the possibility for understanding, require translation and vigilance between an addressor and addressee who are speaking the same language; even more so, obviously, does this occur when phrase universes develop interculturally. The effort in ethnographic work is not so much getting the other right, or presenting a true, albeit critical, account, but first bearing witness to the remarkable and often astonishing conflict of phrases and interests, then finding an idiom for expressing these conflicts. In this sense, then, ethnography is performative and critical but not according to the intentionality of either oneself or another.

An ethnography sensitive to differends is not principally concerned with translation, however. Translation presupposes that shared understanding is possible given current discursive practices from each cultural world. A differend, on the other hand, presupposes that damages are being felt on the margins of discourse and that these damages are being left unexpressed for one reason or another. A *wrong* results, according to Lyotard, when the felt damages cannot find an idiom of expression, or the available idiom is dominated by the other who/which is inflicting damages (1988, 7,

8). The differend is *phrased*, then, through silences or acts of transgression that stop short of ordinary language or, perhaps, bring it to a halt. But expression and perception are not brought to a halt in a differend. Phrasing requires some felt expression, even if it is in the form of a silence. Rather than focusing on the articulate utterances (rule-governed or otherwise) that ostensibly produce shared understanding, an ethnography of differends would embark on an expedition for the asymmetric tone or noise that does not obey normative syntax; the inelegant gesture or oxymoronic juxtapositions that transgress the tacit acceptance of the existing order of things; the inarticulate feeling that runs against the grain of regulative cultural experience; the nonrepresentative form that is created spontaneously and serendipitously but may disappear as quickly as it appears; and, perhaps, the insufferable influences (cultural, political, biological) that often determine fate but remain untouched at a distance.

Further, an ethnography of differends, following Huspek's suggestions for critical ethnography, would be critically self-conscious, not only concerning its own *Weltanschauung* but also with regard to its stated interests and purposes and how these are affected by the discourses of others. It would, therefore, be peripheral to the borderlands as well as its culture/ tradition of origin, hence eminently fallible, and, much like John Cage's musical productions or Karen Finley's performance art, it would not seek validity by appealing to the cognitive genre and its elaborate system of verification procedures. It would be a rhetorical art, and the ethnographer part improvisational actor, part critical and ever-vigilant sentinel.

Turner's phrase "on the pulses" (quoted in Conquergood, 1991, 187) to describe the disposition of the ethnographer would thus be apt for an ethnography of differends to the extent that the pulsations produced by any event are recognized as producing linkages that, at least initially, do not follow a predetermined course and, finally, despite the ethnographer's best efforts, cannot necessarily be reproduced. Whereas ritual assumes a completed form that is reenacted, or *can be* reenacted performatively, "pulses" (think of drives in the Freudian sense) are more akin to quanta that change form the instant they take hold in and through an object of desire or are presented as something to behold. Living "on the pulses" requires an attentiveness to new evocative and expressive forms that attempt to make sense of the conflicts and entanglements that marginal existence presents. An ethnography of differends would be principally concerned with how these new (evocative and expressive) idioms are configured in the immediacy of singular events and then taken up or negated by competing phrases and genres.

The following questions, among many possible others, would seem pertinent for such an oxymoronic ethnography:

- How do addressors, addressees, senses and references come and take their places and compete at the beckoning of an event?

- What kinds of linkages are made between existing forms of a belief or practice and that which challenges that belief and practice?

- How do language practices intermingle and get transcribed through and among diversely gendered and cultured bodies?

- How do competing interests (political forces, moral imperatives, aesthetic preferences, cognitive forms) struggle for control of communication and interpretation when a stranger, or strangers, are present?

- How do different senses of history and purpose collide in the attempt to account for and explain a problematical situation? What are the results?

- What are the ambiguities, equivocalities, uncertainties, damages, and silences that pervade particular intercultural contacts?

Again, in addressing these questions, the ethnographer of differends would not suffer from an illusion of presenting the "true" picture of some "other" world. She or he would remain *"Unheimlichkeit,"* a hostage who maintains a contradictory relationship (with self and other) (1988, 171) and operates according to agonistic notions of linkage, body, and power. What would these agonies look like?

The idea of linkage would not follow what we ordinarily think of as *syntax*, or that which moves along a path known by virtue of its rule-governed, diacritical oppositions (a classically structural rather than post-structural definition).[13] Rather, linkages would take place according to a *paratax*—or an outbreak of phrases that moves more like Gertrude Stein's writing, John Cage's percussive movements, or the way crabgrass grows (1988, 100).[14] Persons who have struggled to communicate with others who speak a different language know how such paratactical linkages are made. They are highly improvisational, contingent, tactical, and often agonizing forms, put together "piecemeal" and pertinent only for that particular moment (see Huspek, 1994, for a nuanced description of this process). Paratactical linkage precedes ritualization, although it can be quite dramatic, conflictual, engrossing, and, at times, damaging. It privileges innovative and wholly experimental ways in which addressors and addressees from different cultures link onto one another's phrases, and how that linking is itself an event to be studied rather than a preliminary means for studying something else. Conventional notions of communication competence falter on this ground to the extent that they hinge on preexisting or idealized rules for linkage—i.e., a syntax—to be learned and used appropriately. Phrasing paratactically is tied to the singular event, rules are discovered according to what happens, and what happens is never the same. This does not mean that the phrase-event is neither real nor false, but "merely what happens, *what is occurring, ce qui arrive, da Fallende*" (1988, 104).

But are not paratactical linkages forms of translation that enable a differend to move into the genre of litigation, so to speak, in which signs and meanings are negotiated for the purposes of the parties involved? And, moreover, are not these linkages made possible by creative speaking-subjects who make a good faith effort to embody the other's language and practices? And, further, are not both of these efforts *universal* prerequisites for creating shared understanding, not to mention constituting some sense of pragmatic justice?

As Lyotard emphasizes throughout *The Differend*, genres of discourse are heterogeneous and unequal, thus any litigation or "negotiation of meanings" between agents of two cultural worlds tends to dissemble, or dissimulate, differences according to the interests of the most powerful party (genre, not person) involved in the differend. This "party" is a "body" of discourse that takes up and takes on various "human" positions (addressors and/or addressees) in a phrase universe (or universes) that includes many possible senses and references. To the extent that "translation" is possible and both parties are satisfied by this translation, there is no differend. To the extent that translation is agonizing or impossible, or is structured explicitly through relations of power that are exclusive, then differends proliferate. Differends are necessary and important, however, since their expulsion, or appearance of expulsion, would mean that political tyranny or, perhaps, some utopian economic vision rules at the expense of other genres, especially those that might hinge on the "ends" of freedom, obligation, and justice. Embodiment presupposes that cultural forms have been taken on intentionally and mobilized for particular ends. Ends, however, are determined by the stakes defined by genres of discourse. The freedom to embody one set of stakes as opposed to another set of stakes depends on one's placement at the margins of *discourses*, and this placement, as Conquergood (1992) shows, is primarily a bodily bearing or movement (kinesis) rather than a becoming (poiesis) or being (mimesis).

As kinesis, the body is not an *intention*, per se, but a *contention*, suffering the pull of any number of discourses and practices. The body, then, in an ethnography of differends, is in continual transgression, much like people with "disabilities" who continually contend with, and necessarily transgress, the normative constructions (language practices, architecture, technology, temporality, and so on) of the "able bodied" world (see Rose, 1994 and in press; Rose and Smith, 1994). A hearing (speaking) person, for example, who attempts communication with a deaf (signing) person is faced with much more than a problem of translation. She or he is faced with the clash of two fundamentally distinct ways of perceiving and expressing discourse—one spatial and visual, the other vocal and aural. To understand the deaf person, the hearing person must prepare for some violence to his or her normative syntactical modalities—the organic body must be placed in a new and different social body, which, in turn, is visually marked by a body of discourse, or discourse's bodies, that continually contend with and violate the normative structures of the hearing world. In a similar manner, to be in a differend is to suffer a disembodiment to the extent that one feels his or her body as something other than his or her own. Power becomes defined by the intensity with which one's body is taken up by a body of discourse, or other discourses' bodies.

As many communication scholars who deploy a critical ethnography have emphasized, power pervades all modalities of linkage and embodiment.[15] Here I have attempted to put a slightly different spin on the notion of power, one that hinges on how genres of discourse battle for and appropriate events. Whereas Conquergood is interested in how marginalized people learn "on the pulses" to become *sophist*-icated counterpublics, and Huspek is interested in ideology critique in "competing" cultures/traditions/structures, my primary concern is in how power is engaged and problematized through a bodily bearing that, by the necessity imposed by the formal properties of that bodily bearing, makes linkages that are perceived as transgressive by the normative structures of a dominant sociocultural world. Such is the case for many people with disabilities, but especially with deaf people, for example, and people who are confined to wheelchairs and "speak" through augmentative or alternative communication devices. For these people, even though the dominant culture has provided them with a technology that "speaks," the feeling of being in perpetual transgression produces damages that are only partially known by the dominant culture primarily because that power does not have an idiom for expressing such damages.

Conclusion

Lyotard's critique of semiotics stems from his vehement objections to the Augustinian pedagogy of signs and sign-referent relations, which, he argues, is not only fallacious but complicitous with a compulsion to convert that which is different into some semblance of the Same. What cannot be assimilated is sacrificed, and the institution of Signs is ostensibly strengthened as a result. In contrast to this particularly strong historical tendency, Lyotard reverts to the pre-Socratic sophists, who, he argues offer a model of simple signs for indeterminate events that is particularly useful for understanding the intricacies of differends and their possible phrasing.

In explicating Lyotard's views, I have recommended that communication research, especially communication ethnography, take up a position on the margins of the field, so to speak, and learn the ways of the sophists, as Conquergood suggests as well. And, as Huspek recommends, in assuming this position, the ethnographer should become critically self-conscious in any attempt to graphically present the practices of the other. I have also suggested that communication ethnography radicalize even further the notions of linkage, body, and power, such that new forms of expression and perception become possible and desirable even though these forms may not be replicable or verifiable according to the stakes of the cognitive genre of discourse. Living on the margins requires this type of break, if we are to follow the suggestions of Lyotard, especially.

Finally, living on the margins, and especially on the margins of the margins, might be compared to living in a dream. Any image seems possible, and the image of self is not one of agency, per se, but more of a patient who suffers any number of persons, events, senses, and references in seemingly random and illogical juxtapositions of the dream-work (see Smith, in press). This suffering can, at times, be joyful, but even the *jouissance* of such a disposition is cradled in an agony of being subjected to a power or powers that can potentially take away, at the slightest whim, whatever has been given. Power plays out desire and desire plays out power often at the expense of whomever is being played. At the margins of the borderlands, as in a dream, senses and references are constantly battling to form addressors and addressees into victims, conquerors, or poets.

Notes

1. Along these same lines see Stewart (1986; 1991). References to *The Differend* are to paragraph numbers rather than pages. This text also has a series of Notices, which are excursus on seminal thinkers in rhetoric, philosophy, and literature. The Notices will be referenced in this essay by name and page number.

2. See especially *The Postmodern Condition, Peregrinations*, and, with Jean-Loup Thebaud, *Just Gaming*.

3. "The differend is the unstable state and instant of language wherein something which must be able to be put into phrases cannot yet be. This state includes silence, which is a negative phrase, but it also calls upon phrases which are in principle possible. This state is signaled by what one ordinarily calls a feeling: 'One

cannot find the words,' etc. A lot of searching must be done to find new rules for forming and linking phrases that are able to express the differend disclosed by the feeling, unless one wants this differend to be smothered right away in a litigation and for the alarm sounded by the feeling to have been useless. What is at stake in a literature, in a philosophy, in a politics perhaps, is to bear witness to differends by finding idioms for them" (Lyotard, 1988, 22).

4. Here I will concentrate on the Sophistic Notices and refer to the Plato and Aristotle Notices only marginally.

5. Lyotard's notion of phrasing is developed throughout *The Differend* and refers to any form of expression. To not phrase is impossible. Even the absence of a phrase where one was expected, is a phrase. Silence is a phrase, as is the twitching of a cat's nose, a mathematical equation, a wink, a nod, and so on. See 1988 (110, 190, 26, 27).

6. Lyotard's notion of sense, here and elsewhere in *The Differend*, is in contrast to the Fregean notion in that Lyotard acknowledges an inflation of senses given the contingencies and multiplicities invoked by phrase universes (see 1988, 54, 55, 74–84 for discussions of Frege and the inflation of sense). This issue is taken up again in the final section of the essay with a particular focus on the difference between translation and differend in communication ethnography.

7. Here Lyotard cites Wittgenstein, *Philosophical Investigations*, section 49.

8. All references to Peirce's Collected Papers (CP) are to volume and paragraph numbers rather than pages.

9. Lyotard uses this phrase as an example in *Discours, Figure*: "When you make a verb with a noun, there is event: the system of rules of the language not only cannot account for this new usage, but is opposed to it, resists it, and between it and the statement the relationship which is established is that of conflict" (1971, 145; quoted in Bennington, p. 77).

10. Brent (pp. 56–57) notes that "Shakespeare's use of language supplied the model for the concept of sign in much of [Peirce's] own work. Peirce often quoted as a poetic version of his own theory of signs this passage from *A Midsummer Night's Dream*:

And, as imagination bodies forth
The forms of things unknown, the poet's pen
Turns them into shapes, and gives to airy nothing
A local habitation and a name.

11. As Shweder (1991, 361n4) has pointed out in the context of acknowledging the existence of "other" cultural realities, abduction "is the faculty of imagination [that] comes to the rescue of sensation and logic by providing them with the intellectual means to see through experience and leap beyond empty syllogisms and

tautologies to some creative representation of an underlying reality that might be grasped and reacted to, even if that imagined reality cannot be found, proved, or disproved by inductive or deductive rule-following." I have taken up the issue of Peirce's abduction and fallibilism in the context of intercultural "realities" in Smith and Shyles (1994).

12. Although Philipsen admits to practicing a more objectivist and normative ethnography, he would also admit, I believe, that certain social forces and power relations that impinge on the shared meanings of a speech community do deserve some form of legitimate explication. Yes, he might say, what is described should be replicable by other ethnographers who go into the same territory, but that does not mean that the ethnographer should be blinded by verification procedures. She or he might also note how the normative structures have changed gradually, been altered directly, or perhaps even shattered and lost. The most fruitful location for investigation, he would continue, is the "new" normative structures and their cross-cultural analogues, especially those analogues that have gone through similar adjustments. If this is a correct interpretation of Philipsen's approach, then questions of transgression and power are by-passed, as is the problematical body. The ethnographer would go directly to the semantico-syntactic structures, unproblematically. Lyotard would object, of course. The structures of discourse are suffused with bodies and power and continually subject to transgression, which makes differends possible—whether, desirable, damaging, sufferable, or emancipatory (along these lines see Huspek, 1993).

13. As defined by Saussure. For critical discussions see Merleau-Ponty "On the Phenomenology of Language" (1968, 84–97) and Lyotard (1971, 93–94). See also Bennington (1988, 58 passim).

14. Lyotard develops the notion of paratax as follows: "The phrase that expresses the passage operator employs the conjunction *and* (*and so forth, and so on*). This term signals a simple addition, the *apposition* [emphasis added] of one term with the other, nothing more. Auerbach (1946: ch. 2 and 3) turns this into a characteristic of 'modern' style, paratax, as opposed to syntax. Conjoined by *and*, phrases or events follow each other, but their succession does not obey a categorial order (*because; if, then; in order to; although* . . .). Joined to the preceding one by *and*, a phrase arises out of nothingness to link up with it. Paratax thus connotes the abyss of Not-Being that opens between phrases, it stresses the surprise that something begins when what is said is said. *And* is the conjunction that most allows the constitutive discontinuity (or oblivion) of time to threaten, while defying it through its equally constitutive continuity (or retention). [. . .] Instead of *and*, and assuring the same paratactic function, there can be a comma, or nothing" (1988, 100).

15. See especially Conquergood, Huspek, West (1993), Smith (1994), Smith and Martinez (1995).

References

Bateson, Gregory. (1972). *Steps to an Ecology of Mind*. New York: Random House.

Bennington, Geoffrey. (1988). *Lyotard: Writing the Event*. New York: Columbia University Press.

Brent, Joseph. (1993). *Charles Sanders Peirce: A Life*. Bloomington: Indiana University Press.

Caputo, John D. (1993). *Against Ethics: Contributions to a Poetics of Obligation with Constant Reference to Deconstuction*. Bloomington: Indiana University Press.

Colapietro, Vincent. (1995). "Immediacy, Opposition, and Mediation: Peirce on the Irreducible Aspects of the Communication Process." *Recovering Pragmatism's Voice: The Classical Tradition, Rorty, and the Philosophy of Communication*, Lenore Langsdorf and Andrew R. Smith, eds. Albany: State University of New York Press.

Conquergood, Dwight. (June 1991). "Rethinking Ethnography: Towards a Critical Cultural Politics." *Communication Monographs* 58: 179–94.

———. (1992). "Ethnography, Rhetoric and Performance." *Quarterly Journal of Speech* 78: 80–123.

Huspek, Michael. (1989/90). "The Idea of Ethnography and its Relation to Cultural Critique." *Research on Language and Social Interaction* 23: 293–312.

———. (1993). "Dueling Structures: The Theory of Resistance in Discourse." *Communication Theory* 3.1: 1–25.

———. (1994). "Critial Ethnography and Subjective Experience." *Human Studies* 17: 45–63.

Jakobson, Roman. (1960). "Closing Statement: Linguistics and Poetics." *Style in Language*. Thomas Sebeok, ed. Cambridge, MA: MIT Press.

Kochman, Thomas. (1981). *Black and White Styles in Conflict*. Chicago: University of Chicago Press.

Kristeva, Julia. (1984). *Revolution in Poetic Language*. Trans. Margaret Waller. New York: Columbia University Press.

Langsdorf, Lenore and Andrew R. Smith (Eds.). (1995). *Recovering Pragmatism's Voice: The Classical Tradition, Rorty, and the Philosophy of Communication*. Albany: State University of New York Press.

Lanigan, Richard L. (1994). "From Enthymeme to Abduction: The Classical Law of Logic and the Postmodern Rule of Rhetoric." *Recovering Pragmatism's Voice: The Classical Tradition, Rorty, and the Philosophy of Communica-*

tion. Lenore Langsdorf and Andrew R. Smith, eds. Albany: State University of New York Press.

Lyotard, Jean-Francois. (1971). *Discours, Figure*. Paris: Klincksieck.

———. (1984). *The Postmodern Condition: A Report on Knowledge*. Trans. Geoff Bennington and Brian Massumi. Minneapolis: University of Minnesota Press.

———. (1988). *The Differend: Phrases in Dispute*. Trans. Georges Van Den Abbeele. Minneapolis: University of Minnesota Press.

———. (1988). *Peregrinations: Law, Form, Event*. New York: Columbia University Press.

———. (1993). *Libidinal Economy*. Trans. Iain Hamilton Grant. Bloomington: Indiana University Press.

Lyotard, Jean-Francois, and Jean-Loup Thebaud. (1985). *Just Gaming* Trans. Wlad Godzich. Minneapolis: University of Minnesota Press.

Merleau-Ponty, Maurice. (1968). *The Visible and the Invisible*. Trans. Alphonso Lingis. Claude Lefort, ed. Evanston, Ill.: Northwestern University Press.

Peirce, Charles Sanders. (1931–35; 1958). *The Collected Papers of Charles Sanders Peirce* (8 vols.). Eds. Charles Hartshorne, Paul Weiss, and Arthur Burks. Cambridge, Mass.: Harvard University Press.

Philipsen, Gerry. (1992). *Speaking Culturally*. Albany: State University of New York Press.

Reusch, Jurgen, and Gregory Bateson. (1968). *Communication and the Social Matrix of Psychiatry*. New York: W.W. Norton.

Rorty, Richard. (1982). *The Consequences of Pragmatism*. Minneapolis: University of Minnesota Press.

———. (1991). *Objectivity, Relativism, and Truth*. Cambridge: Cambridge University Press.

Rose, Heidi. (1994). "Stylistic Features in American Sign Language Literature." *Text and Performance Quarterly* 14: 144–57.

Rose, Heidi, and Andrew R. Smith. (1994). "Sounding Sight and Sighting Sound: The 'Violence' of Linking Deaf and Hearing Worlds." Paper presented to the annual meeting of the Speech Communication Association.

Shweder, Richard A. (1991). *Thinking Through Cultures: Expeditions in Cultural Psychology*. Cambridge, Mass.: Harvard University Press.

Smith, Andrew R. (1990). "Mishima's Seppuku Speech: A Critical-Cultural Analysis." *Text and Performance Quarterly* 10.1: 1–19.

———. (1994). "Phrasing, Linking, Judging: Communication and Critical Phenomenology." *Human Studies* 17: 139–161.

———. (in press) "The Limits of Communication: Lyotard and Levinas on Otherness," *Transgressing Scientific Discourses: Communication and the Voice of Other.* Michael Huspek and Gary Radford, eds. Albany: State University of New York Press.

Smith, Andrew R., and Leonard Shyles. (1994). "On Ethnocentric Truth and Pragmatic Justice." *Recovering Pragmatism's Voice: The Classical Tradition, Rorty, and the Philosophy of Communication.* Lenore Langsdorf and Andrew R. Smith, eds. Albany: State University of New York Press.

Smith, Andrew R., and Jacqueline Martinez. (1995). "Signfying Harassment: Communication, Ambiguity and Power." *Human Studies.* 18:63–87.

Stewart, John. (1986). "Speech and Human Being: A Complement to Semiotics." *Quarterly Journal of Speech* 72.1: 55–73.

———. (Fall 1991). "A Postmodern Look at Traditional Communication Postulates." *Western Journal of Speech Communication* 55: 354–79.

West, James T. (Spring 1993). "Ethnography and Ideology: The Politics of Cultural Representation." *Western Journal of Speech Communication* 57: 209–20.

Part III

Resuscitations of Semiotic Dimensions

Editor's Introduction

D. S. Clarke has published widely on the history and current applicability of semiotic theory. In this chapter he defends the project of semiotic against criticisms like those found in the first four chapters of this volume and in parts of chapters 5 and 6. He anchors his defense in what he takes to be the manifest wisdom and utility of building a science of language on analysis and evolution, that is, on the foundational projects of (a) identifying the simplest, most primitive linguistic signs in order (b) to compare and contrast with them increasingly complex sign levels. This procedure permits one to construct a description of the *necessary* features of language, as contrasted with "those features it *happens* to have because of the contingencies of its historical development." Moreover, "it is the necessary, logical features that seem to be the object of philosophic inquiry, while contingent features are assigned to special sciences such as linguistics and anthropology." Thus Clarke identifies the concerns about language that are central to his disciplinary specialization—philosophical semiotic—and argues that these may be seen to subsume, or at least to be complementary with, the concerns of communication theorists and other disciplinary specialists. He concludes that the central interest of semiotic—"comparing and contrasting interpretation at different sign levels"— is a vitally important project that should proceed despite contemporary philosophical critiques.

The chapter begins with a distinction between the "vertical" semio*tic* theory of Peirce and Morris and the "horizontal" semio*tics* originated by Saussure and developed by Barthes, Jackobson, and others. Clarke remains interested in applying the framework of the former—semiotic—as a means of understanding language use. He maintains, however, that the term "symbol," as in the title of this volume and its companion, is manifestly inadequate "for demarcating conventional or rule governed linguistic signs," and only in this special sense does he endorse progressing "beyond the symbol model." He also argues that any adequate study of language must consider not only its representational functions but also its instrumental and, to some degree, its expressive ones.

The second section of the chapter reviews the impact on language theorizing of three ideals that have directed much of modern philosophy: certainty, simplicity, and comprehensiveness. Each has been modified in the last half-century. Certainty is now universally acknowledged to be unattainable, but some theories that enjoy "virtually unanimous consensus within the scientific community" may serve as an adequately "certain foundation." Evolutionary theory is such a foundation from which language may profitably be viewed. The ideal of simplicity directs language philosophers to the logically necessary, as contrasted with the contingent, features of language use, and this search leads directly to the primitive simple elements that Clarke calls *natsigns*. These are signs that acquire significance through direct associations with either events or responses, such as the sound of the bell learned by Pavlov's dog. Natsigns, Clarke argues "do seem to provide us that sought-for primitive base from which more complex signs can be derived."

Chomsky's critique of Skinner demonstrated the difficulties of conceptually extending such primitives into an account of language in all its complexities. But, Clarke argues, there still exists an alternative: "to start with language use and abstract from its complexity and variety basic logical features capable of extension to more primitive forms of sign interpretation." This move will permit language philosophy to achieve at least a satisfactory degree of both simplicity and comprehensiveness. But it is important to recognize that "features of everyday conversation that resist comparisons and contrasts to the more primitive natsigns and signals" are "less central for semiotic as a branch of philosophy" than the *logical* features of language.

The next section of the chapter discusses some of these "transactional" features. For example, Clarke acknowledges the importance of illocutionary force indicators but maintains that the sentences in which they are expressed also include subject-predicate radicals that may be evaluated as, for example, true or false. Similarly, address terms and pronouns "show" rather than "describe" relative social position, but they are also "indispensable in providing the transactional context in which describing and prescribing take place." Thus a study of these transactional aspects of language is "perfectly consistent with semiotic's central aims of comparing and contrasting logical features of reference and significance present at different sign levels. . . ."

In the final section, Clarke argues that these transactional aspects of language have "far-reaching implications for questions of metaphysics and for the choice of terminology with which to state comparisons between the human and the infrahuman." For example, "the truth value of a knowledge ascription will depend on the relation between speaker and the subject of the ascription in the exchange of information." But, again because of the presence of "sentence radicals with subject-predicate structure" that are embedded in the transactional devices of human discourse, philosophy in general, and especially philosophy of language, continues to manifest a need for, and to profit from, the semiotic project.

Clarke voices exactly the kind of contribution to the conversation that I envisioned when I first planned this volume. His argument for the importance of the disciplinary niche of semiotic contrasts usefully and informatively with my contention that all the disciplines making up the human studies need seriously to consider a *post*semiotic account of the nature of language. Readers can judge for themselves the degree to which Clarke affirms each of the five theoretical commitments making up the symbol model and the extent to which these commitments weaken his claims. They can also assess whether he argues convincingly for philosophy as a *foundational* discipline. But perhaps most importantly, readers might contrast Clarke's decision to begin his account of language with a description of its atoms—its simplest, most primitive sign-radicals—with the argument that any viable account of language must be informatively applicable to paradigm instances of its explanandum and that the paradigm instance of language is naturally occurring conversation. Chapters 1, 2, and 3 of this volume focus on and attempt to explicate what chapter 1 calls articulate contact because this is both the origin and the most profound embodiment of living language. Clarke focuses on natsigns and attempts to explicate such invented examples as "the following phone conversation: 'Hello, Tom; this is Bill. I promise you that John will return the money,'" because these, he believes, are the building blocks into which living language evolves. One might ask what each perspective contributes to an understanding of the nature of language.

7

Semiotic and Transactional Aspects of Language

D. S. Clarke

Introduction

Contributions to interdisciplinary projects always pose problems, given differences in terminology within different fields and between the methodologies employed. The project of this volume, involving as it does so many issues surrounding our understanding of language and its functions, illustrates this difficulty to an unusually high degree. The increasing complexity of community life and the specialization of forms of discourse within social institutions is reflected by the differing philosophic interests in language by those within these institutions. The analyses of Frege directly reflect the interests of a mathematician in the use of language to formulate deductive inferences, those of Carnap and Reichenbach in its use to formulate and test scientific hypotheses, while those of Morris, Skinner, and more recently Fodor and Dretske reflect the interests of experimental psychology in extending to language the methods of the natural sciences. Twentieth-century philosophy has to a considerable extent served as the plain on which battles derived from these differing perspectives have been waged. It should not surprise us then to find those instructing others in the arts of persuasion and social adjustment to be constructing a communication theory that emphasizes interpersonal aspects of language use. How should we respond to their provocative claims?

Let me begin with an attempt to state what I think is the central issue. By the term *semiotic* I shall understand the Medieval theory of signs allied to logic developed by Charles Peirce and later modified by Charles Morris. Unlike recent semiotics (with an 's' after the model of linguistics), this theory emphasizes vertical classifications of signs that compare and contrast the conventional elements of human communication, often referred to within this tradition as *symbols*, with prelinguistic *signals*, signs typically used for communication within animal communities, and with *natural signs*, signs not used for communicative purposes but instead occurring "naturally" within the environments of their interpreters. Semiotics (with an 's') was originated by Saussure (under the heading of "semiology") and later developed by Roland Barthes, Roman Jackobson, and others. In contrast to the Medieval logical tradition, it sought to formulate horizontal classifications comparing and contrasting cultural forms of communication, both linguistic and nonlinguistic, and eventually allied itself with hermeneutics as the interpretation of literary texts and nonlinguistic art forms such as dance, music, and architecture. In other publications (Clarke, 1985, 1990a) I have outlined the divergent directions taken by semiotic and semiotics. Two questions arise for those of us interested in applying the framework of semiotic as a means of understanding language use. First, is it still a viable framework in light of the most recent advances in linguistics and philosophy? And second, if we answer our first question in the affirmative, what modifications must we make in the traditional vertical classifications to maintain its viability?

My procedure will be that of first reviewing briefly in section 2 the rationale for the logical orientation of semiotic and explaining why this orientation serves to emphasize certain features of language use over others. In section 3 the topic is referred to as "transactional aspects" of language. It is to these aspects that communication theorists seem to be appealing when developing their positive account of language use. My contention will be that acknowledgement of such aspects is consistent with the aims of semiotic. Finally, I trace some implications for metaphysics that can be drawn from these transactional aspects.

Throughout the next two parts I will be modifying the traditional vertical classifications of signs. As a preliminary to this, we should recognize at the outset how inadequate is the term 'symbol' for demarcating conventional or rule-governed linguistic signs. Very often single words such as 'stove' or 'black' have been used as examples of symbols. But it has been recognized since Frege and Peirce that the basic units of human communication are complete sentences, such as 'This stove is black,' and since Quine's attack on the analytic-synthetic distinction that these units must be extended to blocks of discourse in which sentences occur. Peirce does list symbols as one of his three trichotomies of signs, along with icons and indices (Peirce 1934, 2.243–2.252). But this is a general heading under which fall what he calls "dicisigns," sentences with subject-predicate structure expressing true or false propositions and arguments as forms of discourse in which some sentences, the conclusions, are inferred from others, the premises.

Moreover, the term 'symbol' is often used to refer to nonlinguistic objects such as wedding rings as signifying marital status, a flag as standing for a nation, or artistic symbols occurring in film, theater, or painting. Such objects are what Morris referred to as "postlinguistic" signs (Morris 1946, 58), signs that derive their significance from linguistic descriptions. I see a wedding ring and interpret its wearer on the basis of background information acquired through language as falling under the noun phrase 'married woman.' The ring itself is not within a distinct level of sign to be compared directly with more primitive signs such as warning cries or naturally occurring events. The more fruitful comparison is between these primitive signs and a sentence such as 'She is a married woman' as embedded within a discourse context. In what follows, therefore, I shall be eschewing use of the term 'symbol' occurring in the title of this volume in favor of terminology that avoids its misleading associations. In this special sense I heartily endorse progressing "beyond the symbol model."

Another weakness of the semiotic tradition is its almost exclusive attention to fact-stating language as a basis for its vertical classifications. Certainly just as central for its comparisons is the prescriptive use of language to influence and control others' actions. In a manner analogous to the way that descriptive language enables a dramatic extension in space and time of the events and objects that we can anticipate, so commands and requests enable an extension of what can be controlled through the actions of others as a means of accomplishing personal and social goals. Their introduction makes possible division of labor and specialization. Instrumental functions are a feature of all signs, and comparisons and contrasts with respect to them are as important as for representational functions. Expressive functions of language are certainly also of interest. They are less amenable to logical analysis, however, and for this reason philosophic descriptions have tended to emphasize similarities and differences betweeen them and the more readily understood representational and instrumental functions of signs.

Semiotic and Some Philosophic Ideals

Three ideals have directed much of modern philosophy: certainty, simplicity, and comprehensiveness. The first ideal of certainty was that of relating all philosophic conclusions to propositions that could survive Descartes's method of doubt. For the empiricist tradition derived from Locke certainty was to be found in the introspective reports of what we experience, with the "mental" defined as the object of these reports. All that we claim to know about the nature of substances, causation, the self, God, or any other philosophical topic was required to be related to this foundation of direct reports of experience. In the early part of this century Russell and the early Wittgenstein construed this empiricist project as that of first constructing an ideal, private language in which such direct reports were to be formulated and then analyzing all standard sentences as either combinations of the so-called "atomic sentences" of this ideal language or as logically related to them.

For reasons familiar to a philosophic audience, but too complicated to enter into here [But see chapter 6. ed.], this ideal of a certain foundation has been abandoned in recent philosophy, both Continental and Anglo-American. *All* statements we make are now acknowledged to be in some degree fallible, including reports of what we experience, and even if such reports were certain or "self-certifying," there are no logical relations, either deductive or inductive, between them and other statements. The effect of this critique has been to undermine the priority of direct experience as the starting point from which philosophical systems are to be constructed. Evolutionary theory, at least in its broad outlines, has received overwhelming evidential support and is now accepted within the scientific community. This theory tells us that human forms of communication are an evolutionary development that have enabled communities to survive in more challenging environments than those of our primate ancestors. Language is accordingly conceived to be an instrument that enables some within a group to convey to others information about distant objects in a way impossible for less developed signaling systems. It also enables control and coordination between community members to an unprecedented degree. A warning cry enables an organism to anticipate and flee from a predator outside its direct field of vision, but the predator must be in the immediate environment of both signaler and audience, and fleeing is an indefinite response. The inclusion within sentences of a distinct subject term with referring function makes it possible to indefinitely extend what is being referred to and specify with great exactness the action being controlled. Language can be viewed as the product of an evolutionary development, continuous with that which had lead earlier to the development of these signaling systems and before that to olfactory, visual, and auditory distance receptors as receivers of information about distant events, and to the evolution of the nervous system within organisms enabling them to modify behavior on the basis of past experience. The scientific theory providing the background for this view of language clearly fails to have the kind of certainty required by early modern philosophy. But it has earned virtually unanimous consensus within the scientific community, and given human fallibility, such consensus seems the best we can muster as a starting point from which conclusions about more controversial issues can be drawn, a starting point just as legitimate as reports of sensations and feelings or the intuitions we may have about the uses of linguistic expressions. In the absence of any other more certain foundation, we therefore accept evolutionary theory as providing us with one of the central viable perspectives from which to view language.

The certain propositions serving as foundation in modern philosophy were assumed to be simple, relative to the complex propositions derived from them or into which they could be analyzed. But pursuit of the second Renaissance ideal of simplicity has been as difficult as that of certainty. We realize now how sophisticated is the use of the elementary atomic sentences of the empiricists, how this use presupposes descriptions of the objects in our environment. But while we may reject modern philosophy's theories, its ideal of simplicity, at least in modified form, seems to be one that philosophy must continue to pursue, if only to retain its identity in contemporary culture. The results of the analyses by the ordinary language philosophers have, after all, been incorporated into contemporary linguistics, and we realize through them how complex and varied language use is. This leads us to ask what is essential or necessary to language use, what are the features that language *must* have to fulfill its basic logical functions, in contrast to those features it *happens* to have because of the contingencies of its historical development. It is the necessary, logical features that seem to be the object of philosophic inquiry, while contingent features are assigned to special sciences, such as linguistics and anthropology.

The senses of 'necessary' and 'logical' used in this characterization are unique to semiotic. In one sense the linguistic modes of reference and signification are not necessary, certainly not physically necessary. It is, after all, consistent with the fundamental laws of physics that the human species never evolved on this planet, that huge asteroids never struck, that the dinosaurs limiting animal development never became extinct, that those events on which our evolution depended never occurred. But given the occurrence of these events, language evolved as an instrument for extending anticipation and control of events. In order for such extension it was *functionally necessary* that conventional signs be developed in which occurred a separate part with a referential role, for without the development of signs with subject-predicate structure the extension would not have been possible. Based on this we can conclude that if there is developed extraterrestial intelligent life it must employ analogues of our sentences if it is to anticipate and control environmental features to the degree possible for the human species. The separate roles of subjects and predicates of sentences are logical in the sense of being roles recognized as distinct for the purposes of deductive and inductive logics in the evaluation of inferences. The interests of these logics and semiotic can be distinguished, but the elements to which their analysis refers are the same.

Vertifical classifications derived from the Medieval semiotic tradition

seem to be relevant to this search for necessary features and allow us to
reintroduce a standard of simplicity in terms of which complex linguistic
signs can be measured. The simple signs are naturally occurring events
lacking features essential for communication. These serve as a base to
compare and contrast first signals without subject-predicate structure and
then isolated sentences, discourse blocks of ordinary language, and finally
the discourse frameworks used within such institutionalized specializa-
tions as mathematics, science, law, literature, and the arts. Simplicity is a
relative concept and is subject to many interpretations. In the context of
comparisons between sign levels it seems best to interpret it in terms of
primitiveness. One type of sign S_1 can be said to be more primitive than
another S_2 if the use of S_2 is possible only on the condition that S_1 is in
prior use, while S_1's use is independent of S_2's. Necessary logical features
of our everyday language are those appealed to in stating these comparisons both to what is primitive in relation to it and to forms of communication whose use is acquired only after specialized training. The central feature is the subject-predicate structure of sentences just described, and the
occurrence within sentences of subject terms with a referring role. Proper
names, definite descriptions, such as 'the old man living next door,' and
general sortal terms, such as 'man' and 'chair,' perform referring roles at
the linguistic level. At more primitive levels this role is performed by devices such as gestures and spatial orientation of a communicator and by
spatial and temporal contiguity of naturally occurring events. At the more
advanced levels of science, reference is accomplished by theoretical terms
such as 'electron' and 'gene.' Semiotic selects out for attention such a
feature because of the comparisons and contrasts between sign levels that
can be based on it.

What are the primitive signs that serve as the base of such comparisons? Certainly not the natural signs of the classical tradition, since their
interpretation seems possible only through the mediation of linguistic
generalizations. A doctor may see a rash as a natural sign or evidence of
scarlet fever, but he or she does so only by identifying the rash as the effect
stated in a linguistic generalization such as 'Scarlet fever is the cause of a
rash of type X.' Clearly natural signs such as these whose interpretation
presupposes language cannot be a primitive base for abstracting necessary
features of language. Derrida's *trace* seems derived from such classical natural signs as footprints in the snow and is intended as a primitive type of
sign more basic than written inscriptions or speech, one that presupposes
neither. But Derrida's formulation of this primitive sign, while suggestive,
is cloaked in mystery: "Origin of all repetition, origin of ideality, the trace
is not more ideal than real, not more intelligible than sensible, not more a
transparent signification than an opaque energy and no concept of meta-

physics can describe it" (Derrida 1974, 65). This does little to advance our understanding of features of language by providing a primitive base of comparison.

Having at least the virtue of explicitness, as well as overcoming the difficulties of the classical natural signs, are the descriptions of sign behavior by John Watson, Morris, and B. F. Skinner derived from models of conditioned reflex and instrumental learning. After pairings of the sound of a bell with the presentation of food, the bell becomes a "substitute stimulus" evoking a reflex response similar to that evoked by the food. In this sense it is a sign of food at a primitive level prior to language use. Also, a flash of red light may be present on a number of trials when a response of bar-pressing is reinforced by a reward. Then normally the red light will acquire significance as a sign of the bar-pressing response. Its interpreter discriminates it from other environmental events as having significance in a way that obviously does not presuppose an ability to communicate with others, much less an ability to use language. Such primitive signs acquiring significance through direct associations with either events or responses I have called *natsigns* (Clarke 1987, Sec. 3.3), an abbrevation of 'natural signs' paralleling Morris's term *comsigns* as an abbrevation of 'communicated signs' (Morris 1938). Despite these verbal origins, natsigns as signs whose significance is derived from direct associations should be clearly distinguished from the postlinguistic natural signs of the classical tradition.

Natsigns do seem to provide us that sought-for primitive base from which more complex signs can be derived. Recent history seems to teach us, however, that behavioral methods cannot be extended from this base to the use of language. Noam Chomsky's critique of Skinner's extension of instrumental learning descriptions to language (Chomsky 1959) notes the radical differences between the interpretation and use of sentences at the linguistic level and what is described in applying associationist learning models, differences that seem to preclude any significant extension of these models. Part of the difficulty may be the sudden jump from natsigns to language made in this behavioral tradition. John McDowell suggests an analogy between primitive signals such as warning cries and the perception of naturally occurring events. A bird call warning of a predator can be regarded, he notes, "as a further mode of sensitivity to the presence of predators, over and above more direct kinds of perception," and the "assertoric core" of linguistic behavior can in turn be regarded as "a descendant, now under intentional control" of such primitive signaling (McDowell 1980). With signals used as an intermediate "substitute stimulus," the eventual extension of conditioned-reflex learning models may seem more reasonable.

McDowell's analysis is directed toward descriptive language with its "assertive core," but it can be readily extended to the use of language to issue commands. A bird's flying off in the presence of a predator certainly promotes its own goals. But these goals may also be promoted by emitting the warning call and enabling others to escape, especially if these others are the bird's offspring bearing its genetic materials or group members providing protection for offspring. Voicing the call thus becomes a way of controlling the behavior of others to promote goals that may be shared within a community, and the "prescriptive core" of intentional commanding seems traceable to such primitive exercises of control.

But even with these refinements and others introduced by the developing disciplines of cognitive science, it seems impossible for a satisfactory extension from primitive signs to language to be achieved within the framework of experimental psychology. We participate in the use of language on the basis of a shared competence in following its rules. We describe language use with normative terms such as 'true,' 'false,' 'justified,' and 'appropriate.' Despite repeated attempts, there has been no successful translation of such terms into the descriptive terminology of the experimental sciences. Failing such translation and the extension of learning models to language use, philosophy's third ideal, comprehensiveness, remains unfulfilled. The study of primitive signs was undertaken in an attempt to understand language as a later evolutionary stage in organic life's anticipation and control of the environment. But the result of applying behavioral methods seems to be that normative features of language use are left unaccounted for.

What is the remedy? One is to simply abandon philosophy's ideals of simplicity and comprehensiveness, allowing them to suffer the same fate as its other ideal of certainty. We would then be left with the diverse studies of language in such disciplines as psychology, linguistics, and anthropology, along with hermeneutic studies of various art forms of the kind practiced within what is called "semiotics." Abandoned would be any attempt to construct a framework that functions to integrate the results of these different disciplines. The effect, I think, would be to impoverish contemporary culture, depriving it of that shared focus of basic concepts that philosophy through much of its history has attempted to provide. The alternative is to start with language use and abstract from its complexity and variety basic logical features capable of extension to more primitive forms of sign interpretation. This extension to the signal and natsign levels may be guided by the results of empirical studies, but the logical concepts are derived from an understanding of language from the perspective of those participating in its use.

Obviously, certain aspects of language will lend themselves to this

type of extension more readily than others. Of central interest will be referential functions of subject terms enabling extensions of reference beyond
that possible for primitive signs. Referring expressions within descriptive
sentences have occupied center stage in the logical tradition. But equally
important are subjects of imperatives such as 'Close the door' in which the
noun phrase 'the door' enables the audience to identify the object upon
which the action of closing is to be performed. Also important are expressive functions of language insofar as they specialize what is combined at
lower levels. An odor may be a natsign of a predator for a deer, signify the
action of fleeing, and arouse the emotion of fear, while a signal such as a
warning cry can also combine these descriptive, prescriptive, and arousal
functions. But at the linguistic level these functions are specialized in differing forms of expression: 'A wolf is approaching' describes, while 'Run to
the house' prescribes, and 'I am afraid' expresses fear. How the conventional rules of language enable such specialization is important in understanding the distinctive features of the linguistic level.

Less central for semiotic as a branch of philosophy are features of
everyday conversation that resist comparisons and contrasts to the more
primitive natsigns and signals. Failure to recognize the special focus of
semiotic is responsible, I think, for some misguided criticisms of attempts
to reestablish semiotic as a viable branch of contemporary philosophy.
These often take the form of objections to the representational-instrumental orientation of semiotic. Hugh Bredin, for example, complains that in
my *Principles of Semiotic* (Clarke 1987) there is no discussion of music as
a distinctive art form (Bedau 1989). The reason for such neglect is that
comparisons and contrasts between music and more primitive forms of
vocal expressions of feelings through groans or laughter are tenuous at
best. Songs of birds and gibbons may be primitive precursors of music at
the subhuman level, but their relationships to the later cultural form is
unclear. Musical compositions do have a structure or "syntax," and it is
certainly important to understand how its ordering of elements is both
similar to and different from that of discursive language and to understand
the extent to which music is or is not representational. But such topics of
aesthetics are not central to semiotic as understood in the Medieval-Peirce
tradition. Similarly, Robert Innis (Innis 1994) objects to the scarcity of
readings in my collection (Clarke 1990a) on iconic representations. Again,
it is important to understand how iconic representations—whether representational (as for maps and diagrams), projective, (a blueprint of a house
to be built), or artistic—differ from discursive means of communication
and how they utilize referential devices. Also, they are present at the level
of signals, as for the nonconventional gesture picturing what it represents
and the warning cry mimicking the sound of a predator. By virtue of such

comparisons, they do have a central position for semiotic. But the primary emphasis for this branch of philosophy is on comparisons and contrasts to signs at all levels, and iconic representations seem to occupy a less prominent place at the level of natsigns. Shadows of objects may be examples, but effects similar to the causes producing them, such as footprints in the snow, a bullet hole, or a fossil (Derrida's traces?), seem to be interpreted only through linguistic mediation.

If iconic representations are indeed confined to language and signaling levels, they would be similar to aspects of conversational language that function to establish and maintain channels of communication between speaker and audience. Borrowing from Bruner, I shall refer to these as *transactional aspects* of language (Bruner 1986). How these aspects are to be understood relative to the goals of semiotic is our next topic.

Transactional Aspects of Language

We recognize now how much of language and nonverbal communication is devoted to establishing a relation between a speaker (or writer) and his or her intended audience. A much-discussed means for establishing this relation is through the use of *illocutionary force indicators*, expressions within sentences that convey to an audience how their descriptive, prescriptive, or expressive contents are to be understood. Austin's performatives, sentences such as 'I promise you that John will return the money' and 'I order you to return the money,' provide examples of this (Austin 1962). Here we distinguish the performative prefixes 'I promise you that . . . ' and 'I order you to . . . ' from the subject-predicate radicals 'John will return the money' and 'return the money' expressing the contents of the sentences. The sentences as wholes, as Austin emphasized, are not descriptions with truth values, and in this sense are not "representational." They are instead used to make a promise and issue an order to an audience through their prefixes. Embedded in these sentences, however, are sentence radicals in which referential roles of 'John' and 'the money' can be distinguished from the predicative role of 'return.' It is the contents expressed by these radicals that are true or false, obeyed or disobeyed. The performative prefixes, in contrast, function to indicate that such contents are to be understood as a promise and order, rather than as a statement, warning, question, request, and so on.

The function of indicating illocutionary force can also be served by psychological and modal prefixes, as illustrated by 'I know that John will return the money,' 'I believe (think) that John will return the money,' 'I intend to repay,' and 'I may repay.' Here 'know,' 'believe' (also 'think'), 'intend,' and 'may' indicate that the content is being conveyed as a guarantee by the speaker, with a hesitation that will offer an excuse if John fails to repay, as an intention, or with lack of commitment. The main verbs of such sentences do not specify the speech act being performed in uttering them in the appropriate conditions, and in this respect they are unlike performative sentences. But they do share with performatives the feature of not being used by the speaker to describe himself, but instead to indicate how the contents are to be understood.

Just as important transactional elements are *addresses*, expressions within language indicating the speaker and intended audience. Addresses commonly occur in greetings ('Hello, Tom') and introductions ('This is Bill') that open up a channel of communication. Consider the following phone conversation: 'Hello, Tom; this is Bill. I promise you that John will return the money.' In it we can distinguish the roles of the names 'Bill' and 'Tom' from the singular terms within the radical 'John will return the money.' 'Bill' is a *source address* indicating the source of the message, while 'Tom' is a *target address* indicating the intended addressee of the information being conveyed. The pronouns 'I' and 'you' within the performative prefix also perform the roles of source and target addresses, since they stand in place of 'Bill' and 'Tom.' These addresses clearly function differently from 'John' and 'the money' as the subjects of the radical, referring expressions that enable identification of objects that may be at considerable distance from the addressee. This is a function that is entirely different from addresses: addresses establish a channel of communication between speaker and audience, while subjects refer and convey (in conjunction with predicates) informational or prescriptive content.

In face-to-face communication, or what is presumably meant by "articulate contact," we can dispense with proper names as addresses. If already introduced, the speakers Bill and Tom need not identify themselves by name. Instead, 'I' and 'you' suffice as indexical addresses indicating speaker and hearer, again with roles distinct from those of referring subjects. Accompanying the use of such pronouns may be titles such as 'Dr.,' 'Professor,' 'Senator' as means for indicating relative social status and power. Military insignias as indicators of rank are another means for indicating who is to order, who to obey, who to regard seriously, who lightly. But there are many others, some more obvious than others. Modes of dress, bearing, and manners are traditional means of the aristocracy for maintaining their ascendancy. Displays of wealth through clothing, cars, houses, and furnishings have become more common, constituting the various "systems" of nonverbal communication described by Roland Barthes (Barthes 1967).

Such devices, whether in the form of force indicators, addresses, or indicators of status, can be said to "show" relative social position rather than to "say" or describe it. They are indispensable in providing the transactional context in which describing and prescribing take place. There are, of course, many other types of devices, either verbal or nonverbal, within conversational language. Saying 'Yes,' grunting 'Uh-huh,' or nodding in agreement are ways of indicating understanding or of endorsing and encouraging what another says, while 'No' and head shaking is taken as opposition. 'Say again' or 'What?' indicates lack of understanding and requests repetition. Most of them are uniquely human and can vary from culture to culture and as such are topics of cultural anthropology. But some aspects of them seem essential for social organization, sharing of information, and coordination of action and at least in rudimentary form can be detected within infrahuman animal communities. The intensity of a dog's snarl can indicate the degree of warning being conveyed. Members of some animal communities can identify the individual source of a signal by its "signature," its distinctive pattern or qualitative aspect. Subordination is indicated by cowering and (in higher primates) baring of teeth in smiles, domination by strutting. The grunts and coos of various species of subhuman primates seem to perform a similar function. These aspects (described in works of ethologists such as Cheney & Seyfarth 1990 and in Sebeok 1990) are of importance for the comparative purposes of semiotic.

Acknowledging all these conversational devices, however, is perfectly consistent with semiotic's central aims of comparing and contrasting logical features of reference and significance present at different sign levels, including the level of natsigns where communication is absent. Transactional elements, both linguistic and nonlinguistic, do indeed provide contexts in which informational, prescriptive, and expressive content is conveyed. It is also true that these elements themselves do not perform representational, instrumental, controlling functions; they themselves neither describe nor prescribe. But radicals embedded in such contexts do have logical structure and do perform such functions. They provide the primary basis for comparisons both "down" to primitive signs and "up" to specialized forms of discourse, and for this reason the chief attention of the semiotic tradition has quite properly been directed toward them.

Metaphysical Implications

While transactional aspects of language force no revision in the central aims of semiotic, they do have far-reaching implications for questions of metaphysics and for the choice of terminology with which to state comparisons between the human and the infrahuman. We have just seen how the personal pronouns in 'I warn you that John will repay' and 'I order you to repay' are not referring expressions within descriptive sentences. They are instead addresses indicating the sources and targets of the messages. Our concept of the self and of a person seems derived from our understanding of the use of personal pronouns. If so, we must conceive of a self or person as related to others through communication as addressor and addressee, as existing in what Charles Taylor aptly calls "webs of interlocution" (Taylor 1989, 36).

Such a conception is inconsistent with the view of the modern Cartesian tradition that the self is a subject of which mental states and processes are predicated. For certain psychological sentences this Cartesian view seems clearly false. Sentences of the form 'I know that p' or 'I believe (think) that p' function to convey the illocutionary force of the proposition p being expressed. As we have seen, the sentences are certainly not used to predicate a state of the speaker but instead to indicate that the subject-predicate proposition p is to be understood as being put forward either as a guarantee or with hesitation, with the pronoun 'I' indicating the speaker. There is no subject having knowledge or a certain belief to be identified, but instead a speaker conveying p with either conviction or qualification.

Third person ascriptions of knowledge and psychological attitudes are also not standard descriptions, though communicative features are less obvious. Ascriptions of knowledge seem to have two basic uses. Sometimes we want to ascertain whether a person is a reliable source of information, as when we ask 'Does he know whether it will rain (the color of the flower, the sidereal period of the moon)?' Such *source knowledge* can be contrasted with *redundancy avoidance knowledge* that is requested by such questions as 'Does she know that it will rain (that the rose is yellow, that the moon's sidereal period is 27.32 days)?' Here a specific proposition follows the verb, and the interest is in avoiding the conveying of information that is not needed. The truth value of a knowledge ascription will depend on the relation between speaker and the subject of the ascription in the exchange of information. For source knowledge only reliability seems essential, while for redundancy avoidance knowledge only true belief is required. (See Clarke 1990b for a discussion of such differences.)

For ascriptions of belief, truth values also seem to shift, with uses being made of them and changing relations between speaker, audience, and the person who is the subject of the ascription. Consider, for example, the sentence 'Smith believes that the gold is hidden in Mammoth Cave.' This could be used to interpret Smith's belief as a means of evaluating it. Suppose both the speaker S and audience A know that what Smith mistakenly takes to be gold is really fool's gold. In such a case S may say to A 'Smith believes that the fool's gold is hidden in Mammoth Cave,' thus interpreting what Smith believes. If the first ascription were true, the second with the substitution would remain true: Smith does really hold the belief, though the belief itself may be assessed as false. We can refer to this as the *interpretive/evaluative* use of 'believe.' In contrast to this, there is another use to predict or explain Smith's behavior. *S* may utter the first sentence to *A* as a means of predicting that Smith will travel to the Mammoth Cave or (if in the past tense) explaining why he went there. In such a case the substitution of 'fool's gold' for 'gold' would not preserve truth. Only belief about gold would successfully predict or explain, assuming normal motivations on the part of Smith.

These two uses of belief ascriptions are interrelated. Very often we wish to influence the conduct of others, and the most effective way is to change their beliefs. Suppose we know that Smith's belief is false, that the gold is not hidden in Mammoth Cave but somewhere else. Then Smith would become our audience for a correction of his belief, and interpretation and evaluation become means for preventing what is predicted. Similar relations hold for explanation. We cannot alter what has occurred, but we can correct a belief explaining its occurrence, and this may prevent a recurrence of that *type* of action. Thus, we may judge that Jones crashed into the embankment because he believed that a highway on a rainy night was safe for fast driving. Informing others of Jones's error may prevent other accidents.

All of this seems obvious enough. But such transactional aspects of ascriptions are inconsistent with principal metaphysical theories about the nature of mentality. Both dualism and materialism assume that ascriptions of beliefs, desires, hopes, and so on are descriptions of matters of fact. They differ only in the way they characterize these facts. For the dualist the facts described are irreducibly mental, not accessible to the methods of the empirical sciences; for the materialist they are physical, whether brain states or abstract functional states mediating between environmental input and response. Having rejected dualism on the basis of convincing criticisms of it over the past fifty years, recent philosophy, certainly of the Anglo-American variety, has opted for materialism. If belief ascriptions (and also ascriptions of desires and hopes) do indeed have the interactive features just described, however, we have a basis for rejecting the original dichotomy. Such ascriptions do not describe matters of fact of any kind, but instead are means for interpreting and evaluating what others say and possibly influencing their conduct.

This conclusion does not by itself have any adverse effects on the project that semiotic sets for itself. But transactional aspects of ascriptions of propositional attitudes do limit the terminology used in semiotic's contrasts and comparisons to primitive levels of sign interpretation. Use of terms such as 'knowledge,' 'belief,' 'thought,' 'desire,' and 'hope' within ascriptions assumes, as we have seen, that the subject of these ascriptions is at least potentially a member of a common linguistic community, one able to use language, provide or receive information, understand corrections or criticisms, and alter behavior on the basis of such criticisms. Such a member exhibits mentality as defined by Brentano in terms of intentionality. If intentionality is confined to language users, it follows that intentional terms cannot be applied to lower animals with which we cannot communicate through language. If we regard mentality as characteristic of organisms with knowledge, belief, thought, and so on then we must restrict it to ourselves and not attempt an extension to other species. This seems to be the central intuition behind the Cartesian division between the human level characterized by intentionality and application of normative concepts and the infrahuman level of mechanical causation. If we were to accept this division, it would seem we must deny any grounds of comparison between the interpretation and use of language and that of more primitive types of signs.

There are reasons, however, for refusing to accept such a conclusion. First, while it does seem illegitimate to extend propositional attitude terms such as 'belief,' 'desire,' and 'hope' to organisms incapable of using language, the extension of nonpropositional terms such as 'expectation,' 'recognition,' and 'want' seems uncontroversial. Propositional attitude ascriptions do normally include radicals with subject-predicate structure, as in 'Smith believes that Bill is hungry.' But 'expect,' 'recognize,' and 'want' do not: we are said to expect rain (rather than that it is raining), recognize a friend, want food. Both experimental psychologists and ethologists commonly extend such terms to lower animals, and there seem to be no philosophical grounds for prohibiting the practice. Selection of the appropriate terminology is thus our means of guarding against the dangers of anthropomorphizing.

There is a second reason for not prohibiting comparisons between sign levels. It is that all levels are represented in human experience. Within language itself we can distinguish, as Strawson noted (Strawson 1960, 208–214), between subject-predicate sentences with count noun subjects and "feature-placing" sentences such as 'It is raining' where reference is limited to the immediate environment. Feature-placing sentences represent a more primitive stage in the development of language before the introduction of nouns enabling reidentification. We signal to each other using nonconventional, iconic gestures, both to represent objects in our environment and to direct the actions of others, and can readily recognize the differences between such gestures and the rule-governed expressions of speech. Natsigns are more difficult to isolate, so language-bound is our interpretation of what we observe. But interpretation of them can be recognized as operating at what is normally a subconscious level of adult experience within a module of the brain only occasionally accessible to consciousness. While listening to the car radio, we see the pothole in the road and swerve to avoid it. Seeing the pothole focuses our attention away from the radio and leads us to expect a jolt on the basis of past associations, while the swerving we learn as a means to avoid what is uncomfortable. Such familiar experiences serve as the basis for the comparisons and contrasts of semiotic, with the findings of experimental psychology and ethology then introduced to identify the different levels of signs in descriptions of various kinds of animal behavior.

And finally, there are types of interspecies communication between us and lower animals, though clearly not of the "dialogic" variety we engage in within our own species. The most widely popularized of these is communication with chimpanzees through manipulable counters (Premack & Premack 1982). More familiar to us are the signals with which we communicate with pets and domestic animals. Our appreciation of bird songs seems to be traceable to a shared sensibility. To account for it Charles Hartshorne notes how aesthetic principles of harmony and variety governing our own artistic productions also seem to explain the songs' origins (Hartshorne 1973). These considerations seem to justify our choice of an intentional vocabulary including 'disciminate,' 'expect,' 'recognize,' and 'want' to describe sentient creatures as primitive as the amoeba capable of learning from experience. This choice seems to be an acknowledgment of the existence of our membership in a community of sentient organisms sharing at least a common capacity to interpret signs. It also acknowledges that all members are different in important respects from rocks, trees, and artifacts (including the most sophisticated computers) incapable of such interpretation.

A myopic humanism would seek to maintain within contemporary culture Descartes's division between ourselves and the rest of animate nature by emphasizing the uniqueness of language as a vehicle of communication. General attacks against the semiotic tradition in American philosophy (as contrasted to specific corrections of mistaken formulations) constitute one form taken by this stultifying anthropocentrism. There certainly are unique features of the language vehicle, and the development of complex transactional elements is one of them. We have seen here, however, that there are elements within infrahuman communication systems that bear some analogy with transactional elements of our own. More importantly, embedded within the transactional devices of human discourse are sentence radicals with subject-predicate structure. It is the special modes of reference and significance of such radicals that is of central interest to semiotic in its project of comparing and contrasting interpretation at different sign levels. The project is of importance, and—notwithstanding what I understand to be the central thrust of this volume—should be allowed to proceed.

References

Austin, J. L. (1962). *How to Do Things with Words*. Cambridge, MA: Harvard University Press.

Barthes, Roland. (1967). *Elements of Semiology*. Trans. A. Lavers and C. Smith. New York: Hill and Wang.

Bredin, Hugh. (1989). "Review of Clarke, *Principles of Semiotic*." *British Journal of Aesthetics*, 29: 186–88.

Bruner, Jerome. (1986). "The Transactional Self" in *Actual Minds, Possible Worlds*. Cambridge, MA: Harvard University Press.

Cheney, Dorothy, and Robert Seyfarth. (1990). *How Monkeys See the World*. Chicago: University of Chicago Press.

Chomsky, Noam. (1959). "Review of Skinner's Verbal Behavior." *Language*, 35: 25–58.

Clarke, D. S. (1987). *Principles of Semiotic*. Boston: Routledge & Kegan Paul.

———. (1990a). *Sources of Semiotic*. Carbondale: Southern Illinois University Press.

———. 1990b). "Two Uses of 'Know'," *Analysis*, 50: 188–90.

Derrida, Jacques. (1974). *Of Grammatology*. Trans. G. C. Spivak. Baltimore: Johns Hopkins University Press.

Hartshorne, Charles. (1973). *Born to Sing*. Bloomington: Indiana University Press.

Innis, Robert. (1994). "The Analytic Telos of Semiotic." *Semiotica*, 98: 163–179.

McDowell, John. (1980). "Meaning, Communication, and Knowledge" in *Philosophical Subjects*. Z. Van Straaten, ed. Oxford: Clarendon Press.

Morris, Charles. (1946). *Signs, Language and Behavior*. New York: Braziller.

———. (1938). *Foundations of the Theory of Signs*. Chicago: University of Chicago Press.

Peirce, Charles. (1934). *The Collected Papers of Charles Saunders Peirce*, Vol. 2. C. Hartshorne and P. Weiss, eds. Cambridge, MA: Harvard University Press.

Premack, D., and A. Premack, A. (1982). *The Mind of an Ape*. New York: Norton.

Sebeok, Thomas. (1990). *Zoosemiotics*. The Hague: Mounton.

Strawson, P. F. (1960). *Individuals*. London: Methuen.

Taylor, Charles. (1989). *Sources of the Self*. Cambridge, MA: Harvard University Press.

Editor's Introduction

Wendy Leeds-Hurwitz's 1989 book, *Communication in Everyday Life* was one of the first thorough accounts of interpersonal communication as a social, rather than psychological process, and her 1993 *Semiotics and Communication: Signs, Codes, Cultures* explores contributions that she believes semiotics can make to the study of speech communication. Her main project in this chapter is to "expand the isolated concept of symbol to include interpretation as an integral element of comunication and of symbol usage, as [her] way of moving 'beyond the symbol model.'" She makes this move because she is "reluctant to reject a theoretical concept which may yet demonstrate its potential value" in understanding human communication.

Leeds-Hurwitz first defines a symbol as "something which stands for something else," distinguishes the present symbol from the typically absent symbolized, and specifies that the symbol-symbolized connection is arbitrary. Then she emphasizes the context-dependence of symbols and elucidates three crucial aspects of this context: event, community, and identity. Event is the midrange category of context (between the narrower speech act and the broader situation), and it frames the verbal or nonverbal symbol for those to whom it is meaningful. A community is a group of people who make, or believe they make, a similar sense of things. Identity subsumes characteristics connected, most often, with individuals. The three interrelate in that identity, as Leeds-Hurwitz puts it, "is often displayed through the use of *symbols* within particular *events* organized and conducted within specific *communities.*" These are some ways context frames symbol interpretation.

The interpretation of a nonverbal symbol, a necklace included on a student-drawn poster, is used to illustrate each feature of context. Leeds-Hurwitz argues that it is appropriate, or even necessary, to consider nonverbal symbols in a book treating language, because of the pervasive presence of nonverbal elements in all living language, which is to say that communication inherently involves both linguistic and nonverbal features. She identifies various events that contribute to the necklace's "layers of meaning." For example, the ritual event of gift-giving at a family birthday party contributed to various persons' interpretations of the necklace, as did the event of the end-of-semester celebration that the poster advertised. Class and extended family communities also contributed to the meaning of the necklace, because, as a symbol, it served as one of the "physical means . . . through which people establish, construct, and maintain group cohesion. . . ." In relation to the necklace, Leeds-Hurwitz's identity has moved "from a teenager given [the necklace] as a present to wear, to a professor using it as a convenient vehicle for explaining a theoretical concept." Leeds-Hurwitz argues that this event-community-identity analysis moves the concept of symbol beyond its traditional representational meaning to its status as a social phenomenon "used in constructing a joint understanding of who we are and what past we share."

The final section of the chapter focuses on symbols in *use* by explicating three constructs central to this process: polysemy, bricolage, and intertextuality. The necklace has multiple meanings for sisters who received similar necklaces from a grandmother living on another continent and for the students who experienced it as a classroom example. Levi-Strauss's term "bricolage" underscores the creative potential of cultural construction, the endless possibilities of juxtaposing one symbol with others. The necklace was in one grouping of objects when sold, in another when given as one of several gifts, and in another when used as an example, and each of these juxtapositions alters its meaning. Intertextuality, as Kristeva uses the term, refers to the multiple references to other events implied in any social use of a symbol. When Leeds-Hurwitz puts on the necklace, she remembers not only her grandmother and the events of receiving her mailed gifts but also the particular class that included it on their poster and the party the poster advertised. "As in the physical world," she concludes, "nothing [in the communicative world] is created *de novo*. We recycle meanings just as we recycle aluminum and newspapers."

The author admits in her conclusion that she comes "from a family of antique collectors, loathe to let go of what others may consider out-of-date, whether furniture or ideas." "Symbol" is for her this kind of construct. If symbols can be understood as *social* phenomena, contexted by event, community, and identity, and interpreted via polysemy, bricolage, and intertextuality, then, she argues, there is no need to move *beyond* symbol theory. Rather, the redefined construct deserves to stay at the center of analyses of verbal and nonverbal communication.

This chapter provides another useful contribution to the interdisciplinary conversation about the symbol model. As Leeds-Hurwitz notes in her conclusion, she would agree with the authors of this book's first four chapters that meaning is a socially negotiated phenomenon and that it is desirable to move beyond individualized, psychologistic accounts of language use to a genuinely social or dialogic understanding. We also share the conviction that language scholars need to attend to both verbal and nonverbal elements of language, especially because they are so indivisible in practice. But Leeds-Hurwitz believes that symbol analysis is a fruitful general strategy for explicating language events, and other chapter authors continue to be convinced that it creates more problems than it solves.

Again, the reader can decide for him or herself whether Leeds-Hurwitz's social account of symbols deals effectively with the conceptual and practical problems created by the two worlds, atomism, and systems assumptions of the symbol model. Her detailed explication of the contributions to social meaning made by intentional actions—*use* of the necklace as a gift, *use* of it as part of a costume, *use* of it as a classroom example—contributes to one way of understanding several overlapping communication events. But I continue to wonder how Leeds-Hurwitz would describe the ontological status of the two elements included in her definition—the "symbol" and the "symbolized." In this chapter, for example, the "symbol" is first identified as the drawing of the necklace on the poster, but in later discussions it is the necklace itself that "stands for" so many other "symbolized" phenomena. Moreover, it is easy to grasp how the necklace itself could be understood as that which is symbolized by the poster drawing, but it is much more difficult to pinpoint the ontological status of the other "symbolized" phenomena that Leeds-Hurwitz's definition requires; for example, "birthday parties and end-of-semester celebrations," "group membership and belonging," or she and her siblings' memories of family experiences. I also wonder how much precision and coherence have been sacrificed when the function of the necklace-as-symbol is variously glossed as "representing," "serving as a statement," "indicating," "reminding," and "identifying." And I question whether the intentional, act-focused account of communicating that is foregrounded, for example, in Leeds-Hurwitz's discussion of bricolage, covers over the degree to which, as Heidegger or Gadamer might put it, humans are *used by* the language that is their way of being-in-the-world. To what degree, in other words, can language and communication scholars writing at the end of the twentieth century continue to maintain that cartesian subjects strategically select and employ units of meaning ("symbols") to negotiate social sense? And could Leeds-Hurwitz use the example of the necklace to say all that she wants to say about polysemy, bricolage, and intertextuality without relying on semiotic vocabulary?

But Leeds-Hurwitz—and others—would doubtless have responses to each of my questions and would raise important parallel questions about the perspective outlined in Part I of this book. Thus the conversation continues.

8

A Social Account of Symbols

Wendy Leeds-Hurwitz

The field of communication has recently shifted emphasis from the study of intention to the study of interpretation, with a consequent shift in emphasis from how individuals convey the meanings they intend to the ways in which meanings and interpretations are jointly constructed within social groups (Leeds-Hurwitz, 1992). If the concept of "symbol" aids the effort to understand the social creation of meaning through communication, and if the social creation of meaning is understood to be a topic of current interest, then the theoretical concept of symbol has not yet lost its value.

In this chapter I propose one way in which the concept of symbol may be rehabilitated, by moving beyond the consideration of symbols as separable, discrete items to what I would term a more adequate, "social" account of symbols. This implies the study of symbols as used by particular people, in a specific context, and the study of the ways in which participants jointly construct the meanings and interpretations of symbols. Introductory comments describing a series of basic concepts entailed by a social account of symbols follow. Six terms are chosen for explication: three are related to the placement of symbols in context, three others relate to the ways people use symbols.

In order to make these theoretical concepts clear, and in order to demonstrate the application of a social approach to actual use of symbols, I describe a single example in detail. The choice of an example of nonverbal behavior in a book ostensibly about language may at first appear bizarre, but there is a theoretical point to be made here. Communication scholars theoretically recognize that language is not synonymous with communication, but they only rarely take this fact into account in their research. The vast majority of communication publications concern language, as if all communication were linguistic. Stewart has proposed that an adequate study of language "becomes synonymous with communication" (1994, p. 143), arguing for the study of language in use. Yet even this expansion of language into the larger realm of communication seems to me incomplete, for communication includes nonverbal aspects as well as linguistic. Nonverbal behaviors are an integral part of communication though they rarely merit treatment as such. Certainly nonverbal communication has been widely studied over the past thirty years, but such studies generally have been conducted by only a small percentage of communication researchers and in separate publications from those investigating linguistic utterances. It is inadequate to include nonverbal behaviors as an afterthought, as a footnote, or as part of communication only at the periphery of our theorizing, ignoring them or treating them separately in practice. These points have certainly been made before, often, but have yet to significantly influence our writing in the discipline. Only when nonverbal and verbal examples alternate in the same publications will we finally have moved from a rhetorical statement that communication is multichannel to a practical acceptance of that point (Birdwhistell 1972; Leeds-Hurwitz 1989).

This then serves as the basis for my choice of a nonverbal example in a book about the nature of language. It is perhaps acceptable for linguists to treat language as self-sufficient, although for the past twenty-five years there have been many who have chosen to do otherwise, including at least some nonverbal aspects of communication in their studies, but it does not seem defensible to me for those who describe themselves as communication scholars to continue this traditional separation of what are clearly interrelated aspects of interaction.

Symbols

Let me turn now to symbols. The definition of symbol chosen here is the broadest possible one: a symbol is something that stands for something else. Two assumptions are implied:

1. The "something that stands for something else" must be present or in some way available during interaction, whereas "that for which it stands" most often is absent. Frequently this is due to the intangible nature of that something for which a symbol stands (as would be the case for an abstract concept, such as "family member").

2. The connection between the two somethings is an arbitrary one. That is, a person who is not told about the connection will not, in general, be able to discern any logical or obvious connection.

It seems to me that this definition stands aside from at least some of the problems implied by much of the semiotic literature as described in Stewart (1994, 1995), problems that perhaps can best be avoided if the topic under study is not limited to words. Words may more readily imply the existence of World 1 and World 2, as described in detail by Stewart, than nonverbal aspects of communication, which have a different nature and may thus escape the problem.

In the following pages, I expand the isolated concept of symbol to include interpretation as an integral element of communication and of symbol usage, as my way of moving "beyond the symbol model." I do this in order to explore one way in which the theoretical concept of symbol may still prove viable, for I am reluctant to reject a theoretical concept that may yet demonstrate its potential value. If exploring the nature, function, and use of symbols contributes to our understanding of human communication, then I would argue that the concept is still viable (as I obviously think it must be, having just published a book on the topic, Leeds-Hurwitz, 1993).

It would be patently absurd to assume that all users of a symbol share some single interpretation of it; instead, what they share is better described as "a system of interpretation" applied to different contexts by the individuals concerned (Valeri, 1987). Cohen has put this particularly well:

> Thus, when we speak of people acquiring culture, or learning to be social, we mean that they acquire the symbols which will equip them to be social.
>
> This symbolic equipment might be compared to vocabulary. Learning words, acquiring the components of language, gives you the capacity to communicate with other people, but does not tell you *what* to communicate. Similarly with symbols: they do not tell us *what* to mean, but give us the capacity to make meaning. Culture, constituted by symbols, does not impose itself in such a way as to determine that all its adherents should make the same sense of the world. Rather, it merely gives them the capacity to make sense and, if they tend to make a similar sense it is not because of any deterministic influence but because they are doing so with the same symbols (Cohen, 1985, p. 16).

Thus participants use symbols during interaction as part of their efforts to jointly create meaning. Symbols do not stand alone as isolates, but rather are supported by and integrated into the meaning structures we erect as we participate in the process of communication.

I am not quite yet ready to reject all structural imagery in my understanding of communication in favor of accepting process, although, as

Stewart (1995) notes, I would certainly argue that it is time to shift the bulk of our theory and research, giving greater consideration to the process of interaction. What I envision may best be described as a fruitful synthesis of what each of these metaphors can contribute. It seems to me that participants generally make use of preexisting elements available to them, revising and reshaping these as necessary, though this does not lead to the implication that we can study process alone. This view rather incorporates process into the older vision of structure, and, if effective, it should lead to a more adequate understanding of communication behavior than assuming either process or structure alone is sufficient (see Leeds-Hurwitz & Sigman with Sullivan, 1995, for elaboration). There must be some building blocks used by people when they interact; I continue to find it useful to call some of these symbols.

Symbols in Context

A symbol does not appear by itself, out of context, with no additional information to guide participants as to its intended meaning. The meaning of a symbol depends heavily upon what have been termed contextual cues (Gumperz, 1982). Context is a large topic, including many issues (Duranti & Goodwin, 1992). Here I present a brief discussion of three crucial aspects of context: event, community, and identity.

Event

Hymes (1972) proposed three levels of context within which any individual example of speaking must be considered: speech act, speech event, and situation. These vary in size, with speech acts (e.g., the telling of a joke) the briefest, speech event (e.g., a conversation) the midrange category, and situation (e.g., an evening spent with a friend) the largest. All three levels have value; for my purposes here, event is the most critical. Event refers to the particular activity, often named, within which a particular utterance or action occurs. It provides the framework within which an utterance or action makes sense. No symbol occurs without some event framing it, for participants make use of symbols to invoke abstract meaning and the meaning must come from somewhere. The nature of the event supplies one critical component of the meaning attributed to a symbol by participants.

Although this hierarchy of act, event, and situation was initially proposed as a way of analyzing speech, the same terms can be appropriately applied to nonlinguistic forms of communication as well. A nonverbal act occurs within an event and a situation just as does a linguistic utterance; both require context for interpretation.

Let me provide an example of how a nonverbal symbol, understood as one particular act, may be framed by a larger set of behaviors, an event. Several years ago a class of mine sponsored a picnic to celebrate the end of the semester. The poster advertising it to the department included caricatures of each member of the class and myself. My caricature wore a necklace, clearly identifiable as one I actually own. That particular necklace had come to have a specific meaning for the course participants. This meaning was not integral to the necklace in any way but acquired through a class discussion about the nature of symbols. One day, trying to explain how meanings become connected to objects that then serve as symbols, I pointed to the necklace I wore, explaining that it conveyed to me not only aesthetic pleasure, for it is beautiful, but, of greater importance, connection to family, since it was a birthday present from my grandmother when I was a teenager.

Since the necklace was used in defining the concept of symbol for a class on semiotic theory, it acquired an additional layer of meaning for those students. In fact, the necklace has at least three layers of meaning. First, it has aesthetic meaning for anyone who views it: it was designed to be beautiful. Second, it represents family to me and members of my immediate family, who understand where it came from and how I was given it. Third, it represents semiotic theory to my students, who used it as a shorthand for the topic of the course when advertising our class picnic. Other students who saw the poster could only understand the first of these three meanings, members of my family, only the first and second, while members of the class knew all three.

In this example, wearing the necklace can be described as an act in Hymesian terms; the caricature of me wearing the necklace is another act. Wearing the necklace originally occurred within a particular event, a class meeting. The caricature was used as part of a poster advertising another event, a class picnic. In fact, a series of events join together to give this particular symbol its meaning for me at the present time. First, there is the event of the original artist making the necklace, who made it beautiful for anyone to appreciate. This event grants some meaning to anyone who views the necklace: it is a recognizable example of wearable art, designed to give aesthetic pleasure to the wearer and the viewers alike. Second, there is the birthday gift-giving ritual within my extended family, through which beautiful and/or functional gifts are exchanged. This event adds meaning only to participants or to those explicitly told about it later. Unlike its role as an aesthetic object, there is nothing intrinsic to the physical necklace that marks its role as a one-time birthday present. Third, there is the classroom discussion of the nature of symbols and how they function, for which my necklace served as an example. This event adds meaning only to those present in the class, which is why my caricature wore the necklace in the poster for the class picnic. It functioned as an inside joke for those in the know, conveying an additional layer of meaning to anyone who had been present for the discussion, and joining them together in their knowledge, just as family members are joined together by their knowledge of family events such as birthday parties.

Jewelry-making, birthday parties, university classes, and picnics are four different types of events brought together through a single symbol, the necklace. The necklace does not "carry" meanings, that is, they are not integral to it. Rather, participants present at particular events negotiate meanings in relation to an object when they perceive it, using it as a conversation or memory trigger, letting it serve to mark the one-time existence of a now completed event.

Events can be classified as to type. Both linguistic and nonlinguistic symbols are often closely allied with ritual behavior. The several types of events involved in this example are all ritualized to some extent. "Ritual" behavior refers to sets of established procedures, to actions intentionally conducted, by some group or community, generally employing symbols (Myerhoff, 1992). Religious rituals are those most people assume when the word ritual is used, since religious celebrations are clearly ritualistic (Turner, 1969). But rituals can be secular as well, that is, they can be a part of the nonsacred aspects of our lives (Moore & Myerhoff, 1977).

For this necklace, only secular rituals were implicated. Of the several possibilities, consider two: birthday parties and end-of-semester celebrations. Gift-giving is a standard component of American birthday parties; a wide variety of possible objects would have served as a symbol constructing and reinforcing the relationship between my grandmother and me. Other years she gave me books, toys, scarves, purses, clothes, or other pieces of jewelry. All of these serve equally successfully as symbols, all taking their meaning from the ritual in which they played a role. Structural equivalents (books or jewelry) are used by the participants (family members) as they construct a particular ritual (the birthday party) and as a way to create meaning (family connection).

Many of my upper-division classes have sponsored some sort of end-of-semester event, whether a party in the classroom or a picnic for the entire department, to mark the completion of a particular course. In that ritual, drawing a caricature of the teacher plays a role as an uncommon but appropriate final marker, and any object of jewelry or clothing identifiable to the other students would have served in lieu of the necklace. Caricatures of the students in the same poster emphasized hairstyle, eye color, particular items of clothing, in short, anything that could be identified as clearly indicative of one individual over others. In fact, I suspect the necklace was included specifically due to the verbal reinforcement of its presence on the day I described symbols—having been pointed out, more students would be likely to recognize it. Again here, structural equivalents (various caricatures) are used by the participants (students) as they construct a particular ritual (the end-of-class party) and as a way to create meaning (group cohesion).

Community

Individual acts of speaking occur not only within particular types of events but also within particular speech communities (Gumperz, 1968; Hymes, 1972; Irvine, 1987). "Community" refers here to any group of people who see themselves as a group and who share expectations. Communities can be large (an entire country in some cases) or small (a couple). They can overlap, permitting multiple membership (the couple lives in some country). They can be divided by physical boundaries (mountains) though more often they are divided by social boundaries alone (political borders). As Cohen (1985) suggests:

> The quintessential referent of community is that its members make, or believe they make, a similar sense of things either generally or with respect to specific and significant interests, and, further, that they think that sense may differ from one made elsewhere (Cohen, 1985, p. 16).

"Speech communities" are specifically those groups whose members share a language and norms of language use. But members of a community do not only talk together, they interact in a wide variety of ways, implying that we need a larger concept than speech community; we need to propose the existence of interaction communities as well (Leeds-Hurwitz, 1989). "Interaction communities" are thus posited as those groups whose members know how to interpret each other's words and actions based on shared knowledge, past experience, and expectations held in common. Speech communities and interaction communities overlap considerably but do not necessarily share identical boundaries. Both types of communities make the distinction stressed by Cohen between group members, who are assumed to share certain assumptions about how to make sense of behavior, and nongroup members, who are assumed to have other assumptions about how behavior makes sense.

In the example of the necklace, each of the events named occurred within a particular interaction community. The making of the necklace occurred in some unrecorded part of Africa, for it is made of African trading beads. The birthday party occurred within a completely different community, my extended family, reaching geographically from Maryland, where the birthday party occurred, to Germany, where my grandmother lived and where she bought the necklace. How it traveled from the jeweler in Africa to the jewelry store in Germany is another story, but the movement demonstrates that communities may be linked by no more than one or a few individuals. The class occurred within yet again a different community, physically located in Wisconsin, more specifically based in the university where I was teaching the course, the University of Wisconsin–Parkside. These communities are not only widely separated geographically but temporally (the individual beads are old, having been made in the 1800s, the necklace was put together and bought and given to me in the 1960s, and I used it as an example for my class in the 1980s). Each of these places and times has its own communities, with their own conceptions of the meaning of the necklace. For the first, it is a form of art; for the second, it is a marker of family; for the third, it is a pedagogic example.

Although the origin of the beads in nineteenth century Africa would be evident to anyone familiar with that particular art form, there is nothing intrinsic to the necklace that would mark it as having connections to Germany, Maryland, or Wisconsin, the other geographic locations of communities for which this particular symbol has meaning. This characteristic of symbols is typical: they are most often arbitrary, that is, the specific nature of the particular object, word, or idea serving as symbol is frequently essentially irrelevant. It is their function and use, not their physical characteristics, that matter most.

It is in part through the continued use of symbols that specific communities establish their definition as a group, and through which they maintain their cohesiveness. Symbols serve as the physical means (or, if linguistic, audible means) through which people establish, construct, and maintain group cohesion within communities. Simply declaring that a particular group will hereby view itself as a coherent community is ineffective and obviously absurd when stated so baldly; but once the members of that group share sufficient history, developing mutual interpretations of the same symbols, their existence as a community is established.

Identity

A community can be described as having a particular identity, but more often the term refers to a single individual. Identity includes who we are, who we understand ourselves to be, and who others consider us to be, as well as the groups within which we act and can reasonably expect to be

understood. Like communities, identities overlap, any one person maintaining multiple identities. I am simultaneously professor; mother; wife;
daughter; member of particular geographic, ethnic, and religious communities; and so on. The three aspects of symbols as used in context described
here—event, community, and identity—are divided for purposes of explication only; they are in fact more closely connected than may have been
evident to this point. *Identity* is often displayed through the use of *symbols* within particular *events* organized and conducted within specific *communities*.

Together with the necklace, I have moved over the years from a teenager given it as a present to wear to a professor using it as a convenient
vehicle for explaining a theoretical concept. When I wear the necklace to a
family gathering, it serves as a statement of group membership and belonging, for ownership of objects given by one family member to another
indicates identity with one particular family in lieu of others. After using it
as a prop, whenever I wore the necklace to class it served as a constant
reminder to my students that they as a group shared knowledge held in
common, apart from other students in other classes. Everyone in the class
could interpret my caricature on the poster, and understood the appropriateness of the necklace as my identifying marker, though they had not
all participated in making the poster. Thus the necklace served to simultaneously construct and reaffirm their identity as members of a particular
class, students sharing not only particular concepts but the same examples
for those concepts.

With these three aspects of context (event, community, and identity)
the concept of symbol can be seen to have moved beyond the traditional
representational meaning (with its frequent implication, in research if not
in theory, of a single meaning that will be consistent for all participants).
Instead, it becomes apparent that symbols are used in constructing a joint
understanding of who we are and what past we share; they are an open
statement of what is important to us. Clearly our social world is not constituted only through words; objects (together with other nonverbal forms
of communication) serve the same purpose in much the same way. They
are not, in the same sense as words, articulate, but they surely are an
integral part of human contact.

Symbols in Use

Symbols are not just scattered haphazardly throughout interaction.
We use symbols in particular ways as we construct meanings jointly within
communities, through events. Three concepts that aid in understanding

how people make use of symbols are polysemy, bricolage, and intertextuality.

Polysemy

Just as a person can have more than a single identity, a symbol can be used to imply more than one meaning. The technical concept polysemy describes the phenomenon of multiple meanings. A symbol may either invoke multiple meanings for a single individual at different times or different meanings simultaneously to different individuals at the same time. In either case, it is the potential multiplicity of meanings that is critical. As a symbol is used again and again, multiple meanings accrue, so the most meaningful symbols often are old rather than new.

My African trading-bead necklace demonstrates polysemy of both sorts. It has been interpreted in different ways by different groups; it also has been interpreted in different ways by a single individual at different times. Although no physical changes occur, it changes socially as different meanings are assigned to it. For members of my family this necklace serves as a reminder of family traditions, such as birthday celebrations, being part of the set of objects given by my grandmother to her granddaughters. My sisters have comparable necklaces of African trading-beads, given during the same year on their birthdays. For all three of us, it is hard to see any one of the necklaces without visualizing a ghost image of the other two and without remembering all the other presents given other years. Since my grandmother lived in another country we rarely saw her; presents permitted her to maintain a concrete and visible presence in our lives. In an important way, the objects chosen as gifts were entirely irrelevant to the process of creating and recreating a family connection over time and distance. Every time any of us had a birthday, as well as every time any of us used (or wore or read) any of the gifts she had sent, that connection was reaffirmed anew. In this way the visible symbols of our relationship with her strengthened her claim to continued active membership in the family, a claim that otherwise might have been weakened considerably by distance and a lack of casual daily familiarity.

At the same time, African trading-beads in the 1960s were not the sort of jewelry our friends' grandmothers were giving them, and so our grandmother's presents served not only as a display of relationship but also as a statement of the character of the giver and the presumed character of the recipient. The trading-bead necklaces convey the message "I am the sort of person who appreciates not only the abstract beauty but who knows the concrete history behind these beads, and you, as my granddaughters, are the same sort of people." Thus, even in the single context of family, the necklace is polysemous, incorporating several meanings. Although I have now used my necklace in teaching semiotic theory, implications do not bleed from one context to another: for my family members, the necklace has developed no connotations of learning semiotic theory.

For my students, the necklace represents all the times I have used whatever stands closest to hand as an example of how we create meaning. It is part of a quite different set of objects: not having seen the other objects my grandmother gave to us, and not having been told about that set, they cannot visualize them. Instead, they draw a connection between this necklace and a piece of white chalk, a connection incomprehensible in the context of family. There is, of course, a specific story behind this. One day I handed a piece of chalk to a student, illustrating the role played by the current speaker in turn-taking and selecting the next speaker. As the students passed the chalk around the room, the role of speaker passed with it. Most of the students looked uncomfortable, uttering no more than a word or two, passing the chalk quickly to someone else. One student, upon receiving it, looked at me, asking "I can really say anything I want?" When I nodded, he began a long and elaborate oral performance of a story, one more appropriate to a college party than a classroom. Several students looked visibly shocked. When finished, he gave me the chalk, and I continued the discussion of conversational turn-taking, commenting not on the content of his story but his ability to determine the length of his own utterance. The story of this event was widely told throughout my department, shared by my students with others not present. For my students, then, the necklace belongs to that set of objects I have used as impromptu props in teaching, having far more in common with a piece of white chalk than with other necklaces.

At the same time that the necklace has served to convey different meanings on different occasions, it is simultaneously capable of conveying multiple meanings to some (not all) of the individuals concerned. As the only individual who was present at both the birthday party and the class discussion, the necklace presumably resonates with the greatest number of meanings for me. Unless I tell them about it, my family members will have no knowledge of the role played by this necklace in a class of mine, seeing it solely as a display of information relevant to the family: as a birthday present from my grandmother, now marking family membership. Having been told about the family meanings of the necklace, my students not only recognize it as a teaching tool but as a marker of family membership, yet it has none of the emotional overtones for them that it has for me and for my sisters (acknowledging family identity being quite different from living it). The concept of polysemy permits (and encourages) researchers to move beyond the more traditional assumption that a symbol stands for a single connection and instead to look for the multiple connections that are likely to exist.

Bricolage

Symbols are not ordinarily employed singly, but in groups. However, each of us creates new groupings each time we speak, or act, bringing together already existing elements in a new, creative way. The creation of something new out of preexisting elements was termed *bricolage* by Levi-Strauss (1966; see also Hebdige, 1979). *Bricolage* focuses on the human ability to be socially creative, on the ability to think about connections not immediately obvious, and particularly on the ability to join together what was never joined before. As Barth points out, "In a civilization, there is a surfeit of cultural materials and ideational possibilities available from which to construct reality" (1993, p. 4). Language makes extensive use of *bricolage*, as we bring together preexisting words in the creation of new and unique utterances. Similarly, nonverbal symbols make use of *bricolage*, as people establish collections of objects that only make complete sense to them, since few others will know the story behind the inclusion of each and every object.

One of the astonishing things about *bricolage* is that the potential of any symbol cannot be readily "used up." That is, despite their past roles, symbols are always available for membership in further new groupings; still another meaning can always be attributed. Sometimes prior use provides lingering connotations, and new uses are startling precisely because participants incorrectly assume they know the "appropriate" grouping within which a particular symbol maintains membership, as it were. What is important to remember is that groupings of symbols are created by humans, who frequently reassemble and recreate them in a multitude of ways.

When my necklace was one of a series of necklaces on display for sale, it was matched with other jewelry in a display case, in a store, to attract buyers. When it was one of a series of presents at a birthday party, it was in a box among other boxes, joined in that context with various other presents. Here it joined not a seller with a buyer but a giver with a recipient. When it was one part of an outfit I wore, it was combined with a skirt, blouse, jacket, and shoes, matched by color and texture. When used in class as a prop, it became one part of a set of objects used to make theoretical concepts clear to my students, a set that also included the chalk described earlier. When drawn on the poster, it was brought together with objects commonly seen at a picnic, such as hot dogs, grills, and picnic tables.

The only consistent element in all of these collections is the necklace. If meaning were inherent in objects, then this necklace could only play a single role, only function as a member of one set, for it would always and consistently invoke the same meaning. But meaning is more accurately to be understood as jointly constructed by the participants in an event, through the use of words and objects and other nonverbal means of communication. Thus the necklace functions appropriately in a (presumably) unlimited number of sets, being given and thus conveying a different meaning within each context.

This example shows the connection I am proposing between structure and process. The necklace is a member of multiple sets (it has a structural identity, in fact it has several) but these sets are created through the process of interaction over time. There is no library where one can go to research the historical connections of symbols; one must learn them gradually over time, as a participant in the groups making use of them. Unlike previous users of the term *bricolage*, my concern here is not primarily with how elements are combined into a single set but rather with the construction of multiple overlapping sets, an expansion of the original use of the term.

Intertextuality

As previously stated, symbols can be reused, they are not in any way "used up" after a single display. In fact, some of their meaning is due to the implications brought to bear on the present use by all past uses. Using a symbol in any event incorporates an echo of all similar past events in which we have participated. The subtle reference to other events, other communities, implied through the use of any symbol, is termed intertextuality (Kristeva, 1969). Texts resonate as it were with prior meanings, according to their uses in prior events. The present is made richer by incorporating references to the past. Group membership is reaffirmed through the implicit statement that individuals who share knowledge of a common past must be members of a common group. As Barth makes clear, "reality construction must be a process of creating connections in people's 'here' and 'now'" (1993, p. 4). Intertextuality provides a point of departure for interpretation; it does not rigidly govern implication but adds a layer of complexity to it.

There are at least three uses of the term intertextuality. The first usage refers to a direct quotation of one text within another, as when one film echoes quite explicitly a scene from a prior film. The second usage is less explicit, suggesting that participants in a particular community will have shared a large number of prior experiences in common and will draw on that experience in interpreting each other's behavior, as when readers of a particular genre know generally what to expect of the next novel in that genre. The third usage is the most implicit, simply pointing out that all conversations in a language draw upon the same resource of words, all interactions are constructed out of the same set of possible actions, therefore one cannot help but repeat choices made previously by others, whether intentionally or not. As Bakhtin has noted:

> Our everyday speech is full of other people's words: with some of them our voice is completely merged, and we forget whose words they were; we use others that have authority, in our view, to substantiate our own words, and in yet others we implant our different, even antagonistic intentions (Bakhtin, 1929/1971, p. 187).

Whether intentional or not, we make considerable use of intertextuality in creating social meanings.

To return to my example, every time I put on the necklace, I think of my grandmother and the gifts she used to send her distant granddaughters. I visualize the small brown envelopes with German stamps sitting on the table for several weeks before any of our birthdays. Their early arrival meant she had remembered us, not just in time, but with time to spare. Since using the necklace as a prop in teaching, I have been unable to wear it without thinking of the students in that class, the party at the end of the semester, or the caricatures of each of them and me included on their poster. The two sets of memories have nothing in common except the fact that they both utilize the same physical item as anchor for the memory. Students who were in that class occasionally remind me that they still remember the necklace and the caricature; they bring it up in conversation as a piece of shared history. This is the contribution of intertextuality: enriching and expanding upon the present by incorporating elements of the past.

Together intertextuality, *bricolage*, and polysemy serve as shorthand, reminding us that we and others have used these and related symbols before, that we are not constructing the social world anew, only reconstructing it from preexisting elements. They remind us that new meanings are made through cannibalizing old meanings, new groupings made out of the constituent elements of old groupings. As in the physical world, nothing is created *de novo*. We recycle meanings just as we recycle aluminum and newspapers. The composition of the present social world owes a heavy debt to the social worlds of the past.

Conclusion

I believe a social account of symbols revivifies the concept of symbol, supporting the suggestion that it be retained in our theoretical vocabulary. I hesitate to reject any concept that may yet prove useful, but then I come from a family of antique collectors, loathe to let go of what others may consider out-of-date, whether furniture or ideas. I would place the major problem in past uses of the term rather than in the essential conceptualization of it and therefore have outlined the requirements for a new usage, termed here a social account of symbols. This new emphasis places symbols in context (including the concepts of event, community, and identity), and analyzes how people use symbols (through polysemy, *bricolage*, and intertextuality). I have intentionally put forth an example that is not linguistic in order to make the argument that communication includes much in addition to language and that it is misleading to separate discussion of nonverbal communication from discussion of verbal utterances. Although they have not been the focus of my discussion, verbal symbols are equally set in context, also contributing to the construction of events, communities, and identities; they equally require an understanding of usage, usefully incorporating the concepts of polysemy, *bricolage*, and intertextuality.

How does this chapter contribute to Stewart's (1995, 1994) proposal to define language as "constitutive articulate contact"? Taken at face value, as a definition of language alone, I have no major problems with his suggestion. It is a different definition than the one to which I have grown accustomed, but it causes me no major problems; clearly I am sympathic with his basic approach, desiring to expand our current conception of what language is and how we must study it. However, at the point where Stewart proposes to view language as an amalgam of verbal and nonverbal, both of which shall be studied as language, I become concerned. Once nonverbal elements are brought into the definition, I would prefer that the focus be shifted from urging an expanded view of language (including nonverbal elements as one part of language) to urging rather a more adequate view of communication (so that researchers would actually understand it to include both verbal and nonverbal elements, and would actually study both simultaneously). I make this potentially trivial distinction because it seems to me that communication scholars should have as their proper subject of study, communication, not language.

Clearly I agree with the constitutive nature of language and communication and the idea that meanings are coconstructed by participants during interaction; that much has been made obvious by the discussion to this point. I also agree that language and communication occur primarily through contact, with a focus on social interaction rather than individual effort, as should also be evident from my extended example. Language, of course, can appropriately be described as articulate. However, I am less comfortable with the implication that all communication is necessarily articulate. An assumption of articulateness serves well for language but is inappropriate for communication, which includes nonverbal aspects inherently inarticulate. Since I have argued that we must include nonverbal behaviors as well as language in our study of communication, I would find it difficult to support a statement that all communication is articulate.

References

Bakhtin, Mikhail. (1971). Discourse Typology in Prose. In *Readings on Russian Poetics: Formalist and Structuralist Views*. L. Matejka and K. Pomorska, eds. (pp. 176–196). Cambridge, Mass.: MIT Press. (Original work published 1929).

Barth, Fredrik. (1993). *Balinese Worlds*. Chicago: University of Chicago Press.

Birdwhistell, Ray. (1972). *Kinesics and Context*. Philadelphia: University of Pennsylvania Press.

Cohen, Anthony P. (1985). *The Symbolic Construction of Community*. London: Tavistock.

Duranti, Alessandro, and Charles Goodwin, eds. (1992). *Rethinking Context: Language as an Interactive Phenomenon*. Cambridge: Cambridge University Press.

Gumperz, John J. (1968). The Speech Community. In *International Encyclopedia of the Social Sciences*, David Sills, ed. 9: 381–86. New York: Macmillan.

Gumperz, John. (1982). *Discourse Strategies*. Cambridge University Press.

Hebdige, Dick. (1979). *Subcultural Style*. London: Methuen.

Hymes, Dell. (1972). Models of the Interaction of Language and Social Life. In *Directions in Sociolinguistics: The Ethnography of Communication* John Gumperz and Dell Hymes, eds., pp. 35–71. New York: Holt, Rinehart and Winston.

Irvine, Judith. (1987). Domains of Description in the Ethnography of Speaking: A Retrospective on the "Speech Community." *Working Papers and Proceedings of the Center for Psychosocial Studies, 11*, 13–24.

Kristeva, Julia. (1969). Le mot, le dialogue et le roman. In *Sémeiotiké: Recherches pour une sémanalyse* (pp. 143–75). Paris: Éditions du Seuil.

Leeds-Hurwitz, Wendy. (1989). *Communication in Everyday Life: A Social Inter-pretation*. Norwood, NJ: Ablex Publications.

————. (1992). Forum Introduction: Social Approaches to Interpersonal Commu-nication. *Communication Theory, 2*: 131–39.

————. (1993). *Semiotics and Communication: Signs, Codes, Cultures*. Hillsdale, NJ: Lawrence Erlbaum Associates.

Leeds-Hurwitz, Wendy, and Stuart J. Sigman with Sheila Sullivan. (1995). Commu-nication Structures and Performed Invocations: A Revision of Scheflen's No-tion of Programs. In *The Consequentiality of Communication*, Stuart J. Sig-man, ed. (pp. 163–204). Hillsdale, NJ: Lawrence Erlbaum Associates.

Levi-Strauss, Claude. (1966). *The Savage Mind*. Chicago: University of Chicago Press.

Moore, Sally Falk, and Barbara Myerhoff (eds). (1977). *Secular Ritual: Forms and Meanings*. Assen, Holland: Royal Van Gorcum Press.

Myerhoff, Barbara. (1992). *Remembered Lives: The Work of Ritual, Storytelling, and Growing Older*. Ann Arbor: University of Michigan Press.

Stewart, John. (1994). Structural Implications of the Symbol Model for Communi-cation Theory: Language as Constitutive Articulate Contact. In *Uses of "Structure" in Communication Studies* Richard L. Conville, ed. pp. 125–53. Westport, CT: Praeger.

Stewart, John. (1995). *Languages as Articulate Contact: Toward a Post-Semiotic Philosophy of Communication*. Albany: State University of New York Press.

Turner, Victor. (1969). *The Ritual Process*. Ithaca, NY: Cornell University Press.

Valeri, Valerio. (1987). On Anthropology as Interpretive Quest. *Current Anthropol-ogy, 28*: 355–57.

Editor's Introduction

John Wilson, a sociolinguist who chairs the Department of Communication at the University of Ulster at Jordanstown, disputes one of the most central arguments of this book's first chapter; namely, that language cannot be both a *way of being* constitutive of humanity and a *system* instrumentally employed by already constituted humans to represent cognitions and accomplish other goals. Language is precisely both of these, Wilson argues. For example, the production of the /in/ vs. /iŋ/ending is a clearly *systematic* contrast that "does not stand for anything other than that very contrast" and is "at the same time functionally part of a speaker's presentation of being." Thus language can be acknowledged to be constitutive and social without any shift in philosophical perspective; as he puts it, "a model of language as an independent symbolic system, systemically interacting with talk in the world will suffice."

Wilson argues that symbol analysis can fruitfully be applied to naturally occurring everyday language. One key to the success of such analysis is for a marker like "So" in such an utterance as "So what do you THI::NK about the bicycles on campus?" (see chapter 1) to be treated "as one of a systemic set of options that function in certain structural positions to indicate a set of meaning potentials." On this view, symbols do not represent objects of cognitions but "first act as instantiations of rules and rule practices." This structural approach to symbols, Wilson maintains, avoids many of the problems of traditional symbol analysis and explains how speakers construct worlds "through language as symbolic choice."

Wilson analyzes material from a corpus of audio recordings of undergraduate Catholic and Protestant students' discussions of "the troubles" within Northern Ireland. He focuses particularly on *discourse markers*, choices speakers make to "bracket units of talk," in utterances such as "oh," "well," and "although." In Goffman's terms, such markers "frame 'understandings through which social life is defined and negotiated'." Wilson claims that questions about the entities or cognitions that such

markers represent or stand for miss the point, because one needs to understand "in what sense is the systemic potential of these forms being used,
worked out, in this particular context of interaction." Responding to this
question will provide insight into how meaning is being constructed. For
example, the *goal* of one speaker's use of "well" is "to indicate that what he
is about to say is not straightforward for him," and that in this context
"*Well* is indicative therefore of a diffidence on the part of the speaker . . . B
is indicating (among other things) that since his experiences of protestants
is limited, any response to the question is not as straightforward as implied
by the question."

A longer series of utterances provide an example of what Wilson treats
as systemic symbolizing via a strategy that other discourse analysts have
termed the "aligning action" of conversational "repair." Aligning actions
have a tripartite structure consisting of a request, a remedy, and an acknowledgment. The issue in the example analyzed is the difference between "political involvement" and "political awareness," which is salient in
the conversational context, because the former could be interpreted to
mean that one is a member of a paramilitary group, and that would be
viewed as a violation of the group norms—or worse. The importance of
the ambiguity is enhanced by the interlocutors' knowledge that their conversation is being audio-recorded. Wilson's point in this case is that, when
viewed from the perspective of the larger context, a marker may be seen as
"meta-conversationally pointing to, representing, a problem within the
talk."

Another, fourteen-line utterance illustrates some implications of the
"choice" to omit "and" in a list of events that could have been verbally
connected—"There's so much unemployment there's so much trouble you
can't travel freely. . . ." Wilson argues that when "and" is omitted, the
utterance is hearable as a holistic surround that might have been turned
into a fractured list of features had the connective been used. He contends
that "when speakers. . . select particular patterns of conjunction in the
presentation of lists, we might learn about the correlation between list
types and speakers' attitudes to the content of what is being listed, or to
the role of such lists within the context of a specific discourse." "Or" and
"but" are other markers that can be analogously analyzed. "By considering
these markers," Wilson summarizes, "we may not only see the direction of
the argument in this part of E's account, but also that he is very aware of
the potential impact of his position relative to the accepted argument that
the troubles are normatively considered to be a bad thing." E's conversational challenges are approached "through the selective use of available
systemic contrasts."

The final section of the chapter explores some relations between "discourse and the life world" by exploring what discourse markers indicate about the way text is adapted to its context. In this case the marker of interest is what Hewitt and Stokes call a "disclaimer," such as "I don't know whether it's a bad sorta thing but . . . ." One of Wilson's points here is that "conversations are not only with those present but also with others not present, and with ourselves in the form of our previous modes of experience," a view that contrasts with both speech act and ethnomethodological analysis, but that is consistent with Gadamer's approach to discourse.

Wilson concludes that analysis of the systemic organization of discourse markers provides insight into "language and its role in the construction of speakers' worlds." The system that is accessed is "independent of interaction but gains existence and potential within interaction." And the speakers' world that is constructed exists not beyond but in the conversational text.

I agree with Wilson that his analysis of these discourse fragments passes the Gadamerian validity test of application. To cite just one example, the argument Wilson makes about the presence or absence of the connective "and" is subtle and informative. Wilson demonstrates throughout that he has a very good ear for some of the moves his interlocutors make as they explicitly and tacitly collaborate to construct meaning. I believe that Wilson's sense of "world" is thinner than, for example, Gadamer's, but Wilson clearly does show how not only micro- but also macro-structures of meaning are accomplished in talk.

But I also believe that Wilson's work here illustrates rather than refutes the claim that the most consequential features of discourse are only accessible when one moves beyond symbol analysis. Wilson asserts without much argument that the "markers" he analyzes are parts of a general "system"—presumably the "language system"—but his analysis itself demonstrates that the larger phenomenon is anything but a "system of *symbols*." His first claim about /in/ and /iŋ/ is revealing in this regard. He argues that a certain percentage operationalization of one or the other "gives a value, stands for, a certain class potential" and concludes that the choice "does not stand for anything other than that very contrast." It is certainly plausible that some indication of social class is accomplished in the consistent use of /in/ or /iŋ/, but the construct, "symbol" is not central or even peripheral to the argument that supports this claim. For one thing, it is difficult to tell how Wilson would identify either the "symbol" or the "symbolized" in this analysis. At one point his claim about the former is linked to the "production" of the phoneme, but ultimately he writes of "90 percent operationalisation." As for the "symbolized," he writes first that /in/ or /iŋ/ stands for "a certain social class potential," and shortly thereafter that it "does not stand for anything other than that very contrast [between /in/

and /iŋ/]." Moreover, symbol model analysis requires a more precise sense of representation than is evidenced by Wilson's equivocal uses of "indicate," "gives a value," and "stands for." Late in the chapter Wilson's dependence on the "symbol" construct lessens to the point of disinterest or irrelevance, so that virtually nothing in the section "Discourse and the Life World" depends on viewing discourse units as symbols. A "sin license" is accomplished, for example, not when a speaker successfully symbolizes something, but when he or she "makes it clear that they are sensitive to the rule they may be about to break."

In short, I believe that this chapter makes some astute and useful observations about the discourse samples analyzed, but virtually none of these observations is dependent on viewing language as a system of symbols. Like Volosinov/Bakhtin in *Marxism and the Philosophy of Language*, the closer Wilson gets to the actual praxis of discursive collaboration the farther he seems to move away from the symbol model.

9

Discourse Worlds and Representation

John Wilson

Introduction

> Language creates society but it does so without ever referring to the
> processes and structures it is creating.
>
> Halliday (1989:136)

> Language cannot be both a *way of being* constitutive of humanity and
> a *system* instrumentally employed by already constituted humans to
> represent cognitions and accomplish other goals.
>
> Stewart (1993:12)

I take Halliday's comment above to be a rejection of Stewart's claims.
Language provides humanity with a way of being because it *does* operate
as an independent system. To take an example from Halliday: he argues, in
the case of language acquisition, that parents do not set about explicitly
creating through their talk (representing) particular social values, norms,
or statuses (modes of being), which they then expect the child to adopt and
accept. At an early age what could we expect a child to understand of such
things? Nevertheless, by the very range of systemic contrasts (language
system) presented to the child, which the child factors as structural evidence, and then represents in the communicative mode with parents and
others, one is marking 'through the grammar' in Halliday's terms, the
confines of the social world—a social world that could not possibility have
been understood in the initial stages as having anything to do with referential aspects of the system, these are only available later to a meta-active
consciousness.

As I have argued elsewhere (see Wilson, 1993a) systemic development within language acquisition operates on two levels. First, the innate factoring suggested by the work of Chomsky delimits which language one is operating in. Here symbols are simply understood as instantiations of their rule potential and their structural possibilities and constraints. Second, an inductive factoring operates that monitors the control of systemic choices at a sociolinguistic level. Differential weightings attached to phonemic contrasts and grammatical choices come to carry social value. For example, children learn to produce the word *thinking* with either an /in/ or /iŋ/ ending (think*in* vs. think*ing*), and they learn to make this selection proportionally relative to selective social factors. Sociolinguistic research has shown that the variable (ing) is proportionally realised as either /n/ or /ŋ/ depending on factors such as class, sex, age, and so on. In one sense we could say that 90 percent operationalisation of /n/ gives a value, stands for, a certain social class potential, but in no way could we argue that such users understand or have ever consciously considered what this proportional delimitation stands for. How could they, because the systemic contrast, as a set of structural choices, does not stand for anything other than that very contrast. It is independent in its operation yet at the same time functionally part of a speaker's presentation of being.

Systemic choices from within language as an independent system allow us to create our world, not as a given, but, in agreement with Stewart, as something we constitute or create through our talk in interaction. In this sense language allows for 'worlding' as defined by Stewart, but we do not need to create any new theory or shift our philosophical perspective in order to accept this point. A model of language as an independent symbolic system, systemically interacting with talk in the world will suffice. In the rest of this chapter I argue this case. I do so within the remit laid down by Stewart's hermeneutic validity test where '. . . the hermeneutic theorist is interested in what the model comes to in its being worked out.'

Natural Language Accounts and Systemic Potential

One of the major problems facing any symbol account of language argues Stewart is how to account for naturally occurring everyday language. He notes the difficulties one might face in attempting to describe what 'so' would stand for in an utterance such as 'So what do you THI::NK about the bicycles on campus.' Any difficulties that Stewart sees here only arise, however, where one imposes a strict correlation between symbols and an objective world. It is possible to see 'so' in another way. It is possible to see this marker as one of a systemic set of options that function in certain structural positions to indicate a set of meaning potentials. Meaning is not imposed here but negotiated relative to a particular choice from a set of choices. In this sense symbols do not primarily represent objects in an objective world or act as representations in a mental world; they first act as instantiations of rules and rule practices.

Saussure implies as much in his discussion of the arbitrary status of language. Symbols have no inherent meaning, they gain meaning in being worked out. Here Stewart might agree, and argue that this working out is a form of what he calls 'worlding.' But such working out is not itself arbitrary, if this were the case all meaning would be created anew each time we spoke and interacted. There are general rule principles and constraints that are adopted in any working out, and it is these rules, their organisation, and their distribution within communication that should be the central goal of a symbol theory. To adapt an example from Saussure, imagine you have a chess board and a list of the rules of chess. You do not, however, have any standard chess pieces, only a series of identical round shapes. Let us further suggest that you are free to modify these shapes in order to distinguish them from each other for the purposes of playing the game of chess. In doing this, one could cut different designs in the shapes, paint them different colours, glue them together in different ways, and so on. The important point is that whatever method we employ will eventually be limited by the rules themselves. Shapes (delimited in whatever way) can only be given meaning (be seen as rook, queen, and so on) in terms of their rule potential. A certain piece is only a queen if defined by a freedom of movement not available to other pieces. This basic and core principle of systemic views of language does not tie analysis to objects in the world, or representations in the mind, but rather to abstract rule formulations that gain/give meaning in their being worked out. If we adopt this approach then many of the problems Stewart has outlined for the symbol model will disappear. To explain this in more practical terms and to take up directly Stewart's challenge of explaining natural language elements like *so* through a symbol model, the rest of this chapter concentrates on describing how discourse markers (such as *so*, for example) may be understood in structural terms and how this understanding reflects the construction of the speaker's world through language as symbolic choice. More directly, we will indicate how the rule potentiality of *so* (and other such markers) gains its meaning in being worked out.

Symbols Markers and Meaning

The analysis that follows builds on work on the function of discourse markers within everyday political accounting (see Wilson, 1993b; Wilson,

1995). The data for analysis is based on audio-recorded discussions involving final-year undergraduate students. Four groups were involved, two Catholic and two Protestant (an average of four students in each group). The aim of the discussion groups was to consider their own views and personal experiences of 'the troubles' within Northern Ireland. The recording was carried out by one of the students themselves and took place in the students' own residences. Talk was initiated using the basic principles of sociolinguistic interviewing as outlined by Labov (1978).

We will approach the accounts produced in these discussions from a discourse analysis perspective. Although the term 'discourse analysis' has been used variously to refer to studies of talk from a range of perspectives (from the historicopolitical through the sociolinguistic to the social psychological; see Ball, 1988; Stubbs, 1983; Brown and Yule, 1983; Potter and Wetherell, 1987), we will adopt a sociolinguistic approach. By this I mean simply that the linguistic construction of talk within its social context of production is a central concern. In the context we are focusing on, our interest relates to linguistic choice in the production of accounts of the troubles within Northern Ireland: specifically, linguistic choice in marking aspects of discourse, the process we will call *discourse marking*.

Discourse marking involves the use of elements within the overall organisation of talk, which function to mark off specific units of discourse structure. In the analysis that follows, these units are considered in their most general sense and range from conjunctions like 'and' and 'but' to larger-scale items such as 'topic prefaces' or 'content disclaimers' (these distinctions are discussed in more detail later).

The Discourse Role of Markers

In her book on discourse markers, Deborah Schiffrin notes that it is not a simple task to define precisely what discourse markers are; she discusses sentence-based, functional, and prosodic means of defining markers and finds all such definitions wanting. Consequently, Schiffrin (1986:31) '. . . operationally defines markers as sequentially dependent elements which bracket units of talk.' This definition suggests that there are some recognisable elements (units of talk) within language that are not sentential (or not only sentential) and that markers function (in part) to sequentially bracket these units.

Some of the most straightforward types of discourse markers are, inter alia, 'oh'; 'well'; 'but'; 'and'; 'although.' Markers like these may act to bind other linguistic elements together (and); they may indicate surprise or recollection (oh!); they can suggest a contrast between forms presented (but); and they may indicate that a predicted next turn will not take the direction one expects (well). Discourse markers may also, however, be considered beyond their purely structural description, and we will be interested in the way in which these discourse functional items are manipulated within account constructions in relation to the presentation of participant views of their own world, as well as their views on this world relative to the worlds of others.

In marking units as particular types, discourse markers may therefore assist us within a larger context of understanding, where the units selected contribute to an overall message or topic construction, and even beyond this to other levels of social understanding; as Goffman (1974:251–69) notes, markers frame 'understandings through which social life is defined and negotiated.'

Structure, Violence, and the Speaker's World

In this section we consider the way in which various accounts of 'the troubles' in Northern Ireland are constructed. Relevant extracts from the recordings mentioned earlier are provided in orthographic form since the location of markers is readily accessible in this format. This is not to say, of course, that a more fine-grained linguistic analysis is not possible nor that the location of such things as stress on markers might not prove useful. Nevertheless, for the purposes of the argument of this chapter a simple orthographic approach is believed adequate.

As an initial example consider the following, which occurred as part of a longer response to a question (put to a Catholic group on their views of Protestants).

> B. I feel I well I don't well I have a few friends that are Protestants I don't have that many and I think that's because of my upbringing I mean I'm a Catholic from a Catholic area I went to a Catholic school and everything else and all my friends, a lot of them . . . most of my friends are all Catholic. But I mean I know Protestants yeah and I mean I don't have anything against them whatsoever I'm not biased or anything.

In the context of this example *B* is attempting to constitute a meaningful response to the question about Protestants. In order to do this he has to take into account a range of factors and balance these in his output. At various points he makes use of those troublesome markers that concern Stewart. For example, how might one indicate what *well* stands for in: 'I *well* / I don't *well*.' . . . Or what about the word *mean* in the utterance *But*

I mean I know Protestants yeah and I mean I don't have anything against them whatsoever I'm not biased or anything. In what sense can the forms *well* and *mean* be said to relate to an aspect of the objective world or be representative of a specific mental state.

To ask such questions is to miss the point, however. The question is in what sense is the systemic potential of these forms being used, worked out, in this particular context of interaction. If we look at the issue from this standpoint, considering the way in which general rules are being employed/manipulated in a specific context, we may gain some insight into how meaning is being constructed in the previously cited example.

In the opening of *B*'s account he seems to have difficulty in constructing what it is he is about to say, it is for this reason that he makes use of *well* (I well/I don't well). His goal is to indicate that what he is about to say is not straightforward for him. So what would the expectations be in this context? The point is that B does not have that many Protestant friends, and he believes as a result his views are affected by this fact. He goes on to explain this point and reveals a sensitivity to his audience (see later) through the interactional marker *I mean*. He uses this to signify his orientation to certain ideas and outcomes. The fact that he has few Protestant friends is not an intentional outcome, it was not a conscious choice but a natural result of being a Catholic from a Catholic area. Once this much is understood, and that any evidence B has for his views on Protestants is limited, he nevertheless makes clear that within these limits he has no reason to be biased against Protestants.

How do we arrive at this conclusion? We know that *well* frequently occurs in those contexts where what is about to be said may not go in the direction of hearer expectations. *Well* is indicative therefore of a diffidence on the part of the speaker and often marks a modification of shared assumptions. B is indicating (among other things) that since his experiences of Protestants is limited, any response to the question is not as straightforward as implied by the question.

The use of *I mean* within talk can be used for a number of purposes. In general, however, it is used to indicate an explanation of ideas and an explanation of intention (Schiffrin, 1987). In B's use of *I mean* it seems to be an example of explaining ideas. In the first case **But *I mean* I know Protestants yeah.** . . . B is contrasting what he is about to say with what he has previously stated. His initial statement suggested he had few Protestant friends and that he was a Catholic from a Catholic area. On this basis his views on Protestants would be limited, but he has views nevertheless. But *I mean* I know Protestants yeah . . . is introduced just in case listeners think B has no specific response to make on the question about Protestants. His use of *I mean* suggests he is sensitive to a possible misinterpretation of his first point about the limits of his knowledge of Protestants, and he is taking the opportunity to clarify his point and to use this as a lead into his final comments: *and I mean I don't have anything against them whatsoever I'm not biased or anything.*

Markers and Presentation

In this section I look in detail at selected aspects of two further examples from the data noted earlier. In both we will see how language-marking provides information on the way participants negotiate meanings and make sense of their own life worlds through linguistic construction.

Example 1

(a)

N. Before I went to Australia I was very involved and listened to all the debates and thought of solutions and every so often . . .

S. You weren't politically involved!

N. Not actually

S. Politically aware

N. Very very politically aware and got upset whenever people came on radio saying certain things and since we went to Australia and learnt the simple fact that outside Northern Ireland nobody gives a shit and that Northern Ireland only matters to people that live inside it and we're outa sight and outa mind and nobody gives a dam what we do. . . .

(b)

N. Nobody gives a fuck and there's nothing I'm gonna do about it and I'm certainly no gonna to change it so let them go ahead and murder away at each other. . . .

(c)

N. So I like to think of myself as not a Northern Ireland person as such now and more of an outsider looking in at the problem because otherwise you just get too filled up with hatred and its not good for anyone.

In these extracts N argues that few people outside the immediate confines of the province of Northern Ireland care what happens to it or its people, and that, as a consequence, why should he care either. In his first comment he suggests that he once did care very much, to the extent that he believed himself to be 'politically involved.'

It is interesting to note that this phrase *politically involved* initiates what is referred to as an *aligning action* (Hewitt and Stokes 1976; cf. McLaughlin, 1984). Such an action arises when participants perceive problems or 'trouble' within the ongoing construction of talk. One type of alignment is what is called a 'repair,' which as the name suggests results in a change to some part (even all) of a previous turn. In our example the 'aligning action' is an example of repair, and this occurs when S questions, or rather rejects, N's claim of 'political involvement' by explicitly stating a disagreement— 'you weren't politically involved.' N accepts this challenge to what he has claimed and modifies his previous phrase from 'politically involved' to 'politically aware.'

The process of repair that had taken place here was initiated not by the speaker himself but by the listener. This is referred to as an 'other initiated' repair, indicating, obviously enough that the repair has been brought about by someone other than the speaker (the alternative, not surprisingly is 'self initiated repair'). According to Remler (1978: cited in McLaughlin, 1984:211) other initiated repair sequences are said to have a tripartite structure consisting of (a) request for repair, the indication that something is wrong; (b) a remedy, the repaired unit; and (c) an acknowledgement, an acceptance/recognition of the repair.

In our example the request for repair takes the form of a challenge to N, the remedy is N's supplied alternative construction, and the acknowledgement is N's acceptance of the challenge put by S ('Not actually . . .').

Now there are a number of interesting points that emerge in the context of this repair, one in particular worth noting is the issue of the call for the repair itself. Why exactly is there a call for repair here? What is it that has been recognised as a potential conversational trouble by S, that is, what is the significant difference between 'political involvement' and 'political awareness' that requires any attention? Obviously, being involved in something is different from simply being aware of something since the former implies a form of action or activity. But in one sense N claims that he has indeed been active, taking part in listening to debates, considering the issues, and, in his words, seeking solutions. This is not the problem, however. Within Northern Ireland to be 'politically involved' can also mean to be active in the construction of the troubles themselves; the term may have specific negative connotations in certain contexts, since it may mean, for example, that one is a member of a paramilitary grouping. The problem here, then, is that S knows N is not politically involved in the negative sense just defined and therefore rejects this possible definition of his claim. N accepts the challenge, recognising perhaps that anyone listening to the tape (as opposed to those present, his peers) might misinterpret what he has said in the way S suggests. As a result N offers another alternative phrase to represent what he had originally intended to mean.

This action is of interest to us here in two senses. First, is the action of 'alignment' not itself a form of marking in a broad sense? After all the function of the alignment is to mark of some aspect of talk as problematic. Second, this example offers some insight into the occasioned and negotiated nature of talk. It is interesting to note, for instance, that N does not in his initial turn say he was 'politically' involved, merely that he was 'very involved.' In the context of this discussion and the context of Northern Ireland itself, to be involved may indicate, however, that one is part of the troubles themselves, that is, to be involved is to be active in a core *political* sense. This is clearly not what N intended, and S is aware that this is the case. But since these participants are friends and know each other well, why has S drawn attention to the possible interpretation of 'involved' as meaning perhaps active in the troubles themselves? S must know that N is not actively involved in any political actions. One reason why this problem arises here, I would suggest, is that this talk is being recorded; it is in some respects, therefore, produced not only for the participants but for another over-hearer who might not understand N's use of 'involved' in the same way as S. This is clearly a potential problem for the participants, and because of the occasioned nature of the way the talk is being produced, this repair sequence may result as a methodological product of the activity (see Wilson, 1987). It may have arisen, that is, because the participants paid attention to listeners not present, as well as those present (see Bell, 1984). This outcome, both in general and specific terms, also has an effect on the overall selection of marking devices, but we will not discuss this issue in detail here (see Wilson, 1993).

The point of this example is that by viewing the interruptive sequence as a form of larger-scale marking we may see it is meta-conversationally pointing to, representing, a problem within the talk. In terms of what we have just suggested this problem is not only highlighted through marking, but such marking calls to mind, brings to the attention of the speakers, not only their ongoing interactional roles but also those roles that may be instantiated within a world of recording. In this recording world, as opposed to simply the in-peer world of friends, certain phrases (for example, *politically involved*) take on other alternative and historically marked interpretations (politically active; part of the troubles). It is hard to see how we could have discovered or highlighted such possibilities without indicating, or separating out the interruptive sequence as being representative of a problematic. Indeed, one can argue that it is not we as analysts who have done this, but it is the participants themselves.

Example 2

(a)

E I suppose I mean its all its all I've ever known . . . there's so much
unemployment there's so much trouble you can't travel freely throughout
the six counties or six counties. I mean its not a normal society and ah at
any time I go away somewhere . . . like my sister lives in Cork or I go to
Dublin or a foreign country em where there is a normal society you know
that you are missing an awful lot like I mean there is a lot of freedom
social freedom and this kinda stuff. . . . I don't know but em the way I feel
about the troubles well sometimes I don't know whether its a bad sorta
opinion but sometimes I feel that the troubles has to keep going on like I
mean the IRA sorta would plant bombs to let people know that everything
isn't normal. Like this Belfast is buzzing thing plant bombs in the Castle
Court and everything just to show that everything isn't normal.

In Example 1, the inevitability of the troubles led one individual to
argue that there was no point in even thinking about the issues. The implication was that there are those who will be involved, and that there isn't
much one can do about it, and that perhaps the best thing is simply to
ignore the whole thing by being like everyone else in the world. In Example 2, there is also an expression of concern about the troubles being inevitable; but there is also a rejection (implicit) of any attempt to resolve one's
position relative to the troubles by ignoring them. This comes through in
this case in the general rejection of 'normality' as a viable concept. From
one perspective things are not normal, consequently when it seems that
normality is being reestablished it becomes necessary to draw attention to
the perspective within which one sees such 'normality' as a fictitious construction; and this is achieved by acts of violence, acts that prove that
normality does not exist.

One of the interesting things about these divergent accounts, from a
structural perspective, is that they reflect a difference in choice of the
distribution of selected discourse markers, in particular the use of *and*. It
is noticeable, for example, that in the first account (Example 1) one finds
fewer uses of the connective. One should note that speakers do not have to
use *and*, they are free, within certain limits, to adopt 'asyndetic' connection, that is, to make use of zero marking. Consider the following:

Example 3

a. There's so much unemployment there's so much trouble

b. There's so much unemployment there's so much trouble you can't
travel freely throughout the six counties or six counties.

In (a) we have a sample from the original text where we have two topics that are not connected by 'and' but that clearly could be:

ai: There's so much unemployment and there's so much trouble

Equally, I believe, you can connect the parts of (b) in a similar way, only this time connecting three elements:

(bi) There's so much unemployment and there's so much trouble and you can't travel freely throughout the six counties.

Now while one might wish to make a stylistic argument about the repeated use of the connective in a case such as (bi), it is acceptable as a possible structural option. Is there any reason, therefore, for E's organisational selection? Can the selection in any way be related to his account as it is constructed?

I believe the response here is yes. The point is that E has a systemic choice here. In his opening statement the points he wishes to make could, of course, be linked with *and*, but using *and* separates the elements in a way that zero marking does not. I don't mean here the obvious point that *and* is absent, but Schiffrin's point that *and* may be used to connect ideas, topics, events, positions, and so on and therefore, by its very use, draws attention to the elements on either side of it as possible entities in their own right.

With zero marking this assumption is removed and we are faced with a list or series, but one that has a holistic flavour. It is as if what combines the elements of the list is an implicit surround, or content, which the use of *and* might disrupt. In E's account the political conflict is fully realised as a set of elements that are both individually identified yet bound together within a single concept of 'the troubles.' The elements in the list have an individuality, but by excluding *and* from the presentation the speaker is attempting to downplay this individuality in an effort to highlight what binds these elements together. The aim is to present 'the troubles' as a single concept, that is, more than the sum of its parts. For E the important thing is not to present a list of individual elements but to indicate the interrelatedness and inter connectedness of these elements; hence, asyndetic connection proves more appropriate.

The issue here is the way in which lists may impact via the use or nonuse of *and*. It has been suggested to me that one can distinguish between planned coordination (as in X, Y, and Z) from unplanned coordination (as in X and Y and Z). To call the second option 'unplanned' suggests that the elements in the list have not been thought out in some sense. Even if this were true, and I have some doubts about this, the result is that it emphasizes the individual elements in the list, it draws attention to their individuality. In planned coordination, however, the list is interpreted as a set of elements bound together, linked, that is, in their commonality or common goal. If this argument is correct it suggests that choices within the process of connective marking may reflect individual styles of thought, and therefore offer an insight into the way an individual views particular issues, problems, or contexts.

What I mean here is that through further study of when speakers (and indeed writers) select particular patterns of conjunction in the presentation of lists, we might learn about the correlation between list types and speakers' attitudes to the content of what is being listed or to the role of such lists within the context of a specific discourse.

Linked to a similar point is the fact that the status of the troubles in Northern Ireland, and their relationship to normality, is further highlighted by the list of places where *E* claims things are normal in comparison to Northern Ireland. This list is tied together by the marker *or*. *Or* is treated similarly to *and* and *but* and defined as a coordinating element. Schiffrin (1987) argues, however, that it differs from these two in that *or* is more hearer-directed. Its main function is to provide a series of options among which the hearer may select.

Example 4

Would you like a cup of coffee or a cup of tea?

Speakers do not have to choose a specific element, of course, they may reject all options or even select all options.

Example 5

Would you like a beer or a whisky?

a. Neither thank you

b. I think I'll have both

The ability to attend to options either operating restrictively, where you select only one member from a set of possibilities, or nonrestrictively, where one selects all the members, reflects what formal analysts normally refer to as the 'exclusive' and 'inclusive' functions of *or* (see, for example, McCawley, 1981; Alwood et al., 1977). Within logic this distinction is introduced in order to reflect the possible contexts where only one or the other of a set of options is possible, as opposed to the context where all options are possible.

Example 6

a. Fred is dead or he is alive (but not both)

b. Mary ate the cake or drank the coffee (or both)

Within interaction Schiffrin suggests that the use of inclusive *or* may provide advantages for the participants. If one gives one's hearers a set of options (a) or (b) or (c), and hearers are free to select either option (a) or option (b) or option (c), then they have a greater freedom of choice. On this basis, Schiffrin (1987:178) argues, a speaker has more chance of having his point accepted, since:

> . . . it minimizes the cost that rejection of any single piece of evidence might have. And the possibility both pieces of evidence will be accepted as cumulative support is itself a means of strengthening a position.

In E's presentation of other places than Northern Ireland, he introduces 'Cork or Dublin or a foreign country' as a set of options connected by or. We are presented with three choices here, and if Schiffrin is right even if we only accept one of these options E's main point will still stand, but if we accept all three then the point that has been made becomes even more strongly encoded.

I think this is clearly the case in E's utterance. If we only accept one of the options (individual areas/countries other than Northern Ireland) as being different from Northern Ireland, then the problems within Northern Ireland are highlighted by their contrastiveness to this other normal society. If we accept all three options as presented then the argument is that Northern Ireland is different from everywhere else in the world. This follows from the logic of accepting the third option, 'a foreign country.' Since the point here is Ireland (Cork and Dublin) and any other country outside Ireland.

This argument sits well with the rest of E's turn, the main thrust of which is the distinction between free societies (normal societies) and those racked by troubles. As E's turn continues, use is made of a different type of marking element, in this case the formulaic phrase 'I mean.' This phrase is used to suggest that what follows it is connected to the previous turn by being a summary, paraphrase, or alternative presentation of the same basic point. The presentation of a set of features describing what life is like in Northern Ireland, noted earlier, was displayed in order to highlight the troubles as a whole, an entity rather than simply a series of connected parts. What follows 'I mean' clarifies this by suggesting that within such a frame, as marked by the list of elements, one could not be describing a normal society.

In the rest of his turn E makes use of the contrastive form 'but' in trying to articulate a specific view. Relative to the content orientation of what he is saying this is not accidental. Consider the following extract:

> I don't know 'but' em the way I feel about the troubles well sometimes I don't whether its a bad sorta opinion 'but' sometimes I feel that the troubles has to keep going on.

In this extract E makes use of the discourse marker 'but' twice, in an attempt to contrast what the speaker believes may be a received opinion, that is, that the troubles in Northern Ireland should stop, with an opinion he would like to present, that is, that the troubles may be a necessary evil. Clearly, there are few, if any, people who wish the violence to continue for its own sake. On the other hand, what one sees as both the cause of the troubles and the solution to the troubles are linked to where one sees the problem residing. If one sees the problem as simply the result of IRA violence then it stops once they stop; if one sees the troubles as a result of the kind of society that Northern Ireland was before the troubles began, then it only stops when that society is changed or destroyed in its original form. But this may actually require the existence of the troubles in order to achieve that end. Not a palatable position, in one sense, but this seems to be what E wishes to get at. Hence, the use of *but* to seemingly contrast what one might have expected with what he is about to say. The use of the marker *well* here also supports this argument as we noted earlier 'well' is used when one is not going to get/give the response one might expect (see Schiffrin, 1987; Owen, 1984). By considering these markers we may not only see the direction of the argument in this part of E's account but also that he is very aware of the potential impact of his position relative to the accepted argument that the troubles are normatively considered a bad thing (see also following).

In this sense E is in a similar position to N, where we saw that outside authorities or considerations may impact on the speaker's choice of presentation. In E's case, however, the issues are larger and more significant. To imply support of violence is problematic, to explicitly indicate support could be illegal. E is faced with a situation of fine judgement in the presentation of what he believes, relative to both others and to himself. This situation is tackled once again through the selective use of available systemic contrasts, in this case what we are calling the system of discourse marking.

Discourse and the Life World

In these brief examples of everyday accounts of the violence/troubles in Northern Ireland. It has been argued that discourse markers provide insight into the way in which participants interactively negotiate their communicative intentions relative to the immediate context of interaction. We have achieved this insight by considering the symbolic potential of markers and their working out in the real world of talk. In terms of the hermeneutic test mentioned earlier we have gained much in the working out of claims, not only systemically but hermeneutically as well. The examples we have considered reflect a basic hermeneutic fact that implicitly pervades the concept of accounting, that is, that the preexisting experiences, historical and cultural, of individuals as they operate within a specific context of understanding are what drives the systemic construction of accounts and their variability:

> . . . relativity to situation and opportunity constitutes the very essence of speaking for no statement simply has an unambiguous meaning based on its linguistic and logical construction, as such, but on the contrary, each is motivated. A question is behind each statement that first gives it its meaning. (Gadamer, 1976: 88–89)

In this section we consider this issue in more detail and explore the way in which preestablished questions might be teased out by considering the process of discourse construction. Or to put it the other way round, we look at what discourse markers tell us about the construction of text relative to its situational production. This is not meant to suggest that there is only a single meaning operative within the text, in any objective sense. Rather, it echos a basic Heideggerian frame, wherein meaning is a product of interaction in which the text, its production, and its interpretation all play a part.

What I want to discuss for the moment is how the concept of normality is effected by one's life world and to explore how accounts as linguistic practices become the site for the struggle of understanding the preexisting meanings speakers bring to a context. We want to reflect on the exercise of having people create accounts for us and how that action forces a selective reaction to meaning construction as a contextual response. By this I simply mean that when we ask (as we did in gaining access to the accounts we have been analysing in this chapter) what people think of violence, what experiences they have of violence, and so on, what we get, as a result, is affected not only by the preexisting meanings the speakers bring of their own relevant experiences but also other preexisting meanings of what or how one should respond to such questions. Consider, for example, the phrase in E's account given earlier, 'I don't know whether its a bad sorta thing but . . .'

This is a classic example of what has been called a 'disclaimer' (Hewitt & Stokes, 1975). This term was introduced to deal with those cases where speakers have recognised a possible violation of some perceived conversational or social norm. In order for the speaker to maintain 'face' (Brown & Levinson, 1978) where such a possible violation is perceived (that is where what the speaker says may be considered problematic and where responsibility for the problematics of the statement will reside with the speaker), it may be necessary for the speaker to 'inoculate' him or herself against any negative perceptions that others may produce of them. Five types of 'disclaimer' are noted by Hewitt and Stokes (see McLaughlin, 1984:202): (a) Hedgeing, (b) credentialling, (c) sin license, (d) cognitive disclaimer, (e) appeal for the suspension of judgement.

> (a) **Hedging:** This refers to those contexts where the speaker modifies in some form their commitment to the truth of what follows and to the potential impact of what they say on others or the context. Examples range from cognitive verbs such as 'I think' or 'I believe' to phrases such as 'I wouldn't know as much as you but . . . .'

> (b) **Credentialing:** This arises where the speaker is about to produce what he or she knows will be construed as a negative statement or claim. As a consequence, the speaker modifies any statement by indicating that they are not unaware of the potential negative typifications they are representing. A classic example here might be something like: 'I've nothing against Protestants/Catholics but . . . .'

> (c) **Sin License:** Here the speaker makes it clear that they are sensitive to the rule they may be about to break, simple cases here are of the type, 'I'm sorry to interrupt you but . . . .'

> (d) **Cognitive Disclaimers:** In this case the speaker indicates their cognitive awareness of the sensitivity of the issues they are about to raise: 'This is going to sound terrible but . . . .'

> (e) **Appeal for the suspension of judgement.** Here the speaker is attempting to provide a frame for what is upcoming in his turn: 'Let me finish before you comment, okay'.

Of this set of disclaimer types, E's statement earlier would seem to be what is referred to as a 'sin licence.' The interesting question then is what is the sin, so to speak, what is the problem that E perceives, or potentially perceives will arise from what he is about to say? Here the context of interpretation overlays what E's view is. He is affected by larger existing meanings, for example that violence is wrong, irrational, and unacceptable. Within such a frame, to express an opposition to the criticism of violence, or to offer any justification for violence, implicit or otherwise, becomes more difficult. In this context, then, the *sin* that E is explicitly marking with a type of disclaimer is that violence may be necessary to make clear to those in Northern Ireland, and those outside Northern Ireland, that everything is not normal. The disclaimer is itself a discourse marker, in the sense of Goffman's claim noted earlier. The phrase attends to an upcoming section of talk and marks it out for a specific type of consideration; in this case in terms of its content claims in relation to issues of what might normally be acceptable in society.

This understanding reflects the layered dimensions of any attempt at understanding discourse production, not only in relation to what others say but of what one says oneself. Our conversations are not only with those present but with others not present and with ourselves in the form of our previous modes of experience (see earlier). This way of looking at conversation is not the classic speech event or ethnomethodological view (see Wilson, 1989) but rather the view one finds espoused, for example, by Gadamer (1975), wherein understanding is the result of our conversation with others. These others need not be only those present, or even others as instantiations of individuals not present (see Wilson, 1987) but rather others as constructed from the interaction of text in construction through preunderstandings and cultural interpretations. This interaction is revealed in part, I believe, through the analysis of discourse markers, because in these we see the frame of something either in mind or that might be brought to mind, in being or in the potentiality for being.

This has been partially revealed in our discussions so far. In the production of N's turn in Example 1, he is not only expressing his views in relation to a question put but bringing into being, into mind, the issue of various states of existence wherein different concerns may operate at different times. Paraphrasing N he seems to suggest that troubles are only troubles for those who create them. Those who live alongside these troubles may be independent of them in some senses, and therefore may create a life world where such troubles are an epiphenonmenon. For E in case (2) normality is an ideal whose very existence is not threatened by the abnormal but rather created by it or through it as some form of dialectic. These are broad themes but ones that recur throughout the accounts.

Within the linguistic structure of accounts we may gain glimpses of the motivating principles of textual production, language is our central clue to a speaker's world. Not a speaker's world beyond the text but instantiated by the text. In analysing accounts it is useful to bear in mind that while variability is inherent, so too is choice. This choice may not be random and unmotivated but structured and ordered with a specific aim in mind. When dealing with the language of accounts it may prove profitable to attend to the issue of choice at the linguistic level and to look for the markers, or guides, which speakers (consciously and unconsciously) provide for us. In doing this we are not imposing some formal straightjacket on interpretation but merely using the elements of the text as given to us by the speakers as a guide to understanding the accounts they provide.

Summary

It has been argued that we may learn much about language and its role in the construction of speakers' worlds by focusing on the systemic organisation of discourse markers. The rule potential of such markers in being worked out can tell us about the speakers and the way they view their interactional context(s). We only achieve this, however, by accepting that there is a system for speakers to draw upon. This system is independent of interaction but gains existence and potential within interaction. The value of this approach has been shown earlier in its working out, and the approach has, in my view, passed Stewart's hermeneutic validity test.

References

Allwood, J. Anderson, L. C. & Dahl, O., (1977) *Logic in Linguistics*. Cambridge: Cambridge University Press.

Ball, T. (1988). *Transforming Political Discourse: Political theory and critical conceptual history*. Oxford: Basil Blackwell.

Bell, A. (1984). Language Style as Audience Design. *Language in Society* (13)2: 145–205.

Brown G, and G. Yule. (1983). *Discourse Analysis*. Cambridge: Cambridge University Press.

Gadamer, Hans-Georg (1975). *Truth and Method*. New York: Seabury Press.

———. (1976). *Philosophical Hermeneutics*. Trans. D. E. Linge, Berkeley: University of California Press.

Goffman, E. (1974). *Frame Analysis*. New York: Harper & Row.

Halliday, M. A. K. (1989). Language and the order of nature. In Nigel Fabb et al., *The Linguistics of Writing*. Manchester: Manchester University Press.

Hewitt, J. P., and R. Stokes. (1975). Disclaimers. *American Sociological Review*, 40: 1–11.

Labov, W. (1978). Notes on Sociolinguistic Fieldwork. Memio.

McCauley, J. D. (1981). Everything Linguists Wanted to Know About Logic: But were Afraid to Ask. Oxford: Blackwell.

McLaughlin, M. (1984). *Conversation. How Talk is Organised*. Beverly Hills, CA: Sage.

Potter J, and M. Wetherell (1987). *Discourse and Social Psychology*. Beverly Hills, CA: Sage.

Remler, J. E. (1978). Some repairs on the notion of repairs in the interests of relevance. *Papers from the Regional Meetings Chicago Linguistic Society*. 14, 291–402.

Schiffrin, D. (1986). Functions of And in Discourse. *Journal of Pragmatics* 10: 41–46.

———. (1987). *Discourse Markers*. Cambridge: Cambridge University Press.

Stewart, J. (May 1993). Beyond the symbol model: Notes towards a post semiotic account of the nature of language. Paper presented at the International Communication Association.

Stubbs, M. W. (1983). *Discourse Analysis*. Oxford: Basil Blackwell.

Wilson, J. (1987). The sociolinguistic paradox: data as a methodological product. *Language and Communication*, 7:161–79.

Wilson, J. (1989). *On the Boundaries of Conversation*. Oxford: Pergamon.

Wilson, J. (1993a). The Study of Communication: Possibly? *Semiotica* 93–½. 123–38.

———. (1993b). Discourse Marking and Accounts of Violence in Northern Ireland. *Text*, 13(3) 455–75.

———. (1995). *Linguistic Forms of Political Life*. London: Longman.

Part IV

Continuing the Conversation

Editor's Introduction

Marcelo Dascal's contribution to this book is unique. On the one hand, he addresses a question different from those considered by other chapter authors. He asks what can be learned about the larger conversation this book fits into by analyzing historically prominent scholarly attempts to move "beyond" a dominant perspective or metaphor. On the other hand, from his perspective as a philosopher working with language pragmatics, he employs his investigation of the "Beyond Enterprise" to explore both the rationale for his weakening commitment to the symbol model and challenges that face scholars interested in moving beyond this metaphor.

The first part of the essay reviews several scholarly works that have contributed to "the Beyond Enterprise," including Dallmayr's *Beyond Dogma and Despair: Toward a Critical Phenomenology of Politics*, Fromm's *Beyond the Chains of Illusions: My Encounter with Marx and Freud*, Neitzsche's *Beyond Good and Evil: Prelude to a Philosophy of the Future*, Skinner's *Beyond Freedom and Dignity*, and Bernstein's *Beyond Objectivism and Relativism: Science, Hermeneutics, and Praxis*.

In the next two sections of the chapter, Dascal describes in detail the "dual nature" of these texts, all of which consist of a "critical component" and a "hope component." Such texts advance five kinds of criticisms of the perspectives they propose to move beyond. The weakest criticism proposes merely to "build upon" the dominant view. A slightly stronger form of criticism consists of showing contradictions, gaps, insufficient development, apparent counterexamples, insufficient grounding, and other forms of intrinsic problems in the view. The most popular form of criticism is "confinement," in which the critical effort is concerned primarily with showing the limitations of the view. This is the move Dascal argues is made in chapter 1 of this book. "Desacralization" is a fourth, stronger form of critique that "consists in showing that, in spite of its widespread acceptance, [the view's] aura of necessity, indispensability, or 'sacredness' is spu-

301

rious." The deepest form of critique is deconstruction, which "undertakes to suppress the very terrain or need for replacing the demolished building by another."

The goal, which the hope component has as its main task to further, is developed in "Beyond" texts in several ways. The first, "liberation," is a dominant theme in all the example texts. In addition, such texts often "develop an alternative" presented as "improvement, reform, or revolution"; they argue for ways of "transcending" the dominant view; or they "reinvent language" by neologizing or attempting to eradicate old metaphors. Sometimes attempts are also made to immunize the proposed alternative from *tu quoque* charges, although, Dascal argues, "Usually . . . *Beyond* . . . texts reveal a surprising naivete concerning the dangers attending the alternatives they propose, which makes them easy prey for *tu quoque* arguments.

Section five of the chapter employs Soteria Svorou's cross-linguistic study of spatial relationships to analyze *Beyond* texts into the object of criticism—the *Landmark*—and the proposed alternative—the *Trajector*. Dascal argues that such texts develop what Svorou calls an *ulterior* relation between Landmark and Trajector, a relation that assumes (a) that the Landmark is a one-dimensional entity, (b) that the Trajector is "located at the region which extends away from the LM and away from an observer," and (c) that the region of the TR is "open to eventual further specification through the context."

The final section of the chapter applies Lakoff's metaphorical analysis to the Beyond Enterprise. Dascal concludes that scholars engaged in this kind of work need to acknowledge the power of the "beyond" metaphor, especially as it "imposes a certain structuration of the field of inquiry." As he argues, the choice of this metaphor "carries with it a 'hidden agenda', not devoid of epistemological and ontological implications," which he sketches. He also argues that the products generated by such scholarly efforts "are not independent of the tools employed in making them," which helps explain why Landmarks such as the symbol model are typically criticized for being static and Trajectors such as the view of language as constitutive articulate contact (chapter 1), or the integrational approach to meaning (chapter 3), are described as dynamic.

Like other meta- or framing comments, Dascal's relativize, in a sense, this entire book. All the chapter authors are forced to reflect on the degree to which their work is characterized by the various features of "Beyond . . ." scholarship. I find this process useful, however, especially because it indicates how I might want to frame my next contribution to this conversation.

10

The Beyond Enterprise

Marcelo Dascal

beyond the stolid iron pond
soldered with complete silence
the huge timorous hills
squat like permanent vegetables

the judging sun pinches smiling
here and there some huddling vastness
claps the fattest finally
and tags it with his supreme blue

whereat the just adjacent valley
rolls proudly his belligerent bosom
deepens his greens inflates his ochres
and in the pool doubles his winnings

e.e. cummings (1991: 938)

We must hold ourselves . . . in readiness to abandon the path we have followed for a time, if it should seem to lead to no good result. Only such 'true believers' as expect from science a substitute for the creed they have relinquished will take it amiss if the investigator develops his views further or even transforms them.

Sigmund Freud (1922: 83)

Section 1

When John invited me to write a paper for *Beyond the Symbol Model*, he believed, in the light of our discussions several years ago, that I would be one of the defenders of the "symbol model" whose limitations the book as a whole purports to transcend. Although, in keeping with the changes in the intellectual landscape by the end of this century, I have been slowly evolving toward a place somewhere beyond the symbol model, I will—and not only for the sake of playing the devil's advocate or satisfying John's expectations—in a certain sense represent "the symbol model" here. For I will be paying close attention to the meaning of certain expressions, especially to the syncategorematic term 'beyond'—which appears prominently in the title of the book.[1] Since I assume that careful linguistic analysis as a way to gain philosophical insights is a hallmark of "the symbol model," I will be acting—at least in this respect—on behalf of that model.

There is, however, a catch to it: in my present view, 'careful linguistic analysis' goes beyond linguistic analysis as traditionally practiced in analytic philosophy, where the aim is to disclose the 'logic' of the ordinary, literal use of a term or concept. After the work of Mary Hesse, George Lakoff, and many others, no appropriate linguistic analysis can overlook the cognitive import of the metaphors we use. In the present case, such an expansion of the notion of 'linguistic analysis' requires close attention to the fact that the theoretical uses of 'beyond' are metaphorical extensions of its primarily spatio-temporal uses. It is the implications of this fact that I purport to bring to the fore here.

Four books bearing the title *Beyond* . . . stand out on my shelves: Skinner (1972), Bernstein (1983), Freud (1922), and—perhaps the hidden inspiration for all of them—Nietzsche's (1989) *Jenseits von Gut und Böse*. Surely there are more, less perspicuous ones. There are also in my files several articles bearing this title.[2] A bibliographic search in a philosophical index yielded many more *Beyond* . . . titles. A sample of the list—which includes, to my surprise, an article by myself (Dascal 1985)[3]—is given in the references. Stewart's project is thus—at least linguistically—in good and productive company. I want to explore the nature of the family resemblance induced among the texts belonging to this company by virtue of the shared metaphor that serves to name and structure them. This exploration, I expect, will shed light on the nature and problems of the Beyond Enterprise in general, as well as in its particular instance, which is the object of this volume. Although admittedly accidental, I think the sample I have hit upon is representative enough for our purposes.

Section 2

Before we open these books or read these articles, we are confronted with their titles—which should be taken very seriously. For they not only are the 'commercial tags,' which will serve to attract the attention of potential customers. They also act as an author's declaration of intentions and as a powerful clue for the 'message' conveyed by their books. Titles deserve, just as any other piece of text, careful syntactic, semantic, and pragmatic analysis.[4]

Two things immediately spring to mind when confronted with the title *Beyond X*. First, that there is something wrong, unsatisfactory, or at least insufficient, with X. Second, that the author proposes a way to overcome the unsatisfactoriness of X. Such titles normally apply, thus, to texts that contain both a *critical* and a *hope* component. No wonder that such texts usually comprise two parts: "The first part of the book deals with what we should leave behind, the last part with what lies beyond" (Kaufmann 1975: preface).[5]

This dual nature of these texts is often marked in their headings themselves, through a peculiar 'division of labor' between title and subtitle, one of them indicating that which is to be transcended and the other that which is supposed to transcend it. The subtitle usually refers to that which is supposed to overcome the deficiencies of X, that is, to the hope component. For example:

Beyond Nihilism: Nietzsche's Healing and Edifying Philosophy (Nimrod 1991).

Beyond Matter and Mind: Natural Sciences Synthesized into Philosophy (Albert 1960).

Beyond Dogma and Despair: Toward a Critical Phenomenology of Politics (Dallmayr 1981).

Beyond the Big Bang: Quantum Cosmologies and God (Drees 1990).

Beyond the Secular Mind: A Judaic Response to the Problems of Modernity (Eildelberg 1989).

Beyond the Chains of Illusions: My Encounter with Marx and Freud (Fromm 1962).

Beyond Belief and Unbelief: Creative Nihilism (Leon 1965).

Beyond Realism and Marxism: Critical Theory and International Relations (Linklater 1990).

Beyond Ethnocentrism: A Reconstruction of Marx's Concept of Science (McKelvey 1991).

Beyond Good and Evil: Prelude to a Philosophy of the Future (Nietzsche 1989).

Beyond Freud: A Study of Modern Psychoanalytic Theorists (Reppen 1985).

Beyond Deficiency: New Views on the Function and Health Effects of Vitamins (Sauberlich and Machlin 1992).

Beyond Deduction: Ampliative Aspects of Philosophical Reflection (Will 1988).

Notice that many of the subtitles attempt to give expression to the sense of *movement* involved in transcending X, by introducing the hope component through such terms as 'toward,' 'prelude,' 'reconstruction,' 'exploration,' 'response,' 'new,' 'synthesis,' 'prolegomena' (van Gelder 1993), 'from . . . to' (Kaufmann 1975), 'design' (Mitroff et al. 1983), 'confrontation' (Sim 1992), and so on. But these explicit markings are, in a sense, redundant. For subtitles following *Beyond X* are normally taken to indicate at least elements that, in the author's view, contribute to elaborating that which transcends X. This is the case, for example, in Bernstein (1983), Conner (1987), Gunn (1983), and Slote (1989). The linguistic order TITLE → SUBTITLE 'naturally' mirrors the diachronic order OLD THEORY → NEW THEORY or the logical order CRITIQUE (DESTRUCTION) → DEVELOPMENT (CONSTRUCTION). As we shall see, this correspondence is anchored in the basic image-schema governing the primary uses of *beyond*.

To be sure, linguistic order can be reversed, as in the following titles:

"Leibniz on the senses and the understanding: Beyond empiricism and rationalism" (Dascal 1985).
Balance and Refinement: Beyond Coherence Methods of Moral Inquiry (De Paul 1993).
Michel Foucault: Beyond Structuralism and Hermeneutics (Dreyfus and Rabinow 1983).
"Technology and an ethic of limits: Beyond utopia and despair" Farrel 1983).
Antonio Gramsci: Beyond Marxism and Postmodernism (Holub 1992).

These reversals seem to belong to the set of devices used in order to increase the 'topicality' of an item, as in "That this is a problem many people have acknowledged" or "My dad, all he ever did was farm and ranch" (Givón 1983: 349). Such devices, according to Givón, serve to mark either higher referential accessibility or increased thematic importance (or both) of the item anteposed. In the case of the titles listed here, although both effects are presumably involved, it seems to me that the pragmatic function of the reversal lies mainly in highlighting the thematic importance of the alternative offered, that is, of the hope component, at the expense of the critical component. The mirroring effect of the linguistic order is deliberately sacrificed for this purpose, but the basic diachronic or logical relation induced by the use of *beyond* is preserved, just as in "The lake, it is beyond the mountain" the spatial order OBSERVER → MOUNTAIN → LAKE, although not mirrored in the sentence, is preserved.

What is *suggested* by a title is part and parcel of what a *pragmatic* analysis seeks to determine: the *speaker's meaning* of the text, that is, the communicative intention the author seeks to convey through it to an audience. What is characteristic of *suggestions*—or, as pragmaticists call them, *implicatures*—is that, although they are conveyed by a text or utterance, they are not *logically necessary* parts of its meaning. This means that, unlike logical implications, they may be *canceled*. For example, if you ask me whether I am enjoying your party and I reply by saying that the food is excellent, you will normally take me to be expressing less than full enjoyment. I can, however, (try to) cancel this implicature by adding: ". . . and the music too, as well as all the rest."[6] An implicature thus functions like a presumption: once detected, it is taken to be present unless some reason is given for suppressing it.

In our case, the *critical* component we have detected has clearly the status of an implicature.[7] This means that one can find *Beyond X* titles where there is no intention of conveying criticism of X, but rather just the intention of developing X, building upon it. Yet, in such a case some effort to cancel the implicature must be made. A case in point is *Beyond Freud* (Reppen 1985), where X (= Freud's theory) is not intended to be criticized. However, the author's awareness of the usual implicature of his title leads him to provide an explicit disclaimer:

> Indeed, the title of this volume, *Beyond Freud*, intends in no way to disparage the originality of psychoanalysis. Instead, it intends to demonstrate how Freud's thinking and how the Freudian text have been used to expand ideas beyond—Freud (Preface, p. vii).

Another example is Sauerblich and Machlin (1992). This book is described in a pamphlet as a "watershed work on the role of vitamins in human health and nutrition." Its novelty—emphasized in the subtitle—consists, however, simply in providing scientific evidence for the role of vitamins in preventing a number of diseases. It certainly does not intend to criticize "deficiency." Nor is its purport to criticize popular beliefs on the beneficial effects of vitamins. It lies *beyond* these beliefs only by providing authoritative "scientific" support for them, thereby showing how vitamins can be used to *overcome* nutritional deficiencies. This fact is reflected in the choice of title and subtitle. A book with the title *Beyond Vitamins* would suggest a criticism of vitamins. Not so with *Beyond Deficiency*, with *vitamins* judiciously appearing in the subtitle, a place usually reserved for the *hope* component.

The *hope* component seems to belong, generally, to a more deeply entrenched layer of meaning of the expression 'Beyond X' than the critical component.[8] This is revealed by the fact that it is harder to cancel. In fact, I have not found, so far, *Beyond X* texts lacking the hope component. This difference in status between the two components is significant and may bear on the nature of metaphorical extension in general and on peculiarities we are here considering. We will return to it later. For the time being it suffices to bear in mind that both are cancelable suggestions— albeit with different degrees of difficulty. Although the hope component is practically always present, it can be construed in quite different ways, ranging from 'extensions' or 'developments' of X, through 'deepenings' or 'radicalizations' of X, up to its 'replacement' by (eventually) 'entirely new alternatives.' Obviously, the particular nature of the hope component is correlated with the nature of the critical component: the more devastating the latter, the more radically new must be the former.

Suggestions and implicatures have to do with the social dimension of meaning, with the interplay between the text and the beliefs, knowledge, and expectations of its intended audience. Every text is designed for some audience (Clark 1992: xviii), and every author takes this fact into account at least to some extent. It stands to reason that *Beyond X* texts are addressed primarily to two kinds of readers/buyers: (a) those who are aware of the unsatisfactoriness of X and (having perhaps suffered from it) are looking for alternatives to X or ways of improving X, and (b) those who naively believe that X is perfectly all right as it stands and are to be awakened from their 'dogmatic sleep' by reading the book: presumably they will be attracted by the surprise that their belief in X is called into question, and their natural curiosity will prompt them to 'call the bluff' and to pay in order to see what the fuss is all about. For the former kind of readers, the *hope-appeal* is dominant; for the latter, the *critical* component. An example of the former customer would be someone who buys, say, *Beyond Conventional Medicine* after years of unsuccessful conventional treatment of his illness. An example of the latter is a Manicheist who never doubted the clearcut and exclusive character of the opposition good/evil, and is struck by the suggestion in Nietzche's title that there may be a third alternative.

The kind of audience primarily envisaged by the author is one of the determinants of the emphasis given to each of the two components and of their particular nature. For example, the intended clients of Dallmayr's (1981) book are political philosophers and scientists who share a "dissatisfaction with the earlier 'behavioral' consensus, which aimed to transform political inquiry into a strictly empirical discipline" (p. vii). For such an audience, there is no need to belabor the critique of the behavioral approach, and the text can be presented as an "outgrowth of the 'post-behavioral' reorientation of the study of politics" (ibid.). Most of the book can be thus devoted to the hope component, that is, to developing an alternative. What it has to overcome is not the behavioral approach (the "dogma" of the title), but the "despair" of theorizing that ensued, leading researchers in the field to turn to "pragmatic problem solving," in the wake of the failure of the "behavioral" attempt to raise their field to the status of a scientific theory.[9] Insofar as it is critical, the book criticizes the narrow view of (scientific) theorizing held by both, the defenders of the behavioral approach and by those who despaired from it. Its hope lies in broadening this view by appealing to the philosophical insights of phenomenology (Merleau-Ponty), which, combined with those of critical theory (Habermas), provide the proper way of revitalizing political theory.

Let us now focus on some of the specific characteristics of the critical and hope components of the Beyond Enterprise.

Section 3

The X in *Beyond X* is, first and foremost, a *landmark*, by reference to which something else—that which is supposed to transcend it—is located. This requires the X to be *salient*, not topographically but culturally, of course. It must possess theoretical significance, historical importance, and widely known status. This is usually taken for granted. Nobody would care to write a book or even an article purporting to go beyond some unknown or unimportant X. No doubt what is important or not is, to some extent, in the eyes of the beholder. But the salience requirement would hardly be satisfied by mere subjective importance per se. If the salience of X is not a cultural given, part of the author's efforts will have to be diverted to proving it. And if it is not immediately transparent in the term chosen for X (as it as it surely is in titles parading "Marx," "Freud," "Postmodernism," "Structuralism," "Good and Evil," "Pleasure-Principle," "Freedom and Dignity"), the preface will set as its main task to make clear the consensual basis on which the salience of X rests (which is what Dallmayr sets out to do regarding the 'dogma' of his title).

The salience of a landmark is closely related to another requirement it must fulfill: *definiteness*. It makes no sense to locate something as "beyond the house" if there are many houses around or as "beyond the border" if there is no clear borderline around. There is, therefore, a presumption of uniqueness and definiteness regarding X. Authors are no doubt aware of the fact that 'postmodernism,' 'marxism,' 'structuralism,' and the like are far from satisfying this presumption. And yet they treat these labels as referring to well-defined theoretical entities. The use of *the* by John Stewart, in the phrase 'the symbol model,' can be seen in this light. Even though he is aware of the fact that there are many varieties of 'symbol models,' he treats them as sharing some core properties that provide a definite referent for the phrase. One may question this assumption, but to his credit it must be said that he at least undertakes to substantiate it, rather than merely taking it for granted.

By virtue of its role in the construction 'Beyond X,' X acquires a further property, not unrelated to the preceding ones, which is crucial for understanding the critical component. It is located *between* the observer and his or her goal. If the observer/author intended only to *locate* something by reference to X, there would be no need to criticize or overcome X. But it is a typical characteristic of the texts in question that they purport to move past X toward that other thing. X is, therefore, broadly speaking, an *obstacle* in the way toward the goal. This is enhanced by the very salience and definiteness of X, which make it difficult to simply ignore or bypass it. The task of the critical component is to handle this 'obstacle.' Its extent, depth, or strength will depend on how much the obstacle is perceived to hinder the author's attempts to reach the goal. Accordingly, it may range from very mild criticism (sometimes disguised as praise) to all-embracing 'deconstruction.' Let us consider these in turn.

1. **Building upon.** I have hedged "obstacle" with the modifier "broadly speaking" precisely in order to account for the cases where criticism seems to be practically absent. As we have seen, sometimes the X is perceived favorably, as something that does not necessarily hinder the attempt to reach the goal, but rather helps. Even in these cases, however, if you have to "climb the giant's shoulders" on your way to the goal, you need to spend some effort to do so: if you want to go "beyond Freud" by relying upon his achievements, you have to learn these achievements in order to become acquainted with that which can be further developed in them. Indirectly, this is a critique, albeit very mild. For it amounts to showing that Freud's theory is not complete or fully developed.

It may be argued—correctly—that the proper place for this "building upon" theme is the hope component, rather than the critical component. And indeed, in many cases, that which is to be built upon is mentioned in the hope-subtitle. What is interesting, however, is that even in its 'proper' hope position, that which is built upon is subject to criticism. A case in point is Fromm (1962), where Marx and Freud are the giants who began to break the "chains of illusion," but did not go far enough, leaving room for the completion of their work by the author. Such a completion requires a critical attitude toward the assumptions and achievements of the giants. Thus,

> Freud's vision was narrowed down by his mechanistic, materialistic phi-
> losophy which interpreted the needs of human nature as being essentially
> sexual ones (Fromm 1962: 26).

and

> Marx was opposed to two positions: the unhistorical one that the nature
> of man is a substance present from the very beginning of history, and the
> relativistic position that man's nature has no inherent quality whatsoever
> and is nothing but the reflex of social conditions. But he never arrived at
> the full development of his own theory concerning the nature of man,
> transcending both the unhistorical and the relativistic positions; hence he
> left himself open to various and contradictory interpretations (Fromm
> 1962: 31).

2. **Inner critique.** A slightly stronger form of criticism consists in dis-
closing in X contradictions, gaps, insufficient development, apparent counterexamples, insufficient grounding, and other forms of intrinsic problems.
To be sure, these may add up to building a case for abandoning X altogether. But, if one places oneself within the 'research programme' (in
Lakatos's sense) represented by X, they may as well function as motivations to correct or improve X rather than for abandoning it.

Thus, the "contradictory interpretations" of Marx's theory are, according to Fromm, partially the fault of Marx himself, but they can be overcome, and once this is done the program can be pursued and brought to
fruition. Hope is not to be sought outside the program in a completely new
framework, but rather inside it. This often requires a reconceptualization
of the program in somewhat broader terms. Unlike Nietzsche, who is critical of "the search for truth" and of the Enlightenment's belief in it,
Fromm—along with Marx and Freud—depicts himself as a true heir to
the Enlightenment, who believes in science, observation, objectivity, and
so on, as the way to freedom. He reconceptualizes this shared program in
terms of the notion of 'humanism':

> The common soil from which both Marx's and Freud's thought grew is, in
> the last analysis, the concept of humanism. Freud's defense of the rights
> of man's natural drives against the forces of social convention, as well as
> his ideal that reason controls and ennobles these drives, is part of the
> tradition of humanism. Marx's protest against a social order in which
> man is crippled by his subservience to the economy, and his ideal of the
> full unfolding of the total, unalienated man, is part of the same humanis-
> tic tradition.

> Different as they were, they have in common an uncompromising will to liberate man, an equally uncompromising faith in truth as the instrument of liberation and the belief that the condition for this liberation lies in man's capacity to break the chain of illusion (Fromm 1962: 25–26).

An interesting example of inner critique occurs when the author himself is the originator of the X. This is the case in Freud's *Beyond the Pleasure Principle*, where he sets out to examine his own earlier assumption of the primacy of the pleasure principle in psychic life. As usual, Freud is very careful in defining what would count as evidence against that assumption:

> . . . even under the domination of the pleasure-principle there are ways and means enough of making what is in itself disagreeable/agreeable . . . ; these cases and situations ending in final pleasure gain . . . are of no help, since they presuppose the existence and supremacy of the pleasure-principle and bear no witness to the operation of tendencies beyond the pleasure-principle, that is to say, tendencies which might be of earlier origin and independent of this (Freud 1922: 16).

The book is a search for such earlier and independent tendencies, whose result is positive. Hence, the basic answer to the question "Is there something *beyond* the pleasure-principle?" is positive too. However, the actual answer is, according to Freud himself, "circuitous."[10] It is not an unqualified "Yes," but rather a "Yes, but," which, according to the logic of *but* (cf. Dascal and Katriel 1977) amounts in fact to a "No." The overall result, thus, is not the unqualified overthrow of the pleasure-principle (a possibility Freud himself does not exclude, as made plain in the quotation used as motto of this paper), but rather its positioning within a more complex stage of the theory, motivated by questions raised within the theory itself.

In general, the upshot of inner critique is to make plain that the criticized views are liable of *reform*. It is 'constructive critique' insofar as it paves the way for further development of a programme or theory, once the detected difficulties are overcome. No wonder that it is directly correlated, thus, with the reform theme in the hope component.

3. Confinement. In most cases, the critical effort is, first and foremost, concerned with showing the limitations of X. This comprises several correlated aspects: first, X is unable to cope with the range of phenomena it is supposed to handle (it does not cure what it is supposed to cure; it does not explain what it is supposed to explain; etc.); second, X artificially restricts the domain of phenomena or of explanatory tools, thereby *exclud-*

ing what should be taken into account; third, reliance on the inefficient X as *the* proper way to handle something imposes on us unwarranted limitations, *confines* us to certain courses of action or modes of understanding, creates in us what psychologists call a 'mental set.'[11] A good portion of the critical part of the texts in my sample is devoted to these (and perhaps other) aspects of the limitations of X.

For example, John Stewart (1995) argues that 'the symbol model' (a) is unable to account for the most basic fact of language use, namely the interactional contact characteristic of natural communicative praxis; (b) arbitrarily excludes from its explanatory arsenal the insights of dialogue-oriented thinkers (Bakhtin, Buber), of ontologically-oriented accounts of language (Heidegger), of hermeneutics (Gadamer), and so on; (c) induces us to think of language in terms of the representational relation, which in turn forces us into a mental set that takes for granted—rather than questions—problematic assumptions such as the "two-world" assumption (language on the one side and the represented world on the other), the compositionality of language (which he labels "atomism"), the dichotomy subject-object, and so on.

Another example is Dallmayr's (1981), who criticizes current political science for its exclusion of relevant philosophical insights, such as those that can be derived from phenomenology. Still another is Bernstein (1983), who contends that the traditional dichotomy objectivism-relativism (and its cognates, rationality vs. irrationality, objectivity vs. subjectivity, realism vs. antirealism) drastically restricts our options. Thereby, it forces those of us who do not want to espouse relativism to accept an uncritical view of the objectivity of science, which does not do justice to the complex nature of scientific practice.

Notice that (1) the present kind of critique is itself a matter of degree: there are stronger and milder forms of limitation and confinement; and (2) at this stage the conclusion might be that, even though X has such drawbacks, it is "the only game in town" (to use a phrase dear to Jerry Fodor). The critic need not provide, at this stage, alternatives that would free us from the limitations of X. From a critical point of view, it is sufficient to show these limitations in order to remove the *blocking* effect they have on further progress.

4. **Desacralization.** Another, stronger form of critique consists in showing that, in spite of its widespread acceptance, X's aura of necessity, indispensability, or 'sacredness' is spurious. A variety of arguments can be used to support this claim. One may resort to history: X came into being in the course of history, at some more or less specific moment; just as it was not there all the time, it is likely to disappear now or in the future. Or

to ontogenesis: X is not innate but acquired; hence, under different contingencies, it is likely not to develop at all. Sociocultural variability may add
further support to the ontogenetic and historical arguments: societies
other than ours (which are not inferior to ours) do not accept X as a
matter of course. By desacralizing X through its historical or sociocultural
relativization, one also reduces the weight of X's *authority*. In so doing,
one is of course paving the way for the *hope* component: X is *not* necessary, *not* ultimately authoritative, and—as other historical periods and cultures show—there are alternatives to X. Rarely, however, the "Beyond . . ."
texts rest content with pointing out *merely existent* alternatives, for they
seek to propose a new, original alternative, even when they make use of
existent elements.

Skinner (1972) offers perhaps the best example of the desacralization
motif, even though he does not resort to the kinds of argument just mentioned. Unlike Freud, Skinner does not proceed in a circuitous way. From
the outset it is clear to him that the sacred notions of freedom and dignity,
as well as all their mentally infected cognates, are unnecessary theoretical
constructs, which a proper science of mind and society can and should do
without. The first task is then to desacralize this entrenched web of interrelated concepts that prevents our progress toward better understanding
and action. Like Descartes, Skinner is confident that the way to progress
passes through the complete overthrow of all the prejudices sanctified by
tradition. The obstacle is construed as immense. The imaginary line linking freedom and dignity is just a minor indication of its extension. All sorts
of usual and apparently harmless concepts belong to it: intention, purpose,
feeling, will, autonomy, value—what not! All of them are interconnected,
however, by a single thread: mentalism. Chapter after chapter Skinner de-
molishes this huge wall, thereby desacralizing not only freedom and dignity but also "the mind" itself. Once this is done, what lies ahead is a
crystal-clear single construct: schedule of reinforcement, which explains
everything that the components of the demolished wall were supposed to
explain, the latter's entrenchment being finally seen for what it is—the
result of mistaking mere by-products for real causes. Were it not for the
fact that hope too is a concept belonging to the wall, we might say that
this vision would flood us in a blissful bath of hope.

Let us pause to reflect on the difference between Skinner's and
Freud's choices of critical strategies. It stems perhaps from the fact that,
while the pleasure-principle is Freud's own creation, freedom, dignity, and
cognates are *not* Skinner's creation, but rather the creation of those who
stand in the way of the development of a scientific psychology and of a
scientific approach to society and politics. Even if critical of his own construct, and even if willing to abandon his earlier path, Freud must do so in

a careful way, so as not to look entirely foolish or unreliable for having taken that path in the first place. Skinner need not have such qualms and can therefore be much more direct and radical in his critique. Consequently, his trajectory can be much more straightforward. He knows what is wrong, how to transcend it, and also what lies ahead. Freud is much more exploratory in his text. Not only is it not clear to him that the supremacy of the pleasure principle is absolutely wrong, but also it is not clear how to prove it is, and particularly what lies ahead, for the region "beyond" is still shrouded in "obscurity" (Freud 1922: 68). Hence his candid words of caution concerning the status of his conclusions, of which he says: "I do not know how far I believe in them" (p. 76). This is a caution, however, which should not prevent him from exploring that region, "by combining facts with imagination," albeit it leads to proposals that "have only a tentative validity" (p. 77).

While Freud's critical stance seems appropriate to a theory in the making, which questions itself and builds upon its self-criticism, Skinner's stance seems more appropriate to pave the way to a radically new theory, which does not want to owe anything to its predecessor. Vis-à-vis X, the former is 'constructive' because it preserves at least part of X's validity, while the latter can afford to be 'destructive' because it sees itself as entirely independent of X. This observation could be generalized: the two first types of criticism here discussed belong to the constructive family, the three last ones to the destructive, and the third shares elements of both.

5. Deconstruction. This is the deepest or strongest form of critique. It does not seek only to demolish a theory, a programme, or a paradigm. It goes deeper than that—'archeological' (Foucault's term)—for it undertakes to suppress the very terrain or need for replacing the demolished building by another.[12] Deconstruction is so radical a critique that it leaves no room for hope. If it succeeds, the absolutely flat landscape it leaves behind has no landmarks left, nothing to go beyond. In its radical form, deconstruction cannot, strictly speaking, be a moment in the Beyond Enterprise. It lacks entirely and deliberately the transcendence motive. It denies the very possibility of a "grand narrative" of progress. Deconstructionists proper do not write Beyond . . . texts.

Yet, paradoxically—that is, by deliberately resorting to paradox—they manage to fit the enterprise. For one thing: their devastating critique of all constructions holds the promise of a construction-free world, a world where subservience to any system, theory, or narrative is perceived as contingent and therefore as not binding; a world where, potentially at least, we can free ourselves of all bonds. Insofar as liberation is one of the key motives in the hope component of the Beyond Enterprise, deconstruction may in principle play the role of its critical counterpart.

If we consider—anachronistically perhaps—Nietzsche to be a practitioner (perhaps the best ever) of deconstruction, we have an example of a *Beyond* . . . text written within this tradition. In his book, Nietzsche indeed seeks to demolish not this or that version of morality in order to replace it by another, but rather to suppress the very need for any morality—leading to a new phase in the 'natural history of morality,' which he calls 'extramoral' (Nietzsche 1966: 44). In order to reach this phase, each moral concept is to be abandoned *along with* its opposite:

> Suppose someone were thus to see through the boorish simplicity of this celebrated concept of "free will" and put it out of his head altogether; I beg him to carry his "enlightenment" a step further, and also put out of his head the contrary of this monstrous conception of "free will": I mean "unfree will" . . . (Nietzsche 1966: 28–29).

Otherwise, we will remain forever prisoners of the conceptual scheme that binds together all such (and other philosophical) concepts, determining the entire field of possible philosophies:

> That individual philosophical concepts are not anything capricious or autonomously evolving, but grow up in connection and relationship with each other; that, however suddenly and arbitrarily they seem to appear in the history of thought, they nevertheless belong just as much to a system as all the members of the fauna of a continent—is betrayed in the end also by the fact that the most diverse philosophers keep filling in a definite fundamental scheme of possible philosophies. Under an invisible spell, they always revolve once more in the same orbit. . . . (Nietzsche 1966: 27)

Freeing ourselves from this and other bonds requires accepting 'superficiality' ("Anyone who has looked deeply into the world may guess how much wisdom lies in the superficiality of men," p. 71), ceasing to overvalue truth ("To recognize untruth as the condition of life," p. 12), becoming able to laugh at those philosophies that take themselves seriously ("as soon as any philosophy begins to believe in itself, it always creates the world in its own image," p. 16), and so on.

All these attitudes, along with many other devices used in the text (arguing for opposite theses, multiplying distinctions, resorting to paradox, etc.), are employed to undermine all forms of dogmatism. And this very uncompromising and deconstructive fight against dogmatism is what produces hope. For it engenders a "spiritual tension" that yields "energies" and freedom that can be put to use to go beyond ("with so tense a bow we can now shoot for the most distant goals," p. 2), even though we may not have a clear idea of these distant goals.[13] Such 'constructive developments' of Nietzche's thought as those of Aloni (1991), Kaufmann (1975), or Leon (1965), however faithful to the source, at least testify to the presence in it of a stimulating hope component.

Section 4

In contrast to the three key properties of the X (cultural salience, definiteness, being an obstacle) that are the target of the critical component, that which lies beyond X, the goal that the hope component has for its main task to further, displays corresponding opposite properties. First, it is *new* and, as such, cannot be well-known, established, that is, culturally salient. Second, it is *open-ended*: being a new theory, in its first stage of elaboration, it lacks definiteness and counts as one of its virtues its vagueness and programmatic character. Third, rather than being an obstacle that blocks the development of the field, it *frees* it from such obstacles and *dynamicizes* the field by creating new alternatives. The hope component highlights these properties. Alas, as we know all too well, the new becomes old and the open-ended is not immune to sclerosis; hence what once furthered dynamism may become a threat to it. Consequently, the hope component has also as a task to thwart these fears, by at least indicating that the new alternative will not fall prey to the same criticisms that led to the fall of its predecessor.

1. Liberation. This is a dominant theme in *Beyond* . . . texts. The critical groundwork, if successful, is supposed to provide the decisive step in freeing the reader from the hold of the limiting conceptual framework. The author, who has been able to detect the limitations of a dominant conceptual framework or practice and free herself from them, not only communicates her findings to the reader, she also presents her achievement as a paradigmatic example. The stronger the bonds, the more valuable is liberation per se. Its sheer possibility generates hope. Hence, the stronger versions of the critical component, which emphasize the stronghold of the chains that bind us, tend to rest content with liberating us from them (through critique), without bothering or perhaps even avoiding to tell us what to do with our newly acquired freedom.

2. Developing an alternative. The euphoria of liberation being ephemeral, hope must be sustained through more substantial means. If not a fully worked out new theory, at least a sketch of what lies ahead, along with a path to reach it, is usually provided. This is itself a display of hope, for it shows that one does not believe that scepticism is the last word.

Sketching an alternative amounts to interpreting criticism not as an aim in itself, but as a step toward something better. Depending on the kind of critique leveled against X, the development of the alternative can be presented as *improvement, reform,* or *revolution.* Freud's tentative addition of basic tendencies other than the pleasure principle to his theory illustrates the first kind. Fromm's *synthesis* between Marx and Freud, which is supposed to overcome the limitations of both, may be an illustration of the second.[14] Skinner's replacement of mental explanations by behavioral ones is certainly an example of the third.

Sometimes the development of the alternative is minimal and consists merely in showing that life is possible without the criticized X (Nietzsche is a case in point). But sometimes, in order to escape charges of vagueness, lack of seriousness, and so on, an effort is made to provide a well-articulated alternative, where the differences with X are made apparent (Kaufmann, Stewart). The danger, of course, is to make it so well-articulated as to become itelf an easy target for the Beyond Enterprise (Skinner's theory is a case in point).

3. *Transcendence.* The hope conveyed by *Beyond . . .* texts is in some cases explicitly (e.g., Cattell 1987, Eildelberg 1989, Aloni 1991, Ferrell 1983, Frankl 1960) and in others implicitly (e.g., Fromm 1962, Kaufmann 1965) related to the hope inherent in transcendentalism, be it religious or secular. I mean by this more than just pointing out the fact that going beyond something is somehow transcending it. Even though many *Beyond . . .* texts purport to reject abstract, idealized, or otherwise 'unrealistic' conceptual frameworks, and to bring us 'down to earth,' they aspire nevertheless to offer a sense of what is *really* real or important. The more radical this departure of earlier conceptions of 'reality' is, the more it brings us to 'another world,' where truth and real hope are to be found. Breaking away from old conceptual tools, old forms of language, old prejudices are means to enter this other world where everything has to be reinvented. Even if all this is done in the name of 'science' or 'reason,' it easily leads to utopia (e.g., Skinner's *Walden Two*).

Cattell's *Beyondism* epitomizes this transcendentalist motive. 'Beyondism' is based on science, more specifically, on sociobiology. It is defined as

> a system for discovering and clarifying ethical goals from a basis of scientific knowledge and investigation, by the objective research procedures of scientific method (Cattell 1987: 1).

Cattell is aware of the fact that the term 'Beyondism' may suggest an afterlife, a suggestion he rejects. And yet, he does not reject the idea of a *future life,* which, though radically different from that portrayed by the revealed religions, is such that "much of [its] emotional meaning for the individual is the same" (p. vii). Cattell's choice of emphasizing the *religious* aspect of his system, its ability to sustain "the emotional restraints and expectations" built up by Christianity (p. vii), while at the same time claiming that it is derived *from* science and created by "rationalists, thinking liberals, sociobiologists, and scientifically progressive, educated persons of all origins" (p. viii) is certainly puzzling. And yet, I surmise, it is not contradictory precisely because it caters to the transcendental motive latent in all versions—scientific, philosophical, or religious—of the Beyond Enterprise.

4. **Reinventing language.** A particularly difficult kind of confinement or limitation the development of an alternative to X has to face is the inadequacy of the extant vocabulary (which in fact reflects the conceptual framework one wants to get rid of) for its purposes. One must get beyond the current vocabulary if one wants to transcend the limitations of the conceputal framework it reflects. But in order to introduce a new vocabulary one cannot but use the existing one, thereby risking not to be able to really transcend X. A widespread solution to this problem is to neologize, either by creating entirely new terms or by hyphenating old ones or else by endowing old terms with new meanings. Heidegger—who is one of the sources Stewart appeals to—was a master neologist, in all its three varieties. Although I have not been able to check this matter systematically, I believe this technique is widespread in *Beyond . . .* texts.

A more subtle way in which 'old' language may undermine the success of the Beyond Enterprise is through the persistence of old root metaphors. Since these metaphors are pervasive and hardly noticed, an effort must be made to become aware of them, to be followed by an attempt to eradicate them, and finally to replace them by new metaphors. As far as I have been able to verify, very little explicit attention has been given in *Beyond . . .* texts to this problem, although some of them no doubt struggle to free themselves from old metaphors and to create new ones. The appeal they make to the old metaphor induced by the term 'beyond' reveals both their lack of awareness of the problem at hand and the possibility of getting rid of metaphor. It is worth noticing, however, that in both respects Freud anticipated much of the current vindication of metaphor's cognitive importance:

> [We are] obliged to operate with scientific terms, i.e. with the metaphorical expressions peculiar to psychology (or more correctly: psychology of the deeper layers). Otherwise we should not be able to describe the corresponding processes at all, nor in fact even to have remarked them. The

shortcomings of our description would probably disappear if for the psychological terms we could substitute physiological or chemical ones.
These too only constitute a metaphorical language, but one familiar to us
for a much longer time and perhaps also simpler (Freud 1922: 78).

5. Tu quoque. It is not easy to immunize the proposed alternative
from the very same kind of criticism addressed against X, especially if that
criticism has been sweeping and 'profound'—as it is supposed to be. For
example, if one has rejected the traditional notions of 'representation,'
'sign,' 'interpretation,' 'justification' as components of the undesirable
'symbol model,' it is not easy to prove that one's alternative conception
does not surreptitiously include remnants of these notions. If, in a postmodern vein, one further rejects the traditional notions of truth, rationality, argumentation, validity, objectivity, and so on, what kind of support
can one claim one's alternative to have? Two possibilities are open in such
a case: either not to propose an alternative or else to express total indifference regarding the status of the alternative or account one proposes.
Both strategies are used by deconstructionists: rejecting the idea that criticism must be 'constructive,' that is, that it must provide alternatives, and
ignoring (or even welcoming) tu quoque arguments against their accounts.[15]
   Usually, however, Beyond . . . texts reveal a surprising naivete concerning the dangers attending the alternatives they propose, which makes
them easy prey for tu quoque arguments. A case in point is Fromm (1962).
There is a kind of paradox in Fromm's attitude, which—perhaps uninten-
tionally—reveals an unexpected meaning in the title of his book—Beyond
the Chains of Illusion. In what is perhaps the best chapter of the book,
Fromm analyzes the fate of Marx's and Freud's doctrines. Both began as
radical innovations, stemming from radical criticism of prevailing ideas
and practices, a criticism that showed such ideas and practices to be illusions. Freud's concept of rationalization and Marx's concept of ideology
both described the nature of these compelling illusions and provided the
tools for getting rid of them. The fate of their doctrines, however, was to
become themselves ideologies. In the hands of organizations (the psychoanalytic establishment, the socialist parties) they became bureaucratized,
thereby losing their vital critical ethos. They became instrumental in leading humans astray from the very same liberating ideas and ideals that had
animated them. In this ideological guise, they became themselves illusions, additional chains to be broken in our path toward liberation. The
way Fromm proposes for breaking these new chains is the return to the
vitality of the original critical power of the very same doctrines that ultimately produced such chains. Fromm's beyond, thus, consists in going
back—with the aim, of course, of leaping ahead. But—one might ask—

what will prevent history from repeating itself? Why should we assume that the illusion-engendering mechanism will not, once more, follow the same track? Why should we presume that the process that led to the ideologization of Freud's and Marx's doctrines is entirely due to causes extraneous to the nature of these doctrines, causes that, if removed, will preserve their liberating power? Couldn't the reason for their petrification lie precisely in the fact that they attempted to transcend their critical/skeptical component, viewing it only as a step toward reaching the truth? Isn't Fromm himself victim of another, deeper illusion—the belief in the possibility of remaining faithful to the ethos both of the liberating power of radical criticism and of the existence and accessibility of truth? It is possible that Fromm's heroic attempt to criticize the ideologized versions of Marx's and Freud's views, while at the same time remaining faithful to their 'core' of truth, illustrates an aspect of the logic of the beyond enterprise: in order to really go beyond, moderate criticism coupled with improvement and/or reform is not enough; once you undertake the beyond move, nothing short of full and radical criticism coupled with all-out conceptual revolution will do; for, if you fall short of that, your move will fall prey to a (justifiable) *tu quoque* argument.

Section 5

The cognitive and linguistic aspects of our handling of spatial relations and motion has been intensively studied by psychologists and linguists, often within a cross-cultural perspective, in the last two decades.[16] The significance of such studies has been broadened by the development of a theory, largely due to George Lakoff, which highlights the fact that both our language and conceptualizations are, for the most part, metaphorically structured.[17] According to this theory, these structuring metaphors are grounded on an 'experiential basis,' where spatial relations occupy a privileged position. It is therefore of primary importance to start from an up-to-date account of the linguistic-cognitive treatment of spatial relations in order to be able to explore their contribution to the metaphorical structuration of other domains. For this purpose, I will rely upon the cross-linguistic study of Svorou (1993), which makes use of much of the preceding literature on the subject and focuses on the front-back axis, which is the one relevant for our purposes.

If one assumes that one of the basic communicative uses of spatial terms is to convey the location of entities and that this is usually done by way of specifying some sort of relation they bear to other entities, a first distinction to be made is that between the entity to be located—the *Tra-*

jector (TR) in Svorou's terminolgy—and the entity with respect to which the TR is located—the *Landmark* (LM).[18] Typically, the relation between these two entities is perceived and linguistically treated as asymmetrical. Such an asymmetry may be construed in different ways. The two entities may be 'objectively' asymmetrical vis à vis their size, orientation, direction of actual or possible motion, and so on. The asymmetry may be induced or projected by a tacit or explicit appeal to an observer who may be the speaker, the addressee, or someone else (Svorou 1993: 9). The asymmetry may also be social or cultural: culturally important, frequently encountered things stand in asymmetrical relation to less important or less frequent ones. Talmy (1983) has observed that in such asymmetrical pairs, the entity usually more likely to be selected as an LM tends to be on the upper end of the scales mentioned herein: larger, more frequently encountered, more culturally significant, and so on. The actual construal of the asymmetry will depend upon the *reference frame* employed by the speaker, and the choice of a particular way of describing a spatial arrangement will depend on several contextual factors.

The term 'beyond' characteristically serves to express an ULTERIOR relation, characterized by the following assumptions: (1) The LM is treated as a one-dimensional entity and (2) The TR is located at the region that extends away from the LM and away from an observer (Svorou 1993: 133). The first assumption implies that the LM is normally treated as devoid of intrinsic orientation. The second assumption implies that the region where the TR is located is 'projected' through an imaginary movement leading from the observer to the LM (this may be the 'movement' of sight). It also implies that that region is 'open' to eventual further specification through the context. The ULTERIOR relation belongs, according to Svorou (1993: 170), to the semantic field of the FRONT-REGION, which also includes, among other things, such relations as OPPOSITE and OBSTRUCTION.

It can easily be seen that most of the mentioned observations and definitions regarding the spatial use of 'beyond' correspond quite straightforwardly to the observations we made regarding its metaphorical use. The correspondence covers the properties of the "X" (i.e., the LM), of the "goal" (the TR), as well as facts such as the intermediary (and hence potentially obstructive) position of the LM in the path leading from the author/observer to the TR, and many others.[19] But it is certainly the *movement* element inherent in the very image-schema that defines ULTERIOR that is picked up as the most significant aspect that informs the metaphorical extension(s) we have been considering, an aspect that is highlighted by the reinforcement of 'beyond' through a 'toward.' This accounts for most of the details of our observations:

1. The field of research is presented by this construction as *dynamic*,

as a *process* whose dynamism has been temporarily blocked but will now be resumed.

2. The LM is responsible for such a blocking. Consequently, it is described as a well-defined position that constitutes a sort of *static* point of equilibrium, as a *consensual* or at least as a *dominant* position, which *blocks* further evolution, because it has led the field to a *dead end*.

3. While the LM *closes* the field of research, the TR is supposed to *reopen* it. Such a feat can be achieved only by a *nonconsensual* proposal, which introduces the necessary *dynamic* imbalance for getting the field *in the move* again.

4. The critique of the LM must demonstrate its consensual (or dominant), static, and blocking character. The first requirement explains the tendency to reduce differences between alleged holders of the LM to a common denominator. Such a presentation of the LM is of necessity simplified and prompts claims by its defenders to the effect that the critic is misrepresenting their positions and attacking a straw man. The second requirement explains the suppression of dynamic or processual components in the presentation of LM: it is a 'mature,' 'fully developed,' 'spelled-out' position; as a 'research programme,' it is kept 'alive' only through minor, ad-hoc, 'degenerative' changes, rather than through 'progressive' innovations or reorganizations. The third requirement explains the emphasis on the stifling effect of LM upon the whole field.

5. By contrast, TR must be presented as held by the underdogs of the field, those whose opinions have not been paid attention to because the consensus considered them 'bizarre,' 'imprecise,' 'unscientific,' 'not well argued for,' and so on. Furthermore, in order to produce the desired dynamization of the field, TR *must* be itself presented as 'open-ended,' as a 'direction' of research, a 'programme' worth pursuing further, rather than as a completely elaborated theory. This explains its *programmatic* character.

6. The overall result of the dynamization due to the use of the *beyond* frame is an emphasis on the *historicity* of theory formation and evolution. The criticized consensual position itself is now viewed as a moment in the historical evolution of the field, rather than as an end point. This explains why even the latest fashionable theories may be challenged by the use of the 'beyond X' frame [Beyond Deconstruction, Beyond Structuralism, Beyond Post-Modernity, etc.], suggesting an even stronger "in the move" effect. At the same time, it explains the always present possibility of *tu quoque*.

7. Just as the critical component that sees in the LM an obstacle is motivated by emphasizing the spatial properties of the movement implicit in the 'beyond' construction, the hope component is motivated by stress-

ing the temporal aspect of such a movement. Hope is indeed a propositional attitude or emotional stance that necessarily refers to the future. It
also implies that the future is somehow better than the present and past.
In other words, the movement from the observer past the LM to the TR is
interpreted as having a clear orientation: *progress*. In this light, the nature
of the LM as an obstacle acquires also a temporal dimension: it is perceived
as blocking the 'course of history' toward upcoming better stages and portrayed as a 'traditional' and 'old' position. The TR, by contrast, should be
depicted as 'nontraditional' and 'new.' Its novelty vis-à-vis the LM is a matter of degree, from minor modifications to major innovations—from small
steps to large steps in the path of progress. So too is the kind and amount
of improvement it contains, from small corrections of mistakes to full-
fledged conceptual revolutions conceived as giant leaps ahead.

8. While progress can in principle be achieved without the need to
overcome obstacles, it seems to be hard to separate it from the notion of
hope. Hence the deeper entrenchment of the hope component in the Beyond Enterprise that was observed in section 2.

Section 6

Why is this metaphor a 'natural'—indeed, a conventional—way of
conceptualizing the abstract domain(s) represented in *Beyond . . .* texts?
One possible way to answer this question is to treat the naturalness of the
metaphor as grounded in 'the structure of our experience.'[20] This would
require us to answer the following questions:

1. What determines the choice of a possible well-structured source domain?

2. What determines the pairing of the source domain with the target
   domain?

3. What determines the details of the source-to-target mapping? (Lakoff
   1987: 276),

by searching our experience for the appropriate 'structural correlations'
between source and target. For,

> there are many structural correlations in our experience. Not all of them
> motivate metaphors, but many do. When there is such a motivation, the
> metaphor seems *natural*. The reason it seems natural is that the pairing

of the source and target domains is motivated by experience, as are the details of the mapping. (Lakoff 1987: 278)

The first question is relatively easy to answer. The ULTERIOR image-schema is pervasive in experience, well-understood, well structured, and correlated with other basic schemas, such as the SOURCE-PATH-GOAL schema.

A possible reply to the second question is that there is a correlation between ULTERIOR experiences (the source) and our personal experiences of intellectual progress (the target). We experience the latter as an oriented process, whereby we pass through a set of stages, in an open-ended series. The essence of this process is the process itself, not any of its particular stages, just as the essence of the ULTERIOR experience is its relational character, which can be reiterated *ad libidum*.[21] Insofar as our personal intellectual progress involves not only learning ready-made concepts or theories but also creating them, thereby contributing to the progress or motion of a field of research, it is relatively unproblematic to extend the correlation, beyond personal progress, to a field's progress.[22]

It is in the third question that we are in for an interesting surprise. It would seem that the kind of progress that most naturally matches the ULTERIOR schema is linear, cumulative progress. And yet, as we have seen, *Beyond* . . . texts more often than not present a different picture of progress: a process of overcoming obstacles, of being forced to abandon earlier achievements that now block our way and beginning anew. This suggests that the significant details of our ULTERIOR and PROGRESS experiences correlated through the metaphorical link are rather those that involve non-linear paths: detours, zigzags, stepping back to leap ahead, trial and error, and so on. There is no doubt that we have such experiences in our intellectual development, just as we have experiences of straight paths and cumulative progress. As we have seen, the Beyond Enterprise allows for both interpretations. But in the majority of cases, it selects the former rather than the latter as its dominant structuring principle.

Section 7

We could no doubt go beyond this initial exploration of the Beyond Enterprise. For reasons that are beyond my control, it had to be interrupted here. Let me outline a few preliminary conclusions that can be drawn so far from this study. This will help to indicate the larger framework within which I locate studies of this kind.

First, we are hardly aware of the fact that the little word 'beyond,' as used in the kinds of texts here examined and in hundreds of similar ones—where it often appears as the first title word—is a powerful metaphor. The reason for this lack of awareness is simply that such a use has become conventionalized in our culture. As a result, it has become remarkably field-independent (as shown by the wide variety of fields covered by our sample). It is, so to speak, a ready-made tool that can be picked up from our conceptual toolbox in order to be easily applied to practically any kind of inquiry.

Second, this tool, is not 'neutral.' For it imposes a certain structuration of the field of inquiry. Its choice carries with it a 'hidden agenda,' not devoid of epistemological and ontological implications. One is that the choice of a 'beyond' framework favors a view of inquiry as dynamic rather than static, as diachronic rather than synchronic, as concerned with both the past and the future. Another is that this dynamic perspective is intrinsically associated with the theme of progress, a fact that endows the Beyond Enterprise with a sort of deep optimism. It conveys the belief that there is always a way—a *tao*—to overcome even the most formidable obstacles to intellectual progress. An additional implication is that the selection of the nonlinear path of progress, implicit in most of the uses of this metaphor we have examined, indicates its 'natural' affinity—albeit unawares—with those epistemologies that emphasize criticism, controversy, crisis, scientific revolution, and other forms of intellectual conflict as the true engines of cognitive evolution.

Third, products are not independent of the tools employed in making them. It is only to be expected that the earlier mentioned properties of the 'beyond' tool be mirrored in the kinds of theories proposed by those who engage in the Beyond Enterprise, as well as in their practices. Thus the models or theories they will tend to reject are those perceived primarily as static. For example, 'the symbol model' is rejected mainly on the grounds that it views language as a system of synchronically fixed signs, each of which functions as a surrogate for that which it represents or stands for. Those that seek to go beyond it propose, instead, a dynamic view of language, based on interaction, dialogue, the fluidity of meaning and interpretation, and so on. Moreover, the inherent optimism of the Beyond Enterprise makes it difficult to reconcile it with theories stemming from the pessimistic theme of 'disenchantment' (to use Weber's term). This raises the question of the precise roles and mutual relationship of the critical and hope components. Disenchantment-motivated approaches tend to deepen and extend the critical component to the point of making hope all but impossible. Beyond-motivated approaches, on the other hand, must sustain hope, and hence their critical components, even when quite radical, always preserve a 'constructive' character; as a result, the product—the alternative view or theory they propose—may often contain elements of the criticized one, in a spirit of constructive eclecticism.

In addition, the nonlinear view of progress and the historicist leaning of the Beyond Enterprise are, of course, intrinsically antipositivistic. For a positivist to write a *Beyond* . . . book would be almost a *contradictio in adjectio*. Almost but not quite. For one thing, Skinner wrote such a book. And this is as it should be. For a metaphor generates a relatively tight conceptual structure and highlights a number of central themes. But the users of the metaphor always have a margin of freedom in its interpretation—including the choice of those themes they see as more central than others. The advantage of resorting to a metaphor-based epistemological analysis lies precisely in that one thereby abandons the positivist dogma according to which the only philosophically respectable concepts are those precisely defined by means of sufficient and necessary conditions.

Fourth, given its widespread and natural use to conceptualize inquiry, 'beyond' belongs perhaps to a set of 'foundational metaphors' in the Western way of understanding intellectual life. Other possible members of this set are 'content' (which rules over the whole domain of meaning), 'field' (which organizes knowledge territorially into disciplines, departments, etc.), 'conduit' (which controls our views on the storage, retrieval, and communication of information and knowledge), and so on. It would be extremely important to clarify this 'foundational status' some metaphors achieve; to analyze their interrelations; and to compare the current Western set of foundational metaphors with those of other cultures or of other periods in Western intellectual history.[23]

Notes

1. I also intended to discuss the closely related prefix 'post' in-such constructions as 'postmodernism' and 'postsemiotic' (Stewart's term), but due to space limitations this will be left for another paper.

2. E.g., van Gelder (1993), whose relevance to the topic of this book is enhanced by its purport of going "Beyond symbolic."

3. This reminded me that I also have a book (Dascal 1983) in a series called *Pragmatics and Beyond*!

4. Here too I am representing—to some extent—"the symbol model," insofar as I am claiming that a title bears an intentional 'message,' that the reader is supposed to find out. If you buy,, say, Marguerite Duras's *L'Amante Anglaise*, you expect to read something about the love life of some English woman. When you discover, after going through more than half of the book, that it deals with an abhorrent murder, where no love nor English women are involved, you begin to look for an explanation—a 'meaning'—for this mismatch between the title and the contents. You may rest content with saying that this is just another gimmick of a

Nouveau Roman author to puzzle her readers or to attract attention. But if you look further, you discover some clues as to how to intepret the title in connection with the contents. To make a long story short (for details, see Dascal and Weizman 1990), Claire, the murderer, often misspells certain words; she is interested in plants, especially in "menthe" (mint), and she grows mint "en glaise" (in potter's clay). So, the 'real' title of the book—if you can say so—is "La menthe en glaise" (The mint in potter's clay) and the actual title is a (deliberate, of course) misspelling of that (both phrases sound exactly alike). Does this mean that the book is about mint cultivation? Certainly not. The book is, broadly speaking, about misspelling, i.e. misrepresentation: about the fact that different persons represent the same event (the murder) along completely different lines, so that no account is an 'objective' rendering of reality. Perhaps this book too belongs to the Beyond Enterprise. Its title might have been 'Beyond Objectivity.'

5. Even though Kaufmann's book does not have 'beyond' in its title, but rather 'without'—which might suggest an exclusive focus on the critical component—it contains also the hope component. Not only does it develop an alternative to what is "left behind," but also emphatically describes it as "new": ". . . [to] develop a new conception of autonomy—a new integrity—a new morality" (ibid.).

6. This is an example of what Grice (1975) calls a *conversational* implicature. The implicature conveyed by the linguistic order of the elements (as in the title → subtitle case) belongs to the class of *conventional* implicatures. For example, *and* carries a conventional implicature of temporal succession: "They got married and had many children." But this can be canceled: "They got married and had many children, but not in that order."

7. Presumably it belongs to the class of 'conventional implicatures,' rather than to the class of 'conversational implicatures.' For more details on the notion of implicature and, in general, on pragmatics, see Dascal (1983).

8. For the notions of 'layer of meaning' and 'entrenchment,' see the "onion model" of meaning proposed in Dascal and Katriel (1977).

9. Notice here the interesting asymmetry between X and Y in the title "Beyond X and Y." One of them having already been left behind, it is the other that now requires attention. For further remarks on the addition of Y to the construction, see note 19.

10. This is only one of the many metaphors of movement abundantly used in Freud's book. See section 4 for a quote from Freud on the metaphorical nature of scientific language.

11. Notice here the reliance on another spatial metaphor, that of the container, whose impact on certain fields may be devastating. For an analysis of one of such fields—the philosophy of mind—see Dascal (forthcoming).

12. On this and other motives in the deconstructionist ethos, see Dascal (1989).

13. In the unpublished project of a preface, the goal is depicted as follows: "I want to found a new caste, an order of superior men where minds in despair will be able to look for advice; men who like me will live not only beyond political and religious confessions, but who will also have gone beyond morality" [from *Werke*, vol. 14, p. 414].

14. It is the emphasis on the common ground shared by Freud and Marx that allows for Fromm's synthesis to be developed. This is a further indication of the predominantly "building" (hope) character of the text. There is no attempt to claim that the axis Freud-Marx itself is to be overcome by such a synthesis. Its basic categories are all right as far as they go: 1. the critical mood; 2. humanism; 3. liberating power of truth. What needs to be done is simply to polish this axis, eliminating apparent irregularities ("contradictions") in it.

15. On this last point, see Dascal (1989).

16. See, for example, Miller and Johnson-Laird (1976), Talmy (1983), Langacker (1987, 1991), Levinson (1992), Svorou (1993), Goldberg (1995).

17. See, for example, Lakoff and Johnson (1980), Johnson (1987), Lakoff (1987), Lakoff and Turner (1989), Turner (1993), Gibbs (1994). For applications of this perspective to philosophical issues, see Dascal (1991; forthcoming).

18. This terminology is that of Langacker. Talmy (1983) employs the terms 'ground' (= LM) vs. 'figure' (= TR), being followed in this by Levinson (1992). Wildgen (1994) makes use of the LM-TR labels.

19. The frequent use, in the sample of texts I have singled out, of the expansion of the basic 'beyond X' to 'beyond X and Y' raises some questions not handled by Svorou. If Y is conceived as between X and TR, along the line defined by the observer and LM, then the one-dimensional assumption about the LM is preserved. On this reading, X and Y would be sequential steps in the path toward TR. But this interpretation is quite unusual in my corpus of texts. Normally, X and Y are taken to form a line perpendicular to the line observer-TR. Thus, Y sort of enlarges the LM, thereby also reinforcing its obstructing character. This is the case, for example, in Skinner (1972), Dallmayr (1981), Nietzsche (1989), and so on.

20. This 'experientialist' way of understanding 'naturalness' is not, of course, the only possible way. Lakoff himself admits that the metaphorical structuration of abstract domains of which we do not have existential experiences, must be based on other forms of correlation, presumably logical ones. In fact, the three questions raised in what follows are entirely general and do not presume experientialist replies. The move, described herein, from the personal experience of intellectual progress to the idea of progress of a field of research (an abstract domain) should be more carefully analyzed in terms of nonexperiential correlations. For lack of space and for simplicity, I will explore here only the experiential notion of naturalness.

21. Cattell's 'Beyondism' seems to capture this purely relational character both linguistically and doctrinally. Linguistically, by nominalizing 'beyond,' it man-

ages to focus on the relational element, letting observer, LM, and TR recede into the background. As a doctrine, it emphasizes evolution as such (much as Rousseau viewed man as characterized not by rationality but by 'perfectibility'), regardless of its particular products at any time, as its main component. The risk of this nominalization-cum-doctrinalization of the dynamic-relational element lies precisely in fixing it, thereby converting it in a nondynamic factor that is liable to block the very dynamism it is supposed to praise.

22. One of the implications of a general constraint on metaphorical mapping recently formulated by Mark Turner forbids "mapping two distinct senses in the source onto one sense in the target" (Turner 1993: 293). In the case we are considering, the converse seems to occur: one sense in the source (the observer-traveler) is successively mapped onto two different senses in the target (the author and the field of inquiry). The questions that arise are: (a) can this occur not successively but in one and the same occurrence of the metaphor? (b) if it occurs, does it violate a corresponding constraint, thus provoking problems of understanding the metaphor?

23. This article was written while I was a fellow of the Institute for Advanced Studies, The Hebrew University of Jerusalem. I wish to thank the Institute for its generous and efficient support. I wish also to thank Alan Gross, a fellow member of the research group, "Leibniz the Polemicist: The pragmatics of theory formation and evolution" (at the Institute), who read earlier versions of this text and provided useful comments. I also thank John Stewart for his patience and helpful corrections of my English.

References

Aloni, Nimrod. 1991. *Beyond Nihilism: Nietzsche's Healing and Edifying Philosophy*. Lanham, MD: University Press of America.

Bachem, Albert. 1960. *Beyond Matter and Mind: Natural Sciences Synthesized into Philosophy*. New York: Vantage Press.

Bernstein, Richard J. 1983. *Beyond Objectivism and Relativism: Science, Hermeneutics, and Praxis*. Philadelphia: University of Pennsylvania Press.

Bock, Gisela, and James Susan (eds.). 1992. *Beyond Equality and Difference*. New York: Routledge.

Cattell, Raymond B. 1987. *Beyondism: Religion from Science*. New York: Praeger.

Clark, Herbert H. 1992. *Arenas of Language Use*. Chicago: University of Chicago Press.

Conner, Frederick W. 1987. "Beyond truth: Santayana on the functional relations of art, myth, and religion." *Bulletin of the Santayana Society* 5:17–26.

Cummings, E. E. 1991. *Complete Poems: 1904–1962.* Edited by G. J. Firmage. New York: Liveright.

Dallmayr, Fred R. 1981. *Beyond Dogma and Despair: Toward a Critical Phenomenology of Politics.* Notre Dame, IN: University of Notre Dame Press.

Dascal, Marcelo. 1983. *Pragmatics and the Philosophy of Mind,* vol. 1. Amsterdam: John Benjamins.

———. 1985. "Leibniz on the senses and the understanding: Beyond empiricism and rationalism." *Iyyun* 34: 201–18 [Hebrew].

———. 1989. "Reflections on the crisis of modernity." In A. Cohen and M. Dascal (eds.), *The Institution of Philosophy: A Discipline in Crisis?* La Salle, IL: Open Court, pp. 217–40.

———. 1991. "The ecology of cultural space." In M. Dascal (ed.), *Cultural Relativism and Philosophy: North and Latin American Perspectives.* Leiden: Brill, pp. 279–95.

———. (forthcoming). "The prison of content."

Dascal, Marcelo, and Tamar Katriel. 1977. "Between semantics and pragmatics: the two types of 'but'—Hebrew 'aval' and 'ela'." *Theoretical Linguistics* 4: 143–72.

Dascal, Marcelo, and Elda Weizman. 1990. "On speaker's meaning in literature." *Hebrew Linguistics* 28/29/30 (Special issue on "Stylistics and the Literary Text"), pp. 9–19 [Hebrew].

De Paul, Michael. 1993. *Balance and Refinement: Beyond Coherence Methods of Moral Inquiry.* New York: Routledge.

Drees, Wilem B. 1990. *Beyond the Big Bang: Quantum Cosmologies and God.* Peru, IL: Open Court.

Dreyfus, Hubert L., and Paul Rabinow. 1983. *Michel Foucault: Beyond Structuralism and Hermeneutics.* Chicago: University of Chicago Press.

Eidelberg, Paul. 1989. *Beyond the Secular Mind: A Judaic Response to the Problems of Modernity.* New York: Greenwood Press.

Ferrell, Donald R. 1983. "Technology and an ethic of limits: Beyond utopia and despair." *American Journal of Theology and Philosophy* 4: 31–48.

Frankl, Viktor E. 1960. "Beyond self-actualization and self-expression." *Journal of Existentialism* 1: 5–20.

Freud, Sigmund. 1922. *Beyond the Principle of Pleasure.* Authorized transl. by C. J. M. Hubback. London: International Psycho-Analytical Press.

Fromm, Erich. 1962. *Beyond the Chains of Illusions: My Encounter with Marx and Freud.* New York: Simon & Schuster.

van Gelder, Timothy. 1993. "Beyond symbolic: Prolegomena to a Kama-Sutra of compositionality." In V. Honavar and L. Uhr (eds.), *Symbol Processing and Connectionist Models in Artificial Intelligence and Cognition: Steps Towards Integration*. New York: Academic Press.

Gibbs, Raymond W., Jr. 1994. *The Poetics of Mind: Figurative Thought, Language, and Understanding*. Cambridge: Cambridge University Press.

Giverz, Harry K. 1973. *Beyond Right and Wrong*. New York: Free Press.

Givón, Talmy (ed.). 1983. *Topic Continuity in Discourse: Quantified Cross-Language Studies*. Amsterdam: John Benjamins.

Goldberg, Adele E. 1995. *Constructions: A Construction Grammar Approach to Argument Structure*. Chicago: The University of Chicago Press.

Grice, H. P. 1975. "Logic and conversation." In P. Cole and J. L. Morgan (eds.), *Syntax and Semantics*, vol. 3. New York: Academic Press, pp. 41–58.

Gunn, J. A. W. 1983. *Beyond Liberty and Property: The Process of Self-Recognition in Eighteenth-Century Political Thought*. Kingston: McGill-Queen's.

Holub, Renate. 1992. *Antonio Gramsci: Beyond Marxism and Postmodernism*. New York: Routledge.

Johnson, Mark. 1987. *The Body in the Mind: The Bodily Basis of Meaning, Imagination, and Reason*. Chicago: The University Chicago Press.

Kaufmann, Walter. 1975. *Without Guilt and Justice: From Decidophobia to Autonomy*. New York: Dell Publishing Company.

Lakoff, George. 1987. *Women, Fire, and Dangerous Things: What Categories Reveal about the Mind*. Chicago: The University of Chicago Press.

Lakoff, George, and Mark Johnson. 1980. *Metaphors We Live By*. Chicago: The University of Chicago Press.

Lakoff, George, and Mark Turner. 1989. *More than Cool Reason: A Field Guide to Poetic Metaphor*. Chicago: The University of Chicago Press.

Langacker, Ronald W. 1987. *Foundations of Cognitive Grammar, vol. 1: Theoretical Prerequisites*. Stanford, CA: Stanford University Press.

———. 1991. *Foundations of Cognitive Grammar*, vol. 2: Descriptive Application. Stanford: Stanford University Press.

Laszlo, Erwin. 1966. *Beyond Scepticism and Realism: A Constructive Exploration of Husserlian and Whiteheadian Methods of Inquiry*. The Hague: M. Nijhoff.

Laudan, Larry. 1984. "Explaining the success of science: Beyond epistemic realism and relativism." In J. T. Cushing (ed.), *Science and Reality*. Notre Dame, IN: University of Notre Dame Press, pp. 83–105.

Leon, Philip. 1965. *Beyond Belief and Unbelief: Creative Nihilism*. London: Gollancz.

Levinson, Stephen C. 1992. "Primer for the field investigation of spatial description and conception." *Pragmatics* 2(1): 5–47.

Linklater, Andrew. 1990. *Beyond Realism and Marxism: Critical Theory and International Relations*. New York: St. Martin's Press.

Madigan, Arthur R. 1991. "Beyond egoism and altruism?." In J. P. Anton (ed.), *Essays in Ancient Greek Philosophy, IV*. Albany: State University of New York Press.

McGrane, Bernard. 1989. *Beyond Anthropology: Society and the Other*. New York: Columbia University Press.

McKelvey, Charles. 1991. *Beyond Ethnocentrism. A Reconstruction of Marx's Concept of Science*. Westport, CT: Greenwood Press.

Miller, George A., and Philip N. Johnson-Laird. 1976. *Language and Perception*. Cambridge, MA: Harvard University Press.

Mitroff, Ian I., Harold Quinton, and Richard O. Mason. 1983. "Beyond contradiction and consistency: A design for a dialectical policy system." *Theory and Decision* 15: 107–20.

Nietzche, Friedrich. 1989. *Beyond Good and Evil: Prelude to a Philosophy of the Future*. Transl. of *Jenseits von Gut und Böse* (1886), by W. Kaufmann. New York: Vintage Books.

Ogilvy, James. 1992. "Beyond individualism and collectivism." In J. Ogilvy (ed.), *Revisioning Philosophy*. Albany: State University of New York Press.

Palmer, Anthony. 1992. "Beyond representation." In A. Phillips (ed.), *The Impulse to Philosophise*. Cambridge: Cambridge University Press.

Pauson, John J. 1966. *Beyond Morality and the Law*. Pittsburgh: Philosophical Press.

Reppen, Joseph (ed.). 1985. *Beyond Freud: A Study of Modern Psychoanalytic Theorists*. London: The Analytic Press.

Sauberlich, H. E., and L. J. Machlin. (eds.). 1992. *Beyond Deficiency: New Views on the Function and Health Effects of Vitamins* (= *Annals of the New York Academy of Science, vol. 669*). New York: The New York Academy of Sciences.

Skinner, B. F. 1972. *Beyond Freedom and Dignity*. New York: Bantam Books.

Slote, Michael. 1989. *Beyond Optimizing: A Study of Rational Choice*. Cambridge, MA: Harvard University Press.

Solomon, Robert C. 1992. "Beyond reason: The importance of emotion in philosophy." In J. Ogilvy (ed.) *Revisioning Philosophy*. Albany: State University of New York Press.

Stewart, John. 1995. *Language as Articulate Contact: Toward a Post-semiotic Philosophy of Communication*. Albany, NY: State University of New York Press.

Stuart, Sim. 1992. *Beyond Aesthetics: Confrontations with Poststructuralism and Postmodernism*. Toronto: University of Toronto Press.

Svorou, Soteria. 1993. *The Grammar of Space*. Amsterdam: John Benjamins.

Swartz, Norman. 1991. *Beyond Experience: Metaphysical Theories and Philosophical Constraints*. Toronto: University of Toronto Press.

Talmy, Leonard. 1983. "How language structures space." In H. L. Pick and L. P. Acredolo (eds.) *Spatial Orientation: Theory, Research and Application*. New York: Plenum Press, pp. 225–82.

Turner, Mark. 1993. "An image-schematic constraint on metaphor." In R. A. Geiger and B. Rudzka-Ostyn (eds.), *Conceptualizations and Mental Processing in Language*. Berlin/New York: Mouton De Gruyter, pp. 291–306.

Urban, Wilbur Marshall. 1949. *Beyond Realism and Idealism*. London: Allen & Unwin.

Wildgen, Wolfgang. 1994. *Process, Image, and Meaning: A Realistic Model of the Meanings of Sentences and Narrative Texts*. Amsterdam: John Benjamins.

Will, Frederick I. 1988. *Beyond Deduction: Ampliative Aspects of Philosophical Reflection*. New York: Routledge.

Contributors

Janet Bavelas is a professor of psychology at the University of Victoria, coauthor of *Pragmatics of Human Communication*, and *Equivocal Communication* and author of *Personality: Current Theory and Research*. She heads an interdisciplinary team of researchers investigating relationships between verbal and nonverbal aspects of "live" communicative events.

Ernst Behler is professor and chair of the Department of Comparative Literature at the University of Washington. His areas of research are European Romanticism, Nietzsche, and contemporary critical theory. He is the editor-in-chief of the complete works of Friedrich Nietzsche in twenty volumes at Stanford University Press.

D. S. Clarke, Jr. is professor of philosophy at Southern Illinois University at Carbondale. His primary research focus is semiotics, and among his most recent works are *Sources of Semiotic, Principles of Semiotic,* and *Rational Acceptance and Purpose.*

Marcelo Dascal is Professor of Philosophy and Dean of the Faculty of Humanities at Tel Aviv University. He is the author of *Leibniz: Language, Signs, and Thought; Pragmatics and the Philosophy of Mind; La Semiologie de Leibniz;* and is the editor or co-editor of twenty books, among them the two-volume *Philosophy of Language: An International Handbook of Research; Cultural Relativism and Philosophy: North and Latin American Perspectives; The Institution of Philosophy: A Discipline in Crisis?;* and *Knowledge and Politics: Case Studies in Relationships between Epistemology and Political Philosophy.*

Wendy Leeds-Hurwitz is professor of communication at the University of Wisconsin-Parkside. In addition to semiotics, her research interests

335

include communication theory, the ethnography of communication, and the history of the study of communication. She is author
of *Communication in Everyday Life*, and *Semiotics and Communication*, and editor of *Social Approaches to Communication*.

Gary Madison is Professor of Philosophy at McMaster University, Canada.
He is the author of *The Phenomenology of Merleau-Ponty*; *Under-
standing: A Phenomenological-Pragmatic Analysis*; *The Logic of
Liberty*, and *The Hermeneutics of Postmodernity: Figures and
Themes*. He has also edited *Working Through Derrida* and *The
Ethics of Postmodernity*.

Giilian L. Roberts has an honours degree in psychology from the University of Victoria. Her coauthored chapter in this volume is based on
her honours thesis.

John Shotter is professor of interpersonal relations in the Department of
Communication, University of New Hampshire. He is author of *Images of Man in Psychological Research*; *Social Accountability and
Selfhood*; *Cultural Politics of Everyday Life*; *Social Constructionism, Rhetoric, and Knowing of the Third Kind*; and *Conversational
Realities: The Construction of Life through Language*. In 1990–
1991 he was the Cornell Distinguished Visiting Professor in Psychology at Swarthmore College and is currently a fellow in the
Center for the Humanities, University of New Hampshire.

Andrew Smith is associate professor of communication studies at Edinboro
University of Pennsylvania. His has authored articles most recently
on the ambiguities of power and sexuality in institutional harrass-
ment cases and co-edited (with Lenore Langsdorf) *Recovering Pragmatism's Voice: The Classical Tradition, Rorty, and the Philosophy
of Communication*.

John Stewart is professor of speech communication and member of the
Critical Theory Faculty at the University of Washington. His articles
address issues in communication theory, philosophy of dialogue,
and philosophy of interpretive research, and he is the author of
*Language as Articulate Contact: Toward a Post-Semiotic Philoso-
phy of Communication*.

John Wilson is professor and chair of the department of communication in
the University of Ulster at Jordanstown. His publications in prag-

matics and sociolinguistics include *On the Boundaries of Conversation* and *Linguistic Forms of Political Life.* He is the editor of an interdisciplinary journal, *Belfast Working Papers in Language and Linguistics.*

Index

abductive logic, 213
agency, 24, 121–122, 137–138
agreement vs. alignment, 46, 141–146
aligning action, 276, 286–287
aliquid stat pro aliquo, 13, 15, 70
alternative and the Beyond Enterprise, 317–318
Antisthenes, 203, 205–207
Apollonian vs. Dionysian spirit, 168
    and language, 172–173, 178–179
Arendt, Hannah, 10
Aristotle, 10, 31, 73–74
articulate contact, 44–48, 100
asyndetic connection, 288–290
atomism commitment of the symbol model, 17–18, 28, 49, 231–233
Augustine of Hippo, 198, 202, 207, 210
Austin, John L., 21, 142, 244–245

Bacon, Francis, 69
Bakhtin, M. M., 1, 3, 5, 38, 40, 45–46, 99, 103–104, 106, 123, 270, 278
Bateson, Gregory, 207
being
    and language, 6, 10–11, 33–34, 77–81
    being-in-the-world, 33–34, 38–40, 66
    vs. knowing, 33–34
Benveniste, Émile, 26, 96n.65
Bernstein, Richard J., 10, 76–77, 111–112, 306, 313
Billig, Michael, 99, 104, 108
bricolage, 254, 268–269
Bruner, Jerome, 244
Buber, Martin, 1, 31, 46

building upon in the Beyond Enterprise, 310–311
Burke, Kenneth, 15

Campbell, John Angus, 31
Cartesian anxiety, 10, 77
Cassirer, Ernst, 39, 111
Catholic-Protestant conflict, 175, 283–293
Cattell, Raymond B., 318–319
certainty in language theorizing, 232, 237–238
Chomsky, Noam, 241
Clark, Herbert H., 139–140, 145
coconstruction, 10, 11, 35–36, 44–48, 53, 150–159
Cohen, Anthony P., 259, 263
collaboration, 10, 11, 35–36
    implicit semantic, 146–149
    explicit semantic, 149–151
    problematic semantic, 151–155
communication
    and language, 36–37
    nonverbal, 22–23, 36–37, 38, 41–43, 47–48, 80, 107, 115, 186, 245, 253–254, 257–258
comprehensiveness in language theorizing, 232, 242
confinement and the Beyond Enterprise, 301, 312–313
Conquergood, Dwight, 215–221
constitutive view of language, 30–33, 41–44, 105–109, 117–120, 189, 275
    incommensurability with semiotic view, 37–41, 54, 60 n.86, 279
context, symbols in, 260–275

sensus communis, 111–115
sentence radicals, 244–246
sin license, 294–295
signifiant-signifié, 26–27
signification and designation, 205–207,
    210–211
sign language, 48
signs, sign relations, 11–14, 236–237
simplicity in language theorizing, 232, 238–
    242
Skinner, B. F., 241, 314–315
Smith, P. Christopher, 37
social constructionism, 100, 114–115
Sophist language theory, 198, 203, 204–
    209, 221–222
speech and thought, 42–44, 80–81
speech community, 263
speaking and thinking, 42–44, 80–81
Stewart, John, 70, 71, 258, 271–272, 279–
    281, 296, 303–304, 309–310, 313
Stokes, R., 286, 294
Strawson, P. F., 249
subject-object split, 29–30, 39–41, 43–44,
    78–80, 84–85, 114, 122
Svorou, Soteria, 302, 321–324
symbol, 12–13, 253–254, 257–260
    context and, 260–265
    in use, 265–270
    language and, 5, 14–15, 236–237
    model, 14–21, 49–51, 253–256, 326–327
    social account of, 257–272
    symbolic marker, 5
system commitment of the symbol model,
    19–20, 29, 50, 280–281

Taylor, Charles, 43, 49, 103, 106–107, 112–
    113, 247
that-it-is vs. what-it-is, 42–44
theory, theorizing, 99, 101, 103–111, 114–
    122
    certainty in language, 232, 237–238
    comprehensiveness in language, 232, 242

three-turn (step) analysis of meaning, 141–
    146
tool (instrumental) commitment of the
    symbol model, 20–21, 29, 39, 50–51,
    86
Tractatus Logico-Philosophicus, 16, 19
transactional aspects of language, 244–246
    vs. logical features, 232
transcendence and the Beyond Enterprise,
    318–319
translation, 85, 87
trajector and landmark and the Beyond En-
    terprise, 302, 309–310, 322–324
truth and language, 180–183
tu quoque and the Beyond Enterprise, 320–
    321
Turner, Victor, 262
two worlds commitment of the symbol
    model, 15, 16–17, 25–27, 29–30,
    37–41, 81–82, 259
    and representationalism, 26–27
    Nietzsche's intrerrogation, 164

validity, hermeneutic, 27–28, 40
    and correspondence, 39–40
Vico, Giambattista, 101, 111
Voegelin, Eric, 46
Volosinov, Valentin, 45–46, 104, 115, 120,
    125, 278
Vygotsky, 99, 104, 112, 125

Wagner, Richard, 167–170
Welt / Umwelt, 31–32, 84
will to power, 170–171
Wittgenstein, Ludwig, 9, 16, 19, 99, 101,
    103–124
words and things, 82
world, 30–33
    and language, 33–41, 76–82, 88
    that vs. what, 42–43
    two worlds commitment of the symbol
    model, 15, 16–17, 25–27, 29–30,
    37–41, 81–82, 259